Microsoft

Publisher 2002

Complete
Concepts and
Techniques

Microsoft
Publisher 2002

Complete Concepts and Techniques

Gary B. Shelly
Thomas J. Cashman
Joy L. Starks

THOMSON
COURSE TECHNOLOGY

COURSE TECHNOLOGY
25 THOMSON PLACE
BOSTON MA 02210

SHELLY
CASHMAN
SERIES®

Australia • Canada • Denmark • Japan • Mexico • New Zealand • Philippines • Puerto Rico • Singapore
South Africa • Spain • United Kingdom • United States

THOMSON

COURSE TECHNOLOGY

Asia (excluding Japan)
Thomson Learning
5 Shenton Way #01-01
UIC Building
Singapore 068808

Latin America
Thomson Learning
Seneca, 53
Colonia Polanco
11560 Mexico D.F. Mexico

Canada
Nelson/Thomson Learning
1120 Birchmount Road
Scarborough, Ontario
Canada M1K 5G4

Japan
Thomson Learning
Nihonjisyo Brooks Bldg 3-F
1-4-1 Kudankita, Chiyoda-Ku
Tokyo 102-0073 Japan

South Africa
Thomson Learning
15 Brookwood Street
P.O. Box 1722
Soverset West 7120
South Africa

UK/Europe/Middle East
Thomson Learning
Berkshire House
168-173 High Holborn
London, WC1V 7AA United Kingdom

Australia/New Zealand
Nelson/Thomson Learning
102 Dodds Street
South Melbourne, Victoria 3205
Australia

Spain
Thomson Learning
Calle Magallanes, 25
28015-MADRID
ESPANA

PHOTO CREDITS: Microsoft Publisher 2002 *Project 1, pages PUB 1.04-05* Hieroglyphics, printing press, print shop, Gutenberg, engraving, Courtesy of ArtToday; *Project 2, pages PUB 2.02-03* Comet, Courtesy of NOAO; planets, Courtesy of JPL; stars, Courtesy of Digital Stock; Girl in telescope, father reading, dad and baby, children at beach, girl in swimsuit, tennis player, child with baseball, tennis racket, baseball bat, Courtesy of ArtToday; *Project 4, pages PUB 4.02-03* Speed limit sign, Courtesy of KPT Metatools; crossing guard and children, Courtesy of Rubber Ball productions; curved road, Courtesy of PhotoDisc, Inc.

ISBN 0-7895-6353-3

4 5 6 7 8 9 10   BC   06 05 04 03

Microsoft
Publisher 2002
Complete Concepts and Techniques

Contents

Preface

The Shelly Cashman Series® offers the finest textbooks in computer education. In this *Microsoft Publisher 2002* book, you will find an educationally sound and easy-to-follow pedagogy that combines a step-by-step approach with corresponding screens. All projects and exercises in this book are designed to take full advantage of the Publisher 2002 enhancements. The popular Other Ways and More About features offer in-depth knowledge of Publisher 2002. The new Learn It Online page presents a wealth of additional exercises to ensure your students have all the reinforcement they need. The project openers provide a fascinating perspective of the subject covered in the project. The project material is developed carefully to ensure that students will see the importance of learning Publisher for future coursework.

Objectives of This Textbook

Microsoft Publisher 2002: Complete Concepts and Techniques is intended for a two-unit course that covers Microsoft Publisher 2002 and desktop publishing. No experience with a computer is assumed, and no mathematics beyond the high school freshman level is required. The objectives of this book are:

- To teach the fundamentals of Publisher 2002
- To expose students to practical examples of the computer as a useful desktop publishing tool
- To acquaint students with the proper procedures to create professional quality publications suitable for course work, professional purposes, and personal use
- To develop an exercise-oriented approach that allows learning by doing
- To introduce students to new input technologies, such as speech and handwriting recognition
- To encourage independent study, and help those who are working alone

The Shelly Cashman Approach

Features of the Shelly Cashman Series *Microsoft Publisher 2002* books include:

- **Project Orientation:** Each project in the book presents a practical problem and complete solution in an easy-to-understand approach.
- **Step-by-Step, Screen-by-Screen Instructions:** Each of the tasks required to complete a project is identified throughout the project. Full-color screens accompany the steps.
- **Thoroughly Tested Projects:** Every screen in the book is correct because it is produced by the author only after performing a step, resulting in unprecedented quality.
- **Other Ways Boxes and Quick Reference Summary:** The Other Ways boxes displayed at the end of most of the step-by-step sequences specify the other ways to do the task completed in the steps. Thus, the steps and the Other Ways box make a comprehensive reference unit.
- **More About Feature:** These marginal annotations provide background information and tips that complement the topics covered, adding depth and perspective.

Other Ways

1. On Format menu click Tabs
2. In Voice Command mode, say "Format, Tabs"

More About

Outsourcing Your Business Cards

For more information on questions to ask your commercial printer before handing off your business cards, visit the Publisher 2002 More About Web page (scsite.com/pub2002/more.htm) and then click Outsourcing Checklist.

■ **Integration of the World Wide Web:** The World Wide Web is integrated into the Publisher 2002 learning experience by (1) More About annotations that send students to Web sites for up-to-date information and alternative approaches to tasks; (2) a MOUS information Web page so students can prepare for the MOUS Certification examinations; (3) a Publisher 2002 Quick Reference Summary Web page that summarizes the ways to complete tasks (mouse, menu, shortcut menu, and keyboard); and (4) the Learn It Online page at the end of each project, which has project reinforcement exercises, learning games, and other types of student activities.

Organization of This Textbook

Microsoft Publisher 2002: Complete Concepts and Techniques provides basic instruction on how to use Publisher 2002. The material is divided into three projects, a Web Feature, five appendices, and a Quick Reference Summary.

Project 1 – Creating and Editing a Publication In Project 1, students are introduced to Publisher terminology and the Publisher window by preparing an advertising flyer with tear-offs. Topics include starting and quitting Publisher; using the New Publication task pane for color and font decisions; editing text and synchronized elements; using Publisher's zoom features; editing graphics; using the Clip Organizer; bulleted lists; formatting, printing, and saving a publication; opening and modifying a publication; adding an Attention Getter; deleting objects; and creating a Web page from the publication.

Project 2 – Designing a Newsletter In Project 2, students create a newsletter using one of the Publisher-designed templates available in the Design Gallery. Topics include identifying the advantages of the newsletter medium and the steps in the design process; editing typical newsletter features including mastheads, multi-column articles, sidebars, pull quotes, and graphics; using the Page Navigation control and pagination; importing text files; using Microsoft Word as an editor; formatting personal information components and Attention Getters; using WordArt; and moving between foreground and background elements. Finally, students check the publication for spelling, use the Design Checker, and then print the newsletter double-sided.

Project 3 – Preparing a Tri-Fold Brochure for Outside Printing In Project 3, students prepare a tri-fold brochure with three panels displaying text, shapes, graphics, a response form, customer address placeholders, and a personalized logo. Topics include the proper use of graphics; inserting a photograph from a file; creating a composite logo using custom shapes; deleting and inserting text boxes; using Smart Tags; grouping, rotating, and overlapping objects; editing form components; and preparing the publication for outside printing by choosing appropriate printing services, paper, and color libraries. This project also illustrates Publisher's Pack and Go feature.

Web Feature – Creating a Web Site with Publisher 2002 In this Web Feature, students are introduced to creating a linked Web site. Topics include converting the tri-fold brochure created in Project 3 into a four-page Web site; editing Web properties for search engine tags; including background music and animation; editing the navigation bar; inserting Web objects, HTML code fragments, and form components; personalizing the Web site with hyperlinks; editing Web Submit and Clear buttons; and viewing and saving the Web site.

Project 4 – Personalizing and Customizing Publications with Information Sets In Project 4, students use information sets to create a letterhead for a construction company and then apply the fields and design scheme to a business card, an envelope, mailing labels, and a calendar. Topics include using layout and ruler guides to assist with design and margins; editing information sets and inserting the components; creating a letterhead with background effects such as tints, shades, patterns, and gradients; inserting and editing a logo; recoloring graphics; and using the Measurements toolbar to format character spacing and placement. Finally, students create an address list and learn how to merge it using field codes in a main publication.

Project 5 – Creating Business Forms and Tables In Project 5, students learn how to use Publisher to create common business forms including an invoice, a coupon, and order forms for both print media and the Web. Topics include creating an invoice template; creating and importing Styles to maintain consistency across publications; using font effects and decorative borders; formatting drop caps, tabs, and margins; inserting a system date; creating and navigating in a table; inserting merged cells and cell diagonals; and attaching a publication to an e-mail message. Finally, students create an electronic order form for e-commerce complete with text fields, option buttons, check boxes, hot spots, submit buttons, animated graphics, and sound.

Integration Feature – Linking a Publisher Publication to an Excel Worksheet In the Integration Feature, students are introduced to linking a publication to an Excel worksheet. Topics include a discussion of the differences among copying and pasting, copying and embedding, and copying and linking; opening multiple applications; and printing Appendices (The book includes five appendices). Appendix A presents an introduction to the Microsoft Publisher Help system. Appendix B describes how to use the speech and handwriting recognition capabilities of Publisher 2002. Appendix C explains how to publish Web pages to a Web server. Appendix D shows how to reset the menus and toolbars. Appendix E introduces students to the Microsoft Office User Specialist (MOUS) Certification program.

Quick Reference Summary In Microsoft Publisher 2002, you can accomplish a task in a number of ways, such as using the mouse, menu, shortcut menu, and keyboard. The Quick Reference Summary at the back of the book provides a quick reference to each task presented.

End-of-Project Student Activities

A notable strength of the Shelly Cashman Series *Microsoft Publisher 2002* books is the extensive student activities at the end of each project. Well-structured student activities can make the difference between students merely participating in a class and students retaining the information they learn. The activities in the Shelly Cashman Series *Publisher 2002* books include the following.

- **What You Should Know** A listing of the tasks completed within a project together with the pages on which the step-by-step, screen-by-screen explanations appear.
- **Learn It Online** Every project features a Learn It Online page comprised of ten exercises. These exercises include True/False, Multiple Choice, Short Answer, Flash Cards, Practice Test, Learning Games, Tips and Tricks, Newsgroup usage, Expanding Your Horizons, and Search Sleuth.
- **Apply Your Knowledge** This exercise usually requires students to open and manipulate a file on the Data Disk. To obtain a copy of the Data Disk, follow the instructions on the inside back cover of this textbook.

- In the Lab Three in-depth assignments per project require students to apply the knowledge gained in the project to solve problems on a computer.
- Cases and Places Up to seven unique real-world case-study situations.

Shelly Cashman Series Teaching Tools

The ancillaries that accompany this textbook are Teaching Tools (ISBN 0-7895-6356-8) and MyCourse.com. These ancillaries are available to adopters through your Course Technology representative or by calling one of the following telephone numbers: Colleges and Universities, 1-800-648-7450; High Schools, 1-800-824-5179; Private Career Colleges, 1-800-477-3692; Canada, 1-800-268-2222; and Corporations and Government Agencies, 1-800-340-7450.

Teaching Tools

The contents of the Teaching Tools CD-ROM are listed below.

- Instructor's Manual The Instructor's Manual includes the following for each project: project objectives; project overview; detailed lesson plans with page number references; teacher notes and activities; answers to the end-of-project exercises; a test bank of 110 questions for every project (25 multiple-choice, 50 true/false, and 35 fill-in-the-blank) with page number references; and transparency references. The transparencies are available through the Figures in the Book. The test bank questions are the same as in ExamView and Course Test Manager.
- Figures in the Book Illustrations for every screen and table in the textbook are available in electronic form. Use this ancillary to present a slide show in lecture or to print transparencies for use in lecture with an overhead projector.
- ExamView ExamView is a state-of-the-art test builder that is easy to use. With ExamView, you quickly can create printed tests, Internet tests, and computer (LAN-based) tests. You can enter your own test questions or use the test bank that accompanies ExamView. The test bank is the same as the one described in the Instructor's Manual section. Instructors who want to continue to use our earlier generation test builder, Course Test Manager, rather than ExamView, can call Customer Service at 1-800-648-7450 for a copy of the Course Test Manager database for this book.
- Course Syllabus Any instructor who has been assigned a course at the last minute knows how difficult it is to come up with a course syllabus. For this reason, sample syllabi are included that can be customized easily to a course.
- Lecture Success System Lecture Success System files are used to explain and illustrate the step-by-step, screen-by-screen development of a project in the textbook without entering large amounts of data.
- Instructor's Lab Solutions Solutions and required files for all the In the Lab assignments at the end of each project are available. Solutions also are available for any Cases and Places assignment that supplies data.
- Project Reinforcement True/false, multiple choice, and short answer questions.
- Student Files All the files that are required by students to complete the Apply Your Knowledge exercises are included.
- Interactive Labs Eighteen completely updated, hands-on Interactive Labs that take students from ten to fifteen minutes each to step through help solidify and reinforce mouse and keyboard usage and computer concepts. Student assessment is available.

MyCourse 2.0

MyCourse 2.0 offers instructors and students an opportunity to supplement classroom learning with additional course content. You can use MyCourse 2.0 to expand on traditional learning by completing readings, tests, and other assignments through the customized, comprehensive Web site. For additional information, visit mycourse.com and click the Help button.

Shelly Cashman Online

Shelly Cashman Online is a World Wide Web service available to instructors and students of computer education. Visit Shelly Cashman Online at scseries.com. Shelly Cashman Online is divided into four areas:

- **Series Information** Information on the Shelly Cashman Series products.
- **Teaching Resources** This area includes password-protected data, Series information, teaching tools, and certification and electronic aids.
- **Community** Opportunities to discuss your course and your ideas with instructors in your field and with the Shelly Cashman Series team.
- **Student Center** Dedicated to students learning about computers with Shelly Cashman Series textbooks and software. This area includes cool links and much more.

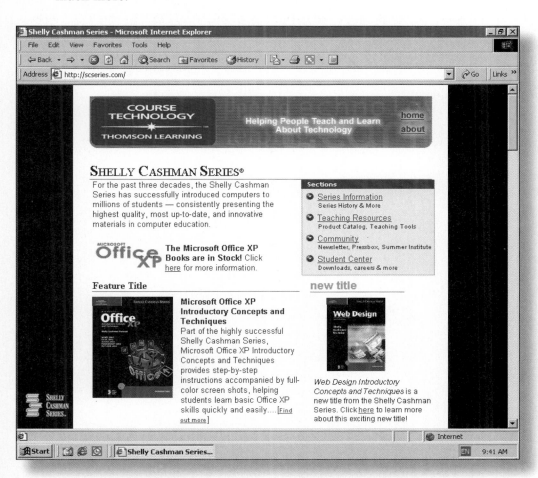

Acknowledgments

The Shelly Cashman Series would not be the leading computer education series without the contributions of outstanding publishing professionals. First, and foremost, among them is Becky Herrington, director of production and designer. She is the heart and soul of the Shelly Cashman Series, and it is only through her leadership, dedication, and tireless efforts that superior products are made possible.

Under Becky's direction, the following individuals made significant contributions to these books: Doug Cowley, production manager; Ginny Harvey, series specialist and developmental editor; Ken Russo, senior Web and graphic designer; Mike Bodnar, associate production manager; Mark Norton, Web designer; Betty Hopkins and Richard Herrera, interior design; Michelle French, Christy Otten, Kellee LaVars, Stephanie Nance, Chris Schneider, Sharon Lee Nelson, Sarah Boger, Amanda Lotter, Michael Greco, and Ryan Ung, graphic artists; Jeanne Black and Betty Hopkins, QuarkXPress compositors; Lyn Markowicz, Nancy Lamm, Kim Kosmatka, Pam Baxter, Eva Kandarpa, Ellana Russo, and Marilyn Martin, copy editors/proofreaders; Cristina Haley, proofreader/indexer; Sarah Evertson of Image Quest, photo researcher; Ginny Harvey, Rich Hansberger, Kim Clark, and Nancy Smith, contributing writers; and Ken Russo, cover design.

Finally, we would like to thank Richard Keaveny, associate publisher; Cheryl Ouellette, managing editor; Jim Quasney, series consulting editor; Alexandra Arnold, product manager; Erin Runyon, associate product manager; Francis Schurgot and Marc Ouellette, Web product managers; Rachel VanKirk, marketing manager; and Reed Cotter, editorial assistant.

Gary B. Shelly
Thomas J. Cashman
Joy L. Starks

Shelly Cashman Series – Traditionally Bound Textbooks

The Shelly Cashman Series presents the following computer subjects in a variety of traditionally bound textbooks. For more information, see your Course Technology representative or call 1-800-648-7450. For Shelly Cashman Series information, visit Shelly Cashman Online at **scseries.com**

COMPUTERS	
Computers	Discovering Computers 2002: Concepts for a Digital World, Web Enhanced, Complete Edition
	Discovering Computers 2002: Concepts for a Digital World, Web Enhanced, Introductory Edition
	Discovering Computers 2002: Concepts for a Digital World, Web Enhanced, Brief Edition
	Teachers Discovering Computers: Integrating Technology in the Classroom 2e
	Exploring Computers: A Record of Discovery 4e
	Study Guide for Discovering Computers 2002: Concepts for a Digital World, Web Enhanced
	Essential Introduction to Computers 4e (32-page)

WINDOWS APPLICATIONS	
Microsoft Office	Microsoft Office XP: Essential Concepts and Techniques (5 projects)
	Microsoft Office XP: Brief Concepts and Techniques (9 projects)
	Microsoft Office XP: Introductory Concepts and Techniques (15 projects)
	Microsoft Office XP: Advanced Concepts and Techniques (11 projects)
	Microsoft Office XP: Post Advanced Concepts and Techniques (11 projects)
	Microsoft Office 2000: Essential Concepts and Techniques (5 projects)
	Microsoft Office 2000: Brief Concepts and Techniques (9 projects)
	Microsoft Office 2000: Introductory Concepts and Techniques, Enhanced Edition (15 projects)
	Microsoft Office 2000: Advanced Concepts and Techniques (11 projects)
	Microsoft Office 2000: Post Advanced Concepts and Techniques (11 projects)
Integration	Integrating Microsoft Office XP Applications and the World Wide Web: Essential Concepts and Techniques
PIM	Microsoft Outlook 2002: Essential Concepts and Techniques
Microsoft Works	Microsoft Works 6: Complete Concepts and Techniques[1] • Microsoft Works 2000: Complete Concepts and Techniques[1] • Microsoft Works 4.5[1]
Microsoft Windows	Microsoft Windows 2000: Complete Concepts and Techniques (6 projects)[2]
	Microsoft Windows 2000: Brief Concepts and Techniques (2 projects)
	Microsoft Windows 98: Essential Concepts and Techniques (2 projects)
	Microsoft Windows 98: Complete Concepts and Techniques (6 projects)[2]
	Introduction to Microsoft Windows NT Workstation 4
	Microsoft Windows 95: Complete Concepts and Techniques[1]
Word Processing	Microsoft Word 2002[2] • Microsoft Word 2000[2] • Microsoft Word 97[1] • Microsoft Word 7[1]
Spreadsheets	Microsoft Excel 2002[2] • Microsoft Excel 2000[2] • Microsoft Excel 97[1] • Microsoft Excel 7[1] • Microsoft Excel 5[1]
Database	Microsoft Access 2002[2] • Microsoft Access 2000[2] • Microsoft Access 97[1] • Microsoft Access 7[1]
Presentation Graphics	Microsoft PowerPoint 2002[2] • Microsoft PowerPoint 2000[2] • Microsoft PowerPoint 97[1] • Microsoft PowerPoint 7[1]
Desktop Publishing	Microsoft Publisher 2002[1] • Microsoft Publisher 2000[1]

PROGRAMMING	
Programming	Microsoft Visual Basic 6: Complete Concepts and Techniques[1] • Programming in QBasic
	Java Programming: Complete Concepts and Techniques[1] • Structured COBOL Programming 2e

INTERNET	
Browser	Microsoft Internet Explorer 5: An Introduction • Microsoft Internet Explorer 4: An Introduction
	Netscape Navigator 6: An Introduction • Netscape Navigator 4: An Introduction
Web Page Creation and Design	Web Design: Introductory Concepts and Techniques • HTML: Complete Concepts and Techniques[1]
	Microsoft FrontPage 2002: Essential Concepts and Techniques • Microsoft FrontPage 2002[2]
	Microsoft FrontPage 2000[1] • JavaScript: Complete Concepts and Techniques[1]

SYSTEMS ANALYSIS	
Systems Analysis	Systems Analysis and Design 4e

DATA COMMUNICATIONS	
Data Communications	Business Data Communications: Introductory Concepts and Techniques 3e

[1]Also available as an Introductory Edition, which is a shortened version of the complete book
[2]Also available as an Introductory Edition, which is a shortened version of the complete book and also as a Comprehensive Edition, which is an extended version of the complete book

Microsoft

PUBLISHER

2002

Microsoft Publisher 2002

PROJECT

Creating and Editing a Publication

You will have mastered the material in this project when you can:

O B J E C T I V E S

- Define desktop publishing
- Start Publisher
- Describe the Publisher window
- Describe the speech recognition capabilities of Publisher
- Edit text in a publication
- Use the zoom buttons to edit
- Edit synchronized elements
- Save a publication
- Edit a graphic using the Clip Organizer
- Save a publication with the same file name
- Print a publication
- Quit Publisher
- Open an existing publication
- Modify a publication
- Add an Attention Getter
- Delete an object
- Run the Design Checker
- Save the publication as a Web page
- Use the Publisher Help system to answer your questions

Helvetica, Anyone?

Typography in the Digital Age

What is a font? If you asked that question 20 years ago, most people — unless they were involved in printing or publishing — probably would stare at you blankly. Nowadays, nearly everyone who uses a computer at home or in the workplace is familiar with the term, font. In the digital age, fonts are the electronic files that contain typefaces in a particular style, such as Times New Roman or Arial (both standard fonts that come with Microsoft applications). Today, thousands of fonts are available, designed to convey your message in a multitude of styles, from casual to formal, whimsical to serious, simple to sophisticated.

The Western system of written communication began with pictograms, which are shapes that portray objects in a language. For example, a stick figure symbolizes man, and a simple building represents shelter.

Next, ideograms evolved, which combine pictograms to represent ideas. For instance, large male and female stick figures combined with a small stick figure could represent a family, and a series of building pictograms could conceptualize a village. Pictograms were followed by phonograms — letters that represent spoken language.

Scribes created the earliest European books, and they painstakingly wrote using a flourishing gothic script.

Johannes Gutenberg, a German goldsmith, experimented in the 1400s with molding and casting metal letters to emulate the scribes'

SETTLEMENT AND PROGRESS
Soldiers first explored Latin America in a ...
families came to the United States seeking ...
The first printing press in the New World ...
Mexico City in 1536; in the United ...

LATIN AMERICA

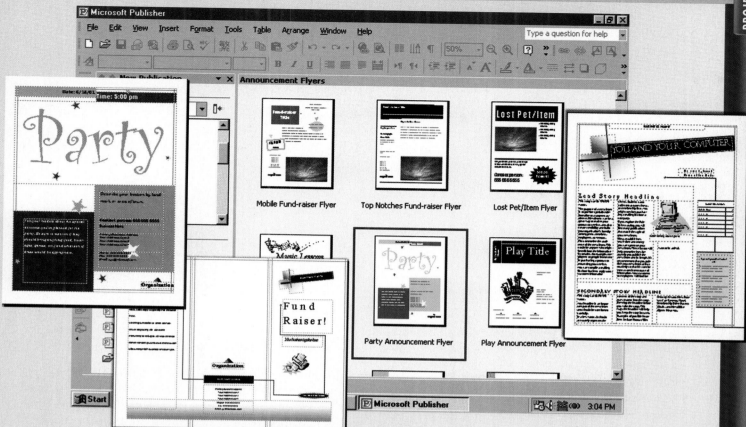

handwriting. His first efforts resulted in more than 300 pieces of type consisting of individual and multiple letters. He put the type together to form words on separate lines, rubbed ink on the letters, and then placed a piece of paper on top of the ink. The last step was to press the paper against the ink to form a good impression of the type. The printing press was born.

Gutenberg's first printing efforts were some small books and a calendar. In 1456, he completed *The Bible of 42 Lines*, which is the oldest printed book in existence in Western society. Historians now credit the publication to him, although during his lifetime he received no credit for his efforts. He also is presumed to have compiled and printed a 748-page encyclopedia by setting type in two columns of 66 lines each.

Printing has come a long way since Gutenberg's day, but some small print shops still prefer to set type by hand as an art form for limited-edition books. In the late 1800s, the Linotype and Monotype machines replaced the painstaking work of setting type manually. Today, designers create digital type with computers, and new fonts are copyrighted daily.

Microsoft features information on many of the latest fonts, as well as typography-related tips and news, at its Web site (microsoft.com/typography).

The fonts you choose for your flyer, your brochure, your correspondence, or your wedding invitations reveal much about your personality and image. Using an appropriate typeface may determine if your reader actually reads your message. Like a fine piece of jewelry, the type should complement your message, not overpower it by being distracting.

Using Publisher 2002 in this book provides you with the latest features of desktop publishing, such as the Design Gallery, that can help you create a variety of high-impact, professional looking publications for your business, organization, school, or home. You can print your publications or publish them to the Web. Wizards, templates, styles, and content are available to help you achieve your desired results.

Type is important, primarily because it allows you to relay information to others. Additionally, type helps you communicate in more subtle ways: it can attract attention, set the style and tone of your documents, and shape how readers interpret your words.

Microsoft Publisher 2002

Creating and Editing a Publication

P R O J E C T

1

CASE PERSPECTIVE

Terry Arslanian, a close friend of yours, is a junior this year at Western College, a Liberal Arts college with 8,000 students, offering a variety of degree programs. Terry recently moved out of the dormitory and has rented a two-bedroom apartment close to campus. Terry wants to find a roommate who also is a student with similar interests and priorities.

Terry has seen flyers around campus advertising everything from cars, to sharing a ride, to typing services. The small tear-off tabs with telephone numbers and information make it easy for interested parties to contact the advertiser. Terry feels quite confident that a flyer advertising for a roommate will fill that empty second bedroom quickly. The college offers an electronic bulletin board where students can post advertisements, as well.

Because of your experience with word processing and the Web, you have agreed to help Terry prepare a flyer with tear-offs at the bottom advertising for a roommate. Together, you decide to use a Microsoft Publisher Sales Flyer with strong, bold headings, descriptive text, and sharp graphics. With your assistance, Terry wants to publish a Web version of the flyer on Western's electronic bulletin board.

What Is Microsoft Publisher?

Microsoft Publisher is a powerful **desktop publishing** (**DTP**) program that assists you in designing and producing professional quality documents that combine text, graphics, illustrations, and photographs. DTP software provides additional tools over and above those typically found in word processing packages, including design templates, graphic manipulation tools, color schemes or libraries, and multiple page wizards and templates. For large jobs, businesses use DTP software to design publications that are **camera ready**, which means the files are suitable for outside commercial printing.

The publishing industry has undergone tremendous change in the past few years due to advancements in hardware and software technology. Books, magazines, and brochures used to be created by slower, more expensive methods such as typesetting — a process that had not changed fundamentally since the days of Gutenberg and his *Bible*. With desktop publishing software, you can create professional looking documents on your own computer and produce work that previously could be achieved only by graphic artists. Both cost and time are significantly decreased. Microsoft Publisher is becoming the choice of people who regularly produce high-quality color publications such as newsletters, flyers, logos, signs, and forms. Saving publications as Web pages or complete Web sites is a powerful feature in Publisher. All publications can be saved in a format that can be easily viewed and manipulated using a browser. Some examples of these publications are shown in Figure 1-1.

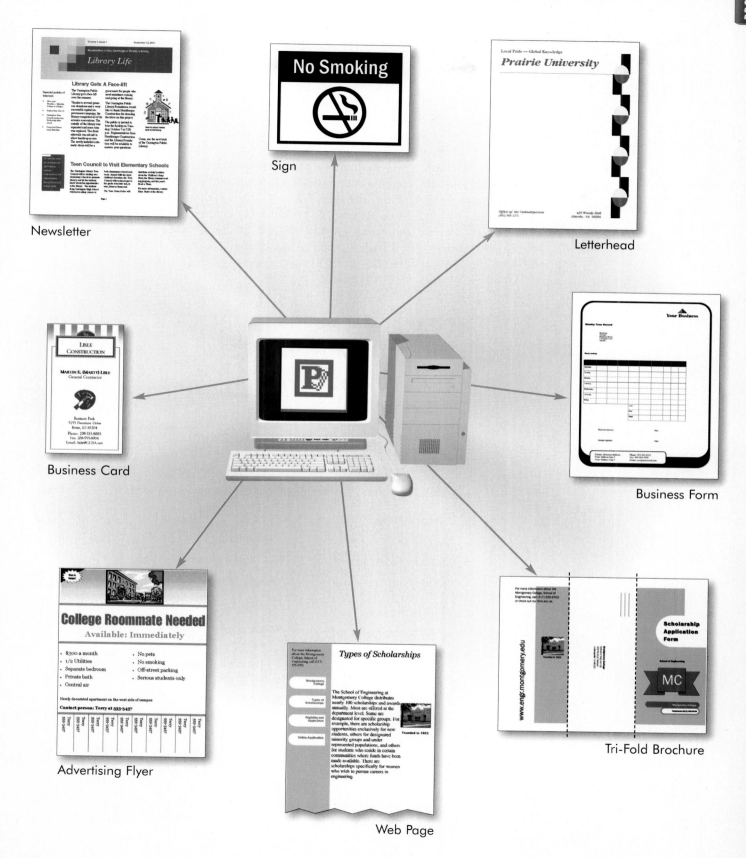

Newsletter

Sign

Letterhead

Business Card

Business Form

Advertising Flyer

Web Page

Tri-Fold Brochure

FIGURE 1-1

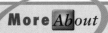

The Publisher Help System

Need Help? It is no further than the Ask a Question box in the upper-right corner of the window. Click the box that contains the text, Type a question for help (Figure 1-5 on page PUB 1.10), type help, and then press the ENTER key. Publisher will respond with a list of items you can click to learn about obtaining help on any Publisher-related topic.

Project One — College Roommate Needed Flyer with Tear-Offs

To illustrate the features of Microsoft Publisher 2002, this book presents a series of projects that use Publisher to create publications similar to those you will encounter in academic and business environments. Project 1 uses Publisher to produce the flyer shown in Figure 1-2. The flyer advertises for a college roommate for Terry Arslanian, who has a two-bedroom apartment close to campus. The heading, College Roommate Needed, is designed to draw attention to the flyer, as is the Attention Getter containing the text, Close to Campus!, in the upper-left corner. An eye-catching graphic of an apartment building is centered at the top. A bulleted list identifies the details about the apartment. Text below the bulleted list explains where the apartment is located and whom to contact. Finally, in the lower portion of the flyer, is a set of tear-offs with Terry's name and telephone number.

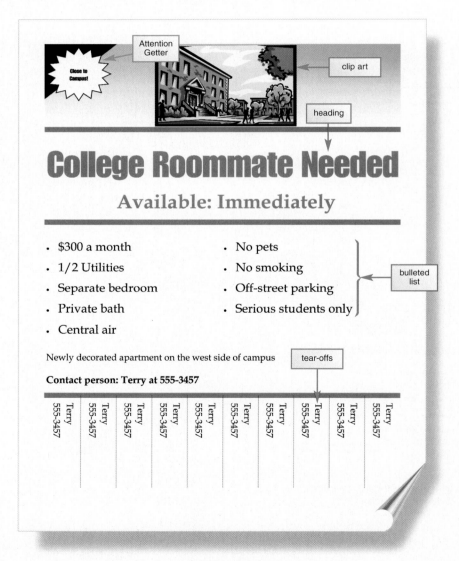

FIGURE 1-2

Starting Publisher

To start Publisher, Windows must be running. Perform the following steps to start Publisher.

 To Start Publisher

1 **Click the Start button on the Windows taskbar and then point to New Office Document.**

The Start menu displays (Figure 1-3). Windows displays a ScreenTip describing the function of the New Office Document command.

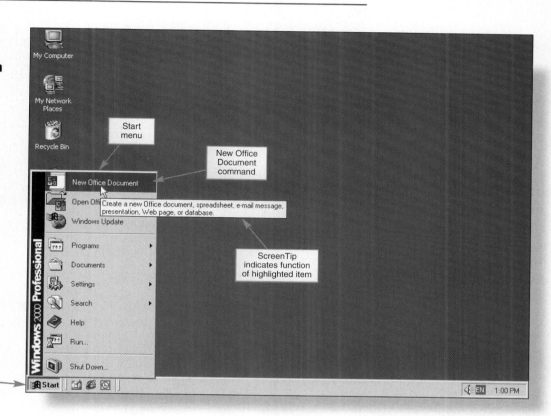

FIGURE 1-3

2 **Click New Office Document. Click the General tab and then point to the Blank Publication icon.**

The New Office Document dialog box displays (Figure 1-4).

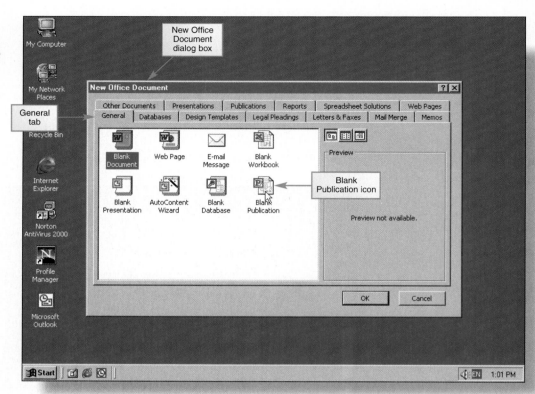

FIGURE 1-4

3 **Double-click the Blank Publication icon. When the New Publication task pane displays, point to Flyers in the By Publication Type list.**

Publisher displays the New Publication task pane on the left and the Quick Publications pane on the right (Figure 1-5). If the Office Assistant displays, right-click the Office Assistant and then click Hide on the shortcut menu. The By Publication Type list displays common types of documents used in desktop publishing.

Other Ways

1. Double-click Publisher icon on desktop
2. On Start menu point to Programs, click Microsoft Publisher on Programs submenu
3. Right-click Start button, click Open, double-click New Office Document, click General tab, double-click Blank Publication icon

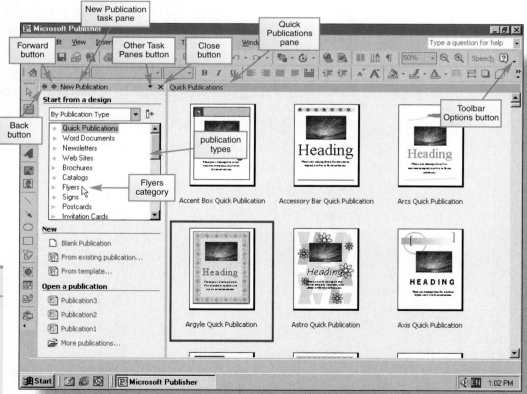

FIGURE 1-5

A **task pane**, such as the one shown in Figure 1-5, enables users to carry out some Publisher tasks more quickly. As you work through creating a publication, you will find that certain Publisher operations result in displaying a task pane. Besides the New Publication task pane shown in Figure 1-5, Publisher provides several additional task panes, including a Clipboard task pane and a Search task pane. These task panes are discussed when they are used. You can display or hide a task pane by clicking the **Task Pane command** on the **View menu**. You can activate additional task panes by clicking the **Other Task Panes button** on the task pane title bar (Figure 1-5) and then selecting a task pane in the list. Using the **Back** and **Forward** buttons on the left side of the task pane title bar, you can move between previously viewed task panes. You also can close the task pane by clicking its **Close button**.

When you start Publisher, the Publisher window displays the same way it displayed the last time you quit Publisher. Thus, if the task pane previously displayed on the left side of the window, and the option to show the task pane was set in Publisher's options (see Appendix D), then the task pane will display when you start Publisher. The same applies to the display configuration of the toolbar.

Three toolbars display on two rows when you first install Publisher: the Standard toolbar, the Connect Frames toolbar, and the Formatting toolbar. These toolbars are discussed later in this project. You can display or hide toolbars by right-clicking any toolbar and clicking the appropriate check boxes, or by clicking Toolbars on the View menu. To change the number of toolbar rows, click the **Toolbar Options button** (Figure 1-5) and then click the appropriate command.

Later in this project, to allow the maximum work space in the Publisher window, you will close the New Publication task pane that displays at startup. For the most efficient use of the toolbars, the buttons are displayed on two rows as shown in Figure 1-5.

Using Publisher's Publication Options to Create an Advertising Flyer

Publisher provides many ways to begin the process of creating a publication. You can:

- Create a publication with a publication wizard
- Create a publication from a design set
- Create a new publication based on an existing one
- Create a publication from a blank page
- Create a publication from a template

Choosing the appropriate one of these methods depends upon your experience with desktop publishing and how you have used Publisher in the past. In this first project, as you are beginning to learn about the features of Publisher, a series of steps is presented to create a publication using a wizard's publication options.

Because composing and designing from scratch is a difficult process for many people, Publisher provides wizards and templates to assist in publication preparation. Publisher has more than 2,000 wizards and templates to create professionally designed and unique publications. A **wizard** is a tool that helps you through the design process by offering you publication options and changing your publication accordingly. Once Publisher creates a publication from the publication options, you then fill in the blanks, replace prewritten text as necessary, and change the art to fit your needs. You also can use the wizard options to design a **template**, which is similar to a blueprint you can use over and over. Once saved, you can edit the elements of the template, just as you do with wizards, to customize them to your situation.

More *About*

Maximizing the Publisher Window

The number of previews you see in a publication's gallery pane may vary depending on the resolution and the size of your window. To make sure you see as many previews as possible, maximize the Publisher window by double-clicking the title bar, or by clicking the Maximize button on the title bar.

More *About*

Task Panes

When you first start Publisher, a small window called a task pane may display docked on the left side of the screen. You can drag a task pane title bar to float the pane in your work area or dock it on either the left or right side of a screen, depending on your personal preference.

More *About*

Task Pane Options

If the task pane does not display on start up, someone may have turned it off. To turn it back on, click Tools on the menu bar and then click Options. If necessary, click the General tab and then click Use New Publication task pane at start up to select the check box.

Microsoft **Publisher 2002**

More About

The Personal Information Wizard

If you have a new installation of Microsoft Publisher on a computer on which Publisher has not been installed before, you may be prompted to fill in fields of personal information. If the Personal Information Wizard displays a dialog box while you are working, you may fill it in for your installation or simply close the dialog box to ignore the personal information fields. You will learn more about personal information fields when they are used.

Creating a Publication Using Publication Options

The New Publication task pane displays a **gallery** of publications organized by publication or by design, on the right side of the Publisher window. The gallery changes based on your publication option choices in the task pane. You will use the **Sale Flyers Publication Gallery** to choose the Apartment for Rent flyer.

Once you choose a publication from the gallery, the task pane will allow you to make choices about the color and font schemes. A **color scheme** is a defined set of colors that complement each other when used in the same publication. Each Publisher color scheme provides a main color and four accent colors. A **font scheme** is a defined set of fonts associated with a publication. For example, a font scheme might be made up of one font for headings, one for body text, and another for captions. Font schemes make it easy to change all the fonts in a publication to give it a new look. Within each font scheme, both a major font and a minor font are specified. Generally, a major font is used for titles and headings, and a minor font is used for body text.

To create the publication using Publisher's publication options, complete the following steps.

Steps To Create a Publication Using Publication Options

1 Click Flyers in the By Publication Type list. Point to Sale in the Flyers category.

The By Publication Type list displays seven types of flyers (Figure 1-6).

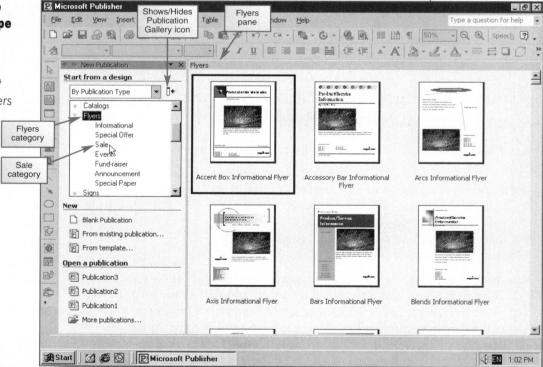

FIGURE 1-6

2 Click Sale in the list. Point to the Apartment for Rent Flyer in the Sale Flyers pane.

The Sale Flyers pane displays (Figure 1-7). Each category of publication type displays a unique publication gallery. A blue box displays around the flyer as you point to it.

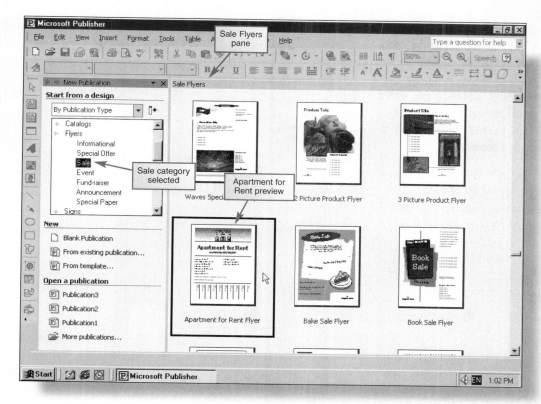

FIGURE 1-7

3 Click the Apartment for Rent Flyer. If a Microsoft Publisher dialog box displays, click its Close button. When the Flyer Options task pane displays, point to Color Schemes.

The gallery closes and the Apartment for Rent Flyer displays (Figure 1-8). The task pane changes to reflect the current publication's options. The Flyer Options task pane displays Publication Designs, Color Schemes, and Font Schemes, as well as options to display the publication with and without graphics, a customer address, and tear-offs.

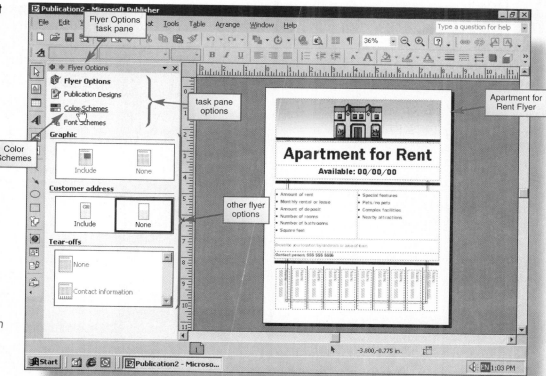

FIGURE 1-8

4 **Click Color Schemes in the Flyer Options task pane. When the task pane changes to Color Schemes, point to the down scroll arrow at the lower-right corner of the Apply a color scheme list.**

The Color Schemes task pane displays a list of color schemes (Figure 1-9). Each color scheme uses colors that complement one another. The main color displays to the left and the four accent colors display to its right.

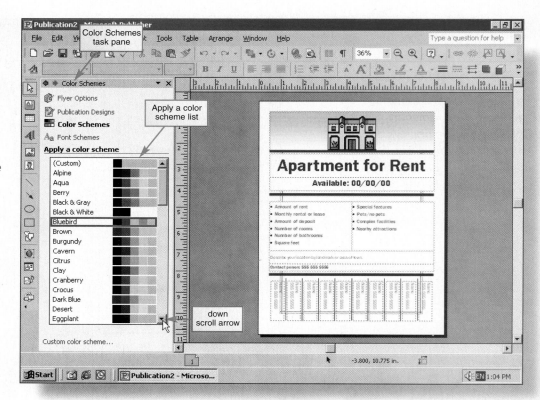

FIGURE 1-9

5 **Click the down scroll arrow until the Parrot color scheme displays. Point to the Parrot color scheme.**

A thin blue box displays around the color scheme as you point to it (Figure 1-10).

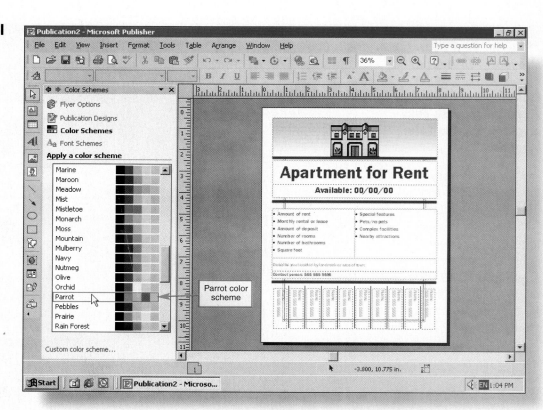

FIGURE 1-10

6 Click the Parrot color scheme. Point to Font Schemes in the Color Schemes task pane.

The Apartment for Rent Flyer displays the new Parrot color scheme (Figure 1-11). The most obvious change to the flyer is the bright red text. The selected color scheme now displays with a heavy blue border in the list.

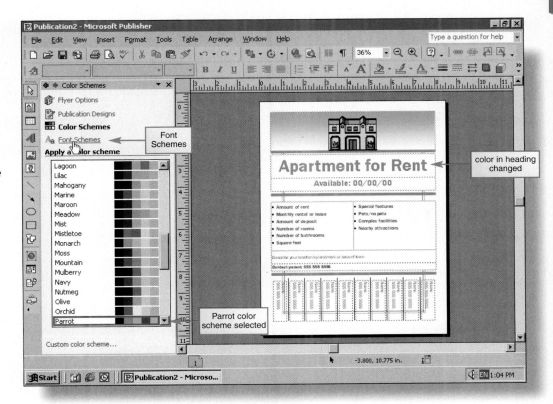

FIGURE 1-11

7 Click Font Schemes in the Color Schemes task pane. When the task pane changes to Font Schemes, point to the down scroll arrow at the lower-right corner of the Apply a font scheme list.

The Font Schemes task pane displays a list of font schemes (Figure 1-12). Each font scheme uses fonts that complement one another.

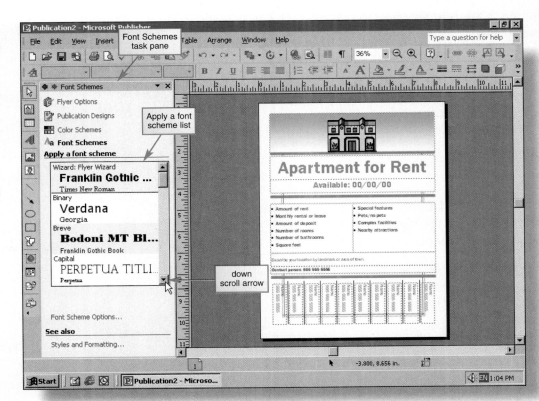

FIGURE 1-12

Microsoft **Publisher 2002**

8 **Click the down scroll arrow until the Impact font scheme displays. Point to the Impact font scheme.**

A ScreenTip displays the name of the scheme, as well as the names of the major and minor fonts used in the scheme (Figure 1-13).

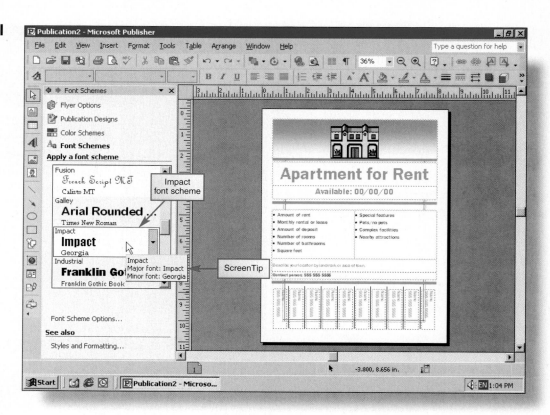

FIGURE 1-13

9 **Click Impact in the Apply a font scheme list. Point to the Close button in the Font Schemes task pane.**

The Apartment for Rent Flyer displays the new Impact font scheme (Figure 1-14). The most obvious change to the flyer is the major font used in the heading, which displays slightly bigger and bold.

10 **Click the Close button in the Font Schemes task pane.**

The task pane closes and the publication, ready to edit, displays in the Publisher workspace.

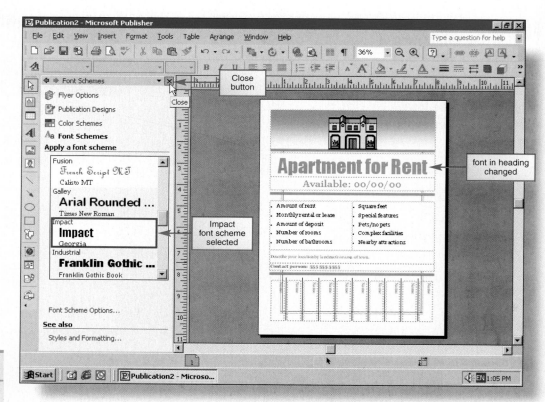

FIGURE 1-14

1. Click Shows Publication Gallery icon in New Publication task pane
2. On Format menu click publication option

The **Flyer Options task pane** displays its option links in the upper portion of the task pane and design choices in the lower portion (Figure 1-8 on page PUB 1.13). Each publication design will differ slightly in its options.

Most publication option task panes display a **Publication Designs option** that offers you the ability to apply a different design from the gallery.

Publication options can be revisited at any time during the design process by clicking the option in the task pane. If the task pane does not display, click Task Pane on the View menu.

The Publisher Window

To illustrate the parts of the Publisher window, a blank publication displays in Figure 1-15. The **Publisher window** includes a variety of features to make your work more efficient and the results more professional. Because Publisher is part of the Microsoft Office XP suite, the window display is similar to other applications in the suite and other Windows-based programs. The main elements of the Publisher window are the workspace, the menu bar, toolbars, and status bar.

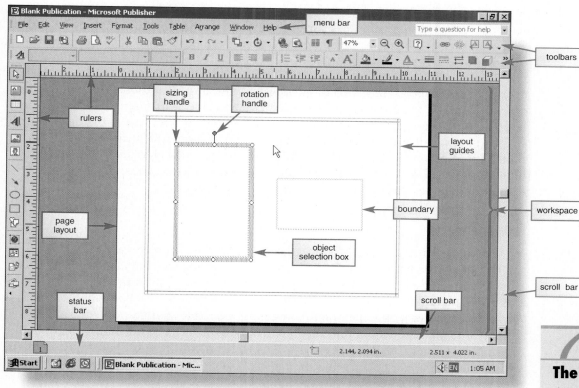

FIGURE 1-15

The Workspace

The **workspace** contains several elements similar to the document windows in other applications, as well as some elements unique to Publisher. As you create a publication, the page layout, rulers, scroll bars, guides and boundaries, and objects display in the gray workspace (Figure 1-15).

Desktop Publishing

Desktop publishing or electronic publishing is an extremely marketable skill in today's information-intensive workplace. For more information about desktop publishing software, visit the Publisher 2002 More About Web page (scsite.com/pub2002/more.htm) and then click Desktop Publishing Software.

More *About*

The Workspace

The workspace is saved with a publication. If you have objects that you might use later, but do not want to include on the page layout, you can move them into the workspace and save them with your publication for later use.

Objects

When clicked, the Design Gallery Object button, on the Objects toolbar, displays a tab for user-defined objects and objects created with other applications. For more information on the use of objects, visit the Publisher 2002 More About Web page (scsite.com/pub2002/more.htm) and then click Object Embedding.

The **page layout** contains a view of the entire page, all the objects contained therein, plus the guides and boundaries for the page and its objects. The page layout can be changed to accommodate multi-page spreads. You also can use the Special Paper command to view your page layout, as it will be printed on special paper, or see the final copy after preparing your publication for a printing service.

Two rulers outline the workspace at the top and left. A **ruler** is used to measure and place objects on the page. Although the vertical and horizontal rulers display at the left and top of the workspace, they can be moved and placed anywhere you need them. You use the rulers to measure and align objects on the page, set tab stops, adjust text frames, and change margins. Additionally, the rulers can be hidden to show more of the workspace. You will learn more about rulers in a later project.

Scroll bars, used to view different portions of the workspace, display at the bottom and right of the workspace.

Publisher's page layout displays the guides and boundaries of the page and its objects. Aligning design elements in relation to each other, both vertically and horizontally, is a tedious task. **Layout guides** create a grid that repeats on each page of a publication. They define sections of the page and help you align elements with precision. Page **margin guides** display in pink. **Grid guides**, which display in blue, assist you in organizing text pictures and objects into columns and rows to give a consistent look to your publication (Figure 1-15 on the previous page).

Boundaries are the gray lines surrounding an object. Boundaries are useful when you want to move or resize objects on the page. Boundaries and guides can be turned on and off using the View menu.

Objects include anything you want to place in your publication, such as text, WordArt, tear-offs, graphics, pictures, bullets, lines, and Web tools. You can choose objects from the Objects toolbar, from the Design Gallery, or insert them from original material. You click an object on the page to **select** it; selected objects display with small squares, called **sizing handles**, at each corner and middle location of the object boundary. A green rotation handle displays connected to each object. A selected object can be resized, rotated, moved, deleted, or grouped as necessary. You will learn more about object manipulation later in the project.

Menu Bar

The **menu bar** is a special toolbar displaying at the top of the window, just below the Publisher title bar (Figure 1-16a). The menu bar includes the menu names. Each **menu name** represents a menu of commands that you can use to retrieve, store, print, and manipulate data on the publication. When you point to a menu name on the menu bar, the area of the menu bar containing the name changes to a button. To display a menu, such as the Edit menu, click the Edit menu name on the menu bar (Figures 1-16b and 1-16c). A **menu** is a list of commands. If you point to a command with an arrow to its right, a **submenu** displays from which you can choose a command. An ellipsis (…) denotes that a dialog box will display when you click that menu command. **Keyboard shortcuts**, when available, display to the right of the menu commands.

Both short and full menus display some **dimmed commands** that appear gray, or dimmed, instead of black, which indicates they are not available for the current selection. A command with a dark gray shading in the rectangle to the left of it on a full menu is called a **hidden command** because it does not display on a short menu. As you use Publisher, it automatically personalizes the short menus for you based on how often you use commands. That is, as you use hidden commands on the full menu, Publisher *unhides* them and places them on the short menu.

Displaying Full Menus

If you prefer to use the full menus in Publisher and do not want to wait for them to display, click Tools on the menu bar and then click Customize. Select the Options sheet in the Customize dialog box and then click Always show full menus to select the check box.

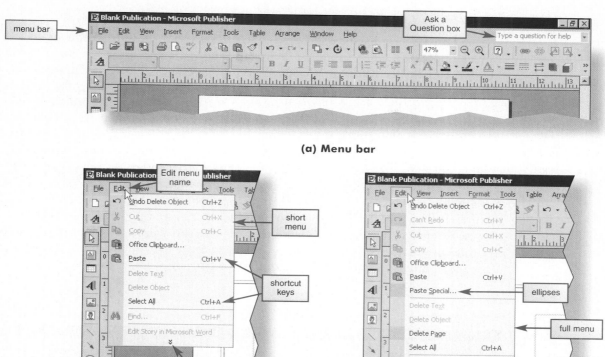

(a) Menu bar

(b) Short Menu

(c) Full Menu

FIGURE 1-16

When you click a menu name on the menu bar, a **short menu** displays listing the most recently used commands (Figure 1-16b). If you wait a few seconds or click the arrows at the bottom of the short menu (Figure 1-16b), the full menu displays. The **full menu** lists all the commands associated with a menu (Figure 1-16c). You can display a full menu immediately by double-clicking the menu name on the menu bar. In this book, when you display a menu, always display the full menu using one of the following techniques.

- Click the menu name on the menu bar and then wait a few seconds.
- Click the menu name and then point to or click the arrows at the bottom of the short menu.
- Double-click the menu name.
- In Voice Command mode, say the name of the menu and then wait a few seconds.

To the right of the menu bar, Publisher displays the **Ask a Question box** (Figure 1-16a). You will learn more about this Help feature later in the project.

Toolbars

Toolbar Buttons

To add a new command button to a toolbar, click Customize on the Tools menu, and then click the Commands tab. You then can drag a command from the Commands tab to the toolbar.

Toolbars contain buttons and boxes that allow you to perform frequent tasks more quickly than when using the menu bar. The menu bar actually is the first toolbar in the Publisher window. When turned on, the **Standard toolbar** (Figure 1-17) displays just below the menu bar. The **Connect Frames** toolbar displays to the right of the Standard toolbar. Immediately below the Standard toolbar, the **Formatting toolbar** displays. Each type of object in Publisher displays its own Formatting toolbar when selected. The toolbars change when you click the object. For instance, in Figure 17, the selected text box displays a Formatting toolbar with font options, whereas a graphic object, such as a picture, will not. The **Objects toolbar** displays on the left edge of the Publisher window and contains buttons for each category of objects you can add to a publication. Additional toolbars, such as the Measurements toolbar, the Picture toolbar, and the WordArt toolbar, are object-specific, which means they only display when you use that specific kind of object. You will learn about other toolbars in future projects. If you do not see a toolbar in the window, click Toolbars on the View menu and then click the name of the toolbar you want to display.

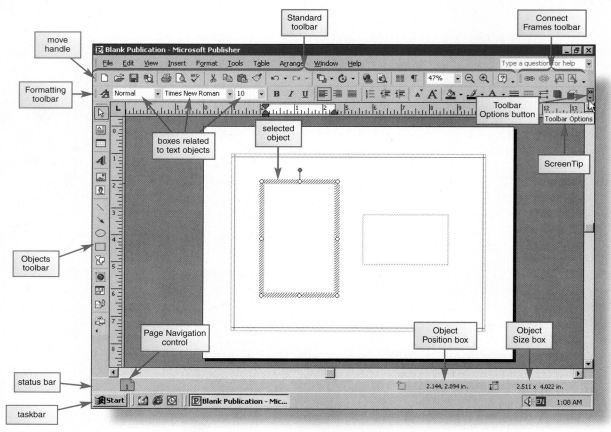

FIGURE 1-17

Each button on a toolbar has a picture on its face that helps you remember its function. In addition, when you move the mouse pointer over a button or box, the name of the button or box displays below it in a **ScreenTip**. Each button and box is explained in detail as it is used in the projects.

The toolbars initially display **docked**, or attached, to the edge of the Publisher window. Additional toolbars may display either stacked below the Formatting toolbar or floating in the Publisher window. A **floating toolbar** is not attached to an edge of the Publisher window. You can rearrange the order of **docked toolbars** and can move floating toolbars anywhere in the Publisher window by dragging them to the desired location.

When you first install Publisher (Figure 1-17), the Standard and Connect Frames toolbars are preset to display on one row, immediately below the menu bar. The Formatting toolbar displays below that. Unless the resolution of your display device is greater than 800 × 600, some of the buttons that belong on these toolbars do not display. Use the **Toolbar Options button** to display these hidden buttons. If more than one toolbar displays on a single row, you can double-click the **move handle** on the left of each toolbar to display more buttons.

Status Bar

Immediately above the Windows taskbar at the bottom of the window is the status bar. In Publisher, the **status bar** contains the Page Navigation control, the Object Position box, and the Object Size box (Figure 1-17). The **Page Navigation control** displays a button for each page of your publication. The current page in a multi-page document will display selected in blue in the Page Navigation control. You may click any page to display it in the workspace. The **Object Position** and **Object Size** boxes are used as an alternative to using the rulers, as guidelines for lining up objects from the left and top margins. The exact position and size of a selected object is displayed in inches as you create or move it. You may choose to have the measurement displayed in picas, points, or centimeters. If no object is selected, the Object Position box displays the location of the mouse pointer. Double-clicking the status bar will display the Measurements toolbar. You will learn more about the Measurements toolbar in a future project.

Speech Recognition

With the **Office Speech Recognition software** installed and a microphone, you can speak the names of toolbar buttons, menus, menu commands, list items, alerts, and dialog box controls, such as OK and Cancel. You also can dictate text and numeric data. Use the **Language bar** (Figure 1-18b) to indicate whether you want to speak commands or dictate entries. You can display the Language bar in two ways: (1) click the Language Indicator button in the tray status area by the clock, and then click Show the Language bar on the menu (Figure 1-18a); or (2) point to the **Speech command** on the **Tools menu** and then click the **Speech Recognition command** on the **Speech submenu**. The Language bar is a floating toolbar that may display transparent, in order to view objects behind it.

> **More About**
>
> ### Docking
>
> You can move a floating toolbar anywhere on the screen by dragging its title bar. You resize a floating toolbar by dragging the edge of the toolbar to the desired size and shape. If you want to return a floating toolbar to its original docked location, simply double-click it. Otherwise, when you drag a toolbar to the edge of the window to dock it, the toolbar snaps into place along the window edge.

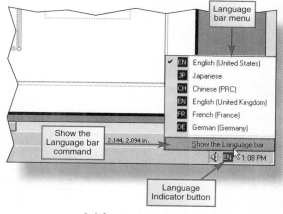

(a) Language Bar Menu

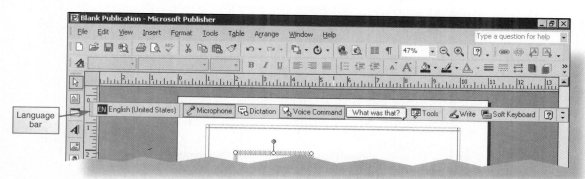

(b) Language Bar

FIGURE 1-18

If the Language Indicator button does not display in the tray status area, and if the Speech command is unavailable (dimmed) on the Tools menu, the Office Speech Recognition software is not installed. To install the software, Publisher will display an installation dialog box when you open the application; or, you may start Microsoft Word and then click Speech on the Tools menu.

Additional information on the Office speech recognition and handwriting recognition services capabilities are available in Appendix B.

Editing Text in a Publication

Most of the publications in the Design Gallery come with text inserted into text boxes. A **text box** is an object in a publication designed to hold text in a specific shape, size, and style. Text boxes can be placed by a wizard or can be drawn on the page using the **Text Box button** on the Objects toolbar. Text boxes can be formatted from the task pane, on the Formatting toolbar, or on the shortcut menu displayed by right-clicking the text box.

A text box has changeable properties. A **property** is an attribute or characteristic of an object. Within text boxes, you can make changes to the following properties: font, spacing, alignment, line/border style, fill color, and margins, among others.

Perform the following steps to edit the text of the flyer.

Editing Text

Editing the flyer involves making changes to the text to fit your needs. Perform the following steps to edit the heading and date on the flyer you created previously.

Steps **To Edit Text**

1 **Click Apartment for Rent in the heading of the flyer. If your page layout is not centered in the workspace, you may drag the horizontal scroll box at the bottom of the workspace.**

*The text box displays its text selected (Figure 1-19). Sizing handles indicate the object can be resized. Publisher displays a ScreenTip immediately below the object. Notice the mouse pointer displays as an **I-beam** as it is moved over text boxes.*

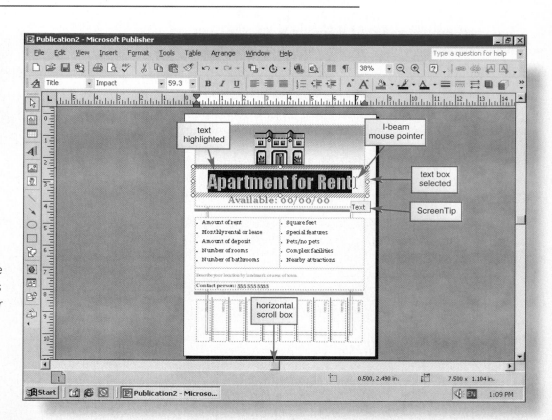

FIGURE 1-19

2 **Type** College Roommate Needed **in the text box. Point to the date text box in the subheading.**

*The selected text is replaced automatically (Figure 1-20). Publisher uses **AutoFit Text** to resize the text automatically so it fits into the allotted amount of space. The font size has been reduced to accommodate the new, longer phrase.*

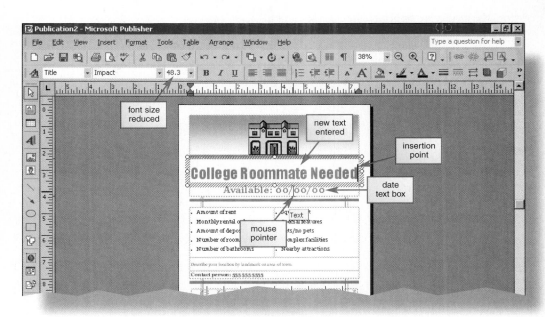

FIGURE 1-20

3 **Click the text, 00/00/00, and then type** Immediately **in the date text box.**

The new text displays (Figure 1-21). The minor font displays in the Font box on the Formatting toolbar.

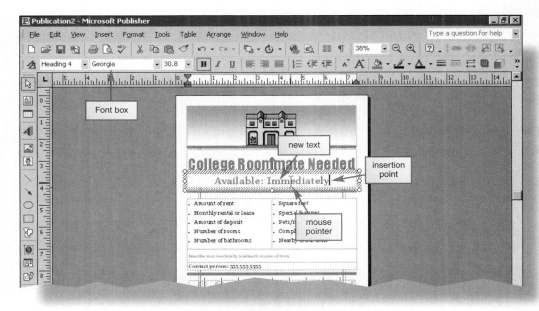

FIGURE 1-21

If text does not fit in a text box, or it seems to run over, it is possible that AutoFit Text has been turned off. The **AutoFit Text command**, available on the Format menu, has three ways to fit text in the text box: None, Best Fit, or Shrink Text On Overflow. **Best Fit** reduces or enlarges text to fill the frame, whereas **Shrink Text On Overflow** reduces text only if you fill the frame. The **None** option does not adjust the size of the text.

Recall that Publisher changes the Formatting toolbar to display buttons associated with specific objects. In Figure 1-21, the Formatting toolbar displays text-related buttons such as Style, Font, Font Size, and alignment buttons, among others.

Flagged Words

Recall that the commands on a shortcut menu differ depending on the object. If you select a word and then right-click it, you can cut, copy, or paste the word from the shortcut menu; however, if the selected word has a red wavy underline below it, you can only spell check it from the shortcut menu.

Publisher automatically checks for spelling errors and duplicate words as you enter text. If you type a word that is not in the dictionary (because it is a proper name or misspelled) a red wavy underline displays below the word. You may right-click the underlined word to see Publisher's suggestions or choose Spelling on the Tools menu to check the spelling of the entire publication.

Zooming to Facilitate Editing

Editing small areas of text is easier if you use the various zoom buttons to enlarge the view of the publication. When viewing an entire printed page, 8½-by-11 inches, the magnification is approximately 38 percent, which makes reading the small text difficult. The **Zoom In button** on the Standard toolbar allows you to increase that magnification. If you click an object before zooming in, Publisher will display the selected object magnified, in the center of the workspace, when you zoom.

The following steps illustrate how to use the Zoom In button to edit the small text below the bulleted list.

 To Edit Text Using the Zoom In Button

1 **Click the text below the bulleted list. Point to the Zoom In button.**

The text is highlighted and the text box is selected (Figure 1-22). Publisher may display a yellow Publisher tip if your installation is fairly recent or you have reset your tips.

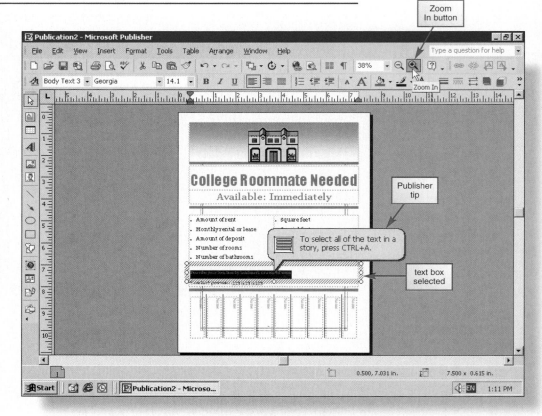

FIGURE 1-22

2 **Click the Zoom In button twice. Type** Newly decorated apartment on the west side of campus **and then point to the telephone number in the Contact person text box.**

The display magnification increases and the new text displays (Figure 1-23). The **Zoom box** *on the Standard toolbar displays 66% (Figure 1-23).*

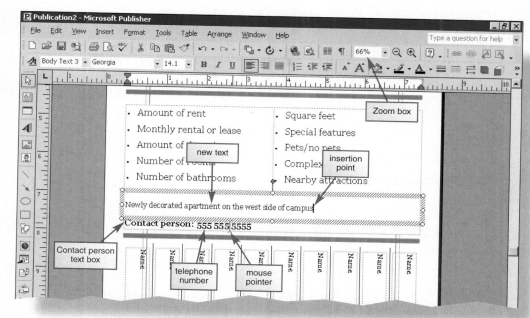

FIGURE 1-23

3 **Click the telephone number. Type** Terry at 555-3457 **to replace the previous text.**

The new text displays (Figure 1-24).

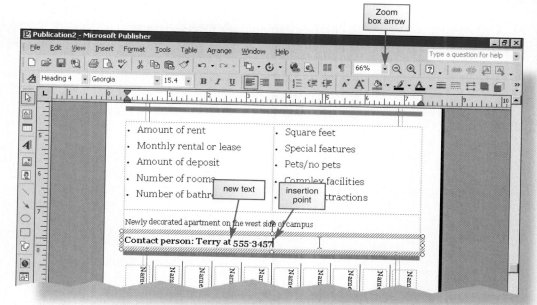

FIGURE 1-24

Publisher also allows you to zoom using the Zoom box on the Standard toolbar. Clicking the Zoom box arrow (Figure 1-24) displays a list of magnifications such as Whole Page, Page Width, and various magnifications. Additionally, you can press the F9 key to enlarge an object to 100% magnification.

Changing the magnification does not change the size of the printed text.

Other **Ways**

1. Click Zoom box arrow on Standard toolbar, click appropriate magnification
2. On View menu click Zoom, click appropriate magnification
3. Press F9
4. In Voice Command mode, say "Zoom In"

Editing a Bulleted List

The Apartment for Rent Flyer contains a bulleted list with samples or ideas for content. **Bullets** are used to draw attention to specific points in your publication. They show emphasis and make your publication lists look more professional. Publisher formats these kinds of text boxes with bullets and columns to make it easier for users to enter their own data.

Perform the following steps to edit the bulleted list.

Steps To Edit a Bulleted List

1 **Click the text in the bulleted list.**

The text is highlighted and the text box is selected (Figure 1-25).

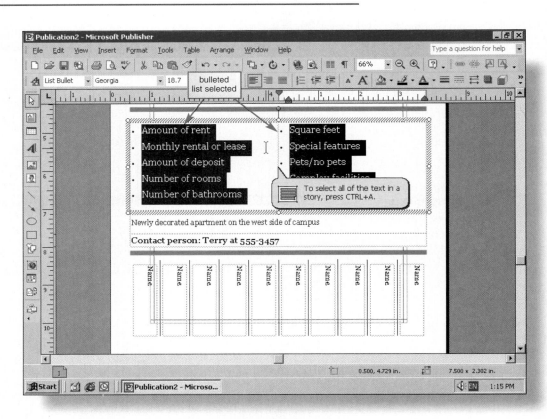

FIGURE 1-25

2 **Type** $300 a month **and then press the ENTER key.**

Publisher begins to rebuild the bulleted list as you enter text (Figure 1-26). The insertion point displays at the second bullet.

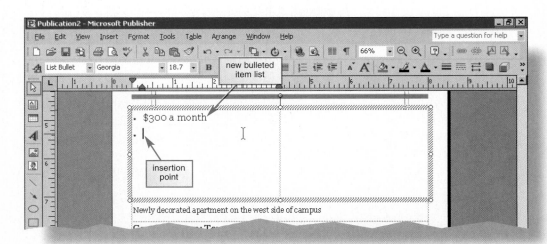

FIGURE 1-26

3 **Type** 1/2
Utilities and
press the ENTER key. Finish
typing the bullets, pressing
the ENTER key after each
item, as displayed in
Figure 1-27.

The bulleted list now is complete (Figure 1-27). The text box is formatted for two columns, so the bullets automatically wrap to the next column as necessary.

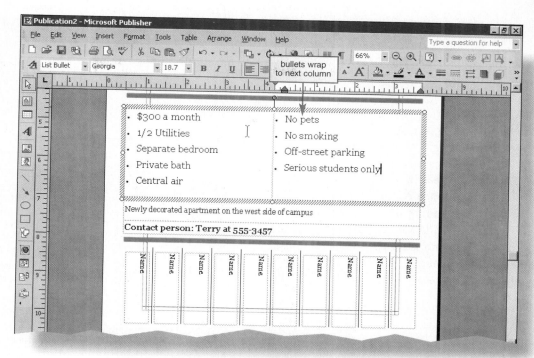

FIGURE 1-27

The bullets displayed in Figure 1-27 are small circles positioned at the beginning of each line. The **Indents and Lists** command on the Format menu displays a list of bullet styles from which you may choose.

Design Gallery Tear-Offs

Publisher provides many design objects such as tear-offs, coupons, and reply forms designed to be perforated or easily torn off from the publication. **Tear-offs** are small tabbed images with some combination of name, telephone, fax, e-mail, or address. Designed for customer use, tear-offs typically are perforated so a person walking by can tear off a tab to keep, rather than having to stop, find a pen and paper, and write down the name and telephone number. Traditionally, small businesses or individuals wanting to advertise something locally used tear-offs; but more recently, large companies are mass-producing advertising flyers with tear-offs to post at shopping centers, display in offices, and advertise on college campuses.

Editing Telephone Tear-Offs

The telephone tear-offs are a repeated design element, **synchronized** to change with editing. This means that when you change the text or format in one tab, Publisher also makes the changes to similar objects so you do not have to change each one manually. Synchronization occurs as soon as you finish editing. It can be cancelled by clicking the Undo button on the Standard toolbar. You can turn the synchronization feature on and off using the **Options command** on the Tools menu.

Synchronization

As you work on a publication, some objects might not retain their formatting because automatic wizard synchronization settings require changing. To change settings, click Tools on the menu bar and then click Options. Click the User Assistance tab and then click the Click to reset wizard synchronizing button. When you turn on synchronization, similar objects automatically change to have the same formatting or content when you make additional changes or click outside the area.

Microsoft **Publisher 2002**

The tear-offs on a standard 8½-by-11-inch piece of paper include 10 text boxes and 9 lines separating them, positioned at the bottom of the page. More repeated design elements will be discussed later.

Perform the following steps to edit the tear-offs.

Steps **To Edit Telephone Tear-Offs**

1 **Click the text in the first tear-off on the left. Depending on your system fonts, the text box may or may not display a placeholder phone number**

The tear-off text box displays selected (Figure 1-28).

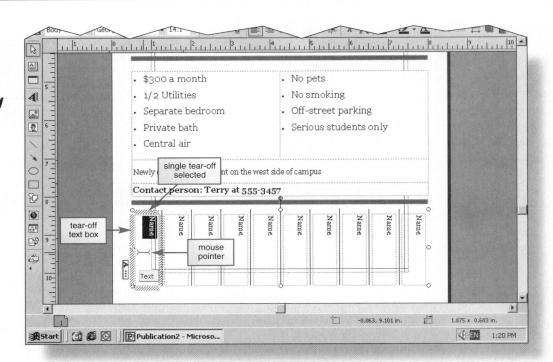

FIGURE 1-28

2 **Type** Terry **and then press SHIFT + ENTER. Type** 555-3457 **on the next line.**

As you begin typing, the insertion point, text, and I-beam mouse pointer display sideways in the tear-off (Figure 1-29).

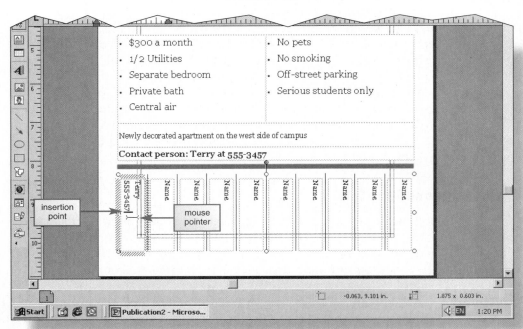

FIGURE 1-29

3 **Click anywhere outside the first tear-off text box.**

All the tear-offs change to display the new text (Figure 1-30).

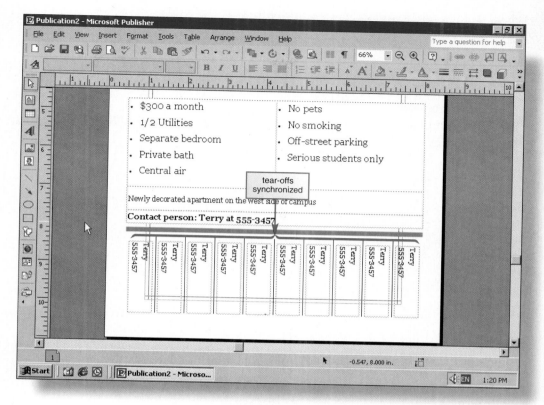

FIGURE 1-30

You may want to have the printed pages perforated at the tear-off lines so they tear easily and consistently. When completed in large batches, perforation costs are relatively small. Most print shops, copy shops, and duplicating services have perforation capabilities.

Saving a Publication

While you are creating a publication in Publisher, the computer stores it in memory. If the computer is turned off or if you lose electrical power, the publication is lost. Hence, it is important to save on disk any publication that you will use later.

Saving a New Publication

The text changes in your publication now are complete. Because you have made so many changes, now is a good time to save a copy of your work. Publisher's Save reminder feature may offer you the chance to save your publication at predetermined intervals during your work session. You may click either the Yes button or the No button when Publisher reminds you to save.

Perform the steps on the next page to save a publication on a floppy disk inserted in drive A using the Save button on the Standard toolbar.

More About

Pressing SHIFT+ENTER

When you press SHIFT+ENTER, you create a manual line break. A manual line break ends the current line and continues the text on the next line. Using a manual line break in a bulleted list will keep the next bullet from displaying as you create a new line. Pressing the ENTER key then will add a new bullet.

More About

Saving

When you save a publication, you should create readable and meaningful file names. A file name can include up to 255 characters, including spaces. The only invalid characters are backslash (\), slash (/), colon (:), asterisk (*), question mark (?), quotation mark ("), less than symbol (<), greater than symbol (>), and vertical bar (|).

Microsoft **Publisher 2002**

Steps **To Save a New Publication**

1 **Insert a formatted floppy disk into drive A on your computer. Click the Save button on the Standard toolbar.**

Publisher displays the Save As dialog box (Figure 1-31). Publisher uses a default file name on unsaved publications. Your default file name may differ. With this file name selected, you can change it by immediately typing the new name.

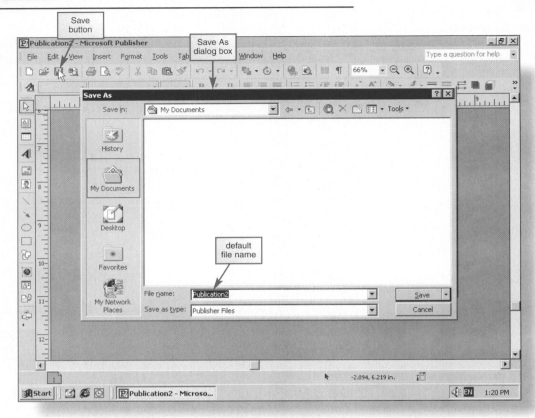

FIGURE 1-31

2 **Type the file name** College Roommate Needed **in the File name text box. Do not press the ENTER key after typing the file name. Point to the Save in box arrow.**

The file name, College Roommate Needed, displays in the File name text box (Figure 1-32). Notice that the current save location is the My Documents folder. A folder is a specific location on a disk. To change to a different location, you use the Save in box.

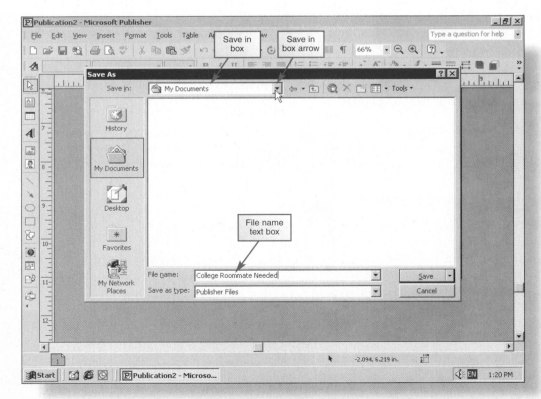

FIGURE 1-32

3 **Click the Save in box arrow and then point to 3½ Floppy (A:).**

A list of the available drives displays with 3½ Floppy (A:) highlighted (Figure 1-33). Your drive letter and list may differ depending on your system configuration.

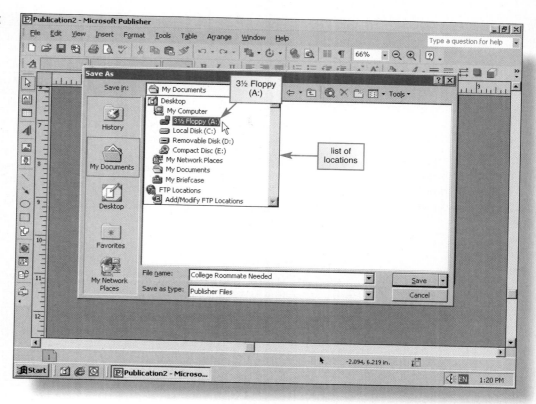

FIGURE 1-33

4 **Click 3½ Floppy (A:) and then point to the Save button in the Save As dialog box.**

The 3½ Floppy (A:) drive becomes the selected drive (Figure 1-34). The names of existing files that are stored on the floppy disk in drive A display. In Figure 1-34, no files currently are stored on the floppy disk.

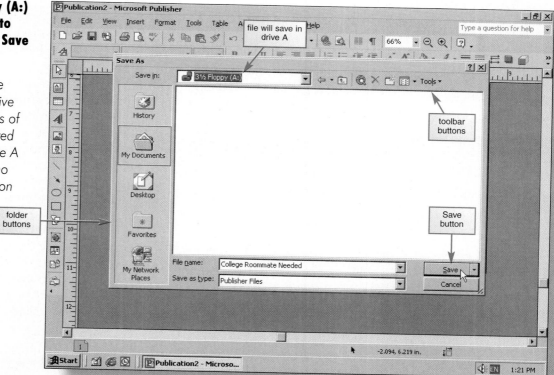

FIGURE 1-34

Microsoft **Publisher 2002**

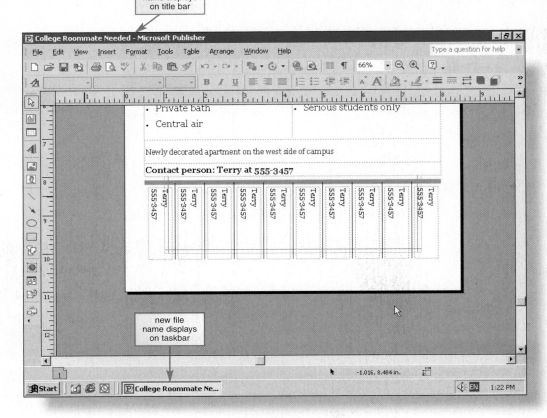

5 Click the Save button.

The saved publication displays with the new file name, College Roommate Needed, on the title bar and on the taskbar (Figure 1-35). Although the publication is saved on a floppy disk, it also remains in memory and displays in the workspace.

FIGURE 1-35

Other Ways

1. On File menu click Save As
2. Press CTRL+S
3. In Voice Command mode, say "File, Save As"

The seven buttons on the Save As dialog box toolbar (Figure 1-34 on the previous page) and their functions are summarized in Table 1-1.

When you click the **Tools button** in the Save As dialog box, a list displays. The **General Options command** in the list allows you to save a backup copy of the publication, create a password to limit access to the publication, and carry out other functions that are discussed later. Saving a backup publication means that each time you save a publication, Publisher copies the current version of the publication on disk to a file with the same name, but with the words, Backup of, appended to the front of the file name. In the case of a power failure or some other problem, use the backup version to restore your work.

You also can use the General Options command on the Tools list to assign a **password** to a publication so others cannot open it. A password is case-sensitive and can be up to 15 characters long. **Case-sensitive** means Publisher can differentiate between uppercase and lowercase letters. If you assign a password and forget the password, you cannot access the publication.

Table 1-1	Save As Dialog Box Toolbar Buttons	
BUTTON	**BUTTON NAME**	**FUNCTION**
⇦ ▾	Default File Location	Displays contents of default file location
🗂	Up One Level	Displays contents of next level up folder
🔍	Search the Web	Starts browser and displays search engine
✕	Delete	Deletes selected file or folder
📁	Create New Folder	Creates new folder
▦ ▾	Views	Changes view of files and folders
Tools ▾	Tools	Lists commands to print or modify file names and folders

The five folder buttons on the left of the Save As dialog box in Figure 1-34 allow you to select often used folders. The History button displays a list of shortcuts to the most recently used files in a folder titled Recent. You cannot save publications to the Recent folder.

When creating file names, you should make them as meaningful as possible. A **file name** can contain up to 255 characters and can include spaces.

Using Graphics

Files containing graphical images, also called **graphics**, are available from a variety of sources. Publisher includes a series of predefined graphics called **clip art** that you can insert into a publication. Clip art is located in the **Clip Organizer**, which contains a collection of clips, including clip art, as well as photographs, sounds, and video clips. The Clip Organizer contains its own Help system to assist you in locating clips suited to your application.

Clip art is an inclusive term given to draw-type images that are created from a set of instructions (also called object-based or vector graphics). **Images** usually are digital photographs, scanned images, or other artwork made from a series of small dots. More information on graphics, animation, and sound is presented in later projects.

Editing a Graphic

Because this flyer is advertising for a roommate in an apartment building, it may be appropriate to choose a graphic that looks more like an apartment building than the house picture supplied by the wizard. A graphic should enhance the message of the publication.

The following steps illustrate how to retrieve an appropriate picture from the Clip Organizer. If you cannot access the graphic described, choose a suitable replacement from your system's Clip Organizer.

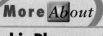

Graphic Placement

The spacing around a graphic should be at least 1/8 inch and should be consistent among the graphics in your publication. You can place the graphic manually or let Publisher maintain the graphic margin and the way text wraps around the pictures. With a graphic selected, clicking Picture on the Format menu allows you to set all four margins as well as text wrapping on the Layout sheet in the Format Picture dialog box.

Graphics on the Web

Microsoft has graphics files you may download from its Web site. To do this, click Clips Online on the Insert Clip Art task pane. If your computer is connected to the Internet, the Clips Online window will display. Follow the instructions to import a graphic or picture.

Steps **To Edit a Graphic**

1 **To view the whole page, click the Zoom box arrow, and then click Whole Page. Point to the graphic of the house.**

The whole page displays (Figure 1-36).

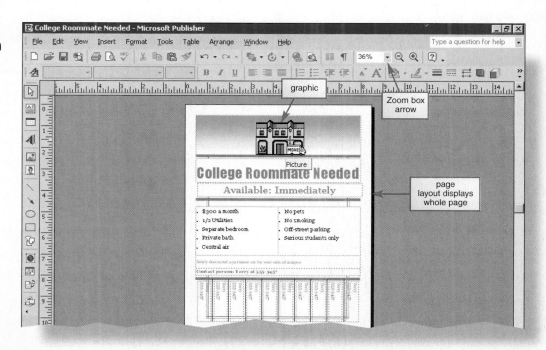

FIGURE 1-36

Microsoft **Publisher 2002**

2 **Double-click the graphic of the house. When the Insert Clip Art task pane displays, if the Search text text box contains text, drag through the text to select it. Type** apartment **and then point to the Search button.**

Publisher displays the Insert Clip Art task pane at the left edge of the Publisher window (Figure 1-37). Recall that a task pane is a separate window that enables you to carry out some Publisher tasks more efficiently. When you enter a description of the desired graphic in the Search text text box, Publisher searches the Clip Organizer for clips that match the description.

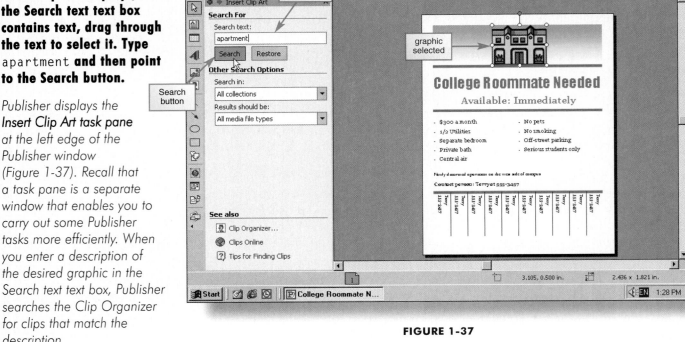

FIGURE 1-37

3 **Click the Search button. Point to the desired graphic and then click the button arrow that displays to the right of the graphic. Point to Insert on the shortcut menu.**

A list of clips that match the description, apartment, displays (Figure 1-38). Your graphics may vary depending on the installation of Publisher or the files on your network. Choose an appropriate graphic from your Clip Organizer.

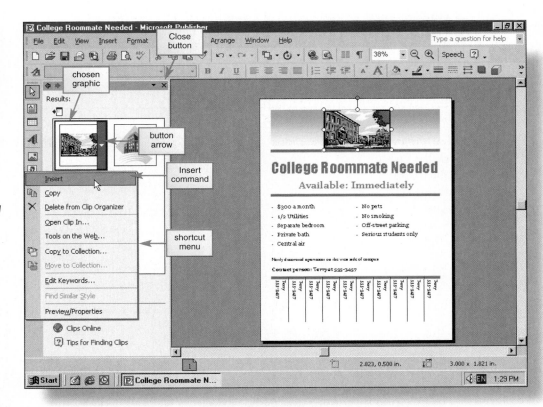

FIGURE 1-38

4 Click Insert. Click the Close button on the Insert Clip Art task pane title bar.

Publisher inserts the clip art into the publication (Figure 1-39). The new image replaces the previous house picture. The size of your graphic may differ.

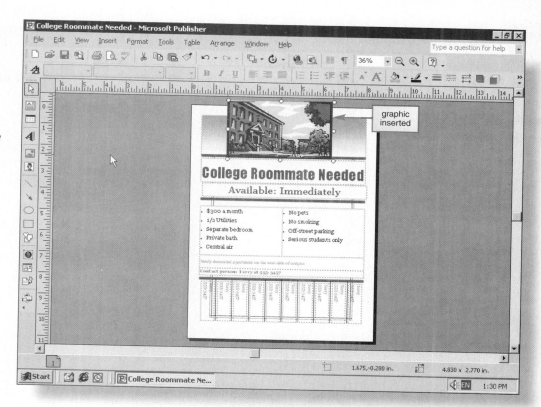

FIGURE 1-39

A **graphic** is any object in Publisher other than a text box. Graphics may include objects from the Clip Organizer, imported images and pictures, drawings, tables, WordArt, shapes, lines, and arrows. Publisher's CD-ROM comes with thousands of graphics including clip art, pictures, sounds, video clips, and animation. A full installation of Publisher copies these clips to the computer's hard disk. Alternately, the clips may remain on the Publisher CD-ROM for insertion as needed. For network installations, ask your instructor for the location of the graphic files.

Graphic files are available from a variety of sources. If you have a scanner or digital camera attached to your system, Publisher can insert the photograph directly from the scanner or camera. Alternatively, you can save the picture into a file and then insert it into the publication at a later time. Some users purchase photographs from local software retailers, have their film developed on a CD-ROM, or locate pictures on the Web.

You can use the Clip Organizer to organize your clips by category or keyword so that finding the one you want is made easier. Some graphics are more suitable for the Web, while others print better on color printers. Future projects discuss the various types of graphic files in detail, including advantages and disadvantages.

Resizing a Graphic

Once you have inserted a graphic into a document, you easily can change its size. **Resizing** includes both enlarging and reducing the size of a graphic. Perform the steps on the next page to resize the graphic.

Steps To Resize a Graphic

1 **If necessary, click the graphic to select it. Point to the upper-left corner sizing handle.**

*The mouse pointer changes to the **Resizer**, an icon to resize objects in Publisher (Figure 1-40). To resize a graphic, you drag the sizing handles until the graphic is the desired size.*

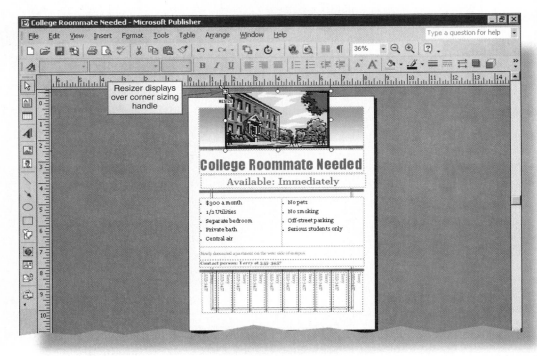

FIGURE 1-40

2 **Drag the sizing handle diagonally inward until the graphic is positioned approximately as shown in Figure 1-41.**

Publisher resizes the graphic (Figure 1-41). When you drag a corner sizing handle, the shape of the graphic remains intact.

Other Ways

1. On Format menu click Picture, click Size tab, enter desired height and width, click OK button
2. Right-click graphic, click Format Picture on shortcut menu, click Size tab, enter desired height and width, click OK button
3. Double-click status bar, enter desired height and width on Measurement toolbar

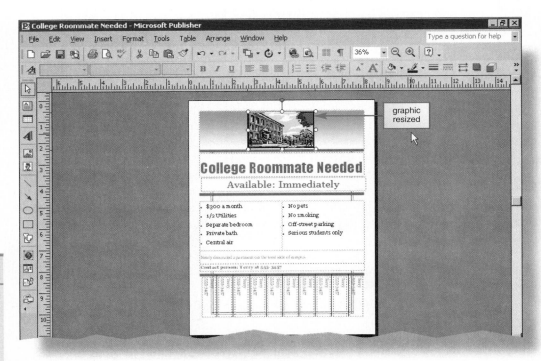

FIGURE 1-41

When you drag a middle sizing handle instead of a corner sizing handle, the proportions of the graphic change, which sometimes causes the graphic to look distorted.

Instead of resizing a selected graphic by dragging the mouse, you also can use the Size tab displayed by clicking Picture on the Format menu or you can use the Measurement toolbar. Either way, you can enter exact height and width measurements.

Sometimes you might resize a graphic and realize it is the wrong size. In these cases, you may want to return the graphic to its original size and start again. You could drag the sizing handle until the graphic resembles its original size. To restore a resized graphic to its exact original size, click the graphic to select it and then click the Format Picture button on the Picture toolbar to display the Format Picture dialog box. Click the Size tab and then click the Reset button. Finally, click the OK button.

Saving an Existing Publication with the Same File Name

The publication for Project 1 now is complete. To transfer the formatting and graphic changes to your file on the floppy disk in drive A, you must save the publication again. When you saved the publication the first time, you assigned the file name, College Roommate Needed. Publisher assigns this same file name automatically to the publication each time you subsequently save it, if you use the following procedure. Perform the following step to save the publication using the same file name.

TO SAVE AN EXISTING PUBLICATION WITH THE SAME FILE NAME

1 Click the Save button on the Standard toolbar.

Publisher saves the publication on a floppy disk inserted in drive A using the current file name, College Roommate Needed. The publication remains in memory and displays on the screen.

If for some reason, you want to save an existing publication with a different file name, click Save As on the File menu to display the Save As dialog box. Then, fill in the Save As dialog box as discussed in Steps 2 through 5 on pages PUB 1.30 through PUB 1.32 using a different file name in the File name text box.

Printing a Publication

Once you have created a publication and saved it on a floppy disk or hard disk, you might want to print it. A printed version of the publication is called a **hard copy** or **printout**. Perform the steps on the next page to print the publication created in Project 1.

More About

The Picture Toolbar

To display the Picture Toolbar, click View on the menu bar, point to Toolbars, and then click Picture. The Picture Toolbar contains buttons to adjust a graphic's color, contrast, brightness, and cropping, among others. You will learn more about the Picture Toolbar when it is used.

More About

Printing

To print multiple copies of the same publication, click File on the menu bar and then click Print. When the Print dialog box displays, type the desired number of copies in the Number of copies text box, and then click the OK button.

Microsoft **Publisher 2002**

1 **Ready the printer according to the printer instructions. Click the Print button on the Standard toolbar.**

A dialog box briefly displays indicating it is preparing to print the publication. A few moments later, the publication begins printing on the printer. The tray status area displays a printer icon while the publication is printing (Figure 1-42).

2 **When the printer stops, retrieve the printout.**

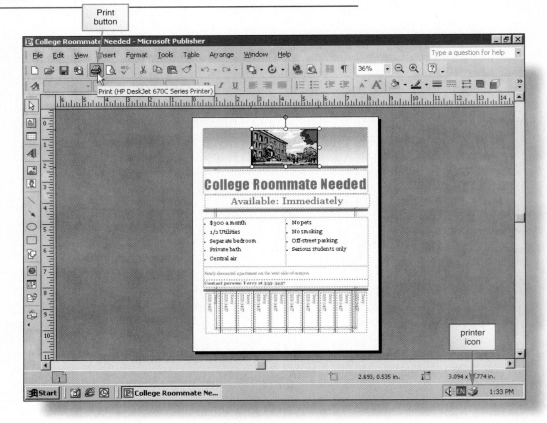

FIGURE 1-42

1. On File menu click Print, click OK button
2. Press CTRL+P, click OK button
3. In Voice Command mode, say "Print"

When you use the Print button to print a publication, Publisher prints the entire publication automatically. You then may distribute the hard copy or keep it as a permanent record of the publication.

If you want to cancel a job that is printing or waiting to be printed, double-click the printer icon in the tray status area (Figure 1-42). In the Printer dialog box, right-click the job to be canceled and then click Cancel Printing on the shortcut menu.

Quitting Publisher

After you create, save, and print the publication, you are ready to quit Publisher and return control to Windows. Perform the following steps to quit Publisher.

To Quit Publisher

1 | **Point to the Close button in the upper-right corner on the title bar (Figure 1-43).**

2 | **Click the Close button.**

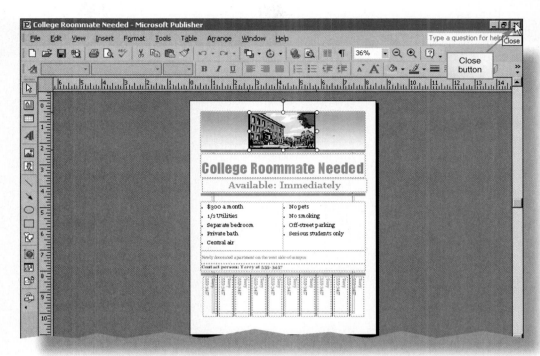

FIGURE 1-43

If you made changes to the publication since the last save, Publisher displays a dialog box asking if you want to save the changes. Clicking the Yes button saves changes; clicking the No button ignores the changes; and clicking the Cancel button returns to the publication. If you did not make any changes since you saved the publication, this dialog box does not display.

Closing a publication is different from quitting publishing. Closing a publication, by clicking Close on the File menu, leaves any other Publisher publication open. If no other publication was open, the Close command displays a blank publication page.

Project 1 now is complete. You created and edited the publication, inserted and resized a picture from the Clip Organizer, printed the publication, and saved it. You might decide, however, to change the publication at a later date. To do this, you must start Publisher again and then retrieve your publication from the floppy disk in drive A.

Other Ways

1. On File menu click Exit
2. Press ALT+F4
3. In Voice Command mode, say "File, Exit"

Opening a Publication

Once you have created and saved a publication, you often will have reason to retrieve it from disk. For example, you might want to revise the publication or print it again. Earlier, you saved the publication created in Project 1 on a floppy disk using the file name, College Roommate Needed. The steps on the next page illustrate how to open the file, College Roommate Needed, from a floppy disk in drive A.

Microsoft **Publisher 2002**

Steps To Open a Publication

1 Click the Start button on the taskbar and then point to Open Office Document (Figure 1-44).

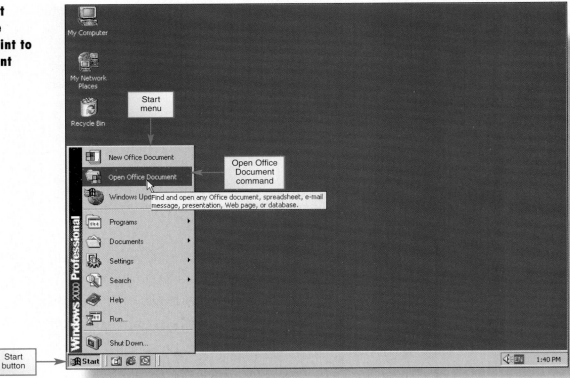

FIGURE 1-44

2 Click Open Office Document. If necessary, click the Look in box arrow and then click 3½ Floppy (A:). If it is not selected already, click the file name, College Roommate Needed. Point to the Open button.

Office displays the Open Office Document dialog box (Figure 1-45). The names of files on the floppy disk in drive A display in the dialog box.

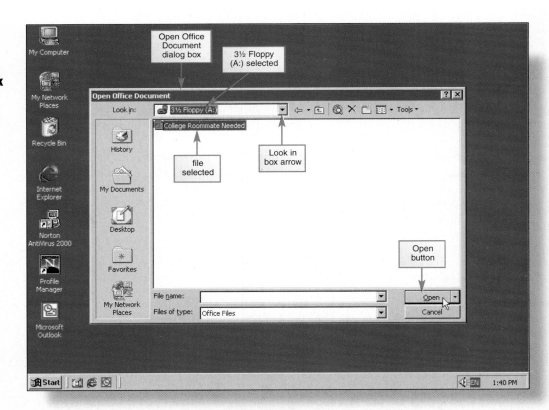

FIGURE 1-45

<table>
<tr><td>3</td><td>**Click the Open button.**</td></tr>
</table>

Office starts Publisher, and then Publisher opens the document, College Roommate Needed, from the floppy disk in drive A. The document displays in the Publisher window (Figure 1-46).

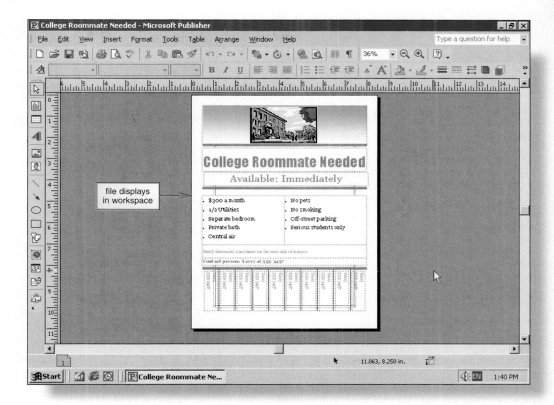

FIGURE 1-46

Modifying a Publication

After creating a publication, you often will find that you must make changes to it. Changes can be required because the document contains an error or because of new circumstances.

Types of Changes Made to Publications

The types of changes made to publications normally fall into one of the three following categories: additions, deletions, or modifications.

ADDITIONS Additional text, objects, or formatting may be required in the publication. Additions occur when you are required to add items to a publication. For example, in Project 1 you would like to add something about the apartment being close to campus in the flyer.

DELETIONS Sometimes deletions are necessary in a publication because objects are incorrect or are no longer needed. For example, to place this advertising flyer on the electronic bulletin board at the college, the tear-offs are no longer needed. In that case, you would delete them from the page layout.

Other Ways

1. Click Open button on Standard toolbar, select file name, click Open button in dialog box

2. On File menu click Open, select file name, click Open button in dialog box

3. Press CTRL+O, select file name, press ENTER

4. In Voice Command mode, say "Open, [file name], Open"

The Design Gallery

The Design Gallery contains an assortment of Publisher-designed attention getting objects such as linear accents, checkerboards, dots, punctuation, and borders. Many of these objects are grouped shapes with color, shading, and shadowing. Others allow you to insert a graphic or text that becomes part of the object. Publisher's design sets, color schemes, and smart object wizards all help you to make attractive decisions about Attention Getters.

MODIFICATIONS If you make an error in a document or want to make other modifications, normal combinations of inserting, deleting, and editing techniques for text and graphics apply. Publisher provides several methods for correcting errors in a document. For each of the text error correction techniques, you first must move the insertion point to the error. For graphic modification, the object first must be selected.

Modifications to the flyer will include moving an object to the corner of the page and editing it.

Adding an Attention Getter to a Publication

Drawing attention to a flyer such as this one is important. You want the customer to notice your flyer over others posted in the same area. The bright red lettering is a start, but adding a graphic to the upper-left corner will help draw attention to the flyer. Publisher has a Design Gallery of objects intended to add flair and style to your publications. The Design Gallery has three tabs: Objects by Category, Objects by Design, and Your Objects (Figure 1-47). A fourth tab called Extra Content displays if you switch design wizards in the middle of creating a publication and some elements in the first design are not included in the new design. The Extra Content tab holds those leftover objects.

Attention Getters display in the Objects by Category sheet. They contain graphic boxes, text frames, geometric designs, and colors intended to draw attention to your publication.

Perform the following steps to add an Attention Getter to the publication.

Steps **To Add an Attention Getter to a Publication**

1 **Click the Design Gallery Object button on the Objects toolbar. If necessary, when the Design Gallery dialog box displays, click the Objects by Category tab, and then point to Attention Getters in the Categories pane.**

The Design Gallery dialog box consisting of three tabbed sheets displays (Figure 1-47).

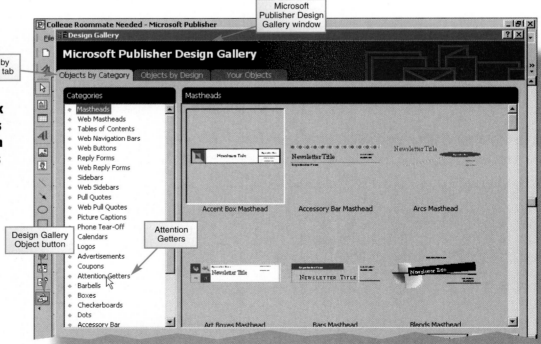

FIGURE 1-47

2 **Click Attention Getters. When the Attention Getters pane displays on the right, click the down scroll arrow until the Corner Starburst Attention Getter displays. Click the Corner Starburst Attention Getter and then point to the Insert Object button.**

The Attention Getters pane displays (Figure 1-48). The Corner Starburst Attention Getter is selected.

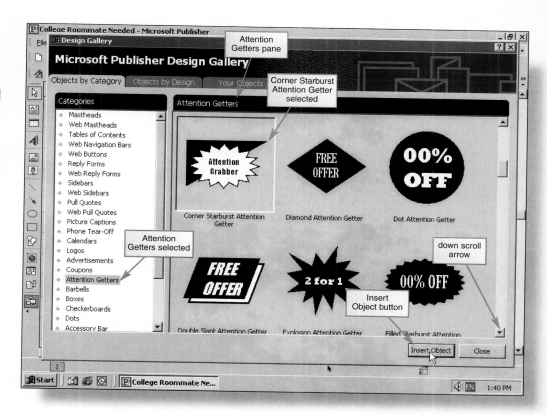

FIGURE 1-48

3 **Click the Insert Object button.**

The Attention Getter displays in the publication (Figure 1-49). A wizard button displays below the Attention Getter. You will learn more about wizards in a later project.

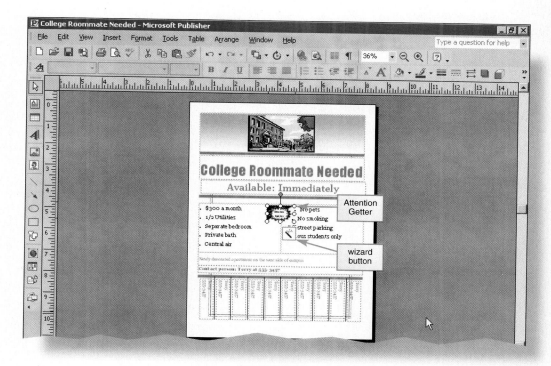

FIGURE 1-49

Other **Ways**

1. On Insert menu click Design Gallery Object

Attention Getters are usually a combination of a shape and text in black and white colors that stand out on the page. The Corner Starburst Attention Getter is suitable for the upper-left corner of a publication. Alternate Attention Getters display in a task pane if you click the wizard button (Figure 1-49 on the previous page).

Each button on the **Objects toolbar** can be used to add objects to your publication. You may want to insert a text box, a picture, or a shape to a publication. In that case, simply click the button on the Objects toolbar and then, on the publication layout page, drag the mouse to the desired size.

Moving an Object

In general, moving an object requires you to select it and then drag it to the desired position. Many objects, however, look better if they are aligned with another object or placed at a margin. Publisher will adjust the placement of an object so it aligns with the page layout guides automatically if you move the object close to the guide. This magnet-like process is called **snapping**. Three variations of snapping are available on the Arrange menu: Snap To Ruler marks, Snap To Guides, and Snap To Objects. All three variations work in a similar manner and apply to both moving and resizing.

Perform the following steps to move the Attention Getter object.

 To Move an Object

1 **Position the mouse pointer over the boundary of the Attention Getter.**

The mouse pointer changes to the Move icon when positioned over the border of an object (Figure 1-50).

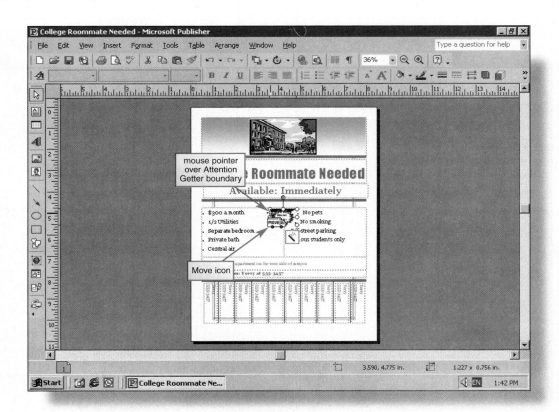

FIGURE 1-50

2 **Drag the Attention Getter to the upper-left corner of the publication.**

The object displays snapped to the guide (Figure 1-51).

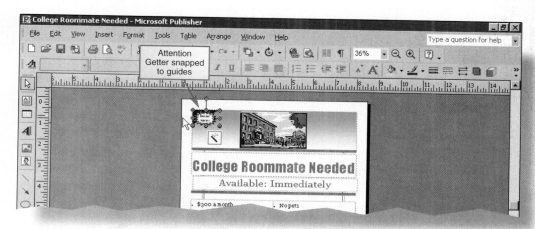

FIGURE 1-51

You may turn on and off the snapping feature by clicking Snap on the Arrange menu, and then clicking the appropriate choice. If you want objects moved very close but not adjacent to other objects, you should turn off the snapping feature. You will learn more about placing objects precisely in a later project.

Editing the Attention Getter

The Corner Starburst Attention Getter is a combination of a shape and a text box. You will edit the Publisher-supplied text to say, Close to Campus! and then use the Resizer to enlarge it. Perform the following steps to edit the text of the Attention Getter.

Steps **To Edit the Attention Getter**

1 **Press the F9 key.**

The object displays centered and enlarged, making it easier to edit (Figure 1-52).

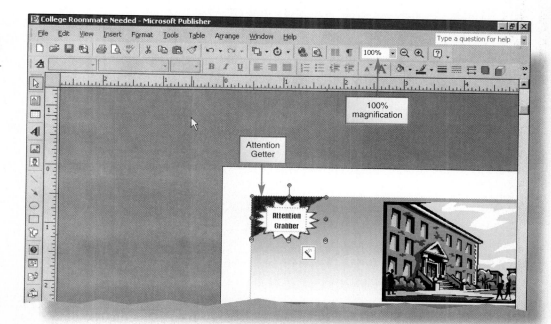

FIGURE 1-52

Microsoft Publisher 2002

2 **Click the text, Attention Grabber.**
Type Close to Campus! **in the text frame.**

The new text replaces the old (Figure 1-53). The AutoFit Text feature adjusts the font size.

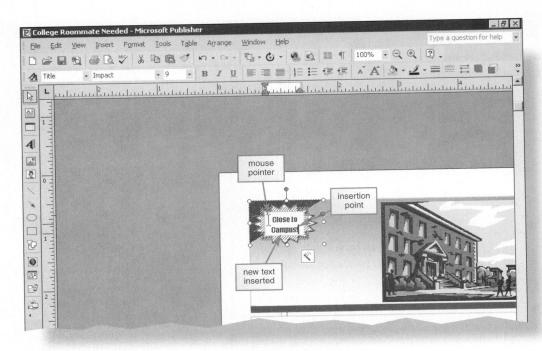

FIGURE 1-53

3 **Drag the lower-right corner sizing handle outward, until the Attention Getter is approximately the size shown in Figure 1-54.**

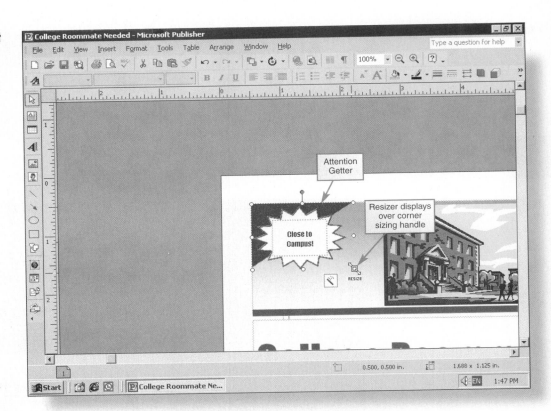

FIGURE 1-54

Should you desire to separate the parts of the Attention Getter and move the text box away from the shape, right-click the Attention Getter and click Ungroup on the shortcut menu.

Deleting an Object from a Publication

It is not unusual to type incorrect characters or words in a text frame, or to change your mind about including an object. If this flyer displays on an electronic bulletin board, the tear-offs are unnecessary. Perform the following steps to delete the tear-offs from the publication.

Steps To Delete an Object

1 **Right-click the workspace. Point to Zoom on the Shortcut menu and then point to Whole Page on the Zoom submenu.**

The shortcut menu displays (Figure 1-55). It contains some of the same view choices as the Zoom box.

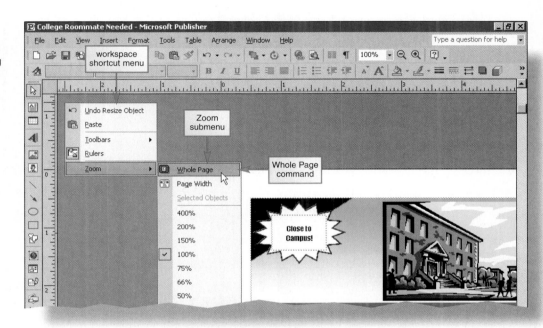

FIGURE 1-55

2 **Click Whole Page. Right-click any of the tear-offs, and then point to Delete Object on the shortcut menu.**

The publication displays in Whole Page view (Figure 1-56). Right-clicking the tear-offs displays a text box shortcut menu.

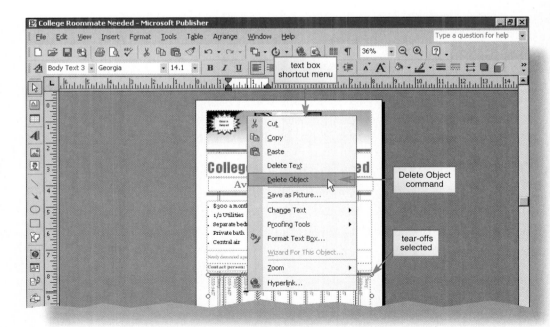

FIGURE 1-56

3 Click Delete Object.

The tear-offs are deleted (Figure 1-57).

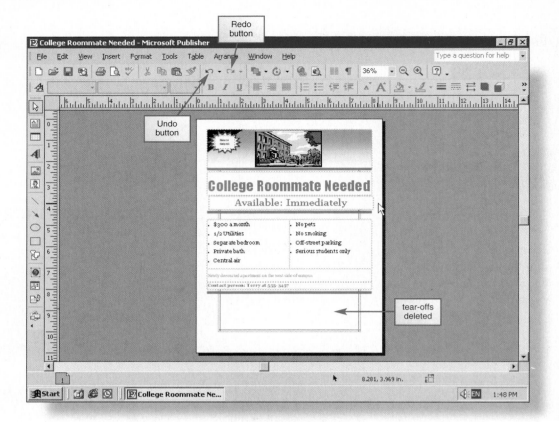

FIGURE 1-57

<table>
<tr><td colspan="2">**Other Ways**</td></tr>
<tr><td>1.</td><td>On Edit menu click Delete Object</td></tr>
<tr><td>2.</td><td>Click graphic, press DELETE</td></tr>
</table>

If you delete an object accidentally, you can bring it back by clicking the **Undo button** on the Standard toolbar (Figure 1-57). If you want to cancel your undo, you can use the **Redo button**. Some actions, such as saving or printing a document, cannot be undone or redone.

You may save your flyer again, if you want to retain the modifications you have made.

Creating a Web Page from a Publication

Publisher can create a Web page from your publication. It is a two-step process. First, Publisher uses a **Design Checker** to look for potential problems if the publication were transferred to the Web. Then the **Save as Web Page command** converts the publication to a Web page.

Running the Design Checker

If your publication contains a layout that is not appropriate, such as overlapping objects, the Design Checker will alert you. If you use links or hot spots to other Web pages within your publication, Design Checker will verify the addresses.

Perform the following steps to run the Design Checker.

Steps **To Run the Design Checker**

1 **Click Tools on the menu bar and then point to Design Checker.**

The Tools menu displays (Figure 1-58).

FIGURE 1-58

2 **Click Design Checker. When the Design Checker dialog box displays point to the OK button.**

The Design Checker dialog box displays options to check partial documents as well as buttons to change the options or cancel (Figure 1-59). Because the publication only has one page, the Pages option button is not available.

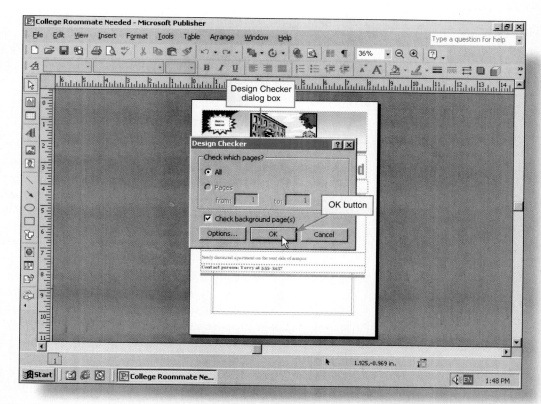

FIGURE 1-59

3 **Click the OK button. If a Design Checker dialog box displays, click Ignore or fix the problem. After a few moments, Publisher's Design Checker indicates that the Design check is complete. Point to the OK button.**

The Design Checker checks the publication for its ability to download, or display, quickly. Certain types of large graphics slow the display process on the Web, as do a large number of fonts and borders (Figure 1-60).

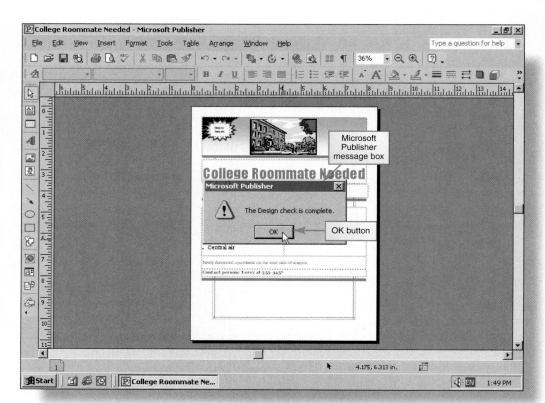

4 **Click the OK button.**

The Design Checker is complete.

FIGURE 1-60

HTML

For more information on HTML including code fragments and Web design issues, visit the Publisher 2002 More About Web page (scsite.com/ pub2002/more.htm) and then click HTML.

If there were problems with your publication, you would have been given the option to ignore, continue, or obtain more information about the problems. For example, if text overlaps an object, the Design Checker offers to convert the text box to a graphic so it will display properly. The Design Checker looks at all graphics and may display suggestions on those that load slowly. Types of graphics will be covered in future projects.

Saving a Publication as a Web Page

The second step is to save the verified Web publication. Normally, Publisher saves a file with the three-letter extension, .pub. The **.pub extension** allows Publisher easily to open your formatted file and assigns a recognizable icon to the shortcut on your disk. Files intended for use on the Web, however, need a different format. A **Hypertext Markup Language** (**HTML**) file is a file capable of being stored and transferred electronically on a file server in order to display on the Web. Publisher can save your file in the HTML format.

Publisher suggests creating a folder to hold each separate publication intended for the Web. A folder is a logical portion of a disk created to group and store similar documents. Inside this folder, Publisher will include the main HTML file, called the index, and copies of the associated graphics. Once created, your publication can be viewed by a Web browser, such as Microsoft Internet Explorer.

The concept of a Web folder facilitates integration of Publisher with other members of the Microsoft Office XP suite and Windows. With Windows, you can choose to use Web style folders on your desktop, which means that the desktop is interactive and all your folders look like Web pages. Publisher also will take care of **uploading,** or transferring, your files to the Web, if you are connected to an Internet service provider or host. See Appendix C for more information on Web folders.

Perform the following steps to save your publication as a Web page.

Steps To Save a Publication as a Web Page

1 **Click File on the menu bar. After a few seconds, when the full menu displays, point to Save as Web Page.**

The File menu displays (Figure 1-61).

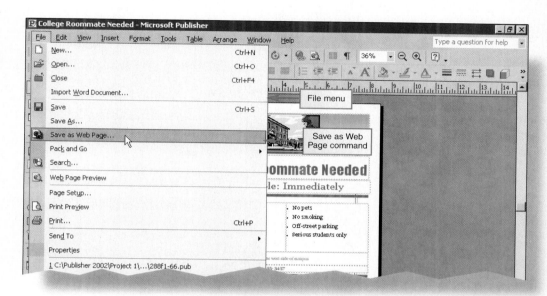

FIGURE 1-61

2 **Make sure a floppy disk is inserted in drive A. Click Save as Web Page. If you are asked to save changes, click the No button. When the Save As dialog box displays, click 3½ Floppy (A:) in the Look in list. Point to the Create New Folder button.**

The Save as Web Page dialog box displays (Figure 1-62). The graphics, text, and links, if any, will save on the floppy disk in drive A.

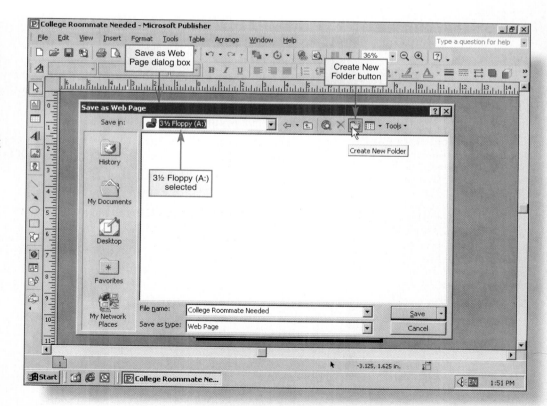

FIGURE 1-62

3 **Click the Create New Folder button. When the New Folder dialog box displays, type** Web flyer **in the Name text box. Point to the OK button.**

The new folder name displays in the Name text box (Figure 1-63).

4 **Click the OK button in the New Folder dialog box, and then click the Save button in the Save as Web Page dialog box.**

The saved files are ready to send to the Web.

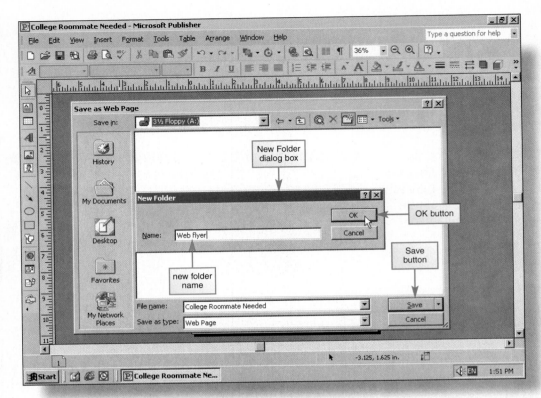

FIGURE 1-63

More About

Folders

You can store publications in any folder on your hard disk, floppy disk, or on a network, but it is a good practice to store them together in a folder that you can find easily when you open or save publications. The preset storage location for publications on a new installation of Publisher is in a folder named My Documents. My Documents can serve as a place to store the publications you use frequently. If you work with many different types of documents, you can organize them in subfolders within the My Documents folder.

Publisher Help System

At any time while you are using Publisher, you can get answers to questions by using the Publisher Help system. Used properly, this form of online assistance can increase your productivity and reduce your frustrations by minimizing the time you spend learning how to use Publisher.

The following section shows how to get answers to your questions using the Ask a Question box. For additional information on using the Publisher Help system, see Appendix A and Table 1-2 on page PUB 1.55.

Obtaining Help Using the Ask a Question Box on the Menu Bar

The **Ask a Question box** on the right side of the menu bar lets you type free-form questions, such as *how do I save* or *how do I create a Web page*, or you can type in terms, such as *copy*, *save*, or *formatting*. Publisher responds by displaying a list of topics related to what you entered. The following steps show how to use the Ask a Question box to obtain information on color schemes.

Steps **To Obtain Help Using the Ask a Question Box**

1 **Type** color schemes **in the Ask a Question box on the right side of the menu bar (Figure 1-64).**

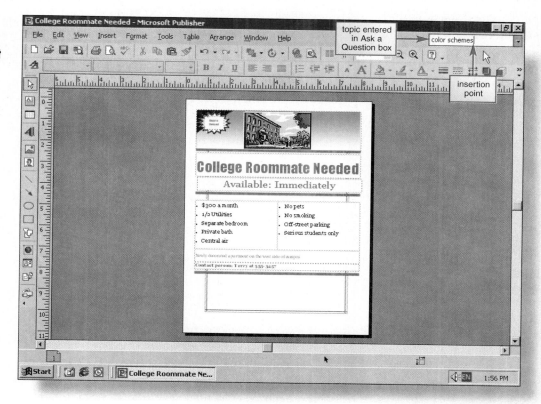

FIGURE 1-64

2 **Press the ENTER key. When the list of topics displays below the Ask a Question box, point to the topic, About color schemes and fill effects.**

A list of topics displays relating to color schemes. The mouse pointer changes to a hand indicating it is pointing to a link (Figure 1-65). Your list may differ.

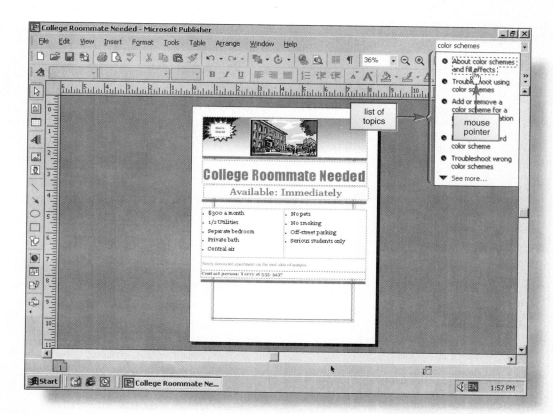

FIGURE 1-65

3 **Click About color schemes and fill effects. When the Microsoft Publisher Help window displays, double-click its title bar to maximize it. Click the What is a color scheme? link.**

Publisher opens a Microsoft Publisher Help window that provides Help information about publication color schemes (Figure 1-66).

4 **Click the Close button on the Microsoft Publisher Help window title bar.**

The Microsoft Publisher Help window closes and the publication displays.

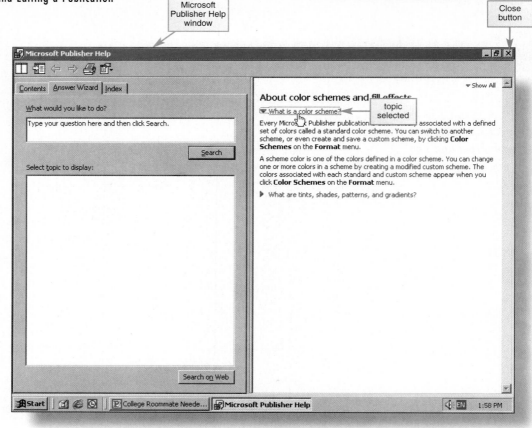

FIGURE 1-66

Links

A link, sometimes called a hyperlink, is text or an icon that when clicked, changes the screen or moves the insertion point to another location. A link also may display an expanded ToolTip or ScreenTip. A link in Publisher's Help system usually displays underlined and in a different color. When clicked, Publisher displays a location with more information on the topic.

The Publisher Help System

The best way to become familiar with the Publisher Help system is to use it. Appendix A includes detailed information on the Publisher Help system and exercises that will help you gain confidence in using it.

Use the buttons in the upper-left corner of the Microsoft Publisher Help window (Figure 1-66) to navigate through the Help system, change the display, and print the contents of the window.

As you enter questions and terms in the Ask a Question box, Publisher adds them to its list. Thus, if you click the Ask a Question box arrow, a list of previously asked questions and terms will display.

Table 1-2 summarizes the 9 categories of Help available to you. Because of the way the Publisher Help system works, be sure to review the rightmost column of Table 1-2 if you have difficulties activating the desired category of Help. Additional information on using the Publisher Help system is available in Appendix A.

Quitting Publisher

To quit Publisher, complete the following steps.

TO QUIT PUBLISHER

1 Click the Close button on the Publisher title bar (see Figure 1-43 on page PUB 1.39).

2 If the Microsoft Publisher dialog box displays, click the No button.

Table 1-2 Publisher Help System

TYPE	DESCRIPTION	HOW TO ACTIVATE
Answer Wizard	Answers questions or searches for terms that you type in your own words.	Click the Microsoft Publisher Help button on the Standard toolbar. Click the Answer Wizard tab.
Ask a Question box	Answers questions or searches for terms that you type in your own words.	Type a question or term in the Ask a Question box on the menu bar and then press the ENTER key.
Contents sheet	Groups Help topics by general categories. Use when you know only the general category of the topic in question.	Click the Microsoft Publisher Help button on the Standard toolbar. Click the Contents tab.
Detect and Repair	Automatically finds and fixes errors in the application.	Click Detect and Repair on the Help menu.
Hardware and Software Information	Shows Product ID and allows access to system information and technical support information.	Click About Microsoft Publisher on the Help menu and then click the appropriate button.
Index sheet	Similar to an index in a book. Use when you know exactly what you want.	Click the Microsoft Publisher Help button on the Standard toolbar. If necessary, maximize the Help window by double-clicking its title bar. Click the Index tab.
Office Assistant	Similar to the Ask a Question box in that the Office Assistant answers questions that you type in your own words, offers tips, and provides help for a variety of Publisher features.	Click the Office Assistant icon. If the Office Assistant does not display, click Show the Office Assistant on the Help menu.
Office on the Web	Used to access technical resources and download free product enhancements on the Web.	Click Office on the Web on the Help menu.
Question Mark button	Used to identify unfamiliar items in a dialog box.	Click the Question Mark button on the title bar of a dialog box and then click an item in the dialog box.
What's This? command	Used to identify unfamiliar items on the screen.	Click What's This? on the Help menu, and then click an item on the screen.

CASE PERSPECTIVE SUMMARY

Terry Arslanian's flyer is complete. With your help, he now has a full-color flyer with tear-offs that he can post at the school, the library, and stores in the area. The flyer consists of a graphic illustrating the purpose of the flyer, a bulleted list identifying characteristics about the apartment, and perforated tear-offs for potential roommates to take with them. The Attention Getter and bright red lettering should attract people to the flyer.

An added enhancement will be the Web page version of the flyer. Terry can publish the Web folder you created on Western College's electronic bulletin board, thus widening his advertising scope.

Project Summary

Project 1 introduced you to starting Publisher and creating an advertising flyer. You learned how to choose a publication wizard and respond to options in the task pane. After selecting color and font schemes, you learned how to edit text frames, bulleted lists, and repeating elements such as tear-offs. You also learned how to use the zoom buttons to assist you in editing. Once you saved the publication, you learned how to change a graphic and move and resize elements on the page layout. In anticipation of posting your publication to the Web, you learned how to delete, insert, and modify objects. You then saved the publication as a Web page in a Web folder, and quit Publisher. Finally, you learned how to use Publisher's Help system.

What You Should Know

Having completed this project, you now should be able to perform the following tasks:

- Add an Attention Getter to a Publication (*PUB 1.42*)
- Create a Publication Using Publication Options (*PUB 1.12*)
- Delete an Object (*PUB 1.47*)
- Edit a Bulleted List (*PUB 1.26*)
- Edit a Graphic (*PUB 1.33*)
- Edit Telephone Tear-Offs (*PUB 1.28*)
- Edit Text (*PUB 1.22*)
- Edit Text Using the Zoom In Button (*PUB 1.24*)
- Edit the Attention Getter (*PUB 1.45*)
- Move an Object (*PUB 1.44*)
- Obtain Help Using the Ask a Question Box (*PUB 1.53*)
- Print a Publication (*PUB 1.38*)
- Open a Publication (*PUB 1.40*)
- Quit Publisher (*PUB 1.54*)
- Resize a Graphic (*PUB 1.36*)
- Run the Design Checker (*PUB 1.49*)
- Save a New Publication (*PUB 1.30*)
- Save a Publication as a Web Page (*PUB 1.51*)
- Save an Existing Publication with the Same File Name (*PUB 1.37*)
- Start Publisher (*PUB 1.09*)

More About

Quick Reference

For a table that lists how to complete tasks covered in this book using the mouse, menu, shortcut menu, and keyboard, see the Quick Reference Summary at the back of this book or visit the Shelly Cashman Series Office XP Web page (scsite.com/offxp/qr.htm) and then click Microsoft Publisher 2002.

More About

Microsoft Certification

The Microsoft Office User Specialist (MOUS) Certification program provides an opportunity for you to obtain a valuable industry credential — proof that you have the Office XP skills required by employers. For more information, see Appendix E or visit the Shelly Cashman Series MOUS Web page at scsite.com/offxp/cert.htm.

Learn It Online

Instructions: To complete the Learn It Online exercises, start your browser, click the Address bar, and then enter `scsite.com/offxp/exs.htm`. When the Office XP Learn It Online page displays, follow the instructions in the exercises below.

1 Project Reinforcement TF, MC, and SA

Below Publisher Project 1, click the Project Reinforcement link. Print the quiz by clicking Print on the File menu. Answer each question. Write your first and last name at the top of each page, and then hand in the printout to your instructor.

2 Flash Cards

Below Publisher Project 1, click the Flash Cards link. When Flash Cards displays, read the instructions. Type 20 (or a number specified by your instructor) in the Number of Playing Cards text box, type your name in the Name text box, and then click the Flip Card button. When the flash card displays, read the question and then click the Answer box arrow to select an answer. Flip through Flash Cards. Click Print on the File menu to print the last flash card if your score is 15 (75%) correct or greater and then hand it in to your instructor. If your score is less than 15 (75%) correct, then redo this exercise by clicking the Replay button.

3 Practice Test

Below Publisher Project 1, click the Practice Test link. Answer each question, enter your first and last name at the bottom of the page, and then click the Grade Test button. When the graded practice test displays on your screen, click Print on the File menu to print a hard copy. Continue to take practice tests until you score 80% or better. Hand in a printout of the final practice test to your instructor.

4 Who Wants to Be a Computer Genius?

Below Publisher Project 1, click the Computer Genius link. Read the instructions, enter your first and last name at the bottom of the page, and then click the Play button. Hand in your score to your instructor.

5 Wheel of Terms

Below Publisher Project 1, click the Wheel of Terms link. Read the instructions, and then enter your first and last name and your school name. Click the Play button. Hand in your score to your instructor.

6 Crossword Puzzle Challenge

Below Publisher Project 1, click the Crossword Puzzle Challenge link. Read the instructions, and then enter your first and last name. Click the Play button. Work the crossword puzzle. When you are finished, click the Submit button. When the crossword puzzle redisplays, click the Print button. Hand in the printout.

7 Tips and Tricks

Below Publisher Project 1, click the Tips and Tricks link. Click a topic that pertains to Project 1. Right-click the information and then click Print on the shortcut menu. Construct a brief example of what the information relates to in Publisher to confirm you understand how to use the tip or trick. Hand in the example and printed information.

8 Newsgroups

Below Publisher Project 1, click the Newsgroups link. Click a topic that pertains to Project 1. Print three comments. Hand in the comments to your instructor.

9 Expanding Your Horizons

Below Publisher Project 1, click the Articles for Microsoft Publisher link. Click a topic that pertains to Project 1. Print the information. Construct a brief example of what the information relates to in Publisher to confirm you understand the contents of the article. Hand in the example and printed information to your instructor.

10 Search Sleuth

Below Publisher Project 1, click the Search Sleuth link. To search for a term that pertains to this project, select a term below the Project 1 title and then use the Google search engine at google.com (or any major search engine) to display and print two Web pages that present information on the term. Hand in the printouts to your instructor.

online

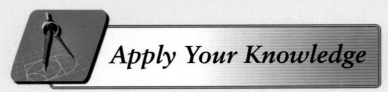

Apply Your Knowledge

1 Editing a Publication

Instructions: Start Publisher. Open the publication apply-1 from the Data Disk. See the the inside back cover of this book for instructions for downloading the Data Disk or see your instructor for information on accessing the files required in this book. The publication is shown in Figure 1-67.

Perform the following tasks.

1. If the task pane does not display, click Task Pane on the View menu. If the displayed task pane is not the Flyer Options task pane, click the Other Task Panes button on the task pane title bar, and then choose Flyer Options.
2. Click Color Schemes in the task pane. When the list displays, click the Field color scheme.
3. Click Font Schemes in the task pane. When the list displays, click the Foundry font scheme.
4. Close the Flyer Options task pane.
5. Drag the text, Corvette for Sale to highlight it. Type Car for Sale in the text box.
6. Select the bulleted list text box below the graphic. Zoom in as necessary. Enter the following bulleted list. The list will wrap around automatically to the next column.

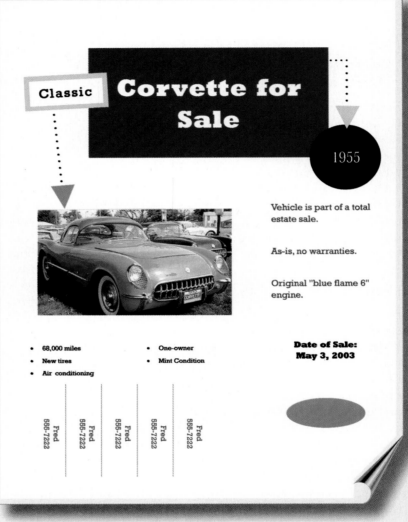

FIGURE 1-67

- 88,000 miles
- New tires
- Added air conditioning

- All leather interior
- Mint condition
- Serious inquiries only

7. Right-click the picture of the car. On the shortcut menu, point to Change Picture, and then click Clip Art. When the Insert Clip Art task pane displays, delete any text in the Search text text box, and then type automobile. Click the Search button.

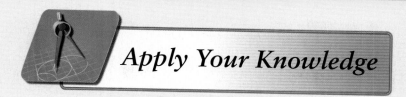

Apply Your Knowledge

8. Select a graphic from your system's gallery. Click the box arrow on the right side of the graphic, and then click Insert on the shortcut menu.

9. If necessary, resize the graphic to make it fit the area vacated by the previous graphic.

10. Click the Design Gallery Object button on the Objects toolbar. When the Microsoft Publisher Design Gallery displays, click Phone Tear-Off in the Categories pane.

11. Click the Insert Object button in the lower-right corner of the Microsoft Publisher Design Gallery window.

12. If Publisher asks you if you want to change to a design that includes contact information tear-offs, click the No button. Drag the tear-offs to the lower empty portion of the publication.

13. Click any tear-off. Click the Zoom In button until the tear-off is easy to read.

14. In the tear-off text box, select the Name and telephone text. Type Fred and then press SHIFT+ENTER. Type 555-7222 and then click anywhere outside the tear-offs.

15. Click File on the menu bar and then click Save As. Use the file name, Car for Sale, and then save the publication on a floppy disk.

16. Print the revised publication.

In the Lab

1 Creating a Sale Flyer

Problem: You are studying for your real estate license and working part-time with the Wright Sell real estate agency. The manager has asked you to create a House for Sale flyer that a homeowner may distribute or place in a protected bin in the yard. Using one of Publisher's Sales Flyers, create the publication shown in Figure 1-68 on the next page.

Instructions: Perform the following tasks.

1. Start Publisher. If the task pane does not display, click Task Pane on the View menu. If the displayed task pane is not the New Publication task pane, click the Other Task Panes button on the task pane title bar, and then choose New Publication.

2. Click Flyers in the publication list, click Sale. Click Borders House for Sale in the Sale Flyers pane.

3. Choose the Teal color scheme and the Etched font scheme.

4. For each text box, select the template text, and then type in the new text.

   a. Replace Organization by typing Wright Sell in the Logo Text text box at the top of the flyer.

   b. Replace House for Sale by typing Home for Sale in the heading.

   c. In the bulleted list on the right, replace the text by entering the following:

   - 40-year old home
   - 4,000 sq. feet
   - Private wooded lot
   - Lakefront property
   - Detached garage
   - 4 bedrooms
   - 3 baths
   - Central air

(continued)

In the Lab

Creating a Sale Flyer *(continued)*

FIGURE 1-68

d. Replace the description text by entering the following paragraph:
   This beautiful, secluded, lakefront home is available immediately with several financing options. Make it your get-away-from-it-all dream home.

e. Enter $300,000 to replace the price.

f. Use your name and telephone number as the contact person.

5. Triple-click the graphic and choose a picture of a house from the Clip Organizer.

6. Save the publication on a floppy disk using the file name, Home For Sale. When prompted to save the new logo to the Primary Business personal information set, click the No button.

7. Print a copy of the flyer.

In the Lab

2 Creating a Sign

Problem: The Read It Now Bookstore you work for has asked you to make a sign for the front door that lists company business hours. Using the Business Hours Sign Wizard, create a sign, as shown in Figure 1-69, listing the days and business hours.

Instructions: Perform the following tasks to create a sign using the data in Table 1-3 on the next page.

1. Start Publisher. If the task pane does not display, click Task Pane on the View menu. If the displayed task pane is not the New from Existing Publication task pane, click the Other Task Panes button on the task pane title bar, and then choose New Publication.

Read It Now Bookstore Hours

Monday	10:00	to	8:00
Tuesday	10:00	to	8:00
Wednesday	10:00	to	8:00
Thursday	10:00	to	8:00
Friday	10:00	to	10:00
Saturday	10:00	to	10:00
Sunday	12:00	to	5:00

Telephone (303) 555-5800

FIGURE 1-69

(continued)

In the Lab

Creating a Sign *(continued)*

2. In the publications list, click Signs. Double-click Business Hours Sign in the Signs pane.
3. Because this sign will be posted in the window of the bookstore, it needs to be clear and easy to read from the sidewalk. Choose the Black and White color scheme. Choose the Wizard: Sign Wizard font scheme.
4. Change the publication heading to say Read It Now Bookstore Hours.
5. The intersection of each row and column in the timetable is a text box. Change the hours in each text box to match Table 1-3.
6. Click the text box below the table. Type Telephone (303) 555-5800 in the bottom text box.
7. Save the publication on a floppy disk with the file name, Business Hours Sign.
8. Print a copy of the sign.

Table 1-3	Read It Now Book Store Hours		
Monday	10:00	to	8:00
Tuesday	10:00	to	8:00
Wednesday	10:00	to	8:00
Thursday	10:00	to	8:00
Friday	10:00	to	10:00
Saturday	10:00	to	10:00
Sunday	12:00	to	5:00

3 Creating a Web Announcement from Scratch

Problem: As assistant to the Events Planner for your park district, you design announcements of community activities. Next month, the park district is sponsoring a senior citizen trip to Blue River Gardens. You prepare the Web announcement shown in Figure 1-70. (**Hint:** Remember, if you make a mistake while creating the publication, you can click the Undo button on the Standard toolbar to undo your mistake.)

Instructions: Perform the following tasks.

1. Start Publisher. On the New Publication task pane, click Blank Publication.
2. Create the objects shown in Figure 1-70 by completing the following steps:
   a. To Create the Masthead:
      (1) Click the Design Gallery Object button on the Objects toolbar. When the Microsoft Publisher Design Gallery displays, click Web masthead in the Categories list. Double-click the Arcs Masthead from the Web Mastheads pane.
      (2) When the masthead displays in the blank publication. Drag it to the top of the page close to the top margin.
      (3) Replace the text, Web Site Title, with Senior Citizen Trip in the masthead. Type July 7, 2002 in the masthead's oval text box. Click the blank text box in the masthead. Type Sponsored by the and then press ENTER. Type Logan Park District to complete the masthead.
   b. To Create the Text Box
      (1) Click the Text Box button on the Objects toolbar. Drag across the area below the masthead on the left side of the page.
      (2) On the Formatting toolbar, click the Font Size box arrow. Click 48. Click the Bold button.
      (3) Type the words Visit Blue River Gardens pressing ENTER after each word.
   c. To Create the Graphic
      (1) Click the Clip Gallery Frame button on the Objects toolbar. When the Insert Clip Art task pane displays, search for a graphic related to the word, garden.

In the Lab

(2) Choose an appropriate graphic and resize it to fit beside the text box.

d. To Create the Bulleted List

(1) Create a large Text Box across the lower portion of the page.

(2) On the Formatting toolbar, click the Font Size box arrow. Click 24.

(3) Click the Bullets button on the Formatting toolbar. If the Bullets button does not display, click the Toolbar Options button on the Formatting toolbar and then click the Bullets button on its list.

(4) Type the following bulleted list:

- Bus will leave at 9:00 a.m.
- Cost is $10.00 per person
- Picnic lunch provided
- Wear comfortable walking shoes
- Bus will return at 4:00 p.m.
- Call 555-1815 for reservations

JULY 7, 2002

Senior Citizen Trip

Sponsored by the
Logan Park District

Visit
Blue
River
Gardens

- Bus will leave at 9:00 a.m.
- Cost is $10.00 per person
- Picnic lunch provided
- Wear comfortable walking shoes
- Bus will return at 4:00 p.m.
- Call 555-1815 for reservations

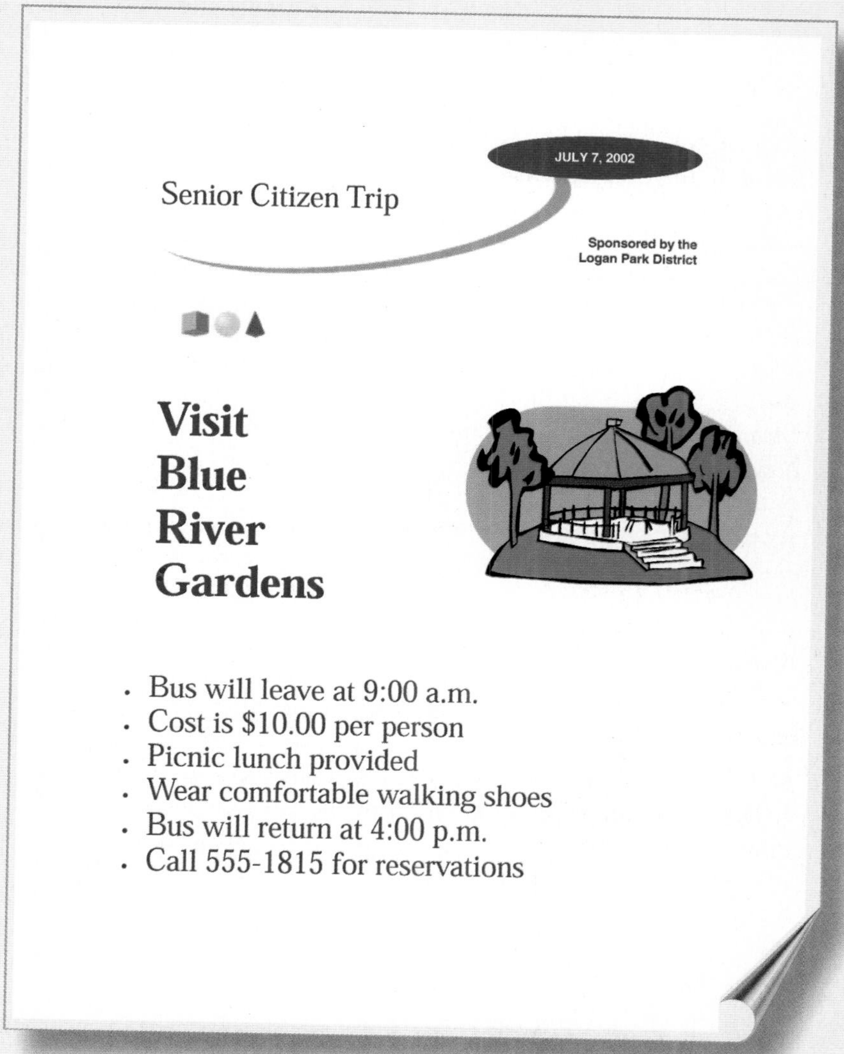

FIGURE 1-70

3. Display the Color Schemes task pane. Choose Dark Blue from the list.

4. Run the Design Checker. Fix any problems.

5. Save the publication as a Web Page. Create a folder on your floppy disk named Web announcement. Save the file with Blue River Gardens Trip as the file name.

6. Click the Web Page Preview button on the Standard toolbar to view the announcement.

7. Close the Web Page Preview window by clicking the Close button on the title bar.

8. Print the Web announcement.

Cases and Places

The difficulty of these case studies varies:
▶ are the least difficult; ▶▶ are more difficult; and ▶▶▶ are the most difficult.

1 ▶ Use the Flyers Wizard titled Car Wash Fund-raiser Flyer to create a flyer for your club's upcoming 5K walk-a-thon. The walk-a-thon is Saturday, September 18 from 10:00 a.m. to 2:00 p.m. Use the name of your own school and address in the appropriate areas. The starting location is the College Library parking lot.

2 ▶ You are the secretary for the Computer Technology Department at the University. Part of your job is to let students know the advising hours during registration periods. Using the Business Hours Sign Wizard, create a sign listing advising hours. Change the heading to Advising Hours. Change the times to Monday and Wednesday from 8:00 a.m. to 5:00 p.m.; Tuesday and Thursday from 12:00 p.m. to 8:00 p.m.; and Friday from 8:00 a.m. to 3:30 p.m. In the lower text box list the advisement telephone number: 555-HELP, and the office number, SL 220.

3 ▶▶ Your high school has asked you to create a flyer for the upcoming 10-year class reunion. Use the concepts and techniques presented in this project to create the flyer with information from your high school. Be sure to include at least two bulleted items in a list, an Attention Getter, and insert an appropriate graphic from the Clip Organizer or the Web.

4 ▶▶ Start the Play Announcement Flyer Wizard to create a flyer for a local dramatic production. Use the Cranberry color scheme and the Fusion font scheme. Use the techniques in Project 1 to edit the text as follows: The name of the play is *Quadrille*. The author is Noel Coward. The dates are October 8, 9, and 10. The time is 8:00 p.m. at the Theatre in the Round. The ticket price is $9.00. Choose an appropriate graphic from the Clip Organizer searching for the word, entertainment. Add an Attention Getter in the lower-right corner. You may delete the sponsor logos, or edit them as you desire.

5 ▶▶ Create an advertising flyer to advertise your word processing/desktop publishing business. Use a wizard that includes tear-offs and a graphic, such as the Pets Available Flyer. Decide where you might place such a flyer and think about how you could attract the most attention as you plan your publication. Describe your services. Include the features in a bulleted list. Include a graphic related to desktop publishing, such as a printer. Use tear-offs with your name and e-mail address.

6 ▶▶▶ Many communities offer free Web page hosting for religious organizations. Using a one-page design wizard, such as a flyer or sign, create a Web page for a local house of worship. Include the name, address, telephone, worship and education hours, as well as the name of a contact person. If possible, include a photo or line drawing of the building. Run the publication through the Design Checker and then save it in its own folder as a Web page.

Microsoft Publisher 2002

Designing a Newsletter

You will have mastered the material in this project when you can:

OBJECTIVES

- Describe the advantages of using the newsletter medium
- Identify the steps in the design process
- Create a newsletter
- Edit a newsletter template
- Change pages using the Page Navigation Control
- Insert and delete pages in a newsletter
- Edit a masthead
- Import text files
- Toggle newsletter views
- Save a newsletter
- Edit personal information components
- Edit a design set
- Create columns in a text box
- Edit an Attention Getter
- Replace graphics
- Add a Pull Quote
- Edit and delete sidebars
- Insert a WordArt object
- Add automatic page numbers to the Master Page
- Identify foreground and background elements
- Check a newsletter for errors
- Print a two-sided newsletter

Quick Reads

Newsletters Get the Word Out

Newsletters are a powerful tool for communicating ideas and information. Each year an estimated 250,000 newsletters are published regularly in the United States and thousands more can be read on the Internet. The popularity of print and online newsletters is growing as computer users discover desktop publishing software and the dynamic formatting features of programs such as Publisher 2002. In this project, using the Newsletter Wizard, you will create *Library Life*, a newsletter designed to inform the community about the programs and services offered by the Carrington Public Library.

The two-page newsletter contains articles, regular features, dates, and graphics. The desktop aspects of design and production available with Publisher make it easy and inexpensive to produce printed publications such as newsletters. In addition, newsletters provide a forum for entertainment, education, and advertisement of dated information. They are more focused in scope than newspapers and include a myriad of design possibilities and appeal.

Newsletters are inexpensive, effortlessly passed along, and they make good reading material in reception and waiting areas.

From the church bulletin to the homeowners association, a newsletter exists to suit every interest. The *At-Home Dad* newsletter, in an online edition and a print version, is devoted to providing connections and resources for fathers who stay home with their children. *The Nutrition Connection* is a newsletter dedicated to helping you feel your best. *Storm Track* is a publication to which weather buffs can subscribe that features storm chasers in pursuit of cumulonimbus clouds, severe storms, and tornadoes.

Other specialty newsletters have been created, such as *Catnip* for feline lovers, published by Tufts University School of Veterinary Medicine, *ChildFree Network* for individuals without children who desire equity in the corporate world, and *Naturally Well* for health-conscious individuals interested in homeopathic remedies.

Baby boomers' interests account for an increase in specialized publications. For example, *Homeground*, a quarterly newsletter started by a former gardening columnist, and *Virtual Garden*, on the Internet, are among the newsletters filling the gardening niche. Health and nutrition

newsletters have become very popular in the last ten years; among the titles are *Health After 50*, *Nutrition Advocate*, and *Health Wisdom for Women*.

Internet users can find an abundance of online publications, some of which are available in printed versions as well. Investors might surf to investing Web sites that feature articles from *Investor's Business Daily* or *The Online Investor*, a newsletter providing data, research, and tips for the online trader. Sports lovers will find the *Penn State Sports Medicine Newsletter* or *Tennis Weekly*, where they can read all the latest headlines from the world of tennis. Scientists can discover *The American Astronomer*, the *Electronic Zoo*, and *Syzygy*, which is an earthquake prediction newsletter. Many Web sites exist to help Internet newsletter readers find exactly what they are looking for, providing links to thousands of electronic magazines and newsletters. Readers can browse the category listings or enter search words to find newsletters on the topics of their choice.

Whether you are telling the world about your company's products and services, or trying to get your neighbors excited about a community fund-raiser, newsletters help you get the word out.

Microsoft Publisher 2002

Designing a Newsletter

PROJECT

2

CASE PERSPECTIVE

The Carrington Public Library serves the small town of Carrington, Missouri. Besides the normal book checkout program, the library offers a reading room, children's center, computer lab, and community meeting space. Teresa Hall, the head librarian, has plans for new programs, but must start by getting an approval from the Library Foundation Board and then getting the word out to the community. Teresa has asked you to prepare a sample newsletter that she can show to the board members. She will ask them to pay for printing and mailing costs if they approve the newsletter.

Along with the usual volume, date, and organizational information, the library newsletter should include articles of interest, and a section that recognizes young students for their reading accomplishments. Teresa wants a monthly feature called Bookworm's Corner, which gives a short review of a new book at the library.

Teresa has written and typed several articles to include in the first issue. She wants bright, attractive colors; boxes; and graphics. You will use Microsoft Publisher's Newsletter Wizard to publish the two-page, three-column newsletter.

Introduction

As discussed in Project 1, desktop publishing is becoming the most popular way for businesses of all sizes to produce their printed publications. The desktop aspects of design and production make it easy and inexpensive to produce high-quality documents in a short time. **Desktop** implies doing everything from a desk, including the planning, designing, writing, layout, cutting, and pasting, as well as printing, collating, and distributing. With a personal computer and a software program such as Microsoft Publisher, you can create a professional document from your computer, such as the newsletter you will create in this project. Newsletters are a popular way for offices, businesses, and other organizations to distribute information to their clientele. A **newsletter** usually is a multi-page publication, double-sided, with newspaper features such as columns and a masthead, and the added eye appeal of sidebars, pictures, and other graphics. Using Publisher eliminates the cost and time of sending the newsletter to a professional publisher.

Project Two — Library Life Newsletter

Project 2 uses a Publisher Newsletter Wizard to produce *Library Life*, the newsletter shown in Figures 2-1a and 2-1b. This semi-monthly publication informs the public about services offered by the local library. The library's two-page newsletter contains articles, features, dates, and graphics.

Volume 1, Issue 1   September 12, 2003

Newsletter of the Carrington Public Library

Library Life

Library Gets A Face-lift

Special points of interest:

- Now open: Monday – Saturday 9:00am to 10:00pm
- Read-a-thon, Dec 10
- Carrington Teen Council meets every Wednesday after school
- Computer Classes every Saturday

The Carrington Public Library got a face-lift over the summer.

Thanks to several generous donations and a very successful capital improvement campaign, the library completed all of its exterior renovations. The outside of the library was repainted and some trim was replaced. The front sidewalk was rebuilt to allow handicap access. The newly installed automatic doors will be a

great asset for people who need assistance coming and going at the library.

The Carrington Public Library Foundation would like to thank Hershberger Construction for donating the labor on this project.

The public is invited to tour the facility on Tuesday, October 7 at 7:00 p.m. Representatives from Hershberger Construction and the Library Foundation will be available to answer your questions.

Back to school means back to the library

Come, see the new look of the Carrington Public Library.

Teen Council to Visit Elementary Schools

The Carrington Library Teen Council will be visiting area elementary schools to promote literacy and let the students know about fun opportunities at the library. Ten students from Carrington High School will host reading corners at

both elementary schools next week. Armed with the latest children's favorites, the Teen Council will read passages to the grade-schoolers and, in turn, listen to them read.

The Teen Council also will

distribute activity booklets about the Children's Story Hour, the library summer reading program, and this year's Read-a-Thon.

For more information, contact Katie Starks at the library.

Page 1

(a)

(b)

...ton Public Library

Rapid Readers

Aaron Gibson	Benny Tran
Josh Stewart	Jason Coleman
Ashley Harris	Lacey Montgomery
Andrew Greg	Adam Freetam
Samantha Borman	Maria Joper

Reading is FUNdamental!

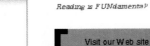

Visit our Web site
www.carrington.lib.mo.us

Bookworm's Corner

He was born two hundred years before his time, but he faced the world in a way that only modern people can imagine. Orie, named Orson Amos, was born in Old Westport, into a very poor family. Influenced by traders and trappers who came into his father's store along the Missouri River, Orie met all problems and all events in his own forthright manner.

As the West expanded, he made his way across the continent, at one time serving as a cook for gold miners in South Dakota. He endured floods, Indian uprisings, economic failures and disappointment in romance and he handled it all despite his lack of education and money. And with all of life's obstacles, Orie never lamented his fate and never complained. He

was too occupied looking for solutions. In his own vigorous, creative way, he always succeeded.

Read Orie! You may end up thinking you were born too late.

Orie! By Elsie Amos Montgomery

Page 2

FIGURE 2-1

Microsoft **Publisher 2002**

Newsletters

Many newsletters are published regularly on the Web. To look at some samples and for more information on newsletter content, visit the Publisher 2002 More About Web page (scsite.com/pub2002/more.htm) and then click Newsletters.

The Newsletter Medium

Newsletters have several advantages over other publication media. They are easy to produce. Brochures, designed to be in circulation longer as a type of advertising, usually are published in greater quantities and on more expensive paper than newsletters and are, therefore, more costly. Additionally, newsletters differ from brochures in that they commonly have a shorter shelf life, making newsletters a perfect forum for dated information.

Newsletters are narrower and more focused in scope than newspapers; their eye appeal is more distinctive. Many organizations and companies distribute newsletters inexpensively to interested audiences, although that is beginning to change. Newsletters are becoming an integral part of many marketing plans because they offer a legitimate medium by which to communicate services, successes, and issues. Table 2-1 lists some benefits and advantages of using the newsletter medium.

Table 2-1	Benefits and Advantages of Using a Newsletter Medium
AREA	**BENEFITS AND ADVANTAGES**
Exposure	An easily distributed publication — office mail, bulk mail, electronically A pass-along document for other interested parties A coffee table reading item in reception areas
Education	An opportunity to inform in a nonrestrictive environment A directed education forum for clientele An increased, focused feedback — unavailable in most advertising
Contacts	A form of legitimized contact A source of free information to build credibility An easier way to expand a contact database than other marketing tools
Communication	An effective medium to highlight the inner workings of a company A way to create a discussion forum A method to disseminate more information than a brochure
Cost	An easily designed medium using desktop publishing software An inexpensive method of mass production A reusable design

Starting Publisher

To start Publisher, Windows must be running. Perform the following steps to start Publisher.

TO START PUBLISHER

1 Click the Start button on the Windows taskbar and then click New Office Document.

2 When the New Office Document dialog box displays, if necessary, click the General tab and then double-click the Blank Publication icon.

3 If the Publisher window is not maximized, double-click its title bar to maximize it.

4 If the New Publication task pane does not display, click View on the menu bar and then click Task Pane.

5 If the Language bar displays, click its Minimize button.

You may recall that Publisher's New Publication task pane displays publication types, commands to begin new publications, and the names of previously opened publications on your computer.

Designing a Newsletter

Designing an effective newsletter involves a great deal of planning. A good newsletter, or any publication, must deliver a message in the clearest, most attractive, and effective way possible. You must clarify your purpose and know your target audience. You need to gather ideas and plan for the printing of the newsletter. Finally, you must determine the best layout for eye appeal and reliable dissemination of content. Table 2-2 outlines the issues to consider during the design process and their application to newsletters.

Table 2-2 Design Process Issues	
DESIGN ISSUE	**NEWSLETTER APPLICATION**
Purpose	To communicate and to educate readers about the organization
Audience	Local interested clientele or patrons, both present and future
Gather data	Articles, pictures, dates, figures, tables, discussion threads
Plan for printing	Usually mass-produced, collated, and stapled
Layout	Consistent look and feel; simple, eye-catching graphics
Synthesis	Edit, proofread, and publish

Creating a Newsletter Template Using a Wizard

You can type a newsletter from scratch by choosing a blank publication from the task pane, or you can use a wizard and let Publisher format the newsletter with appropriate headings, graphics, and spacing. You can customize the resulting newsletter by filling in the blanks and selecting and replacing objects.

Microsoft Publisher has many of the design planning features built into the software. Publisher has 25 different kinds of publications from which you may choose, each with its own set of design wizards and templates, more than 2,000 in all. Recall from Project 1, a **wizard** is a tool that guides you through the design process by offering choices and changing the publication accordingly. Once Publisher creates a publication from a wizard, you then can use it as a template to fill in the blanks, replace prewritten text as necessary, and change the art to fit your needs. Along the way, Publisher periodically may remind you to save your work. As you work through the project, you will be instructed to save the newsletter shown on page PUB 2.21; however, you may save at any time. Perform the steps on the next page to create a newsletter template.

More About

Design Issues

The steps in good design and attractive layout are similar to the steps in designing any new product, program, or presentation. For more information on design, visit Publisher 2002 More About Web page (scsite.com/pub2002/more.htm) and then click Design Issues.

To Create a Newsletter Template

1 **Click Newsletters in the New Publication task pane. If necessary, click the down scroll arrow until the Pixel Newsletter preview diaplays. Point to the Pixel Newsletter preview.**

Publisher displays the New Publication task pane on the left and the previews on the right in the Newsletters pane (Figure 2-2). The list of previews may display differently on your computer.

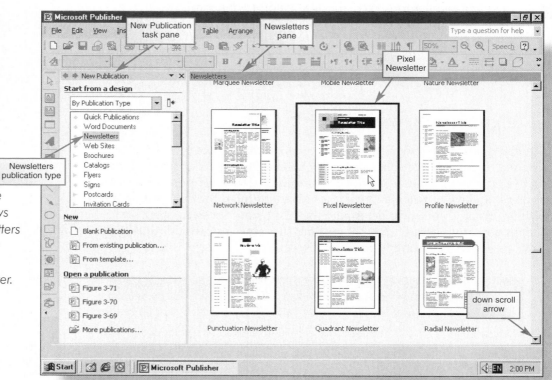

FIGURE 2-2

2 **Click the Pixel Newsletter preview. If a Microsoft Publisher dialog box displays, click its Close button. When the Newsletter Options task pane displays, point to Color Schemes.**

In the workspace, page 1 of the Pixel Newsletter displays (Figure 2-3). Newsletter options for two-sided printing and no customer address display in the Newsletter Options task pane.

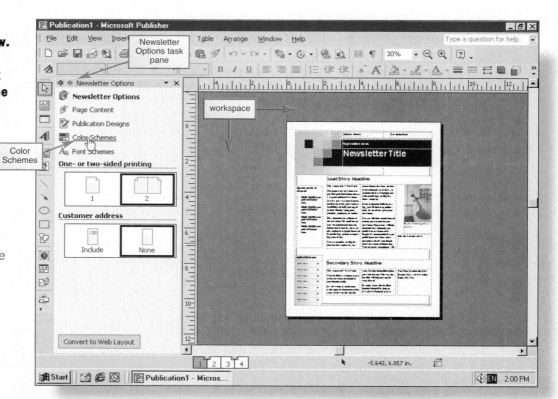

FIGURE 2-3

3 Click Color Schemes. In the Apply a color scheme list, click Mountain. Point to Font Schemes.

The newsletter displays with the Mountain color scheme (Figure 2-4).

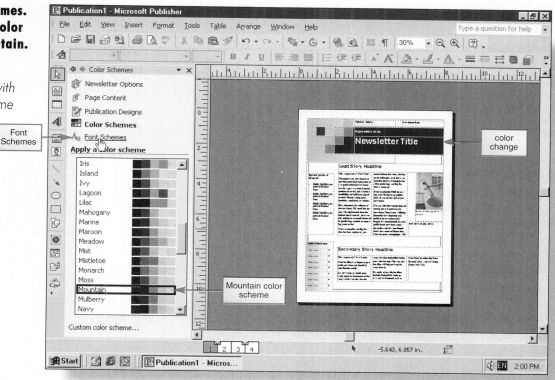

FIGURE 2-4

4 Click Font Schemes. In the Apply a font scheme list, if necessary, scroll down and then click the Textbook font scheme. Point to the Close button in the Font Schemes task pane.

Publisher displays the newsletter with the Textbook font scheme (Figure 2-5).

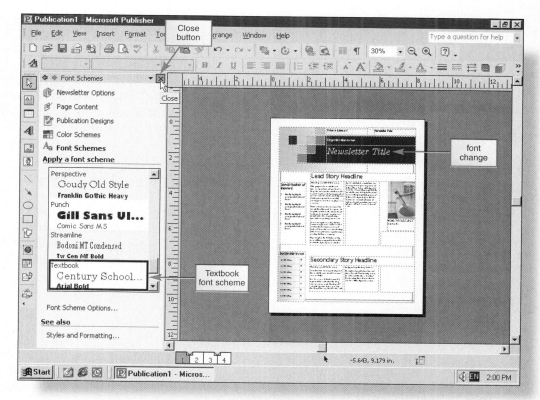

FIGURE 2-5

Microsoft **Publisher 2002**

5 **Click the Close button in the Font Schemes task pane. Right-click the workspace, click Zoom on the shortcut menu and then point to Whole Page on the Zoom submenu.**

The Zoom submenu displays magnifications (Figure 2-6).

6 **Click Whole Page.**

The first page of the Pixel Newsletter displays.

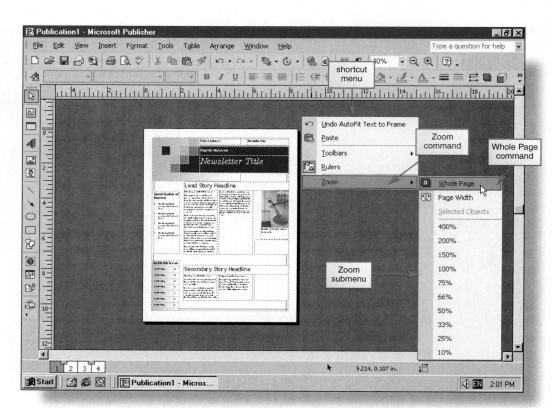

FIGURE 2-6

Design Sets

Each Publisher-designed newsletter is part of a design set, which is a collection of related publication types that share a consistent color scheme, design, and look. For example, a master set includes a business card, a company letterhead, and a company brochure, each with a matching design. To view design sets and their elements, click the Design Gallery Object button, and then click the Objects by Design tab.

You can revisit newsletter options to make changes by clicking View on the menu bar and then clicking Task Pane.

Any publication you choose in the Publications list is a Publisher-designed publication. You may use these publications, of course, as part of Publisher's licensing agreement. Using proven design strategies, Publisher places text and graphics in the publication at appropriate places for a professional-looking newsletter.

Editing the Newsletter Template

As the first step in the design process, the purpose of a newsletter is to communicate and educate its readers. Publisher places the lead story in a prominent position on the page, and uses a discussion of purpose and audience as the default text.

The following pages discuss how to edit various articles and objects in the newsletter.

Pagination

Publisher's Newsletter Wizard creates four pages of text and graphics. This template is appropriate for some applications, but the library wants to print a single sheet, two-sided newsletter. Page 4 of the newsletter contains objects typically used on the back page, so you will delete pages 2 and 3. Follow the steps to change and delete pages.

To Change and Delete Pages in a Newsletter

1 **Click the page 2 icon on the Page Navigation Control.**

Pages 2 and 3 display (Figure 2-7). The Page Navigation Control displays the selected pages in blue.

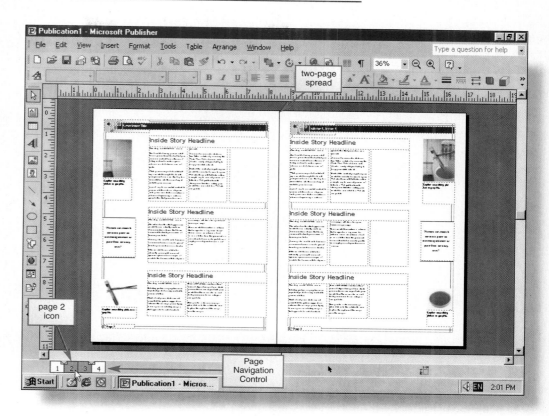

FIGURE 2-7

2 **Click Edit on the menu bar and then click Delete Page. When the Delete Page dialog box displays, if necessary, click the Both pages option button to select it. Point to the OK button.**

Publisher displays a dialog box with options for deleting either or both pages (Figure 2-8).

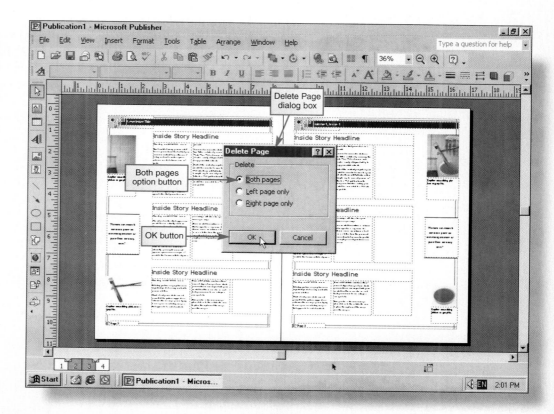

FIGURE 2-8

Microsoft **Publisher 2002**

3 **Click the OK button. If a Microsoft Publisher dialog box displays to confirm deleting all the objects, click the OK button.**

Publisher deletes pages 2 and 3 and displays the back page as the new page 2 (Figure 2-9).

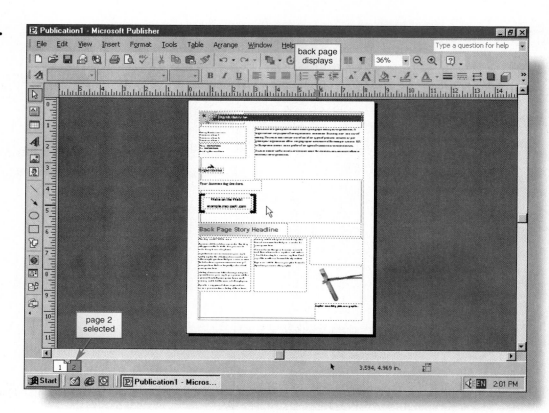

FIGURE 2-9

Inserting pages in a newsletter is just as easy as deleting them. The Page command on the Insert menu provides the option of inserting a left- or right-hand page, as well as choices in the types of objects to display on the page. When you choose to insert or delete when working on the first or last page, Publisher will warn you of pagination problems and will offer you a confirmation button.

With the newsletter containing two pages, you are ready to edit the graphics and articles.

Editing the Masthead

Most newsletters and brochures contain a masthead such as the ones used in newspapers. A **masthead** is a box or section printed in each issue displaying information such as the name, publisher, location, volume, and date. The Publisher-designed masthead, included in the Pixel Newsletter design set, contains several text boxes, rectangles, and lines (Figure 2-10). The colored rectangles and text create an attractive, eye-catching graphic that complements the Pixel Newsletter design set. You need to edit the text boxes, however, to convey appropriate messages.

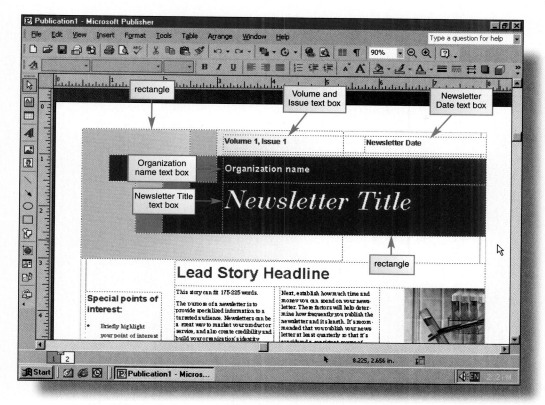

FIGURE 2-10

More *About*

Pagination

You cannot actually move a page to a different location in a publication. You can, however, insert a new page and then move existing content there. On the Insert menu, click Page and choose the location. Next, in the Page Navigation Control, click the page icon you want to move. Press CTRL+A to select all the objects. Cut and paste into the new page.

Publisher incorporates four text boxes in the Pixel Newsletter masthead. The newsletter title displays in a text box layered on top of a blue rectangle. Two text boxes display in the upper part of the masthead for the volume and date. Across the top of the newsletter title is a fourth text box for the Organization name. You will edit this name later in this project.

Editing Techniques

Publisher uses text-editing techniques similar to most word processing programs. To insert text, position the insertion point and type the new text. Publisher always inserts the text to the left of the insertion point. The text to the right of the insertion point moves to the right and downward to accommodate the new text.

The BACKSPACE key deletes text to the left of the insertion point. To delete or change more than a few characters, however, you should select the text. Publisher handles selecting text in a slightly different manner than word processing programs. In Publisher, you select unedited default text, such as placeholder titles and articles in the newsletters with a single click. To select individual words, double-click the word, as you would in word processing. To select larger portions of text, drag through the text. To select all the text in a text box, press CTRL+A.

Perform the steps on the next page to practice some of these techniques as you select and edit text.

More *About*

Deleting

Whether to delete using the BACKSPACE key or the DELETE key is debated hotly in word processing circles. It really depends on the location of the insertion point in the publication. If the insertion point already is positioned left of the character you want to delete, it makes more sense to press the DELETE key instead of repositioning the insertion point just to use the BACKSPACE key.

Steps **To Edit the Masthead**

1 **Click the page 1 icon on the Page Navigation Control. Point to the text, Newsletter Title.**

Page 1 displays (Figure 2-11).

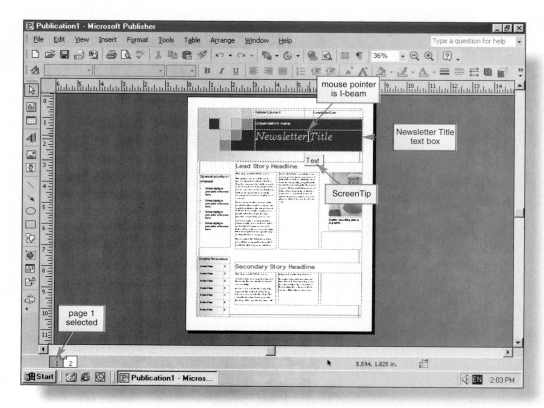

FIGURE 2-11

2 **Click Newsletter Title. Press the F9 key to view the masthead more closely.**

Publisher selects the entire text because it is placeholder text (Figure 2-12). Pressing the F9 key zooms the magnification to 100%. Because the text box is a layered object on top of a blue rectangle, the highlight color is yellow.

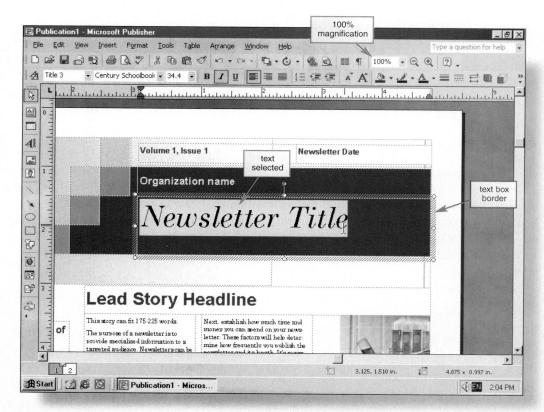

FIGURE 2-12

3 **Type** Library
Life **in the text
box. Point to the
Newsletter Date text box.**

*Publisher replaces the text
using the font from the
design set (Figure 2-13).
Because fonts are sometimes
printer-dependent, your font
may differ from the one
shown.*

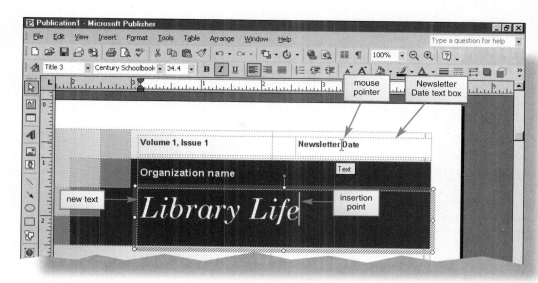

FIGURE 2-13

4 **Click Newsletter
Date.**

*Publisher selects the entire
date because it is place-
holder text, designed to be
replaced (Figure 2-14).*

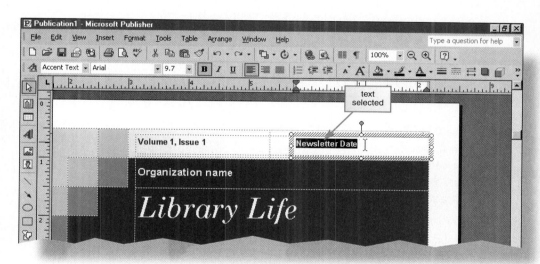

FIGURE 2-14

5 **Type** September
12, 2003 **in the
text box.**

*The masthead edits are
complete (Figure 2-15).*

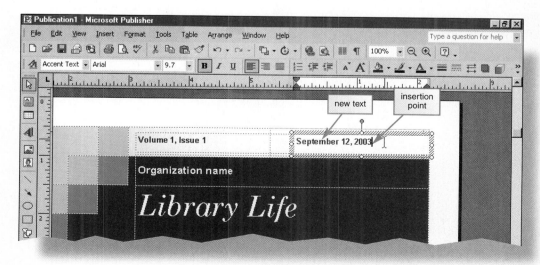

FIGURE 2-15

Microsoft Publisher 2002

More About

Importing HTML as Text

Publisher accepts many types of files including plain text, spreadsheet data, and files from the many versions of popular text editing and word processing programs. To see a listing of the types of files Publisher accepts, click the Files of Type box arrow in the Insert Text dialog box. Publisher will not import HTML as text into a text box. You can import, however, HTML code fragments such as scrolling marquees, counters, or scripting languages. Simply click HTML Code Fragment on the Insert menu.

Importing Files

Publisher allows users to import text and graphics from many sources into its publications. Publisher accepts imported objects from a variety of different programs and in many different file formats. Gathering data of interest to the readers is an important phase in the design process. The stories for the newsletter are provided on the Data Disk associated with this textbook. See the inside back cover of this book for instructions for downloading the Data Disk or see your instructor for information on accessing the files required for this book. **Downloading** means moving data or programs from a larger computer to a smaller one. Publisher uses the term **importing** to describe inserting text or objects from any other source into the Publisher workspace.

Replacing Default Text Using an Imported File

Publisher suggests that 175 to 225 words will fit in the space allocated for the lead story. This Publisher-designed newsletter uses a three-column text format that **wraps**, or connects, the running text from one column to the next. Perform the following steps to import a text file from a floppy disk and replace the Publisher-supplied default text.

Steps To Replace Default Text

1 **With the Data Disk in drive A, scroll down until the Lead Story article displays. Read the article. Click the article to select it.**

Publisher selects the entire article (Figure 2-16). At 100% view, the Lead Story article can be edited easily. Reading the article will provide you with valuable suggestions about the design process of newsletter publications.

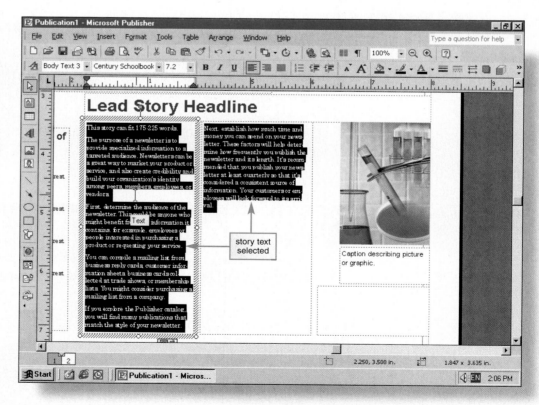

FIGURE 2-16

2 Click Insert on the menu bar, and then point to Text File.

Publisher displays the Insert menu (Figure 2-17).

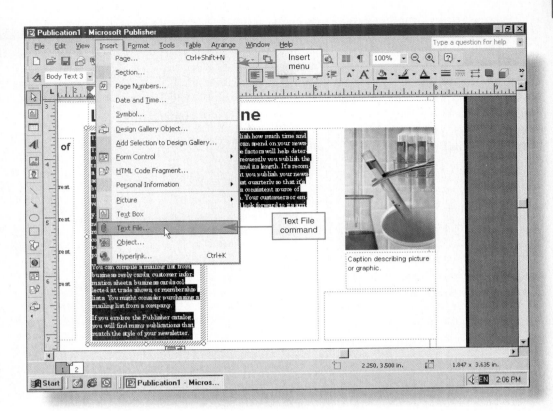

FIGURE 2-17

3 Click Text File. When the Insert Text dialog box displays, click the Look in box arrow, and then click 3½ Floppy (A:) in the Look in list. Point to the Face-lift file name.

The data files on the floppy disk display in the list below the Look in box (Figure 2-18). Your list of files may differ.

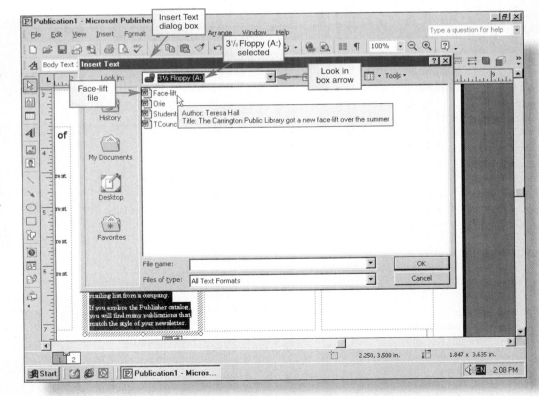

FIGURE 2-18

4 Double-click the Face-lift file name. If a Microsoft Publisher dialog box about file conversion displays, click the OK button. When the article displays, point to Lead Story Headline above the article.

Publisher replaces the selected default text with the Face-lift article (Figure 2-19). The article wraps, or connects, across the columns. The Go to Previous Frame button *displays above the last column. When clicked, Publisher will select the previous column of the story.*

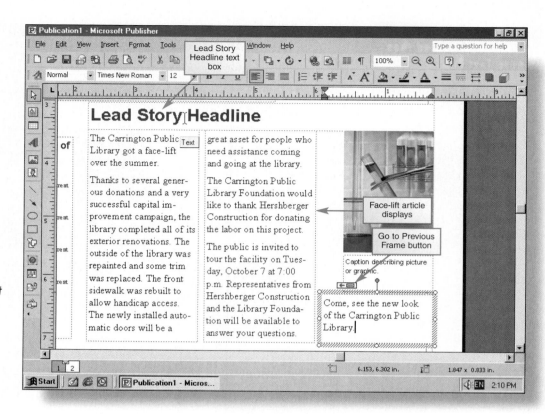

FIGURE 2-19

5 Click Lead Story Headline. Type `Library Gets A Face-lift` to replace the default headline.

Publisher displays the new headline (Figure 2-20).

Other Ways

1. Right-click article, click Change Text on Shortcut menu, click Text File
2. In Voice command mode, say "Change Text, Text File, [select file], OK"

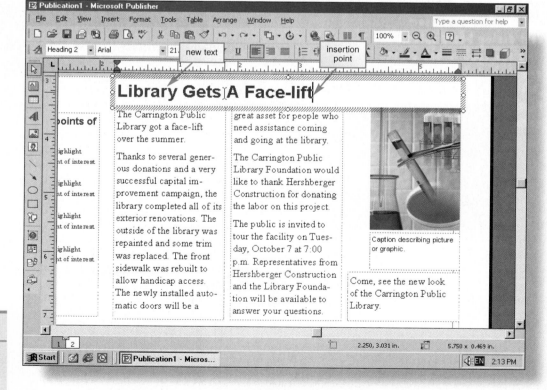

FIGURE 2-20

Continuing a story across columns or text boxes is one of the features that Publisher performs for you. If the story contains more text than will fit in the box, Publisher displays a message to warn you. You then have the option of connecting to another box or continuing the story on another page. Publisher will add the continued notices, or **jump lines**, to guide readers through the story.

The F9 **function key** toggles between the current page view and 100% magnification. **Toggle** means the same key will alternate views, or turn a feature on and off. Editing text is much easier if you view the text box at 100% magnification or even larger. Page editing techniques, such as moving graphics, inserting new boxes, and aligning objects, more easily are performed in **Whole Page view**. Toggling back and forth with the F9 key works well. You also may choose different magnifications and views in the **Zoom list** on the Standard toolbar.

Importing Text for the Secondary Article

The next step is to import the text for the secondary article in the lower portion of page 1 of the newsletter as explained in the steps below.

TO IMPORT MORE TEXT

1 Click the Zoom box arrow on the Standard toolbar and then click Whole Page in the Zoom list. Click the secondary story article to select it.

2 Click Insert on the menu bar and then click Text File.

3 If not already selected, click 3½ Floppy (A:) in the Look in list.

4 Double-click the TCouncil file name.

5 Click the headline, Secondary Story Headline, to select it.

6 Type Teen Council to Visit Elementary Schools to replace the headline of the article.

Figure 2-21 shows the completed article at 75% magnification. Your screen may differ slightly, depending on the fonts your computer uses.

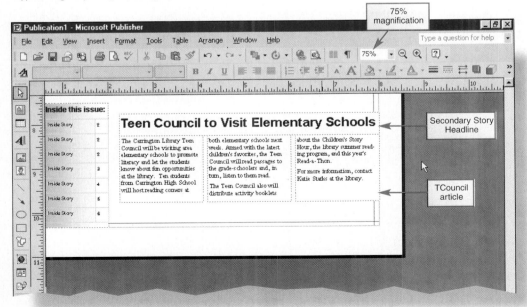

FIGURE 2-21

More About

Zooming

To adjust the size of the characters on the screen, you can click the Zoom In or Zoom Out button; click the Zoom box arrow and then select the desired percentage, magnification style, or type a percentage of your choice in the Zoom box. To have the screen redraw even faster during the zooming, you can reduce the quality of the picture display by clicking Pictures on the View menu.

Importing Text on the Back Page

The final steps to finish the articles in the newsletter involve importing text for the book review.

TO IMPORT THE BACK PAGE STORY

1 Click the page 2 icon on the Page Navigation Control.

2 Click the Back Page Story article in the lower part of the page.

3 Click Insert on the menu bar and then click Text File.

4 If not already selected, click 3½ Floppy (A:) in the Look in list.

5 Double-click the Orie file name.

6 Click the Back Page Story Headline.

7 Type Bookworm's Corner to replace the headline.

The book review article and headline display (Figure 2-22).

Text Columns

Publisher provides two ways to create text in columns: connected text boxes and columns. The Newsletter template creates separate text boxes and connects them as frames. You also can use multiple columns within one text box. Either way, the text will flow automatically, and jump lines will guide the reader. If you want separate stories in adjacent columns on the same page, or if you want your story to have unequal column widths, use separate text boxes.

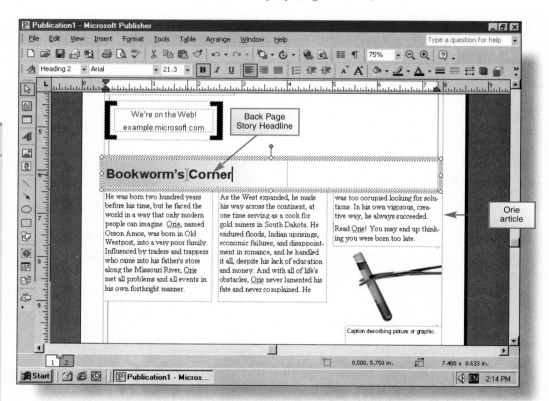

FIGURE 2-22

All the articles for the newsletter now are complete. Importing the articles instead of typing them saves time and adds the convenience of using word processing. Publisher accepts most file formats from popular word processing programs and text editors. Once imported, Publisher lets you edit the articles using Microsoft Word when you right-click and then click Change Text on the shortcut menu. Editing your articles with Word allows you to manipulate the text using the full capabilities of a word processing program.

Saving an Intermediate Copy of the Newsletter

A good practice is to save intermediate copies of your work. That way, if your computer loses power or you make a serious mistake, you always can retrieve the latest copy from disk. Use the Save button on the Standard toolbar often, because you can save time later if the unexpected happens.

With the masthead edited and the text files imported, it is now a good time to save the entire newsletter before continuing. For the following steps, it is assumed you have a floppy disk in drive A.

TO SAVE AN INTERMEDIATE COPY OF THE NEWSLETTER

1 Click the Save button on the Standard toolbar.

2 Type Library Newsletter in the File name text box. If necessary, select 3½ Floppy (A:) in the Save in list.

3 Click the Save button in the Save As dialog box. If Publisher displays a dialog box asking if you want to save a new logo, click the No button.

Publisher saves the publication on a floppy disk in drive A using the file name, Library Newsletter (Figure 2-23).

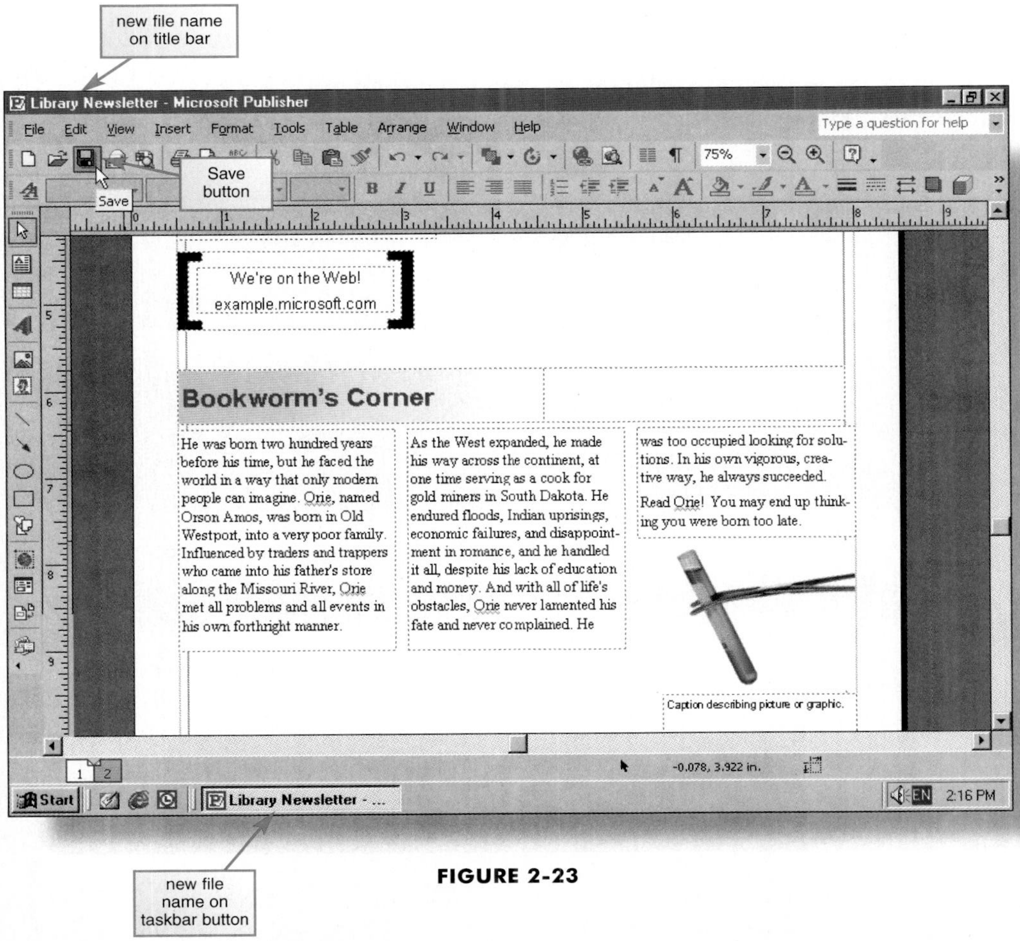

FIGURE 2-23

new file name on title bar

new file name on taskbar button

More About

Hyphenation

You can change the number of hyphens that are added automatically to the text. You might want to achieve a more even right edge, reduce white gaps in the text, or reduce the number of hyphens and short syllables. On the Tools menu, point to Language, and then click Hyphenation. To achieve a different effect, change the number in the Hyphenation zone in one of the following ways: for a more even right edge and fewer white gaps in the text, reduce the number; for fewer hyphens and fewer short syllables before or after hyphens, increase the number.

More About

Importing Files

In order to import all manner of word processing documents, you must have chosen to perform a full installation of Microsoft Publisher. Publisher will remind you to reinsert the Publisher CD-ROM if it needs more information about the type of file you are trying to import.

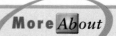

Personal Information Sets

Publisher maintains four Personal Information Sets: Primary Business, Secondary Business, Other Organization, and Home/Family. Every new publication has the Primary Business Personal Information Set selected by default. You can apply a different Personal Information Set to the publication, however. Simply, click Personal Information on the Edit menu, and then click the appropriate set.

Working with Personal Information Sets

Publisher permits you to store four unique sets of personal information for use at work and home. The name of the organization, the address, the telephone number, and other pieces of information such as tag lines and logos are stored in Personal Information Sets. In **Personal Information Sets**, Publisher can keep track of data about you, your business, an organization affiliation, or other personal information that you might use to create publications. In this newsletter, you will edit the text box for the Organization name, Address lines, Phone, Fax, and Email. You will learn more about permanently changing personal information components in a future project.

Editing the Personal Information Components

Both pages of the newsletter contain an Organization name text box. Editing one of these text boxes automatically changes the other. Additionally, after typing the name of your organization, Publisher can reuse the text in other publications, if it is saved as a personal information component. A **personal information component** is a text box that contains information about the organization from the Personal Information Set. This information can carry over from one publication to the next. For example, the name of the company might display at the top of the newsletter, on the business cards, and on the letterhead stationery.

Perform the following steps to edit personal information components for this publication only.

Steps **To Edit Personal Information Components**

1 With page 2 still displayed, scroll if necessary to click the Organization name text box in the upper-left corner. If necessary, press the F9 key to display the text box at 100% magnification.

The text box displays at 100% magnification (Figure 2-24). Your Personal Information Set may display a different Organization name in the text box.

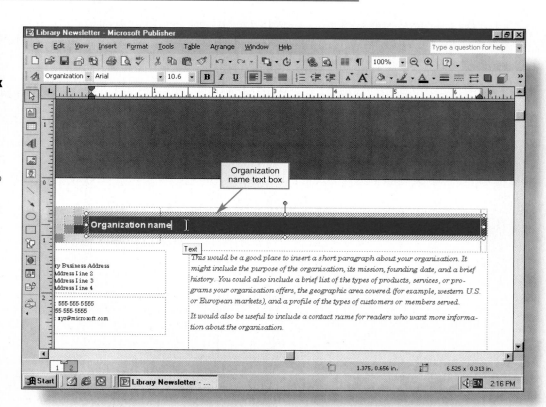

FIGURE 2-24

2 **Drag through the text in the Organization name text box, and then type** Newsletter of the Carrington Public Library **in the text box.**

Newsletter of the Carrington Public Library replaces the previous Organization name (Figure 2-25). Because it is part of the Personal Information Set, Publisher changed the Organization name text box on page 1 as well (shown in Figure 2-41 on page PUB 2.33).

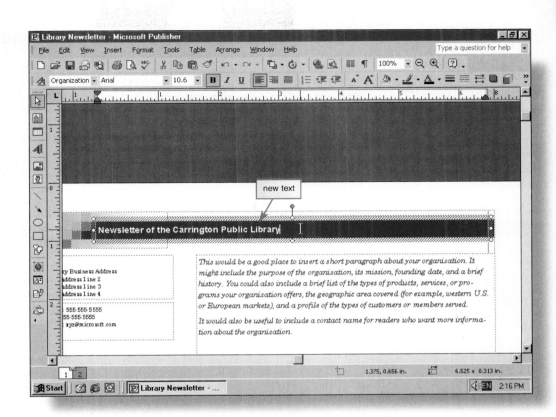

FIGURE 2-25

3 **Repeat Step 2 to edit the text boxes for the Address lines and Phone, Fax, and Email as shown in Figure 2-26. Zoom as necessary. As you type, press the ENTER key for new lines of text inside the Address and Phone, Fax, and Email text boxes.**

The edited personal information components display in the newsletter (Figure 2-26).

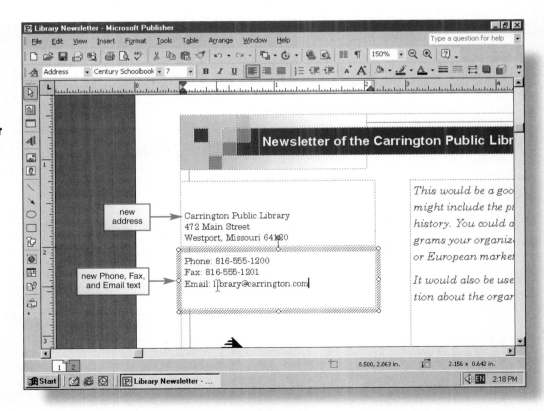

FIGURE 2-26

Microsoft **Publisher 2002**

4 **Scroll down the page to display the text box containing the words, Your business tag line here. Drag through the text to highlight it.**

The text in the business tag line displays selected (Figure 2-27).

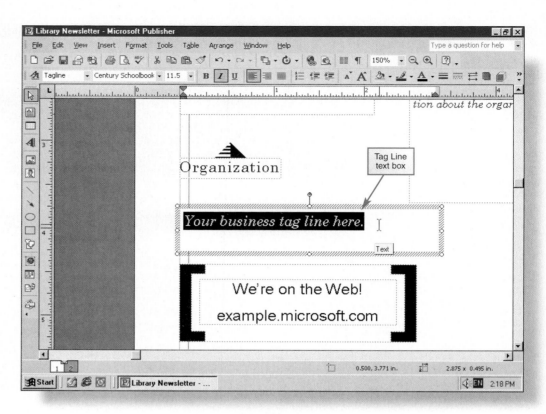

FIGURE 2-27

5 **Type** Reading is FUNdamental! **to replace the text.**

The new tag line displays (Figure 2-28). The red wavy line indicates the word is not in Publisher's dictionary, because of the unusual capitalization.

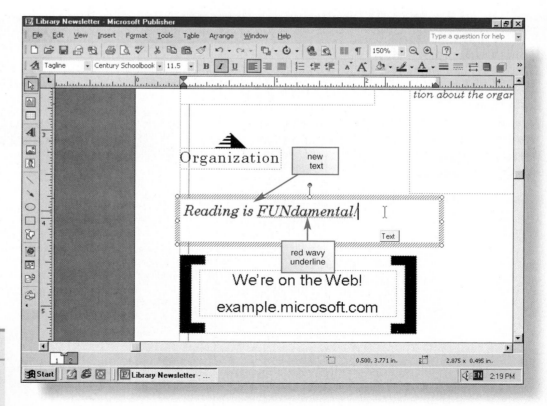

FIGURE 2-28

Other Ways

1. On Edit menu click Personal Information
2. In Voice command mode, say "Edit, Personal Information"

Each personal information component has its own preset font, font size, and text alignment. If desired, you can make changes to the formatting for individual publications. If you want to keep Publisher from synchronizing, or repeating, the changed component on other pages, click Undo on the Edit menu.

Editing the Design Set

Page 2 of the *Library Newsletter* contains several objects that are part of the Pixel Newsletter design set. A **design set** is specific to the type of publication and chosen design scheme. Recall that an object in Publisher is any text box, shape, border, image, or table inserted in the publication. The Pixel Newsletter design set contains another text box, a logo, and an Attention Getter on the back page, among other objects.

Creating Columns within a Text Box

The text box in the upper-right corner of page 2 is not large enough to hold the file you will import containing a list of students. Wrapping the text to another box makes it more difficult for the reader to follow. Reducing the font size decreases readability, and the page does not contain enough room to make the box larger. One solution is to create columns within the box itself, so the list can flow downward and then to the right.

Follow these steps to import the text and format the columns.

> **More About**
>
> ### Fitting Text into Text Boxes
>
> When you cannot fit all the required text into a text box, you might try one of these alternatives: create columns within the text box, turn on automatic copyfitting, increase the size of the text box, decrease the font size, reduce the margins within the text box, tighten character spacing, reduce line spacing, delete some text or choose a different font entirely.

Steps **To Import the Student List and Create Columns**

1 **Press the F9 key to view the whole page. Point to the text in the upper-right text box.**

Publisher displays page 2 (Figure 2-29). You also may display the whole page by clicking the Zoom box arrow, and then clicking Whole Page in the Zoom list.

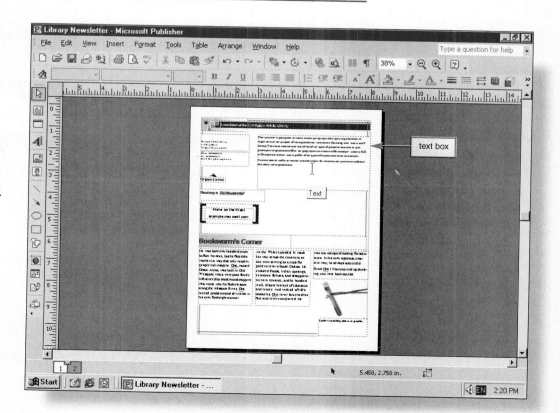

FIGURE 2-29

2 Click the text and then press the F9 key to enlarge the view to 100%.

The text box displays enlarged (Figure 2-30).

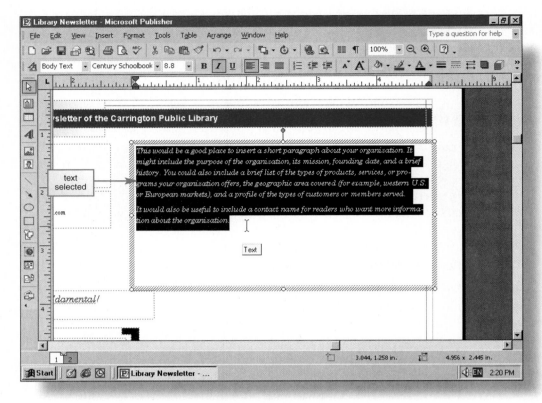

FIGURE 2-30

3 Click Insert on the menu bar, and then click Text File. If not already selected, click 3½ Floppy (A:) in the Look in list. Double-click the Students file in the list. When the Microsoft Publisher dialog box displays, point to the No button.

A Publisher dialog box displays because the student list is too large to fit in the box (Figure 2-31). Clicking No allows you to connect the boxes for yourself or format the text differently.

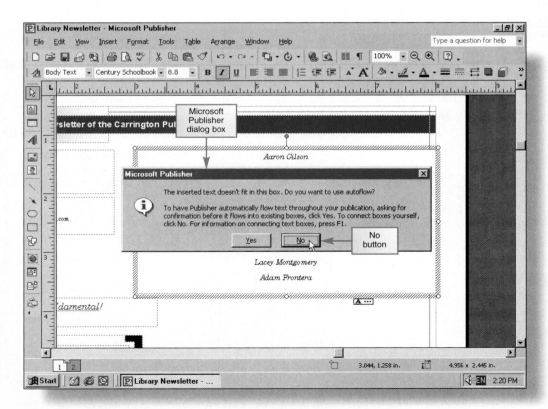

FIGURE 2-31

4 **Click the No button. Point to the Columns button on the Standard toolbar.**

A Text in Overflow indicator displays (Figure 2-32). The rest of the student list is stored in an overflow area, similar to the Clipboard, waiting to be edited or moved to another text box.

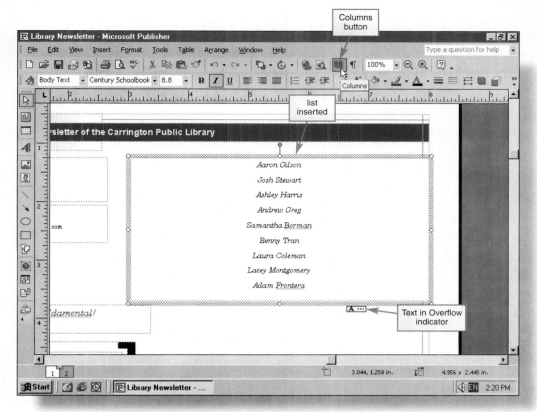

FIGURE 2-32

5 **Click Columns. When the choices display, point to 2 Columns.**

The column choices display (Figure 2-33).

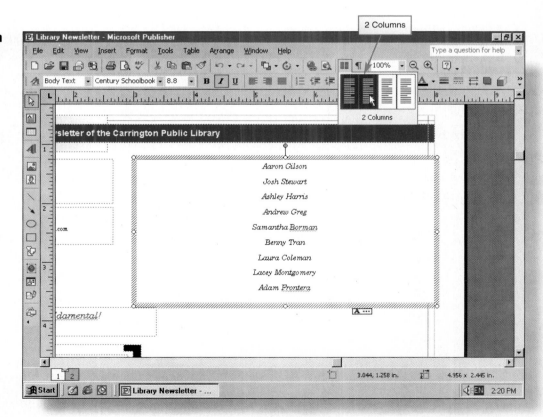

FIGURE 2-33

6 Click 2 Columns. Point to the top center sizing handle.

The list displays in a two-column format (Figure 2-34). The mouse pointer changes to the Resize icon when positioned over a sizing handle.

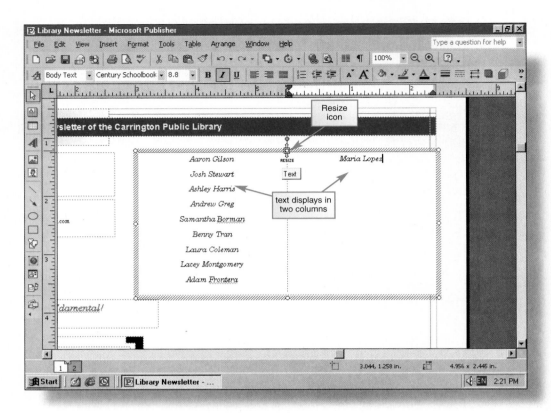

FIGURE 2-34

7 Drag the Resize icon down until the text box is approximately 1.5 in. tall as displayed on the status bar.

The names in the text box display in two even columns (Figure 2-35).

Other Ways

1. Right-click text box, click Format Text Box, on Text Box sheet click Columns
2. While typing text, press CTRL+SHIFT+ENTER to insert column break

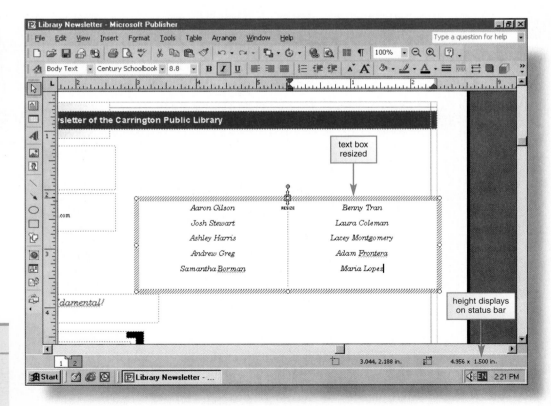

FIGURE 2-35

With an imported list, it is easier to create columns within one text box than wrap the list to the next box. All columns within a single text box are the same width; however, you can adjust the space between columns and the location in the text where the second column begins. Separate stories in adjacent columns would require separate text boxes, as would stories across pages.

Editing the Attention Getter

As discussed in Project 1, Attention Getters are eye-catching graphics and text that draw attention to a location on the page. The Pixel Newsletter design set uses a rectangle, two outside brackets, and a text box grouped together as an Attention Getter on the back page. Perform the following steps to add color and change the text in the Attention Getter.

More About

The Connect Frames Toolbar

If you decide to connect text across frames, the Connect Frames toolbar contains buttons to help you create text box links, remove those links, and go to a previous or next connected text box. If the Connect Frames toolbar does not display, click Toolbars on the View menu, and then click Connect Frames.

Steps **To Edit the Attention Getter**

1 **Press the F9 key to view the whole page. Point to the Attention Getter, We're on the Web!**

The Attention Getter is a rectangle, two brackets, and a text box (Figure 2-36). If the AutoFit text feature has been turned off, your Attention Getter may display less text.

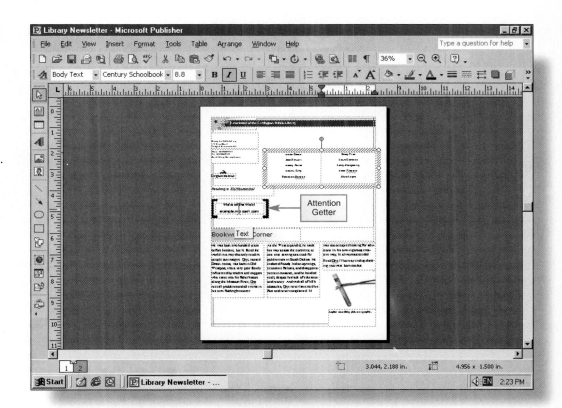

FIGURE 2-36

2 **Click the Attention Getter text box and then press the F9 key. Type** Visit our Web site **and then press the ENTER key. Type** www.carrington.lib. mo.us **to complete the text. If the entire text does not display, point to AutoFit Text on the Format menu, and then click Best Fit.**

The new text displays (Figure 2-37). Publisher resizes the text as necessary.

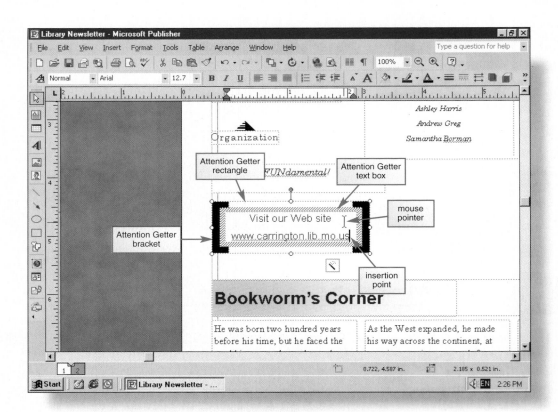

FIGURE 2-37

3 **Click the rectangle outside of the Attention Getter text box. Point to the Fill Color button arrow on the Formatting toolbar.**

The rectangle is selected (Figure 2-38).

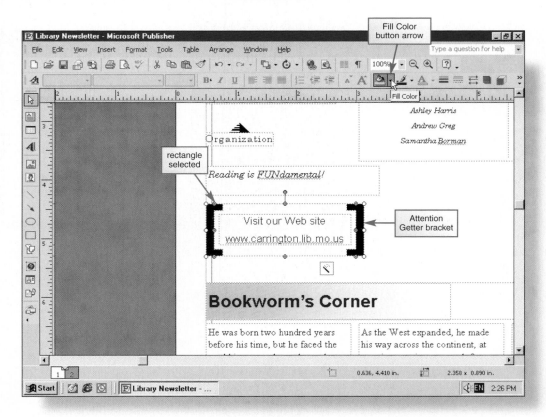

FIGURE 2-38

4 **Click the Fill Color button arrow. Point to Accent 2 in the scheme colors area.**

The Pixel Newsletter color scheme displays in the Fill Color menu (Figure 2-39). Your colors may vary.

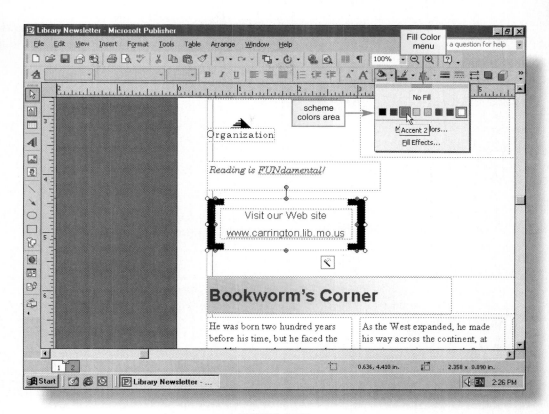

FIGURE 2-39

5 **Click Accent 2.**

The Attention Getter rectangle's fill color changes (Figure 2-40). The Attention Getter now is complete.

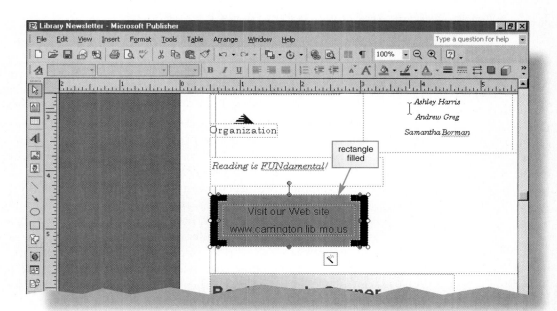

FIGURE 2-40

Other Ways

1. Right-click Attention Getter, click Change Text on shortcut menu
2. Right-click Attention Getter, click Format Text Box on shortcut menu

Graphics

For tips on using graphics effectively in a presentation, visit the Publisher 2002 More About Web page (scsite.com/pub2002/more.htm) and then click Discovering Presentation.

Clip Art

For samples of shareware clip art available on Web sites, visit the Publisher 2002 More About Web page (scsite.com/pub2002/more.htm) and then click Discovering Clip Art.

You can edit the text, text color, fill color, borders, and shadows of Attention Getters. Publisher's Design Gallery has other styles and shapes from which you may choose, as well.

Deleting the Logo

The Pixel Newsletter design set displays an organization logo on the back page (Figure 2-40 on the previous page). A **logo** is a personal information component that varies with each Personal Information Set. Because the library has no logo, perform the following steps to delete the logo.

TO DELETE THE LOGO

1 Right-click the logo on the back page.

2 Click Delete Object on the shortcut menu.

If you delete an object by accident, click the Undo button on the Standard toolbar. The Edit menu also contains a Delete Object and an Undo command.

Using Graphics in a Newsletter

Most graphic designers employ an easy technique for deciding how many graphics are too many. They hold the publication at arm's length and glance at it. Then, closing their eyes, they count the number of things they remember. Remembering more than five graphics indicates too many, two or less indicates too few. There is no question that graphics can make or break a publication. The world has come to expect them. Used correctly, graphics enhance the text, attract the eye, and brighten the look of the publication.

You can use Publisher's clip art images in any publication you create, including newsletters. Publisher also accepts graphics and pictures created by other programs, as well as scanned photographs and electronic images. In newsletters, you should use photographs for true-to-life representations, such as pictures of employees and products. Graphics, on the other hand, can explain, draw, instruct, entertain, or represent images for which you have no picture. The careful use of graphics can add flair and distinction to your publication.

Graphics do not have to be images and pictures. They also can include tables, charts, shapes, lines, boxes, borders, pull quotes, and sidebars. A **sidebar** is a small piece of text, set off with a box or graphic, and placed beside an article. It contains text that is not vital to understanding the main text; it usually adds interest or additional information. Tables of contents and bulleted points of interest are examples of sidebars. A **pull quote** is an excerpt from the main article to highlight the ideas or to attract readers. As with other graphics, it adds interest to the page. Pull quotes, like sidebars, can be set off with a box or graphic (Figure 2-41).

You will edit the sidebar and insert a pull quote later in this project.

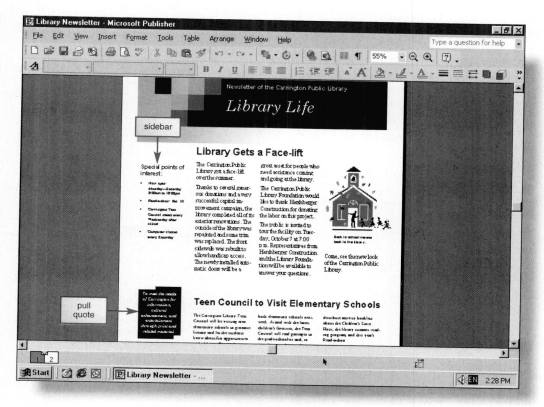

FIGURE 2-41

More *About*

Sidebars

This More About box is an example of a sidebar. The Shelly Cashman Series textbooks use sidebars to offer more information about subjects in the text, as well as to direct readers to Web pages about the topic. The Other Ways feature also is a sidebar.

Deleting a Sidebar

The sidebar in the Pixel Newsletter is a table of contents. Because the newsletter now has only two pages, a table of contents is not necessary. Perform the following steps to delete the sidebar.

TO DELETE THE SIDEBAR

1 Click the page 1 icon on the Page Navigation Control. If the whole page is not in view, press the F9 key to display it.

2 Right-click the table of contents sidebar table located to the left of the secondary story.

3 Click Delete Object on the shortcut menu.

4 If a shaded background rectangle still displays, repeat Steps 2 and 3 to delete it also.

This table was an index used to locate articles in longer newsletters. Many newsletters have a **table of contents**, not only to reference and locate, but also to break up a long text page and attract readers to inside pages. Tables can be used for purposes other than displaying contents and page numbers. You will learn more about tables in a later project.

More *About*

Microsoft Certification

The Microsoft Office User Specialist (MOUS) Certification program provides an opportunity for you to obtain a valuable industry credential — proof that you have the Office XP skills required by employers. For more information, see Appendix E or visit the Shelly Cashman Series MOUS Web page at scsite.com/offxp/cert.htm.

Replacing a Graphic

As you may remember from Project 1, the clip art provided with Publisher has assigned keywords to make finding clips easier. Instead of searching through thousands of graphics for just the right picture, you may type in a keyword or words and Publisher will display only the graphics related to those keywords. You may add additional keywords to stored clips or assign keywords to new and imported clips. Perform the following steps to find an appropriate graphic for the lead story.

Steps **To Replace a Graphic**

1 **Double-click the lead story graphic. When the Insert Clip Art task pane displays, drag through any text that may display in the Search text text box.**

The Insert Clip Art task pane displays (Figure 2-42). The Picture toolbar also may display.

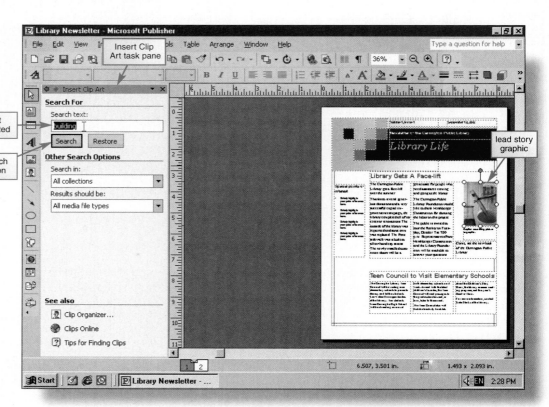

FIGURE 2-42

2 Type school **in the Search text text box and then click the Search button. Point to an appropriate graphic and then point to the box arrow.**

The clips associated with the keyword, school, display (Figure 2-43). Your clips may be different.

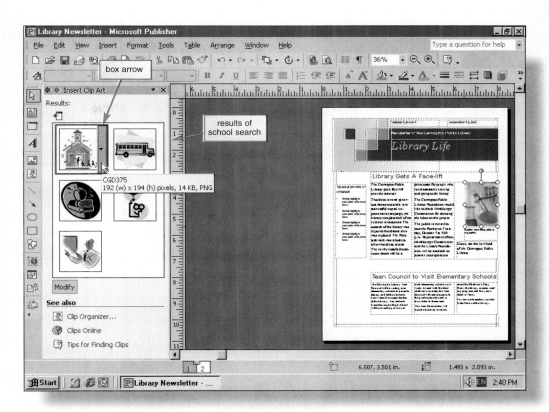

FIGURE 2-43

3 **Click the box arrow beside an appropriate graphic. When the menu displays, point to Insert.**

The graphic's menu displays (Figure 2-44).

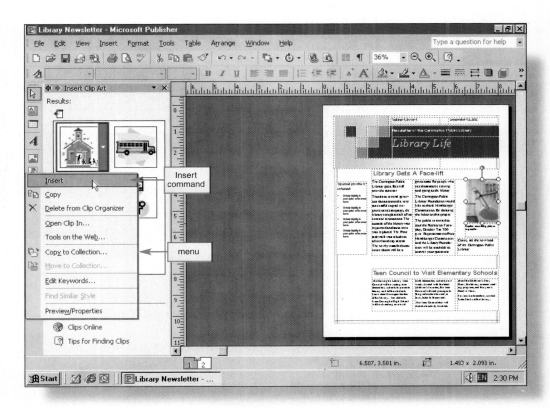

FIGURE 2-44

Microsoft **Publisher 2002**

4   Click Insert. Click the Close button on the Insert Clip Art task pane title bar.

The graphic displays to the right of the original one (Figure 2-45). Your graphic may display differently, or it may replace the old graphic.

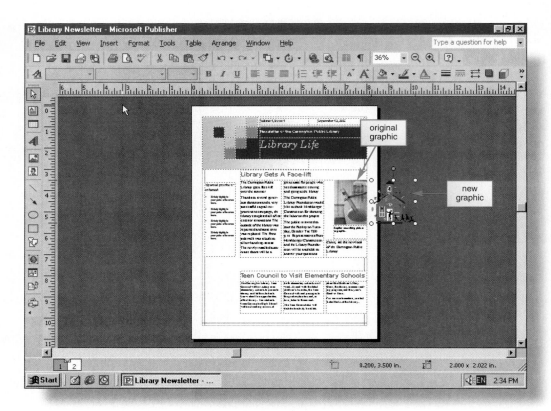

FIGURE 2-45

5   If both graphics display, right-click the original graphic and point to Delete Object on the shortcut menu.

The shortcut menu displays (Figure 2-46).

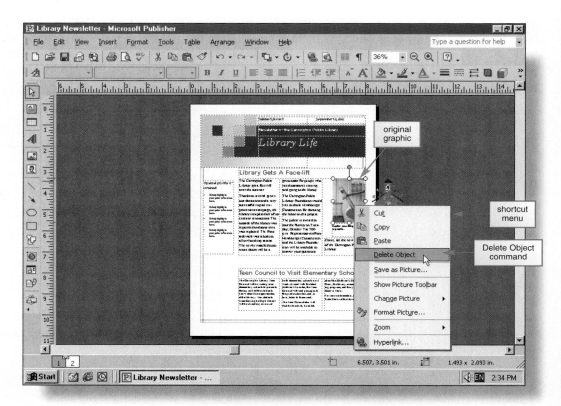

FIGURE 2-46

6 **Click Delete Object. Drag the graphic left to fill the space vacated by the previous graphic.**

The graphic fills the space left by the original one (Figure 2-47).

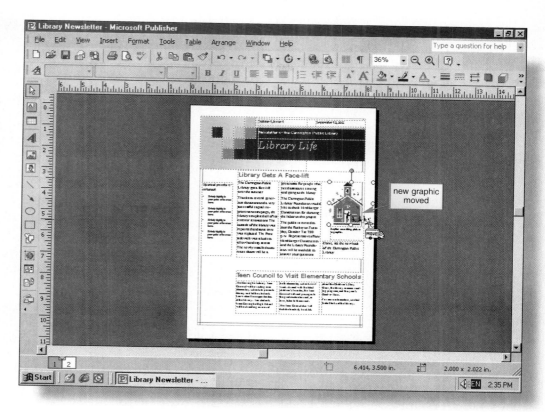

FIGURE 2-47

7 **Press the F9 key to view the graphic at 100% magnification. Point to the caption below the graphic.**

The graphic displays at 100% magnification (Figure 2-48).

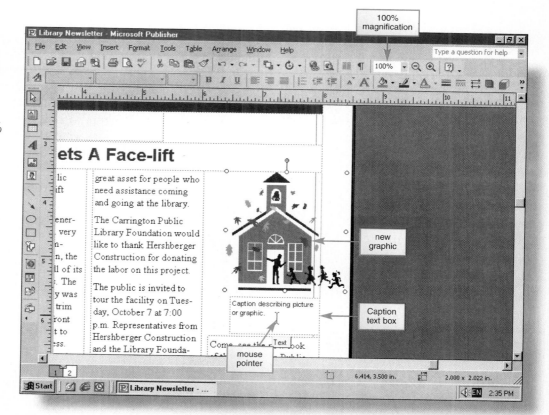

FIGURE 2-48

Microsoft **Publisher 2002**

8 **Click the caption. Type** Back to school means back to the library. **to replace the text. If the Picture toolbar displays, click its Close button.**

The caption is replaced (Figure 2-49).

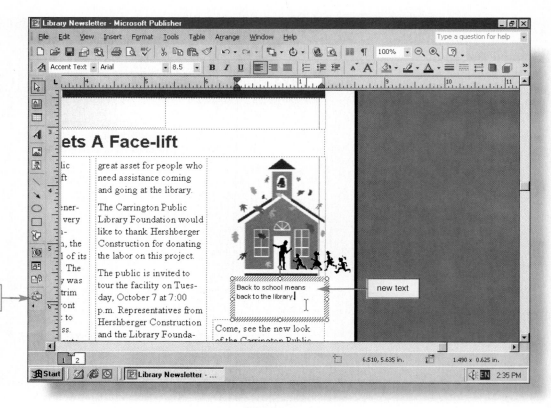

Design Gallery Object button

new text

FIGURE 2-49

Other Ways

1. On Insert menu click Picture, click Clip Art
2. Right-click Picture, click Change Picture on shortcut menu, click Clip Art
3. In Voice command mode, say "Insert,Picture, Clip Art"

Graphics in the **Clip Organizer** are not all the same size. Some of the images and clip art are **portrait oriented,** which means they are taller than they are wide. The opposite graphic orientation is **landscape.** When you change graphics, your choice may alter both the way the columns look and where the columns break. You may want to experiment with dragging the picture in small increments to make the columns symmetrical. The text automatically wraps around the graphic in the newsletter. The column breaks do not have to match the project newsletter exactly.

More About

Portrait and Landscape

The terms portrait and landscape are used to refer to more than just graphic orientation. Portrait also refers to printing a document so the short edge of the paper is the top of the page. Landscape printing assumes the long edge to be the top of the page.

More About

Lines

If you want to use lines as borders or for decoration, click the Line or Arrow button on the Objects toolbar and draw across the page. The Formatting toolbar then displays buttons you can use to format the line or arrow. You also can double-click the line to display the Format AutoShape dialog box.

Graphics in the Clip Organizer are proportional, which means the height and width have been set in relation to each other, so as not to distort the picture. If you resize the graphic, be sure to hold down the SHIFT key while dragging the corner sizing handle as described in Project 1. Shift-dragging maintains the graphic's proportional height and width.

Adding a Pull Quote

People often make reading decisions based on the size of the text. Bringing a small portion of the text to their attention, using a pull quote, invites readership. Pull quotes are especially useful for breaking the monotony of long columns of text. Desktop publishers also use pull quotes to add visual interest. Finally, pull quotes and sidebars are good multiple entry devices, offering readers many ways to digest information. Layout specialists say article titles and pull quotes should outline the intended message.

The final step to complete page 1 is to create a pull quote using Publisher's Design Gallery. The pull quote graphic in this newsletter will contain the motto of the library and be placed appropriately on the page to draw the reader's attention. Follow these steps to add a pull quote to the publication.

Pull Quotes

When you create a pull quote, use a large, bold font to make it really stand out from the rest of the text. You also can add shading behind the text, add a decorative border above or below the text, or create hanging quotation marks around the text.

Steps To Add a Pull Quote

1 **Press the F9 key to view all of page 1, and then click the Design Gallery Object button on the Objects toolbar. When the Design Gallery dialog box displays, click Pull Quotes in the Categories pane. Scroll to display the Top Notches Pull Quote, and then click the Top Notches Pull Quote preview. Point to the Insert Object button.**

The previews display in alphabetical order in the pane (Figure 2-50). Top Notches Pull Quote is selected.

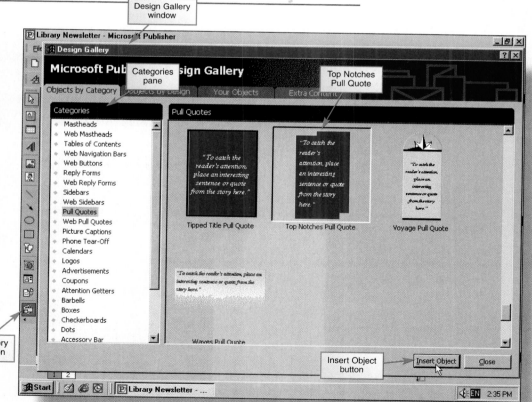

FIGURE 2-50

Microsoft **Publisher 2002**

2 **Click the Insert Object button. When the newsletter again displays, drag the pull quote to the left side, below the Special points of interest sidebar.**

The pull quote displays below the sidebar (Figure 2-51).

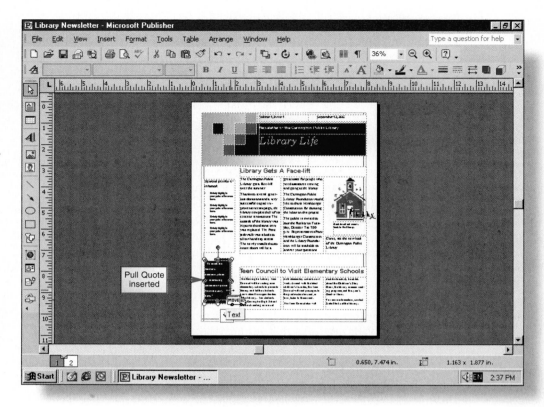

FIGURE 2-51

3 **Click the pull quote and then choose 150% on the Zoom menu to facilitate editing. Click the text of the pull quote.**

The text is selected (Figure 2-52).

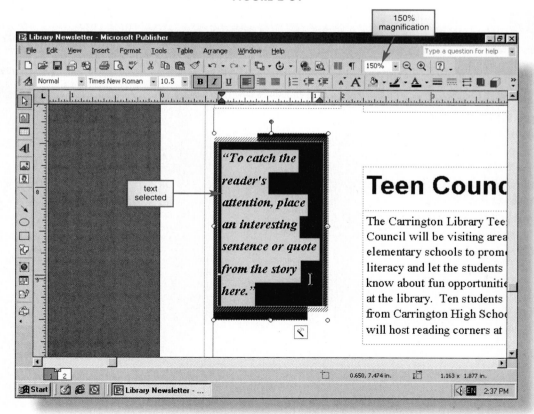

FIGURE 2-52

4 Type the text as displayed in Figure 2-53.

The new text replaces the pull quote text (Figure 2-53).

5 If the text does not display completely, point to AutoFit Text on the Format menu, and then click Best Fit.

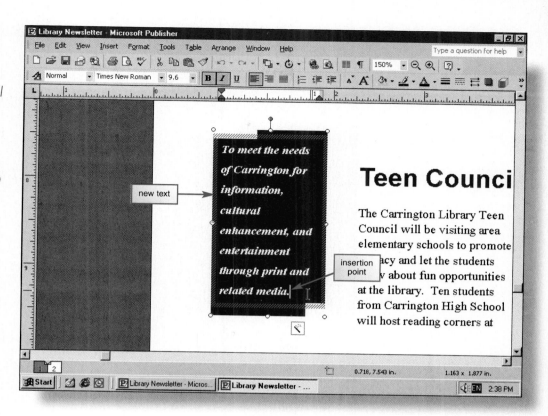

FIGURE 2-53

The pull quote fills the gap left by the table of contents sidebar. The proportion and balance of two graphics beside the text enhance the layout.

Editing the Sidebar

The sidebar of the newsletter contains a list of dates to remember. Sidebars should be placed close to their related text or in a prominent place. Although the sidebar is not vital to understanding the main text, it is important and adds interest.

Using the editing techniques you learned in Project 1, edit the text of the sidebar to create the object as shown in Figure 2-54.

TO EDIT THE BULLETED TEXT BOX SIDEBAR

1 Scroll up to display the sidebar on page 1.

2 Click the bulleted list and then type the text shown in Figure 2-54 on the next page. Press SHIFT+ENTER at the end of lines within the bullets. Press the ENTER key after each bulleted item is entered.

The edited sidebar displays as shown in Figure 2-54.

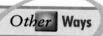

Other Ways

1. On Insert menu click Design Gallery Object
2. In Voice Command mode, say "Design Gallery Object"

More About

Typing

Publisher tries to help you as you type. This AutoCorrect feature, similar to the same feature in word processing applications, will format text and correct some misspellings for you as you type. For instance if you type 2nd, Publisher will convert it to 2nd. If you type teh and then press the SPACEBAR key, Publisher will convert it to the word, the. If you wish to undo an AutoCorrect, point to the smart tag below the word. When it changes to the AutoCorrect Options button, click it, and then click Change back.

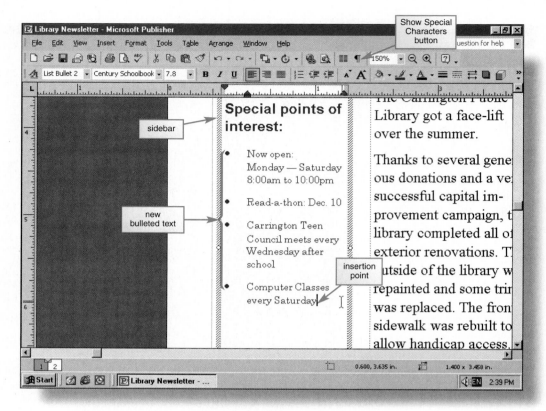

FIGURE 2-54

If you have any word processing experience, you may know that SHIFT+ENTER is called a manual line break. Use a manual line break when you have short lines or want to advance the insertion point to a new line without new paragraph formatting. The manual line break is especially useful when wordwrap creates ragged lines or poor hyphenations. Press the ENTER key when you want a paragraph break between each line. Normal formatting, or bullets, applies when you use a paragraph break. If you want the special characters for line and paragraph breaks to display on the screen, click the Show Special Characters button on the Standard toolbar (Figure 2-54).

Replacing the Graphic on Page 2

The graphic on page 2 does not have anything to do with the book review article. Graphics placed by the wizard are meant to be changed. Perform the following steps to replace the graphic provided by the wizard on page 2 with an article-specific graphic.

TO REPLACE THE GRAPHIC ON PAGE 2

1 Click the page 2 icon on the Page Navigation Control. Click the Zoom arrow on the Standard toolbar and then click Whole Page in the Zoom list.

2 Double-click the graphic. Type book in the Search text text box, and then click the Search button.

3 Select an appropriate graphic, and then click the graphics arrow. Click Insert on the menu.

4 Close the Insert Clip Art task pane. If necessary, close the Picture toolbar.

5 If necessary, delete the old graphic and move the new one to its place. Resize and zoom as necessary.

6 Click the caption and type the text from Figure 2-55.

Your graphic may be a different size than the one shown in Figure 2-55.

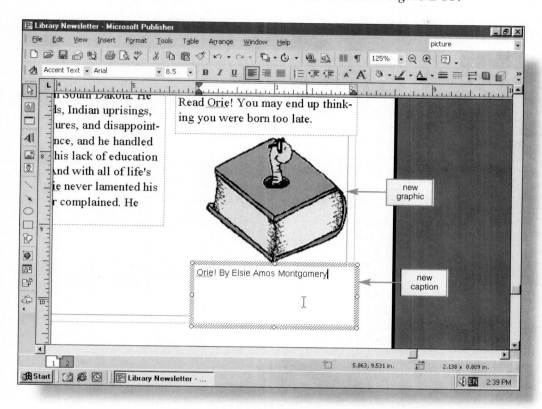

FIGURE 2-55

WordArt

WordArt is a program that works with Publisher to create fancy text effects. A WordArt object is actually a graphic and not text at all. Publication designers typically use WordArt to catch the reader's eye with fancy headlines and banners. WordArt uses its own toolbar to add effects to the graphic.

Inserting a WordArt Object

The final graphic to add to the newsletter is a headline for the Student List. Headlines can be text, formatted to draw attention; however, using WordArt increases the number of special effect possibilities and options.

Perform the steps on the following pages to add a WordArt object as the headline for the Student article in the newsletter.

More About

WordArt Objects

Keep in mind that WordArt objects are drawing objects and are not treated as Publisher text. Thus, if you misspell the contents of a WordArt object and then spell check the publication, Publisher will not catch the misspelled word(s) in the WordArt text.

To Add WordArt to the Newsletter

1 Click outside the graphic and then zoom to Whole Page view. Click the Insert WordArt button on the Objects toolbar. When the WordArt Gallery window displays, point to an appropriate style.

The WordArt Gallery window displays (Figure 2-56).

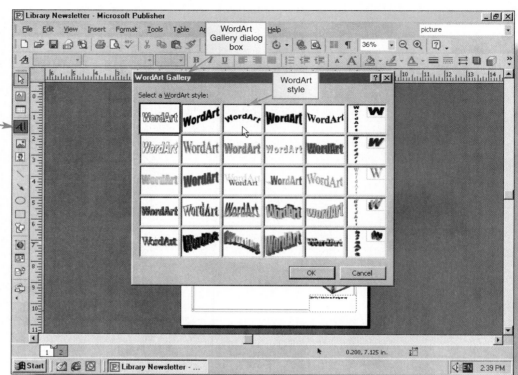

FIGURE 2-56

2 Double-click the style. When the Edit WordArt Text dialog box displays, type Rapid Readers to replace the default text, and then point to the OK button.

Rapid Readers replaces the text in the text area (Figure 2-57). Your font may vary.

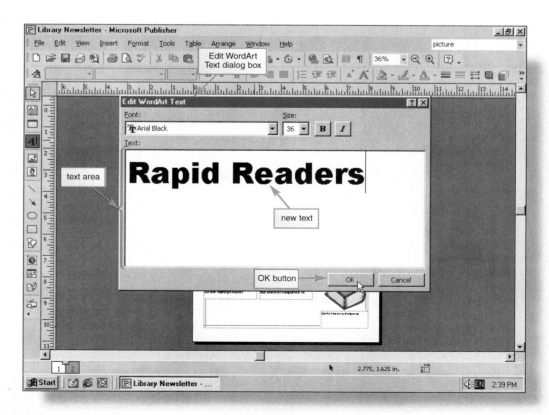

FIGURE 2-57

3 **Click the OK button.**

Publisher displays the WordArt object and the WordArt toolbar (Figure 2-58).

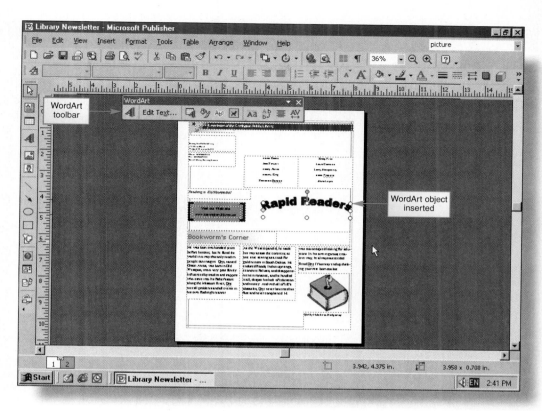

FIGURE 2-58

4 **Drag the WordArt object above the student list. Point to the WordArt Same Letter Heights button on the WordArt toolbar.**

The WordArt object displays above the list (Figure 2-59).

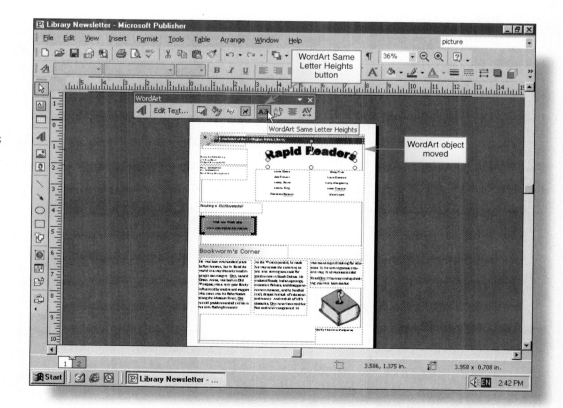

FIGURE 2-59

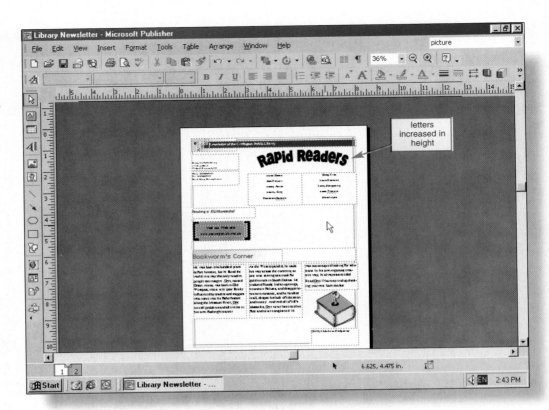

FIGURE 2-60

5 Click the WordArt Same Letter Heights button and then click the newsletter anywhere outside the WordArt object.

The newsletter with the WordArt object displays (Figure 2-60).

Other Ways

1. Click Insert WordArt button on WordArt toolbar
2. In Voice command mode, say "WordArt"

More About

Objects on the Background

Text boxes for page numbers and headers/footers are not the only objects that display in the background on the Master Page. A watermark is a lightly shaded object displaying behind everything else on the page. For example, you can place a light gray graphic or a gray WordArt object such as the word, Confidential, on the Master Page of a publication. It then faintly displays behind text on the foreground.

WordArt includes options for spacing, rotating, shadows, and borders, as well as many of the same features Publisher provides on its Formatting toolbar, such as alignment, bold, italics, underline, and fonts.

Adding Page Numbers to the Master Page

Page numbering on a two-page newsletter probably is not as important as it is for longer publications. Many readers, however, reference articles and points by page numbers. Part of the design process is to provide a consistent look and feel to the layout, so page numbers can furnish a reference for the organization in designing future, perhaps longer, newsletters. Additionally, certain features always may appear, for example, on page 2. Placing page numbers in prominent locations, or using fancy fonts and colors, can make numbering a design element in and of itself.

The next steps in this project describe how to add page numbers to the center of each page at the bottom of the newsletter by creating a text box and moving it to the publication's Master Page. The **Master Page** is a blank sheet located behind your publication where you place objects that will display on every page, such as headers and footers, page numbers, and logos. Most publication objects, such as text and graphics, actually lie in front of the Master Page, allowing the format to display from behind. You can insert and edit these recurring objects in two ways. If you want an object to display on every page, you can move it to the Master Page, or you can go to the Master Page view, and create the object there.

Inserting Automatic Page Numbers on the Master Page

Perform the following steps to create the text box, insert the automatic page number, and then send it to the Master Page so it will display on all pages.

 Steps To Insert Automatic Page Numbering on the Master Page

1 Click the Text Box button. Drag the mouse to form a rectangle in the lower portion of the page in the center.

Publisher displays a selected, rectangular text box with an insertion point (Figure 2-61). Your display may differ due to the size of your graphic. You may want to place your page number text box even lower on the page.

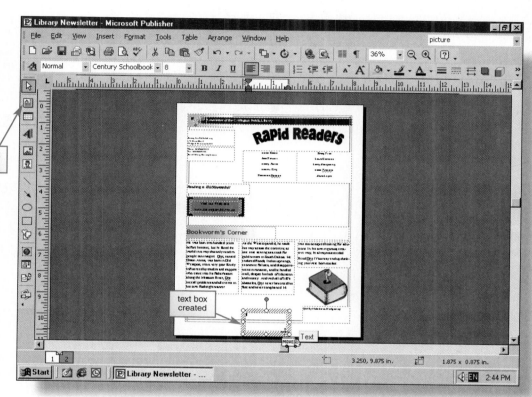

FIGURE 2-61

2 Press the F9 key to view the text box at 100% magnification. Type the word Page in the text box and then press the SPACEBAR to insert a space.

The word, Page, displays in the text box (Figure 2-62).

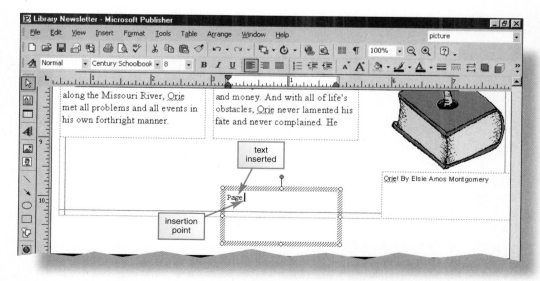

FIGURE 2-62

3 Click Insert on the menu bar and then point to Page Numbers.

The Insert menu displays (Figure 2-63).

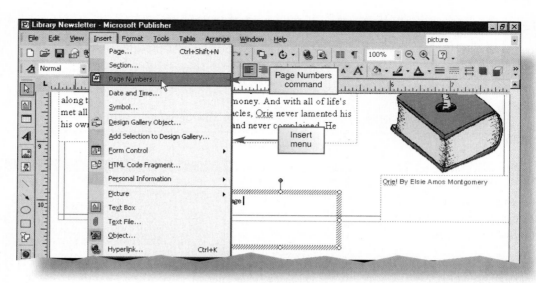

FIGURE 2-63

4 Click Page Numbers. When the Page Numbers dialog box displays, point to the OK button.

The Page Numbers dialog box offers choices for Position, Alignment, and whether or not to show the page number on the first page (Figure 2-64).

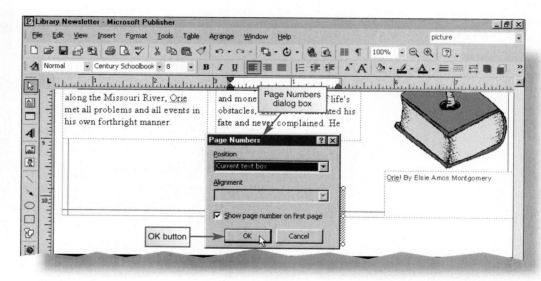

FIGURE 2-64

5 Click the OK button.

The page number displays in the text box (Figure 2-65). Publisher automatically reflects the current page number. Page 1 will display the correct page number as well.

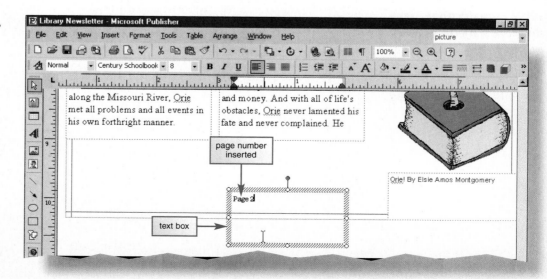

FIGURE 2-65

6 **Click Arrange on the menu bar. Point to Send to Master Page.**

The Arrange menu displays (Figure 2-66).

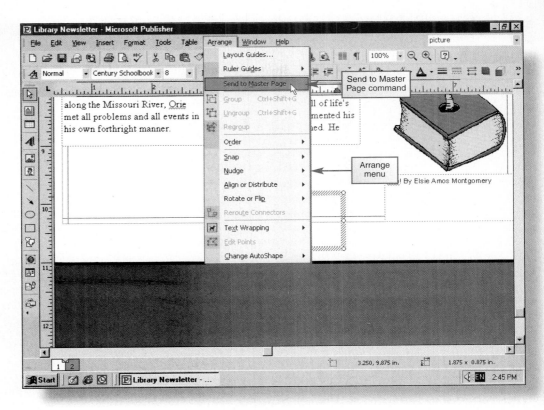

FIGURE 2-66

7 **Click Send to Master Page. When the Microsoft Publisher dialog box displays, point to the OK button.**

A Publisher dialog box displays, informing you that the text box was moved to the Master Page (Figure 2-67).

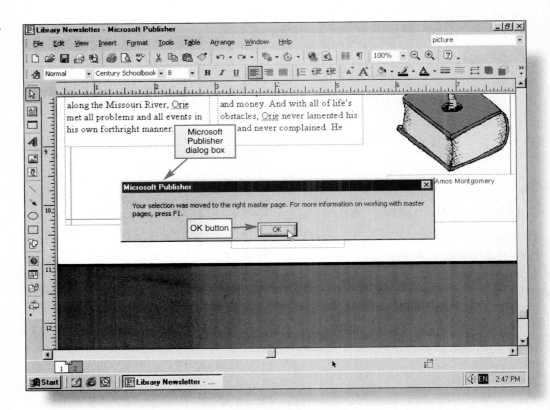

FIGURE 2-67

8 **Click the OK button.**

The page displays with the text box moved to the Master Page (Figure 2-68). The text box no longer is selected.

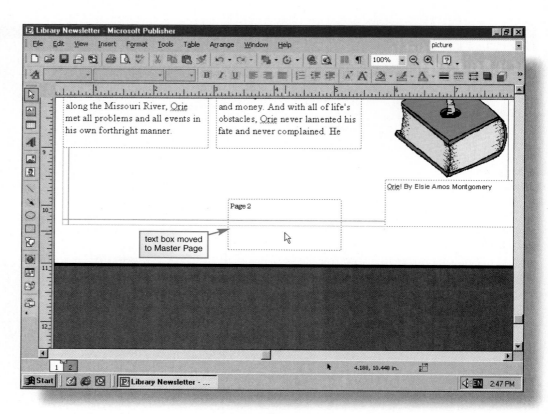

FIGURE 2-68

Backgrounds on the Master Page

If you want the Master Page background not to display on a given page, such as a page number text box on page 1, click Ignore Master Page on the View menu.

Logical choices for a text box on a Master Page might include personal information, dates, times, headers and footers, and page numbers. Options on the Insert menu allow you to insert dates and times derived from the operating system that will update automatically when the publication is edited or printed.

Many newsletters have a Master Page texture or pattern on each page. As with watermarks, a Master Page pattern can provide additional interest and contrast. By creating a text box on the Master Page, you can use fill colors or gradient patterns from the color scheme to add singularity to your newsletter.

If an object disappears when you move it to the Master Page, it does not mean that it becomes invisible; rather, it may be behind another object in the foreground. Typically, items in the foreground, or in the front, which partially cover an item in the Master Page, need to be transparent. The combination keystrokes of CTRL+T will convert selected objects into transparent ones. Should you change your mind, CTRL+T is a toggle; press it again to turn transparency off and make the foreground object opaque again.

Checking a Newsletter for Errors

The final phase of the design process is a synthesis involving editing, proofreading, and publishing. Publisher offers several methods to check for errors in your newsletter. None of these methods is a replacement for careful reading and proofreading. Similar to the spell checking programs in word processing applications, Publisher looks for misspelled words, grammatically incorrect sentences, punctuation problems, and mechanical errors in text boxes.

Spelling and Grammar Errors

As you type text into a text box, Publisher checks your typing for possible spelling and grammar errors. If a typed word is not in the dictionary, a red wavy underline displays below it. Likewise, if typed text contains possible grammar errors, a green wavy underline displays below the text. You can check the entire newsletter for spelling and grammar errors at once or as you are typing.

When a word is flagged with a red wavy underline, it is not in Publisher's dictionary. A flagged word is not necessarily misspelled. For example, many names, abbreviations, and specialized terms are not in Publisher's main dictionary. In these cases, instruct Publisher to ignore the flagged word. To display a list of suggested corrections for a flagged word, right-click it, and then click a replacement word on the shortcut menu.

When using imported text, as in the newsletter, it may be easier to check all the spelling at once. Publisher's check spelling feature looks through the selected text box for errors. Once errors are found, Publisher offers suggestions and provides the choice of correcting or ignoring the flagged word. If you are creating this project on a personal computer, your text boxes may contain different misspelled words, depending on the accuracy of your typing.

More *About*

Spelling Options

On the Tools menu, the Spelling command allows you to access Spelling Options for use in checking the spelling of the publication. Included in the Spelling Options dialog box are check boxes for checking the spelling as you type, flagging repeated words, and ignoring words in uppercase, among others.

Smart Tags

A **Smart Tag button** is a button that automatically displays on the screen when Publisher performs a certain action, such as identifying a misspelled word. When the button displays, you may click it to display a menu of actions associated with the button's concept. Table 2-3 summarizes the smart tags available in Publisher.

With the AutoCorrect Options and Smart Tag Actions, Publisher notifies you that the smart tag is available by displaying a **smart tag indicator** on the screen. The smart tag indicator for the AutoCorrect Options smart tag is a small blue box. The smart tag indicator for the Smart Tag Actions smart tag is a purple dotted line. If you want to display the Smart Tag button, point to the smart tag indicator.

Clicking a Smart Tag button displays a menu that contains commands relative to the action performed at the location of the smart tag. For example, if you want to add a name in your Publisher document to the Outlook Contacts folder, point to the purple dotted line below the name to display the Smart Tag Actions button. Then, click the Smart Tag Actions button to display the Smart Tag Actions menu. Finally, click Add to Contacts on the Smart Tag Actions menu to display the Contacts dialog box in Outlook.

Table 2-3	Smart Tags in Publisher	
BUTTON	**SMART TAG**	**MENU FUNCTION**
☑	AutoCorrect Options	Undoes an automatic correction, stops future automatic corrections of this type, or displays the AutoCorrect Options dialog box
📋	Paste Options	Specifies how moved or pasted items should display, e.g., with original formatting, without formatting, or with different formatting
⑤	Smart Tag Actions	
	• Person name	Adds this name to Outlook Contacts folder or schedules a meeting in Outlook Calendar with this person
	• Date or time	Schedules a meeting in Outlook Calendar at this date or time
	• Address	Adds this address to Outlook Contacts folder
	• Place	Adds this place to Outlook Contacts folder or schedules a meeting in Outlook Calendar at this location

Microsoft **Publisher 2002**

Table 2-4   Design Checker Options
DESIGN ERRORS
Empty frames
Covered objects
Text in overflow area
Objects in nonprinting region
Disproportional pictures
Spacing between sentences

Design Checker

A third way Publisher checks a publication for errors is with the Design Checker. The Design Checker looks for errors related to design issues and object interaction, providing comments and correction choices. Design errors are the most common type of problem when submitting a publication to a professional printer. In a later project, you will learn that, in addition to the interactive design checker, Publisher's Pack and Go Wizard checks for errors related to embedded fonts and graphics. Table 2-4 lists errors detected by the Design Checker.

Checking the Newsletter for Spelling and Grammar Errors

The Spelling command displays on the Tools menu. As you perform the following steps to check your newsletter for spelling and grammar errors, you may encounter spelling mistakes you have made while typing. Choose to correct those errors as necessary. Perform the following steps to check the newsletter for spelling and grammar errors.

 To Check the Newsletter for Spelling and Grammar Errors

1 **With page 2 of the Library Newsletter** still displayed, click the book review article. Click Tools on the menu bar, point to Spelling, and then point to Spelling on the submenu.

The Spelling submenu displays (Figure 2-69).

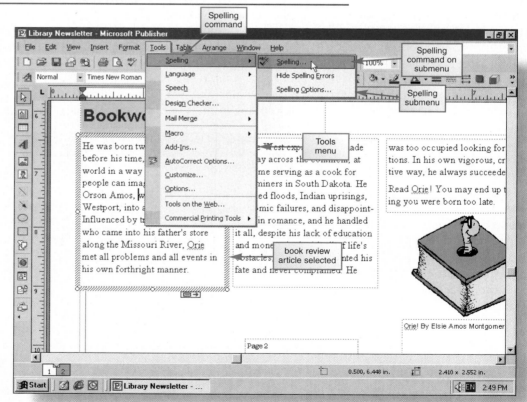

FIGURE 2-69

2 Click Spelling. When the Check Spelling dialog box displays, point to the Ignore All button.

Publisher flags the name, Orie, as shown in Figure 2-70. Because this is a personal name and spelled correctly, you will ignore this flag for all occurrences.

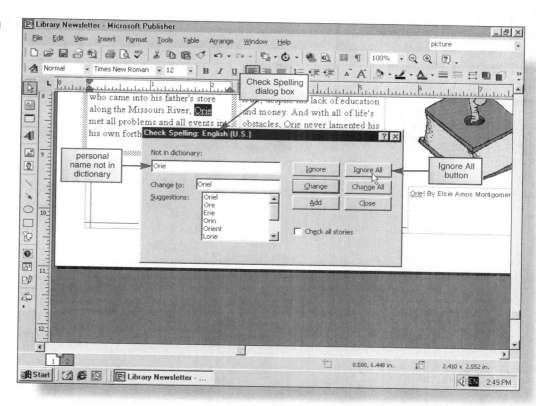

FIGURE 2-70

3 Click the Ignore All button. When the Microsoft Publisher dialog box displays, point to the Yes button.

Publisher did not find any more errors in the book review article. It displays a dialog box that asks if you want to check the rest of the publication (Figure 2-71).

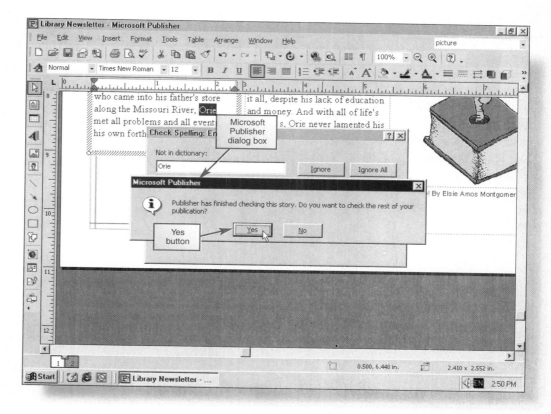

FIGURE 2-71

Microsoft **Publisher 2002**

4 **Click the Yes button. When the Check Spelling dialog box again displays, point to the Ignore button.**

Publisher flags the error in capitalization (Figure 2-72). The Check all stories check box now displays with a check mark.

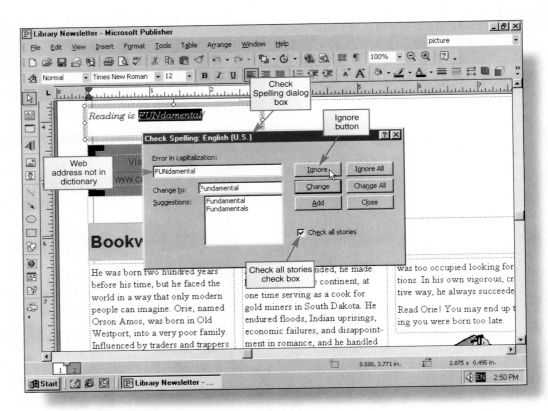

FIGURE 2-72

5 **Click the Ignore button. If Publisher flags the Web address or other personal names in the Student list, click the Ignore button for each. If you have other errors, choose appropriate measures to fix or ignore them. When the check spelling process is complete, a dialog box will display. Point to the OK button.**

Publisher displays a dialog box informing you that the process is complete (Figure 2-73).

6 **Click the OK button.**

1. Click Spelling button on text Formatting toolbar
2. In Voice command mode, say "Spelling"

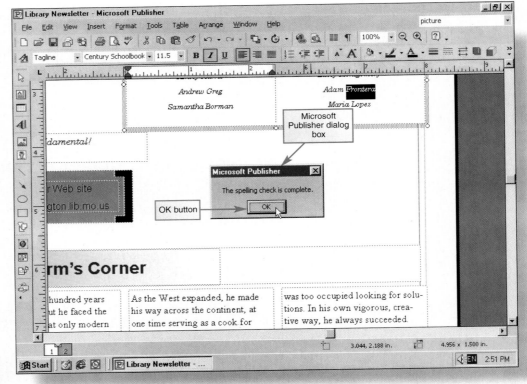

FIGURE 2-73

Even if text is checked for spelling before it is imported, Publisher flags words, phrases, and punctuation not found in its dictionary. The process is worth the time it takes, but again, there is no substitute for proofreading the text yourself.

Checking the Newsletter for Design Errors

You now are ready to check the newsletter for design errors as you did in Project 1. The Design Checker can check single pages or entire publications, for a specific type of error or all types of errors. Perform the following steps to have Publisher check for all kinds of design errors throughout the newsletter.

TO CHECK THE NEWSLETTER FOR DESIGN ERRORS

1 Click Tools on the menu bar and then click Design Checker. When the Design Checker dialog box displays, if necessary, click All to select it.

2 Click the OK button.

3 If the Design Checker finds errors, choose to fix or ignore them as necessary. When the Design Checker terminates, click the OK button.

If you have made errors in placing graphics or WordArt objects, you may have to accept or ignore other Design Checker recommendations.

If you resized any graphic in the newsletter, Publisher's Design Checker will warn you that the graphic may not be proportionally correct. At that time, you may choose to resize the graphic or ignore the change.

The newsletter is complete, and should be saved again before printing. Follow this step to save the newsletter using the same file name.

TO SAVE AN EXISTING NEWSLETTER USING THE SAME FILE NAME

1 With your floppy disk in drive A, click the Save button on the Standard toolbar.

Publisher saves the publication using the same file name, Library Newsletter, on the floppy disk in drive A.

Printing a Two-Sided Page

Printing the two pages of the newsletter back to back is a process that is highly dependent upon the printer. Some printers can perform duplex printing, which prints both sides before ejecting the paper, while other printers require the user to reload the paper manually. If you are attached to a single-user printer, you must check the printer's documentation to see if it supports double-sided printing. If you are connected to a network printer, you probably will need to feed the paper through a second time manually.

The steps on the next page illustrate how to print the first page and then manually feed the page through a second time. Adjust the steps as necessary for your printer.

More About

Web Design

For more information on the design problems associated with loading Web pages quickly, visit the Publisher 2002 More About Web page (scsite.com/pub2002/more.htm) and then click Web Design.

More About

Network Printing

If your network printer seems to lock up or prints only part of the page, it may not have enough memory to store the large print files that Publisher creates. Consider one of the following solutions: wait until everyone else has printed before sending your publication, print your publication in black and white instead of color, choose to print lower-resolution graphics using your printer's Advanced Settings button, change the spool settings or print directly to the printer by clicking Spool Settings on the Details tab in your printer's Properties dialog box, or finally, print the text only and then send the paper through a second time for the graphics.

If the problem continues, ask your network supervisor to check the printer's memory setting. The memory setting on your printer driver influences your printer's ability to reproduce your publication. If your printer driver's memory setting is too low, the publication may not appear complete when printed. Sometimes freeing hard drive space improves printer performance, as well.

Steps **To Print a Two-Sided Page**

1 **If necessary, click the page 1 icon on the Page Navigation Control. Ready the printer according to the printer instructions. Click File on the menu bar and then click Print. When the Print dialog box displays, click Current page in the Print range area. Point to the OK button.**

The print dialog box displays (Figure 2-74). Your dialog box may differ.

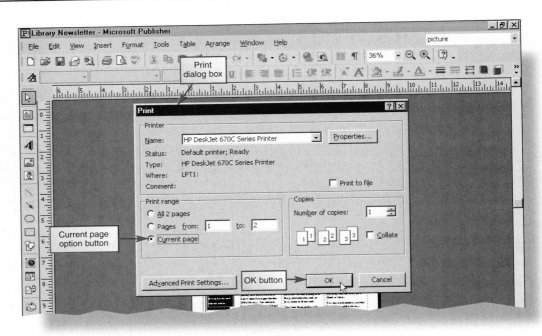

FIGURE 2-74

2 **Click the OK button. When printing is complete, retrieve the printout.**

The printed newsletter is shown in Figures 2-1a and 2-1b on page PUB 2.06. Publications with many graphics and fonts take longer to print than plain text documents.

3 **After retrieving the printout, wait a few seconds for it to dry. Reinsert the printout in the manual tray of the printer; usually blank side down, top first. Click the page 2 icon on the Page Navigation Control. Click Print on the File menu and then repeat Steps 1 and 2 to print page 2 of the newsletter.**

Retrieve the printout from the printer.

Other Ways

1. Click print button on Standard toolbar
2. Press CTRL+P

If you have an option button or an Advanced Print Settings button in your Print dialog box (Figure 2-74), you may be able to duplex print. Check your printer documentation, or click the button for more information.

If you are unsure how to load the paper, you can run a test page through the printer. Mark an X in the upper-right corner of a blank sheet, and then insert the sheet into the printer, noting where the X is. If your printer has a Manual Feed button or Paper Source list box, be sure to click Manual. Print the first page. Note where the X is in relation to the printed page and turn the paper over to print the other side accordingly.

In a later project, you will learn more about types of paper best suited for printing on both sides, as well as how to prepare a publication for a printing service.

The newsletter now is complete. Perform the following step to quit Publisher.

TO QUIT PUBLISHER

1   Click the Close button in the Publisher window.

Publisher closes and the Windows desktop displays.

CASE PERSPECTIVE SUMMARY

The Carrington Library newsletter is complete. The library's information is located in the masthead and in the Personal Information Sets. You imported several articles, written by Teresa Hall, for the front page of the newsletter. Teresa likes the graphics you chose.

On the back page, you inserted WordArt for the Rapid Readers heading, and formatted the list in two columns. The book review is complemented by an appropriate graphic. The library's motto displays prominently, as does the library's Web address in an Attention Getter.

The library is pleased with the effect, the quick turn around, and the professional look of its new newsletter. It is equally pleased that future newsletters will be easy to create using this template.

Project Summary

Project 2 introduced you to the design process and the newsletter medium. You used the Publisher Newsletter Wizard to design a template for editing. Using the Pixel Newsletter style, you learned how to edit a masthead, import text from other sources, and add appropriate graphics. You also learned how to insert and delete pages in a newsletter and incorporate personal information components. With WordArt, you inserted a fancy headline with special text effects. You added page numbers to the Master Page and used the Spelling and Design Checker features to identify spelling, grammar, and design errors. Finally, you printed the newsletter double-sided and saved it on a floppy disk.

What You Should Know

Having completed this project, you now should be able to perform the following tasks:

▶ Add a Pull Quote *(PUB 2.39)*
▶ Add WordArt to the Newsletter *(PUB 2.44)*
▶ Change and Delete Pages in a Newsletter *(PUB 2.11)*
▶ Check the Newsletter for Design Errors *(PUB 2.55)*
▶ Check the Newsletter for Spelling and Grammar Errors *(PUB 2.52)*
▶ Create a Newsletter Template *(PUB 2.08)*
▶ Delete the Logo *(PUB 2.32)*
▶ Delete the Sidebar *(PUB 2.33)*
▶ Edit Personal Information Components *(PUB 2.22)*
▶ Edit the Attention Getter *(PUB 2.29)*
▶ Edit the Bulleted Text Box Sidebar *(PUB 2.41)*
▶ Edit the Masthead *(PUB 2.14)*
▶ Import More Text *(PUB 2.19)*
▶ Import the Back Page Story *(PUB 2.20)*
▶ Import the Student List and Create Columns *(PUB 2.25)*

▶ Insert Automatic Page Numbering on the Master Page *(PUB 2.47)*
▶ Print a Two-Sided Page *(PUB 2.56)*
▶ Quit Publisher *(PUB 2.57)*
▶ Replace a Graphic *(PUB 2.34)*
▶ Replace Default Text *(PUB 2.16)*
▶ Replace the Graphic on Page 2 *(PUB 2.42)*
▶ Save an Intermediate Copy of the Newsletter *(PUB 2.21)*
▶ Save an Existing Newsletter Using the Same File Name *(PUB 2.55)*
▶ Start Publisher *(PUB 2.07)*

More About

Quick Reference

For a table that lists how to complete tasks covered in this book using the mouse, menu, shortcut menu, and keyboard, see the Quick Reference Summary at the back of this book or visit the Shelly Cashman Series Office XP Web page (scsite.com/offxp/qr.htm), and then click Microsoft Publisher 2002.

Learn It Online

Instructions: To complete the Learn It Online exercises, start your browser, click the Address bar, and then enter scsite.com/offxp/exs.htm. When the Office XP Learn It Online page displays, follow the instructions in the exercises below.

1 Project Reinforcement TF, MC, and SA

Below Publisher Project 2, click the Project Reinforcement link. Print the quiz by clicking Print on the File menu. Answer each question. Write your first and last name at the top of each page, and then hand in the printout to your instructor.

2 Flash Cards

Below Publisher Project 2, click the Flash Cards link. When Flash Cards displays, read the instructions. Type 20 (or a number specified by your instructor) in the Number of Playing Cards text box, type your name in the Name text box, and then click the Flip Card button. When the flash card displays, read the question and then click the Answer box arrow to select an answer. Flip through Flash Cards. Click Print on the File menu to print the last flash card if your score is 15 (75%) correct or greater and then hand it in to your instructor. If your score is less than 15 (75%) correct, then redo this exercise by clicking the Replay button.

3 Practice Test

Below Publisher Project 2, click the Practice Test link. Answer each question, enter your first and last name at the bottom of the page, and then click the Grade Test button. When the graded practice test displays on your screen, click Print on the File menu to print a hard copy. Continue to take practice tests until you score 80% or better. Hand in a printout of the final practice test to your instructor.

4 Who Wants to Be a Computer Genius?

Below Publisher Project 2, click the Computer Genius link. Read the instructions, enter your first and last name at the bottom of the page, and then click the Play button. Hand in your score to your instructor.

5 Wheel of Terms

Below Publisher Project 2, click the Wheel of Terms link. Read the instructions, and then enter your first and last name and your school name. Click the Play button. Hand in your score to your instructor.

6 Crossword Puzzle Challenge

Below Publisher Project 2, click the Crossword Puzzle Challenge link. Read the instructions, and then enter your first and last name. Click the Play button. Work the crossword puzzle. When you are finished, click the Submit button. When the crossword puzzle redisplays, click the Print button. Hand in the printout.

7 Tips and Tricks

Below Publisher Project 2, click the Tips and Tricks link. Click a topic that pertains to Project 2. Right-click the information and then click Print on the shortcut menu. Construct a brief example of what the information relates to in Publisher to confirm you understand how to use the tip or trick. Hand in the example and printed information.

8 Newsgroups

Below Publisher Project 2, click the Newsgroups link. Click a topic that pertains to Project 2. Print three comments. Hand in the comments to your instructor.

9 Expanding Your Horizons

Below Publisher Project 2, click the Articles for Microsoft Publisher link. Click a topic that pertains to Project 2. Print the information. Construct a brief example of what the information relates to in Publisher to confirm you understand the contents of the article. Hand in the example and printed information to your instructor.

10 Search Sleuth

Below Publisher Project 2, click the Search Sleuth link. To search for a term that pertains to this project, select a term below the Project 2 title and then use the Google search engine at google.com (or any major search engine) to display and print two Web pages that present information on the term. Hand in the printouts to your instructor.

online

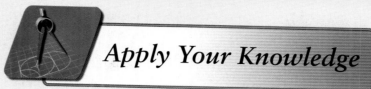

Apply Your Knowledge

1 Editing a School Newsletter

Instructions: Start Publisher. Open the publication, Apply-2, from the Data Disk. See the inside back cover for instructions on downloading the Data Disk or see your instructor for information on accessing the files required in this book. The first page of the publication is shown in Figure 2-75.

Perform the following tasks.

1. On page 1 highlight the text, The Weekly Warrior, in the vertical masthead. Type The Warrior Journal to replace the text.

2. In the lower center of the page, right-click the sidebar table titled, Inside this Issue. Click Delete Object.

3. Click the Design Gallery Object button on the Objects toolbar and then click the Pull Quotes category. Insert the Nature Pull Quote. Drag it to the empty space left by the deleted sidebar.

4. Select and copy the next to the last sentence of the article titled, Housing Shortage on Campus. Click the pull quote text. Paste the sentence into the pull quote.

5. Delete the picture of the student. Use the Insert Clip Art task pane to find a different picture of students. Drag the picture to the end of the article.

6. Drag a corner sizing handle to resize the picture proportionally until it fits in the third column.

7. Click the Organization name text box on the left side of the masthead. Click the Fill Color button and choose a color from the Scheme colors.

8. Click the page 2 icon on the Page Navigation Control. Use the Edit menu to delete pages 2 and 3.

9. On the back page, click the colored rectangle in the upper-left portion of the page. Zoom as necessary. Replace the text with information from your college or business. Use your school or business Web page address (URL) in the Attention Getter.

10. Click File on the menu bar and then click Save As. Save the publication using Warrior Journal Newsletter, as the file name. Print the revised newsletter, double-sided.

FIGURE 2-75

BUSINESS NAME

The Weekly Warrior

Dates of Interest

- *Frat Pledge Week: Sept. 22–27*
- *Swing Choir Try-Outs: Sept. 18–19*
- *Last Day to Add a class: Sept. 15*

Inside this

Professor Profile	2
Letters to the Editor	2
Greek Row	2
Arts & Entertainment	3
All Around Campus	4
Sports	5
Schedule of Classes	6

Volume 5, Issue 1   August 25, 2003

Fall Classes Begin

Classes began today with one of the largest enrollments in recent years. With fall semester enrollment on the rise administrators seem to be proving that their efforts to work with students and create a more student–friendly atmosphere are effective. Administrators were on hand to greet students and parents moving into dorms across the campus this past weekend.

The Bursar's Office will stay open late every night this week, to accept payments and change registration for students adding and dropping courses. You may pick up deferment forms in Gyte 241. Students who owe housing deposits should see their building coordinator before Friday.

The newest degree on campus is an associate degree in Web design. Students can take 30 credit hours in information system courses, web development, and

Students have mixed feelings about the new parking spaces.

general studies require–

Housing Shortage on Campus

As Central College expands and enrollment increases, students are finding it more and more difficult to secure housing on campus.

Freshmen and Sopho–

mores must live in campus approved housing. The dormitories have been full since July 1. The College Housing Board recently approved Stevenson Hall and Quad Towers as ap–

proved housing, pending completion of their cafeterias. Both units are accepting applications. Freshmen and Sophomores must file a housing arrangement contract with the Uni–

In the Lab

1 Creating a Special-Purpose Newsletter

Problem: You are a teacher of fifth grade students at a local elementary school. You thought the students and parents might find a monthly newsletter interesting and informative. Students could write the articles concerning happenings in the school and in your classroom, and you could include dates of future events and projects (Figure 2-76a). In addition, you would like to include a monthly feature called "Caught Being Good," a list of students who have gone out of their way to do something good and caring in the classroom (Figure 2-76b). Using Publisher's Newsletter Wizard, create a two-page, double-sided newsletter with columns.

Instructions: Perform the following tasks.

1. Start Publisher.
2. Click Newsletters in the Publications list. Select the Kid Stuff Newsletter. Choose an appropriate color and font scheme in the task pane.
3. Make the following changes on page 1:
   a. Change the newsletter title to Fifth Grade News.
   b. Change the Lead Story Headline to Fifth Grade Goes on Field Trip.
   c. Change the Secondary Story Headline to Science Fair News!
   d. Change the Organization name to Brown Elementary.
   e. In the bulleted list sidebar, change the title to Specials Each Week and then in the list, type the following: `Monday: Music, Tuesday: Gym, Wednesday: Art, Thursday: Computers, Friday: Library`, each with a separate bullet.
   f. Delete the table sidebar and insert a WordArt object in its place. When the styles display, choose a top to bottom display. Type `First Issue` as the text.

Fifth Grade News

Fifth Grade Goes on Fieldtrip

This story can fit 175-225 words.

The purpose of a newsletter is to provide specialized information to a targeted audience. Newsletters can be a great way to market your product or service, and also create credibility and build your organization's identity among peers, members, employees, or vendors.

First, determine the audience of the newsletter. This could be anyone who might benefit from the information it contains, for example, employees or people interested in purchasing a product or requesting your service.

You can compile a mailing list from business reply cards, customer information sheets, business cards collected at trade shows, or membership lists. You might consider purchasing a mailing list from a company.

If you explore the Publisher catalog, you will find many publications that match the style of your newsletter.

Next, establish how much time and money you can spend on your newsletter. These factors will help determine how frequently you publish the newsletter and its length. It's recommended that you publish your newsletter at least

quarterly so that it's considered a consistent source of information. Your customers or employees will look forward to its arrival.

Science Fair News!

This story can fit 75-125 words.

Your headline is an important part of the newsletter and should be considered carefully.

In a few words, it should accurately represent the

contents of the story and draw readers into the story. Develop the headline before you write the story. This way, the headline will help you keep the story focused.

Examples of possible headlines include Product Wins

Industry Award, New Product Can Save You Time!, Membership Drive Exceeds Goals, and New Office Opens Near You.

Brown Elementary

Volume 1, Issue 1

Newsletter Date

Specials Each Week
☺ Monday: Music
☺ Tuesday: Gym
☺ Wednesday: Art
☺ Thursday. Computers
☺ Friday: Library

First Issue

FIGURE 2-76a

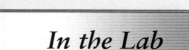

In the Lab

g. On the WordArt toolbar, click the Shading button (third from the right), and choose a blue foreground color. Right-click the WordArt object and then, click Format WordArt on the shortcut menu. Choose blue for both the Fill Color and Line Color.

4. Use the Page Navigation Control to move to page 2. Delete pages 2 and 3.

5. Make the following changes to the back page:

a. Change the back page story headline to, This Month's Spelling Words.

b. Use a keyword to locate and insert graphics about children.

c. Delete the logo on the back page.

d. Click the text box in the upper-right corner. Click Format on the menu bar and then click Text Box Properties to change the text box to contain two columns. With the text still selected, type the following names on separate lines: Jared Allen, Dara Arslanian, Fredrick Carl, Marsha Louks, Katie Marie. Then, press CTRL+SHIFT+ENTER to create a column break. Continue the list by typing: Michael Montgomery, Hannah Murphy, Jon Reneau, Nathan Thomas, Rebecca Witte, each on a separate line.

e. Add a WordArt text box with the text, Caught Being Good, positioned above the list. Stretch the text to fit the box. Add an Attention Getter under the list. Enter Students are cool! to replace the text.

6. Spell check and design check the newsletter.

7. Save the newsletter on a floppy disk using the file name, Kids Newsletter, and print a copy.

Caught Being Good

Jared Allen	Michael Montgomery
Dara Arslanian	Hannah Murphy
Fredrick Carl	Jon Reneau
Marsha Louks	Nathan Thomas
Katie Marie	Rebecca Witte

Students are cool!

FIGURE 2-76b

2 Creating a Masthead from Scratch

Problem: The accounting firm of A. W. Wright and Associates has asked you to create a masthead for its newsletter. Mr. Wright wants you to incorporate the company logo and colors in the masthead. You decide to use a rectangle, two lines, three text boxes, a graphic, and a WordArt object for the newsletter title.

Instructions: Perform the following tasks to create the masthead shown in Figure 2-77 on the next page.

1. Start Publisher. From the New Publication task pane, click Blank Publications.

2. Using the Rectangle button on the Objects toolbar, draw a large rectangle across the center of the page, toward the top. Click the Fill Color button, and choose an orange color in the Scheme colors.

3. Using the Line button on the Objects toolbar, draw a line across the top of the rectangle extending beyond its edges, as shown in Figure 2-77. Draw another line on the left extending down the page. Hold down the SHIFT key while you draw to keep your lines straight. Use the Line/Border Style button on the Formatting toolbar to make both lines 8 pt and orange.

4. Using the Insert Clip Art task pane, find a clip related to teamwork. Insert the graphic and move it to the right of the rectangle.

(continued)

In the Lab

Creating a Masthead from Scratch *(continued)*

5. For the newsletter title, draw a WordArt object just inside the rectangle. Type `The Wright Choice` in the dialog box. Use the shape and font settings shown in Figure 2-77.

6. Use the Text Box button on the Objects toolbar to create a text box to hold the words, Newsletter of A. W. Wright and Associates. Use a bold font, and place the text box at the approximate location shown in Figure 2-77.

7. Create two small text boxes below the name of the company. Type `Volume 7, Issue 12` in the first text box. Type `December 17, 2003` in the second text box. Using the shortcut menu, change each box's Line/Border Style to a thin line.

FIGURE 2-77

8. Use the Design Checker to correct any errors in the publication.

9. Save the publication on your floppy disk using the file name, Wright Masthead.

10. Print a copy of the masthead.

3 Looking at Publisher's Newsletter Options

Problem: You work in the public relations department of an architectural firm. Your supervisor wants to publish a weekly newsletter for customers and potential clients, but would like to see some samples first. You decide to use Publisher's Newsletter Wizard to give him a variety from which he may choose.

Instructions: Using the techniques presented in this project, access the New Publication task pane, and choose five different newsletter previews, one at a time, that you have not used before. Below are some general guidelines.

1. Click each of the options in the Newsletter Options task pane. Make a note of the default values for each newsletter.

2. Print page 1 of each newsletter.

3. Identify the parts of the newsletter on the printout. Label things such as the masthead, color and font schemes, personal information components, sidebars, pull quotes, attention getters, and all objects.

4. Pick your favorite of the five newsletters. For that one, print all the pages and identify any different components or objects. If possible, print double-sided.

5. Let your instructor look at all the printouts.

Cases and Places

The difficulty of these case studies varies:
▶ are the least difficult; ▶▶ are more difficult; and ▶▶▶ are the most difficult.

1 ▶ Use the Checkers Newsletter to create a letterhead for your personal use. Delete all the pages except page 1. Delete all the objects on page 1 except the masthead and the checkers graphic across the bottom. Put your name in the Newsletter Title and your address and telephone number in the Volume and Issue and Newsletter Date text boxes.

2 ▶ Use the Newsletter Wizard titled Voyage Newsletter, to create a two-page newsletter for the Seniors Abroad Club. This local club of senior citizens gets together to take group trips. For the newsletter title, use Seniors on the Go, and place today's date in the masthead. Include an article headline for the lead story, which concerns the club's most recent trip to London (you may use the default text), and a secondary article headline that tells how to pack light for the Orient. Add a list of dates for upcoming trips to Quebec, Paris, and Tokyo in the Special Points of Interest sidebar. Replace the graphics with suitable pictures from Publisher's Clip Organizer.

3 ▶▶ You are associate editor of *The Weekly Warrior*, a two-page newsletter for students at Central College. Last week's edition is shown in Figure 2-75 on page PUB 2.59. Volume 4, Issue 2 is due out in three weeks. Using the same masthead and design set, your assignment is to decide on a feature article for *The Weekly Warrior* newsletter and develop some announcements. Select a topic about your school that would interest other students, such as extracurricular activities, the fitness center, the day-care center, the bookstore, the student government organization, registration, the student body, a club, a sports team, etc. Obtain information for your article by interviewing a campus employee or student, visiting the school library, or reading brochures published by your school. Use appropriate clip art graphics, sidebars, and pull quotes. Design and spell check your final product, making corrections as necessary. Print a double-sided hard copy.

4 ▶▶▶ Ask a local civic group or scouting organization for a sample of its newsletter. Try to recreate its style and format using a blank publication page in Publisher. Use Publisher's Design Gallery and Personal Information Sets to customize the newsletter. Print your final product and compare the two.

5 ▶▶▶ Many clubs and organizations put their newsletters out on the Web. Browse the Web and look for examples of newsletters. Note how many pages, graphics, and articles they use. Look at their mastheads and logos. Then, using a Publisher Newsletter Wizard, create a newsletter for a club or organization with which you are affiliated. Include at least three articles, one sidebar or pull quote, a masthead, and several graphics. Use the Create Web Site from Current Publication command on the File menu to create a group of files for posting to the Web.

Microsoft Publisher 2002

PROJECT

3

Preparing a Tri-Fold Brochure for Outside Printing

You will have mastered the material in this project when you can:

OBJECTIVES

- Discuss advantages of the brochure medium
- Use the Brochure Options task pane
- Edit placeholder text and personal information sets
- Edit a story in Microsoft Word
- Delete and insert text boxes
- Use the AutoCorrect Options Smart Tag
- Rotate and move text boxes
- Describe the use of photographs versus images
- Insert a photograph from a file
- Create a logo from scratch using AutoShapes
- Create a composite object in the scratch area
- Create an AutoFit, transparent text box
- Group and ungroup objects
- Edit a sign-up form
- Preview a brochure before printing
- Choose appropriate printing services, paper, and color libraries
- Prepare a publication for outside printing
- Use the Pack and Go Wizard

The Paper Trail

Producing Publications with a Personal Touch

The 1991 movie, *Green Card*, portrayed the madcap antics of Georges, a French composer, and Bronte, a well-to-do American, as they try to convince the authorities that their marriage is legitimate. The goal is to secure Georges a green card, a document that has the power to transform his life. In many ways, individuals' lives are defined by a paper trail of documentation.

A newborn receives a birth certificate to declare that he or she is indeed a real person. From that point on, a succession of documents tracks his or her progress through life and even beyond. Medical records, diplomas, military orders, marriage certificates, wills, contracts, drivers licenses, and resumes, are among the many publications organized in the personal filing cabinets of the general population.

In addition, a number of other publications, such as the *Holy Bible*, the *Koran*, or the *Talmud*, as well as the works of countless great thinkers and authors, influence the minds and personalities of people. Yet, the most personal and gratifying kinds of publications are those created by the individuals themselves; whether they are works of art, words of poetry, letters, journals, term papers, newsletters, flyers, personal greetings, business cards, or brochures, whatever the medium, individual creativity provides the most significant sense of accomplishment.

Still, for many people, the mere act of creating any publication ranks high in difficulty. You have a powerful tool, however, with the Publisher Brochure Wizard that you will use to create a tri-fold brochure. The brochure medium is intentionally tactile, making it an effective communication tool. Whether you want to advertise an event or service or provide information to a large audience, brochures are a popular type of promotional publication. Brochures can be produced quickly with lots of color and graphics. Strategically placed, they reach a wide audience and can influence and educate.

Publisher allows you to choose from a variety of brochure types and designs. Then, you can edit and delete text to fit your personal, academic, or professional needs. Enhancing your brochure using photographs and images adds a special touch. Publisher also makes it possible to combine numerous shapes to create a logo of your design. As you examine the Objects by Category in the Design Gallery, you will find a large selection of objects to insert into your brochures and other publications.

Finally, you will learn about packaging the publication for the printing service using the Pack and Go Wizard. The productivity tools of Publisher 2002 make it easy to produce professional-looking publications with a personal touch.

Microsoft Publisher 2002

Preparing a Tri-Fold Brochure for Outside Printing

CASE PERSPECTIVE

The School of Engineering at Montgomery College in Indianapolis, Indiana, offers 17 majors with more than 300 students. Graduates of the engineering program are in great demand by high-tech businesses throughout the state, as Indiana moves forward with its Hold On To Technology initiative. Many local scholarships have been funded.

As a student worker in the Financial Aid office, you have been asked to create a scholarship brochure that advertises these scholarships along with an application form. Your supervisor, Andrea Walter, would like a full-color, tri-fold brochure on glossy paper. The office has budgeted the money to send the final copy to a printing service. The brochure should include information about the scholarships, school, and college; an application form; the Montgomery College logo; and the school's Web site address.

You decide to use Publisher to set up a tri-fold brochure for outside printing. After printing a copy for Andrea's approval, you package the publication on a floppy disk along with all of the items the printing service will need to produce large quantities.

Introduction

Whether you want to advertise a service, event, or product, or merely want to inform the public about a current topic of interest, brochures are a popular type of promotional publication. A **brochure**, or pamphlet, usually is a high-quality document with eye catching color and graphics, created for advertising purposes. Businesses that may not be able to reach potential clientele effectively through traditional advertising, such as newspapers and radio, can create a long-lasting advertisement with a well-designed brochure.

Brochures come in all shapes and sizes. Colleges and universities produce brochures about their programs. The travel industry uses brochures to entice tourists. Service industries and manufacturers display their products using this visual, hands-on medium.

Project Three — Tri-Fold Scholarship Brochure

Project 3 uses Publisher to illustrate the production of the two-page, tri-fold brochure shown in Figure 3-1. The brochure informs the public about engineering scholarships at the local college. Each side of the brochure has three panels. Page 1 contains the front and back panels, as well as the inside fold. Page 2 contains a three-panel display that, when opened completely, provides the reader with more details about the scholarships and an application form.

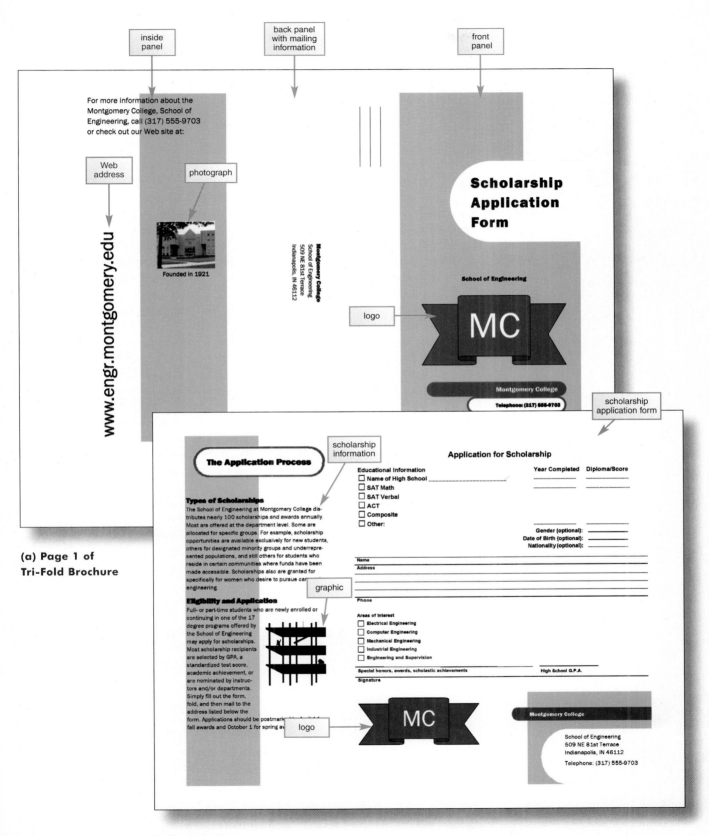

**(a) Page 1 of
Tri-Fold Brochure**

**(b) Page 2 of
Tri-Fold Brochure**

FIGURE 3-1

On page 1 (Figure 3-1a on the previous page), the front panel contains shapes, text boxes, and a photograph, designed to draw the reader's attention and inform the reader of the intent of the brochure. The back panel, which displays in the middle of page 1, contains the name of the school, the mailing address, and a place for the applicant to enter a return address. The inside fold, on the left, contains information about the college, with a colored background and graphic.

The three inside panels on page 2 (Figure 3-1a) contain more information about scholarships, graphics, and a form the reader may use to apply.

The Brochure Medium

Brochures are professionally printed on special paper to provide long-lasting documents and to enhance the graphics. The brochure medium is intentionally tactile. Brochures are meant to be touched, carried home, passed along, and looked at again and again. Newspapers and fliers usually are produced for short-term readership on paper that soon will be thrown away or recycled. Brochures frequently use a heavier stock of paper so they can stand better in a display rack.

The content of a brochure needs to last longer too. On occasion, the intent of a brochure is to educate, such as a brochure on health issues in a doctor's office; but more commonly, the intent is to market a product or sell a service. Prices and dated materials that are subject to frequent change affect the usable life of a brochure.

Typically, brochures use a great deal of color, and they include actual photographs instead of drawings or graphic images. Photographs give a sense of realism to a publication and should be used to show people, places, or things that are real, whereas images or drawings more appropriately are used to convey concepts or ideas.

Many brochures incorporate newspaper features, such as columns and a masthead, and the added eye appeal of logos, sidebars, shapes, and graphics. Small brochures are separated into panels and folded. Larger brochures resemble small magazines, with multiple pages and a stapled binding.

Brochures, designed to be in circulation for longer periods as a type of advertising, ordinarily are published in greater quantities and on more expensive paper than newsletters, and are, therefore, more costly. The cost, however, is less prohibitive when produced **in-house** using desktop publishing rather than hiring an outside service. The cost per copy is sometimes less than a newsletter because brochures are produced in mass quantities.

Table 3-1 lists some benefits and advantages of using the brochure medium.

Brochures

Many brochures are published regularly on the Web. To look at some samples and for information on brochure content, visit the Publisher 2002 More About Web page (scsite.com/pub2002/more.htm) and then click Brochures.

Table 3-1	Benefits and Advantages of Using the Brochure Medium
AREA	**BENEFITS AND ADVANTAGES**
Exposure	An attention getter in displays A take-along document encouraging second looks A long-lasting publication due to paper and content An easily distributed publication — mass mailings, advertising sites
Information	Give readers an in-depth look at a product or service An opportunity to inform in a nonrestrictive environment An opportunity for focused feedback using tear-offs and forms
Audience	Interested clientele and retailers
Communication	An effective medium to highlight products and services A source of free information to build credibility An easier method to disseminate information than a magazine

In addition to the intent and content of the brochure, you must consider the shape and size of the page when designing this type of publication. Publisher can incorporate a variety of paper sizes from the standard 8½-by-11-inch to 8½-by-24-inch. You also can design smaller brochures, such as those used as liner notes for CD jewel cases or inserts for videotapes. In addition, you need to think about how the brochure or pamphlet will be folded. Publisher's Brochure Wizard can create three or four panels. Using the Page Setup options you may create special folds, such as book or card folds.

Starting Publisher

To start Publisher, Windows must be running. Perform the following steps to start Publisher.

TO START PUBLISHER

1. Click the Start button on the Windows taskbar and then click New Office Document.
2. When the New Office Document dialog box displays, if necessary, click the General tab and then double-click the Blank Publication icon.
3. If the Publisher window is not maximized, double-click its title bar to maximize it.
4. If the New Publication task pane does not display, click View on the menu bar and then click Task Pane.
5. If the Language bar displays, click its Minimize button.

You are now ready to use Publisher's New Publication task pane to create a tri-fold brochure.

More About

Starting Publisher

Microsoft Windows provides many ways to start Publisher. You have been using the Open Office Document command on the Start menu. You also can click Programs on the Start menu and then click Microsoft Publisher. If you have installed the Office toolbar, you may have a button on your desktop for Publisher. In addition, you can right-click the desktop, click New on the shortcut menu, and then click Microsoft Publisher Document. Finally, you can open any Publisher file by double-clicking its icon.

Creating a Tri-Fold Brochure

Publisher-supplied templates and wizards use proven design strategies and combinations of objects, which are placed to attract attention and disseminate information effectively. The options for brochures differ from other publications in that they allow you to choose from page sizes, special kinds of forms, and panel/page layout options.

Making Choices in the Brochure Options Task Pane

For the scholarship brochure, you will use the Capsules Informational Brochure as a template, making changes to its page size, customer address, sign-up form, color scheme, and font scheme. **Page size** refers to the number of panels in the brochure. The **Customer address** selection offers choices to include or not to include the customer's address in the brochure. **Form** options, which display on page 2 of the brochure, include None, Order form, Response form, and Sign-up form. The **Order form** displays fields for the description of items ordered as well as types of payment information. The **Response form** displays check box choices and fields for comments. The **Sign-up form** displays check box choices, fields for time and price, as well as payment information. Table 3-2 displays the task pane selections you will make in the steps on the next pages.

Table 3-2 Task Pane Selections

BROCHURE OPTIONS	SELECTION
Page size (Panels)	3-panel
Customer address	Include
Form	Sign-up form
Color Scheme	Harbor
Font Scheme	Industrial

Steps **To Choose Brochure Options**

1 **Click Brochures in the New Publication task pane. If necessary, click the down scroll arrow in the Informational Brochures pane until the Capsules Informational Brochure preview is visible. Point to the preview.**

Publisher displays the Brochure Publication Types on the left and the previews on the right in the Informational Brochures pane (Figure 3-2). The list of previews may display differently on your computer.

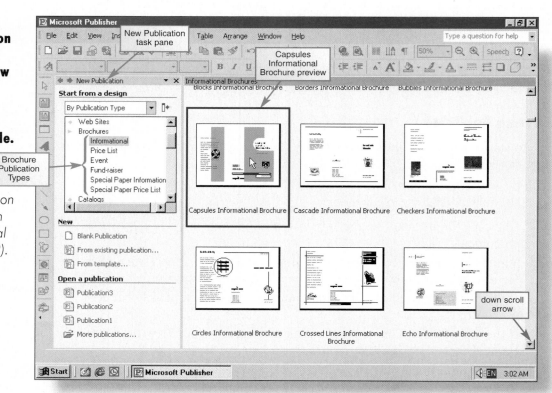

FIGURE 3-2

2 **Click the Capsules Informational Brochure preview. When the Brochure Options task pane displays, if necessary, under Page size, click 3-panel. Under Customer address, click Include. Under Form, click Sign-up form. Point to Color Schemes in the Brochure Options task pane.**

The selected brochure options for page size, customer address, and sign-up form display (Figure 3-3).

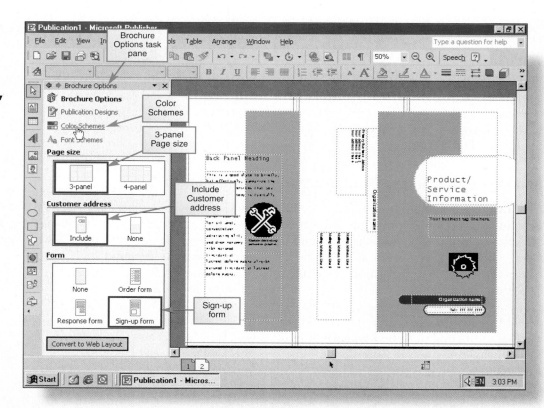

FIGURE 3-3

3 Click Color Schemes, and then click Harbor in the list. Point to Font Schemes in the Color Schemes task pane.

The brochure will use colors from the Harbor color scheme (Figure 3-4).

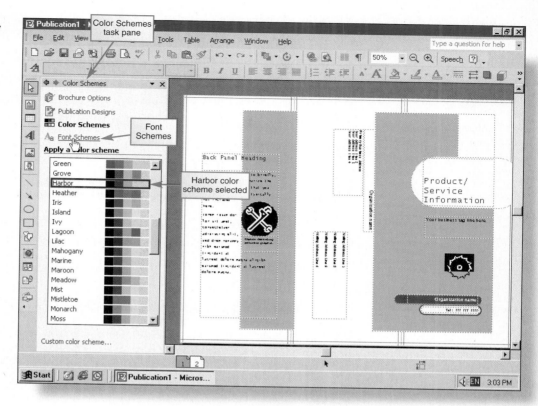

FIGURE 3-4

4 Click Font Schemes and then click Industrial in the list. Point to the Close button in the Font Schemes task pane.

The Industrial Font Scheme includes Franklin Gothic major and minor fonts (Figure 3-5).

5 Click the Close button. When Publisher completes the changes to the publication, click the Zoom box arrow and then click Page Width.

The Brochure Wizard makes the appropriate changes to the publication. (The changes are shown in Figure 3-6 on the next page.) The publication, ready to edit, displays in the Publisher workspace.

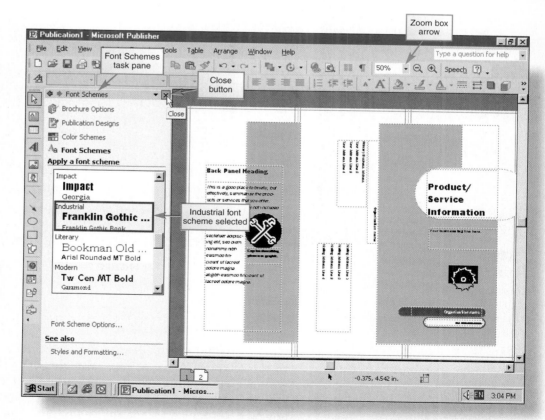

FIGURE 3-5

Now that several important options have been chosen, it is a good practice to save the publication. Perform the following steps to save the publication with the file name, Scholarship Brochure.

TO SAVE THE PUBLICATION

1 Click the Save button on the Standard toolbar.

2 Type Scholarship Brochure in the File name text box. If necessary, select 3½ Floppy (A:) in the Save in list.

3 Click the Save button in the Save As dialog box. If Publisher asks if you want to save the new logo to a personal information set, click the No button.

Publisher saves the publication on a floppy disk in drive A using the file name, Scholarship Brochure (Figure 3-6). The three panels of page 1 display.

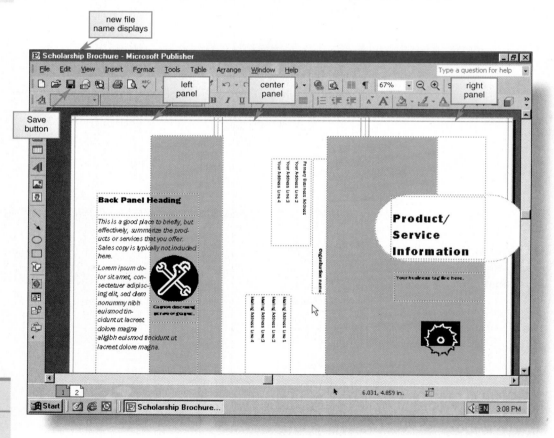

FIGURE 3-6

Editing Text with Publisher and Microsoft Word

Editing text in the brochure involves selecting the current text and replacing it with new, appropriate text in one of two ways: you can edit text directly in Publisher or use Word to facilitate editing. If you only need to edit a few words, it is faster to use a Publisher text box and the accompanying Publisher tools. If you need to edit a long story, however, perhaps one that appears on different pages in a publication, it may be easier to edit the story in Word. Both Publisher and Word use smart tags to facilitate editing.

Editing Text with Publisher

Publisher inserts **placeholder text** in its supplied templates, which may be selected by a single click. Other small text boxes may be **personal information components** that are designed to be changed or personalized for a company. The best way to select personal information text is to drag through the text. When you change a personal information component, all matching components in the publication change due to synchronization.

Perform the following steps to edit both placeholder and personal information text in the brochure.

 To Edit Text in the Brochure Using Publisher

1 **Click Product/ Service Information in the right panel on page 1.**

The placeholder text is selected with a single click (Figure 3-7). This text is the title of the brochure.

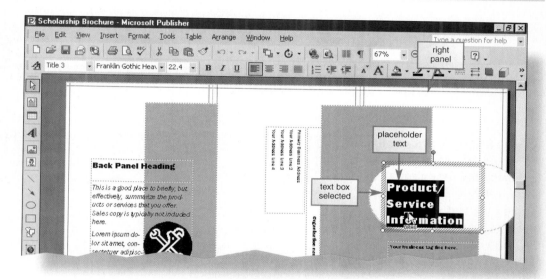

FIGURE 3-7

2 **Press the F9 key. Type** Scholarship Application Form **to replace the title text. Drag through the tag line text in the text box below the title.**

The new title text displays (Figure 3-8). The personal information component text, Your business tag line here., is selected by dragging.

FIGURE 3-8

3 **Type** School of Engineering **to replace the text. Point to the down scroll arrow on the vertical scroll bar.**

The new text for the tag line displays (Figure 3-9).

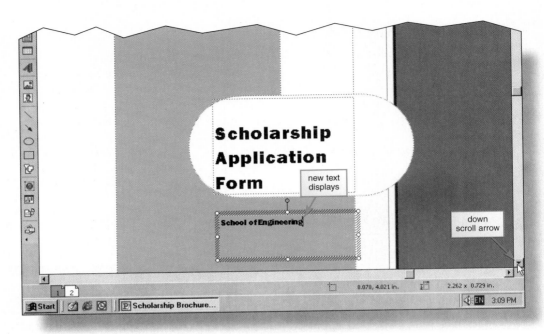

FIGURE 3-9

4 **Click the down scroll arrow several times to display the Organization name text box. Drag through the text and then type** Montgomery College **to replace the text. Click the Telephone placeholder text.**

Organization name is replaced with Montgomery College (Figure 3-10). Notice the Organization name text box in the middle panel changes as well.

5 **Type** Telephone: (317) 555-9703 **to replace the text.**

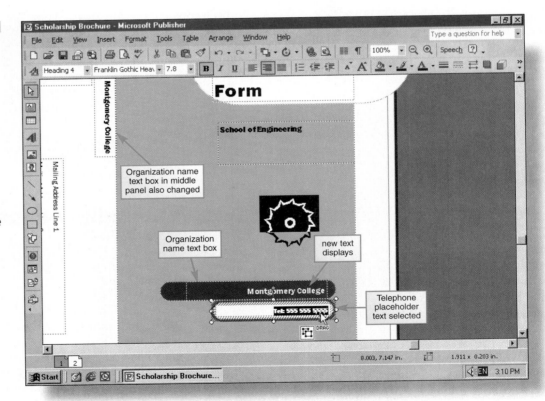

FIGURE 3-10

Use the same scrolling and editing techniques to edit other text boxes in the brochure is indicated by the following steps. Recall that larger portions of text are selected quickly by clicking inside the text box and then pressing CTRL+A.

TO EDIT OTHER TEXT BOXES

1 On page 1, click the caption of the picture in the left panel. Type `Founded in 1921` to replace the caption.

2 Click the Return Address text box in the upper-right corner of the middle panel.

3 Press CTRL+A to select all the text in the text box.

4 Type 20 underscores and then press the ENTER key. Repeat to create a total of four lines.

5 Click the Mailing Address text box in the center of the middle panel.

6 Type `School of Engineering` and then press SHIFT+ENTER. Type `509 NE 81st Terrace` and then press SHIFT+ENTER. Type `Indianapolis, IN 46112` to complete the mailing address.

7 Press CTRL+A to select all the text in the Address text box. On the Standard toolbar, click the Copy button.

8 Click the page 2 icon on the status bar. In the right panel, click the text box below Montgomery College that displays underscores. On the Standard toolbar, click the Paste button.

9 Click outside of the text box and then, on the Standard toolbar, click the Undo button to cancel synchronization.

10 Click the Main Inside Heading at the top of the left panel and then type `The Application Process` to replace the text.

The headings, placeholder text, and personal information components have been edited.

The underscores in Step 8 above were created due to synchronization of text boxes when you edited the return address on page 1.

Editing Text with Microsoft Word

Editing text using Word has several advantages. The Word toolbars display allowing you take advantage of available Word features, such as grammar checking or revision tracking. The story displays in a Word window allowing you to see it more easily. You do not have to zoom back and forth for editing purposes.

Few disadvantages exist for larger portions of text. One disadvantage may be that you must have Word installed on your computer to use that feature — otherwise the command is dimmed. It would not make much sense to use Word to edit a very small passage.

Publisher's Edit menu contains the command, Edit Story in Microsoft Word. When you click the command, selected text opens in a Word window. Table 3-3 displays the new text for the stories on page 2 of the brochure. Perform the steps on the next pages to use Microsoft Word to edit the stories in the scholarship brochure.

Table 3-3 Text for Page 2	
HEADING	**STORY TEXT**
Types of Scholarships	The School of Engineering at Montgomery College distributes nearly 100 scholarships and awards annually. Most are offered at the department level. Some are allocated for specific groups. For example, scholarship opportunities are available exclusively for new students, others for designated minority groups and underrepresented populations, and still others for students who reside in certain communities where funds have been made accessible. Scholarships also are granted specifically for women who desire to pursue careers in engineering.
Eligibility and Application	Full- or part-time students who are newly enrolled or continuing in one of the 17 degree programs offered by the School of Engineering may apply for scholarships. Most recipients are selected by GPA, a standardized test score, academic achievement, or are nominated by instructors and/or departments. Simply fill out the form, fold, and mail to the address listed below the form. Applications should be postmarked by April 1 for fall awards and October 1 for spring awards.

Microsoft Publisher 2002

Steps **To Edit a Story in Microsoft Word**

1 **If necessary, click the page 2 icon on the status bar. Click the Zoom box arrow and click Page Width. Click any text in the middle panel.**

A portion of the text displays selected (Figure 3-11).

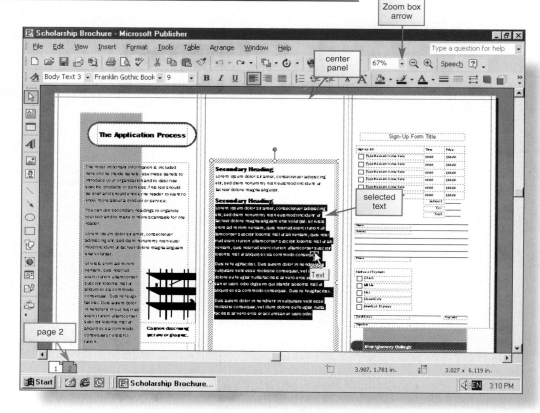

FIGURE 3-11

2 **Click Edit on the menu bar and then, when the full menu displays, point to Edit Story in Microsoft Word.**

The Edit menu displays (Figure 3-12).

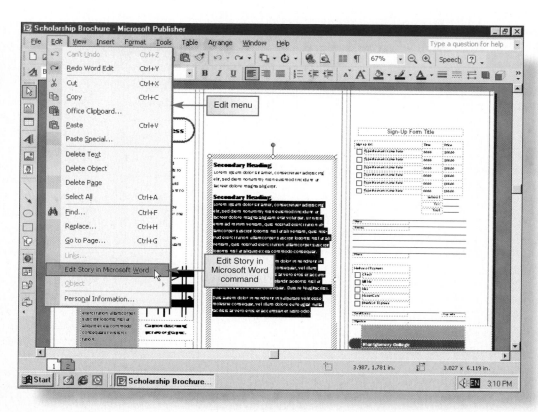

FIGURE 3-12

3 **Click Edit Story in Microsoft Word.**

Publisher opens a second window named Document in Scholarship Brochure – Microsoft Word (Figure 3-13). Notice a Word application button displays on the Windows taskbar.

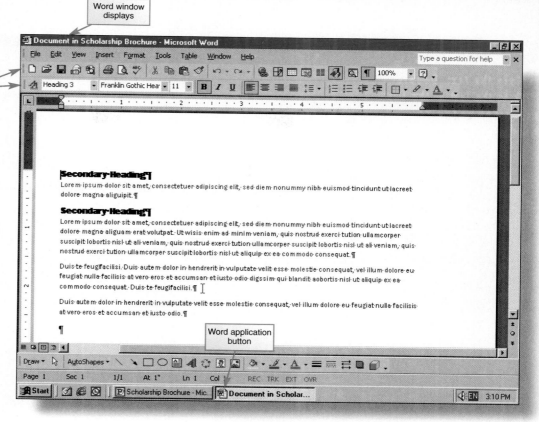

FIGURE 3-13

4 **Click to the left of the first Secondary Heading to select the entire line.**

The heading displays selected (Figure 3-14).

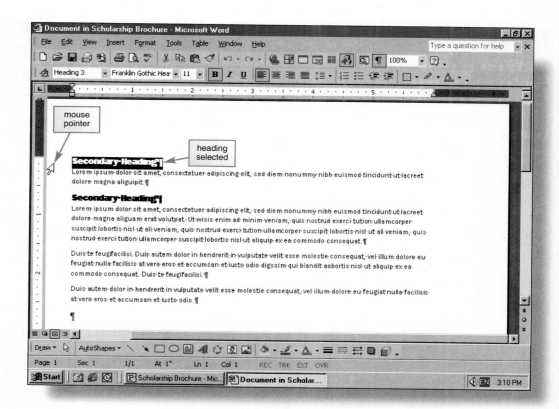

FIGURE 3-14

5 **Type** Types of Scholarships **to replace the text. Double-click to the left of the first paragraph under the heading.**

The new title displays and the paragraph is selected (Figure 3-15). Because you are now editing in Microsoft Word, the red wavy spell check lines display under the Latin placeholder text.

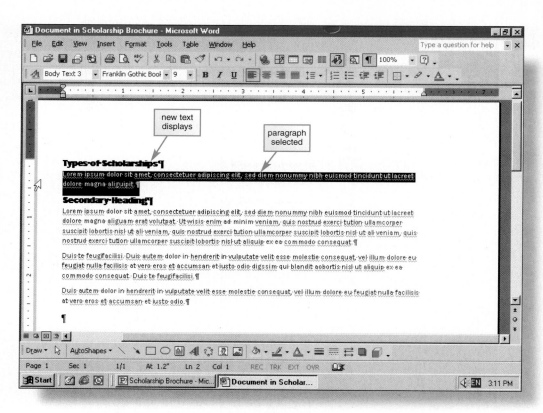

FIGURE 3-15

6 **Type the text for the Types of Scholarships article from Table 3-3 on page PUB 3.13. Double-click to the left of the second heading.**

The article displays (Figure 3-16).

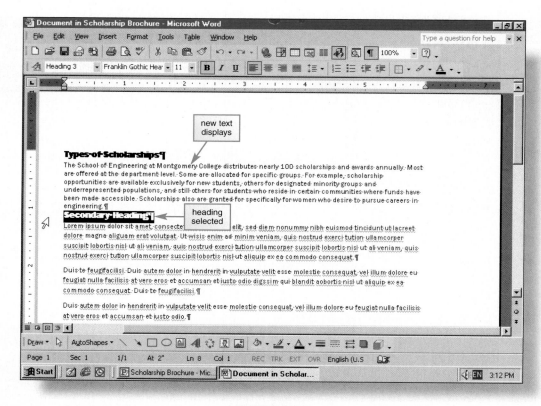

FIGURE 3-16

7 **Type** Eligibility and Application **to replace the text. Drag down the left of the paragraphs in the second story to select all the paragraphs.**

The second heading displays (Figure 3-17). All the remaining paragraphs are selected.

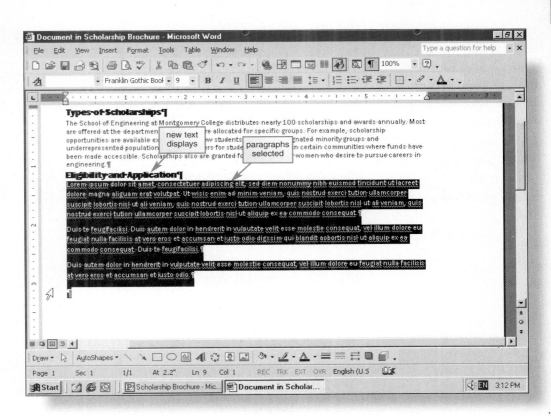

FIGURE 3-17

8 **Type the text for the Eligibility and Application article from Table 3-3. Point to the Close button on the title bar of the Document in Scholarship Brochure – Microsoft Word window.**

The second article displays (Figure 3-18).

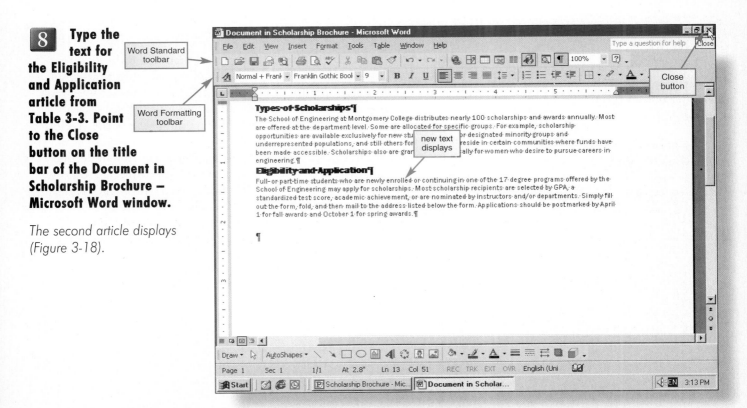

FIGURE 3-18

Microsoft **Publisher 2002**

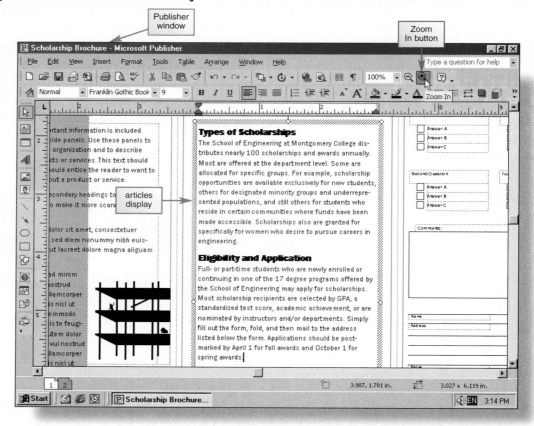

FIGURE 3-19

9 Click the Close button. On the Publisher Standard toolbar, click the Zoom In button twice to more easily read the text.

Publisher closes the Word window and displays the edited articles in the middle panel (Figure 3-19).

Other *Ways*

1. In Voice Command mode, say "Edit, Edit Story in Microsoft Word"

More *About*

Editing Text

You can edit text directly in Microsoft Publisher or in Microsoft Word. If you only need to edit a few words, it is faster to stay in Publisher. If you need to edit a long story that appears on multiple pages in a publication, it may be easier to edit the story in Microsoft Word. Or, you may be more accustomed to working in Word and want to take advantage of available Word features, such as grammar checking and revision tracking.

Recall that Publisher automatically checks for spelling errors and duplicate words as text is entered. Word does the same thing. If you type a word that is not in the dictionary (because it is a proper name or misspelled), a red wavy underline displays below the word. You may right-click the underlined word to see Word's suggestions or click Spelling and Grammar on the Tools menu to check the spelling of the entire publication.

Because you are using Word to edit text, you may see a green wavy underline that indicates a grammar error. Right-click the underline to see Word's suggestions for changing the grammar or click Spelling and Grammar on the Tools menu.

When Publisher opens Word, two Word toolbars display: Standard and Formatting (as shown in Figure 3-18 on the previous page). The **Word Standard toolbar** contains buttons to assist you with file management, inserting objects, and making changes to the view. The **Word Formatting toolbar** is similar to Publisher's Formatting toolbar when text boxes are selected. It contains buttons to edit the font, alignment, style, and indentations. A third toolbar, the Word Web toolbar, may display as well. The **Word Web toolbar** contains buttons to move from document to document as well as to the Web.

Manipulating Text Boxes

You can delete and insert text boxes as well as the text inside them. Several text boxes of the Capsules Informational Brochure will not be included in the final product. Others need to be added. The ability to move, align, and rotate text boxes provides additional flexibility. It is this flexibility that makes Publisher so useful. Desktop publishers can start from scratch and create their own text boxes, or manipulate publisher-supplied text boxes and graphics to suit their needs.

Deleting Text Boxes

Simply selecting text and then cutting or deleting that text leaves an empty text box on the page. To delete unnecessary text boxes, you select the entire object rather than just the text.

Perform the following steps to delete text boxes beginning on page 2 of the publication.

More About

Line Spacing in Publisher

If you need to change the line spacing of a text box in order to make it fit or display better, you can adjust the line spacing. On the Format menu, the Line Spacing command displays three choices. You may change the spacing between lines, before paragraphs, and after paragraphs. Pressing CTRL+1 or CTRL+2 changes the line spacing to single or double, respectively. Publisher 2002 contains a new button for line spacing that can be added to the Formatting toolbar.

 To Delete Text Boxes

1 If necessary, click the page 2 icon on the status bar. Click the Zoom box arrow and then click Whole Page. Right-click the story on the left panel. Point to Delete Object on the shortcut menu.

The shortcut menu for text boxes displays (Figure 3-20).

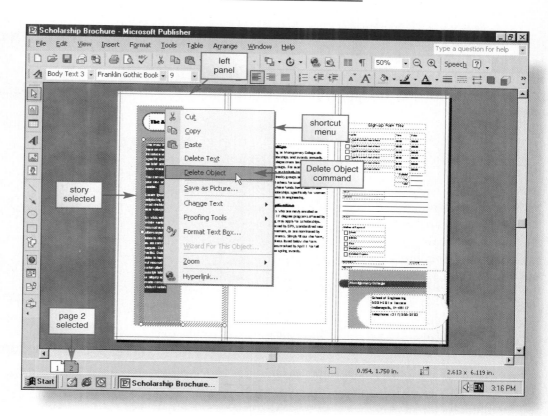

FIGURE 3-20

2 Click Delete Object. Point to the page 1 icon on the status bar.

The story text box is deleted (Figure 3-21).

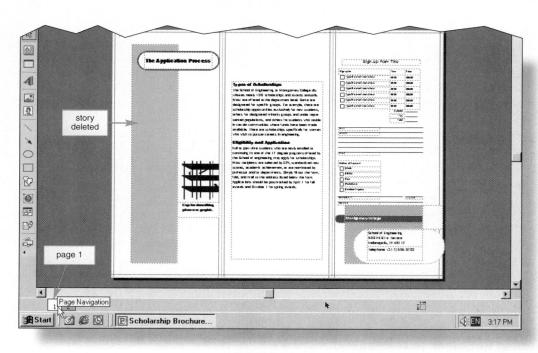

FIGURE 3-21

3 Click the page 1 icon. Right-click the story in the left panel and then point to Delete Object on the shortcut menu.

The story will be replaced with a Web address later in the project (Figure 3-22).

4 Click Delete Object. Repeat the process to delete the Back Panel Heading text box on Page 1.

The story and heading in the left panel of page 1 are deleted (shown in Figure 3-23).

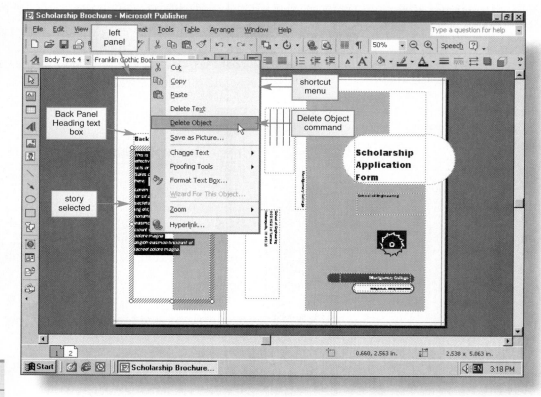

FIGURE 3-22

Other Ways

1. On Edit menu click Delete Object
2. Select object (not text), press DELETE
3. Select object, in Voice Command mode, say "Delete"

The shortcut menu changes depending on the type of object clicked. Notice in Figure 3-22 that the text box shortcut menu includes commands to delete the text and delete the object, among other commands.

Inserting Text Boxes and Using the AutoCorrect Smart Tag

In the following steps, you will click a Smart Tag button in one of the text boxes. Recall that a smart tag displays to help you edit text in Publisher and Word. The smart tag you will use is called AutoCorrect Options. The **AutoCorrect Options button** displays after an automatic correction or change is made, such as a lowercase letter changing to a capital or a Web address that changes automatically to a hyperlink. Recall that a smart tag indicator displays first as a small, blue box when you rest the mouse pointer near text that was changed; it then becomes a button icon when you point to it. You may click the Smart Tag button to display a shortcut menu. The **AutoCorrect Options menu** displays commands to undo, turn off that type of correction for good, or connect to the AutoCorrect dialog box to adjust settings.

Two different text boxes will replace the back panel heading and story created by the Brochure Wizard. The first text box will display some instructions; the second will display the college Web address.

More About

Smart Tags

Smart tags are new in Office XP. For more information about smart tags and how they are used in other Office applications, visit the Publisher 2002 More About Web page (scsite.com/pub2002/more.htm) and then click Word Smart Tags.

Steps **To Insert Text Boxes and Use the AutoCorrect Smart Tag**

1 **Click the Text Box button on the Objects toolbar. Move the mouse pointer to the upper part of the left panel on page 1.**

The mouse pointer displays as a cross hair (Figure 3-23).

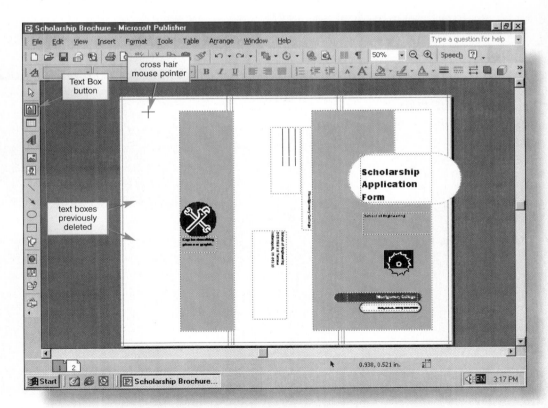

FIGURE 3-23

Microsoft **Publisher 2002**

2 Drag a square at the top of the panel approximately 2.500 × 1.000 in. as displayed in the Object Size box on the status bar. Release the mouse button. Point to the Font Size box arrow on the Formatting toolbar.

The new text box displays (Figure 3-24).

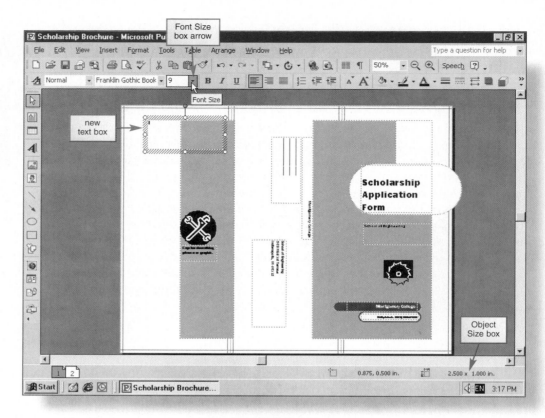

FIGURE 3-24

3 Click the Font Size box arrow and then click 12 in the list. Press the F9 key. Type For more information about the Montgomery College School of Engineering, call (317) 555-9703 or check out our Web site at: **in the new text box.**

The text displays (Figure 3-25).

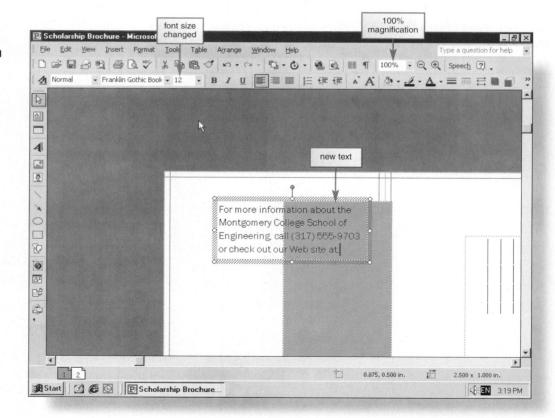

FIGURE 3-25

4 **Click the Text Box button on the Objects toolbar again. Below the previous text box, drag a new text box approximately 4.750 × .500 in. Release the mouse button. Point to the Font Size box arrow on the Formatting toolbar.**

The text box displays (Figure 3-26). Do not be concerned if the text box runs over into the workspace.

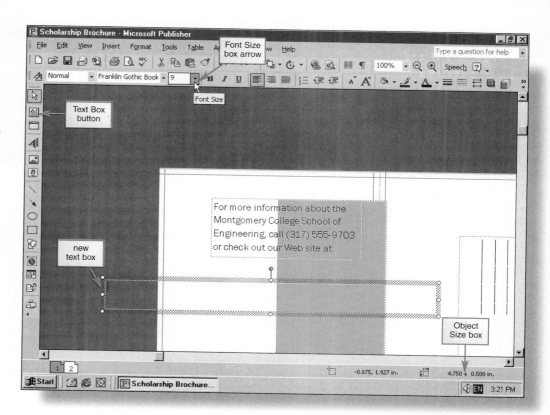

FIGURE 3-26

5 **Click the Font Size box arrow and then click 28 in the list. Click the Bold button. Type** www.engr.montgomery .edu **in the text box. Publisher will change the lowercase w to uppercase W as you type.**

The smart tag displays as a blue small rectangle (Figure 3-27).

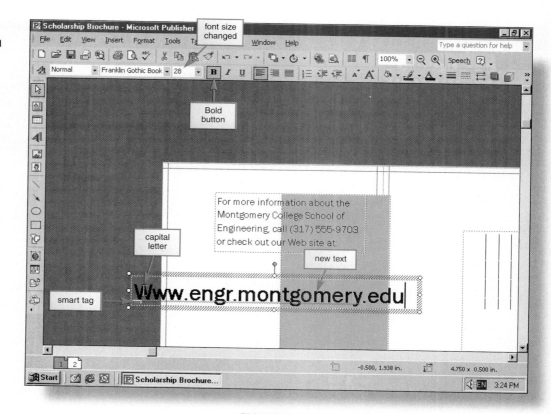

FIGURE 3-27

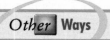
6 **Point to the uppercase W and then point to the smart tag that displays below it. When it changes to the AutoCorrect Options button, click the button arrow. Point to Undo Automatic Capitalization on the menu.**

The AutoCorrect Options menu displays (Figure 3-28).

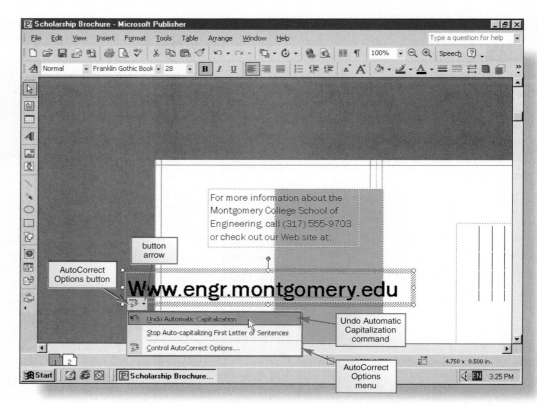

FIGURE 3-28

7 **Click Undo Automatic Capitalization. Right-click the red wavy underline and then point to Ignore All on the shortcut menu.**

The Web address is not in Publisher's dictionary (Figure 3-29). The uppercase W becomes a lowercase w.

8 **Click Ignore All.**

Other Ways

1. On Insert menu click Text Box
2. In Voice Command mode, say "Insert, Text Box"

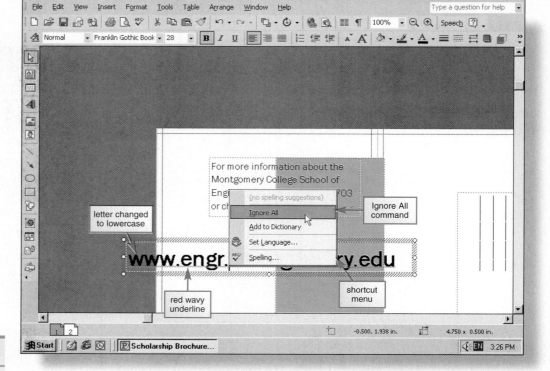

FIGURE 3-29

This Web address does not display the standard http:// prefix; rather, it begins with www. Because the prefix is missing, Publisher does not try to convert the Web address to a hyperlink.

In the next steps, you will rotate the Web address text box and move it to the left side of the panel.

Rotating Objects

Selected objects, such as text boxes, are rotated easily by dragging the rotation handle. The **rotation handle** is a small green circle with an attached line to the text box itself. **Shift-dragging** the rotation handle moves the selected object by 15-degree intervals.

More About

Rotating Objects

You can rotate objects in many ways. To rotate an object on its base, hold down the CTRL key and drag the green rotation handle. To rotate objects by 90 degrees, on the Arrange menu point to Rotate or Flip, and then select an option. To rotate an object an exact number of degrees, right-click the object, on the shortcut menu click to format the object, and then, on the Size tab, enter the number of degrees.

Steps To Rotate an Object

1 If necessary, click the Web address text box. Point to the rotation handle that displays above the text box.

When you point to the rotation handle, the mouse pointer changes to a circular arrow (Figure 3-30).

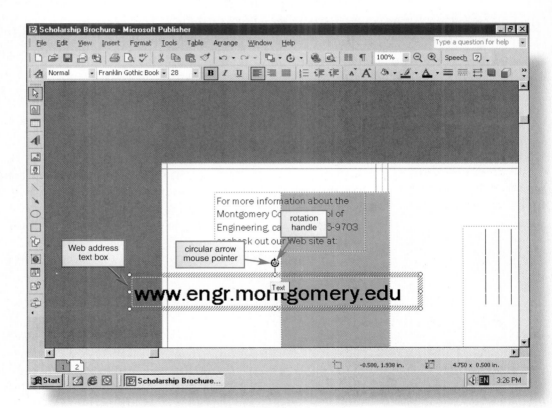

FIGURE 3-30

2 **Press and hold
down the SHIFT key
and then drag the rotation
handle until the text box
frame displays vertically.
When it is straight, release
the mouse button first, and
then release the SHIFT key.**

*The Web address text box
displays in a vertical position
(Figure 3-31).*

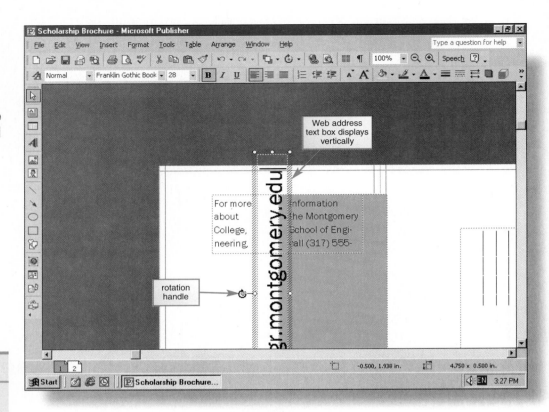

FIGURE 3-31

Aligning Objects

Moving text boxes is similar to moving other objects in Publisher. One way is to select the text box and then drag it to the new location. To move and align a text box more precisely in relationship to another object, click Align or Distribute on the Arrange menu, and then choose to align the left, right, top, bottom or center of the objects.

Perform the following steps to align the Web address text box with the rectangle on the left panel.

Steps **To Align Objects**

1 Press the F9 key to view page 1 in its entirety. Point to the edge of the Web address text box. When the mouse pointer changes to the Move icon, drag the Web address text box left and down slightly so it does not overlap any other object.

The Web address text box is easier to read when placed on the white background (Figure 3-32).

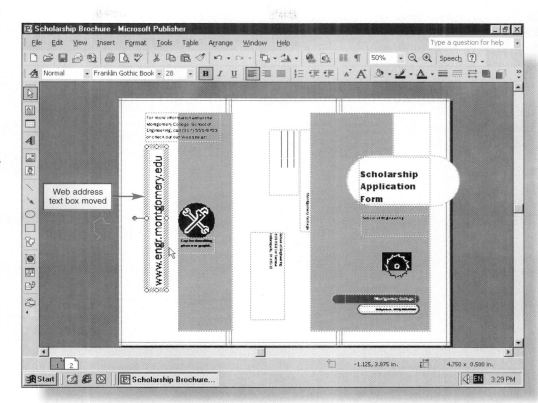

FIGURE 3-32

2 With the Web address text box still selected, press and hold down the SHIFT key, and then click the color-filled rectangle in the left panel.

Both objects are selected (Figure 3-33).

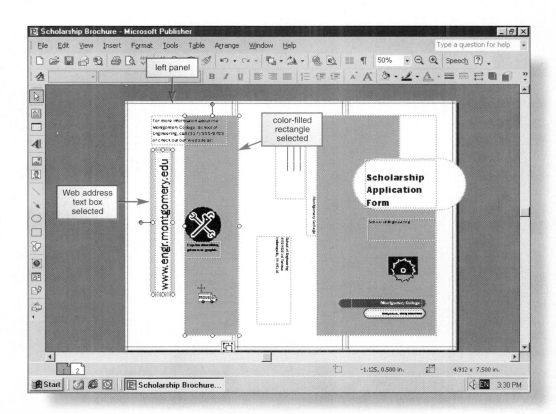

FIGURE 3-33

3 **Click Arrange on the menu bar. When the full menu displays, point to Align or Distribute, and then point to Align Bottom on the Align or Distribute submenu.**

The Align or Distribute menu displays many alignment choices (Figure 3-34).

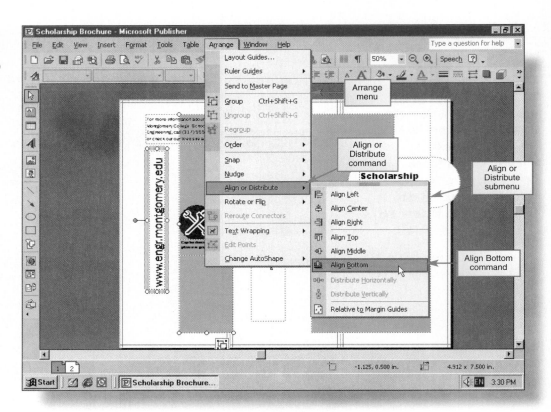

FIGURE 3-34

4 **Click Align Bottom.**

The Web address text box and the rectangle are aligned along their bottom edges (Figure 3-35).

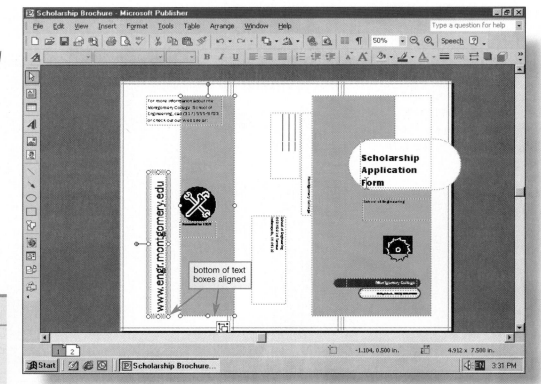

FIGURE 3-35

Other Ways

1. Click appropriate alignment button on Standard toolbar
2. Right-click object, click Align or Distribute on shortcut menu
3. In Voice Command mode, say "Arrange, Align or Distribute"

The **Align Bottom command** aligns the lower borders of selected objects on the page. Similarly, Align Top aligns the upper borders of the objects. Left and Right alignment move in the direction of the command as well.

Using Photographs and Images in a Brochure

The advent of inexpensive photo CDs and digital cameras has increased exponentially the possibilities for photographic reproduction in publications. Regular cameras using popular types of film now can take pictures and have them digitized, a process that previously required digital cameras. **Digitizing** means converting colors and lines into digital impulses capable of being read by a computer. Digitized photographs and downloaded graphics from the Web, combined with high-resolution production from scanners, create endless possibilities. Small businesses now can afford to include photographs in their brochures and other types of publications.

Publisher can accept photographs and images from a variety of input sources. Each graphic you import has a file name, followed by a dot or period, followed by a three-letter extension. Publisher uses **extensions** to recognize individual file formats. Table 3-4 displays some of the graphic formats that Publisher can import.

Table 3-4 Supported Graphic Formats	
GRAPHIC FORMAT	*FILE EXTENSION*
Computer Graphics Metafile	.cgm
CorelDRAW!	.cdr
Encapsulated PostScript	.eps
Graphics Interchange Format	.gif
Joint Photographic Experts Group	.jpeg or .jpg
Kodak Photo CD or Pro Photo CD	.pcd
Macintosh PICT	.pct
PC Paintbrush	.pcx
Portable Network Graphics	.png
Tagged Image File Format	.tif
Microsoft PhotoDraw or PictureIt!	.mix
Windows Bitmap File	.bmp
Windows Enhanced Metafile	.emf
Windows Metafile	.wmf
WordPerfect Graphics	.wpg

More *About*

Clip Art

For additional samples of clip art available on the Internet, visit the Publisher 2002 More About Web page (scsite.com/pub2002/more.htm) and then click Discovering Clip Art.

More *About*

The Microsoft Web Page

Microsoft supplies many free graphics and add-ins for your Microsoft Office products that you may download from the Microsoft Web site. To do this, click Help on the menu bar and then click Office on the Web. When your browser displays the site, follow the link to Office Update.

Inserting a Photograph from a File

Publisher can insert a photograph into a publication by accessing the Clip Organizer, by externally importing from a file, by directly importing an image from a scanner or camera, or by creating a new drawing. The sequence of steps on the next pages illustrates how to insert a previously scanned photograph from a file into the brochure. The photograph for the brochure is provided on the Data Disk. See the inside back cover of this book for instructions for downloading the Data Disk or see your instructor for information on accessing the files required for this book.

Steps **To Insert a Photograph from a File**

1 **Insert the Data Disk in drive A. See the inside back cover of this book for instructions for down loading the Data Disk or see your instructor. If necessary, click the page 1 icon on the status bar and then click the picture/caption grouped object in the left panel. Click the picture again to select only the picture from the group. Right-click the picture and then point to Change Picture on the shortcut menu.**

The Change Picture menu displays (Figure 3-36). Clicking one object in a group a second time selects only that object. The selected object displays a filled sizing handle with an x in it.

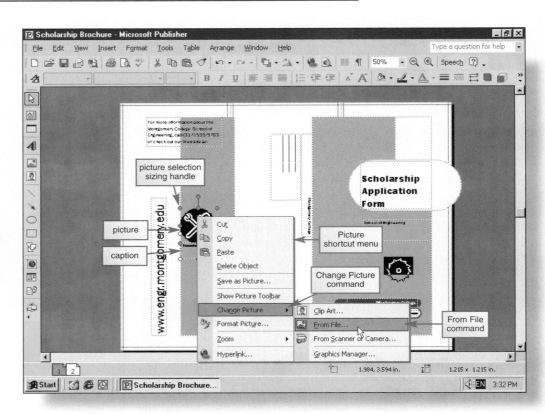

FIGURE 3-36

2 **Click From File. When the Insert Picture dialog box displays, click the Look in box arrow and then click 3½ Floppy (A:) in the list. Point to the file name, college.**

The list of picture format files on drive A displays (Figure 3-37). The college picture is stored as a JPEG image scanned from an actual photograph.

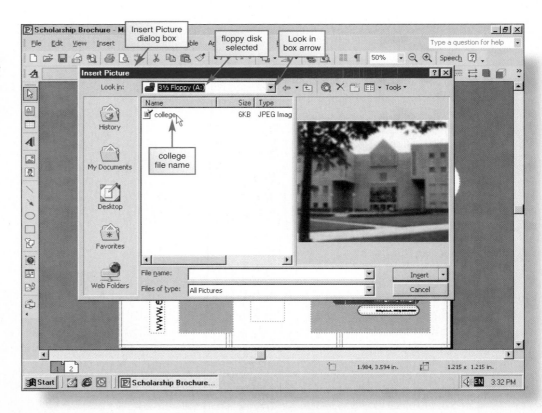

FIGURE 3-37

3	**Double-click the file name, college. When the picture displays in the brochure, drag its border until the picture displays centered within the rectangle.**

The college picture replaces the original picture (Figure 3-38).

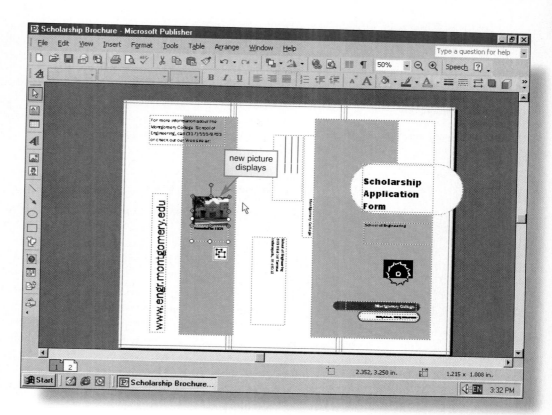

FIGURE 3-38

Publisher resizes replacement clip art and photographs to match the size and shape of the wizard-placed graphic without distorting the picture. If you import a picture into a spot where no picture was placed previously, you may have to resize it yourself.

Another common method of creating new image files, other than scanning, is to use **illustration software**. Designed for artists, illustration software packages such as CorelDRAW! and Adobe Illustrator create graphics to import into desktop publishing software.

Deleting a Graphic

The graphic in the right panel of page 1 will be replaced by the college logo, so it must be deleted. Perform the following steps to delete the graphic in the right panel.

TO DELETE A GRAPHIC

1. Click the graphic in the right panel of page 1.

2. Press the DELETE key

In addition to the clip art images included in the Clip Organizer, other sources for clip art include retailers specializing in computer software, the Internet, bulletin board systems, and online information systems. Some popular online information systems are The Microsoft Network, America Online, CompuServe, and Prodigy. A **bulletin board system** is a computer system that allows users to communicate with each other and share files. Microsoft has created a special page on its Web site where you can add new clips to the Clip Organizer.

Other Ways

1. On Insert menu point to Picture, click From File

2. In Voice Command mode, say "Insert, Picture, From File"

More *About*

Positioning Objects

You can drag objects to new positions or you can press and hold down the ALT key while pressing the arrow keys to nudge objects to new positions. If you increase the magnification of the monitor, you can resize and reposition objects precisely. For instance, at 400% magnification, you can move an object .003 inch by pressing and holding down the ALT key and then pressing an arrow key. The Arrange menu also contains options for nudging and aligning. The Measurements toolbar allows you to type in exact horizontal and vertical positions.

Creating a Logo from Scratch

Many types of publications use logos to identify and distinguish the page makeup. A **logo** is a recognizable symbol that identifies a person, business, or organization. A logo may be composed of a name, a picture, or a combination of symbols and graphics. In a later project, you will learn how to add a permanent logo to an information set for a company.

Creating a Shape for the Logo

The logo in the scholarship brochure is a combination of a shape and a text box. Created individually in the workspace and then grouped together, the logo easily is positioned and sized to the proper places in the brochure. The logo appears both in the front panel below the brochure title and below the sign-up form in the center panel of page 2.

The background of the logo is from the AutoShapes menu. Accessed from the Objects toolbar, the **AutoShapes** menu displays seven categories of shapes you may use as graphics in a publication. These shapes include lines, connectors, basic shapes, block arrows, stars and banners, among others. AutoShapes differ from WordArt in that they do not contain text; rather, they are graphic designs with a variety of formatting options, such as color, border, size, and shadow.

The following steps illustrate creating the logo in Publisher's workspace to the right of the brochure.

Steps To Create a Shape for the Logo

1 **If necessary, click the page 1 icon on the status bar and then increase the magnification to view the whole page. Drag the horizontal scroll box to the right, to view more of the workspace. Point to the AutoShapes button on the Objects toolbar.**

The brochure moves left as you scroll right, providing more workspace area (Figure 3-39).

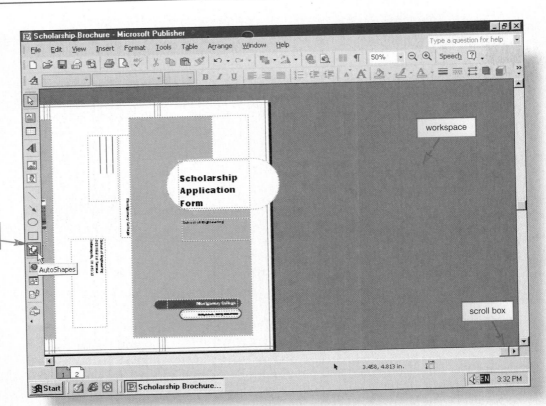

FIGURE 3-39

2 **Click the AutoShapes button. Point to Stars and Banners on the AutoShapes menu and then point to Up Ribbon.**

The AutoShapes menu displays (Figure 3-40). Up Ribbon is the first button in the third row.

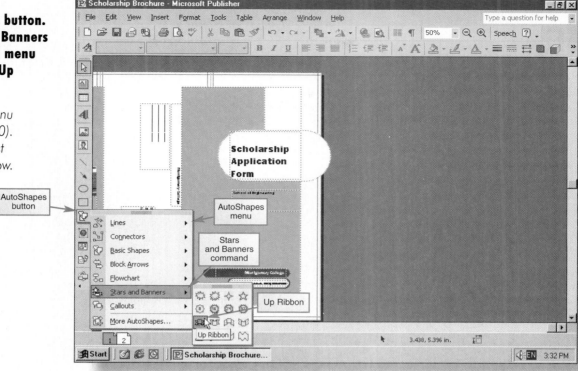

FIGURE 3-40

3 **Click the Up Ribbon AutoShape and then move the mouse pointer to an open space to the right of the brochure. Drag down and to the right until the shape is approximately 3.000 × 1.500 in. as displayed in the Object Size box on the status bar. Release the mouse button and then point to the Fill Color button arrow on the Formatting toolbar.**

The workspace displays the ribbon shape for the logo (Figure 3-41). The Object Size box displays the size of the object.

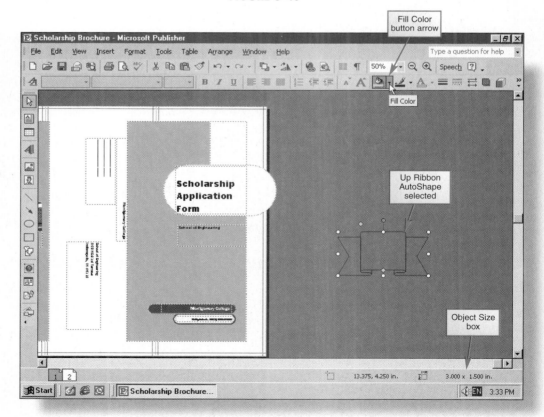

FIGURE 3-41

4 Click the Fill Color button arrow.

When the Fill Color menu displays, point to Accent 1 on the menu (Figure 3-42).

5 Click Accent 1.

The Up Ribbon's fill color changes to dark green to match the brochure's Harbor color scheme (as shown in Figure 3-43).

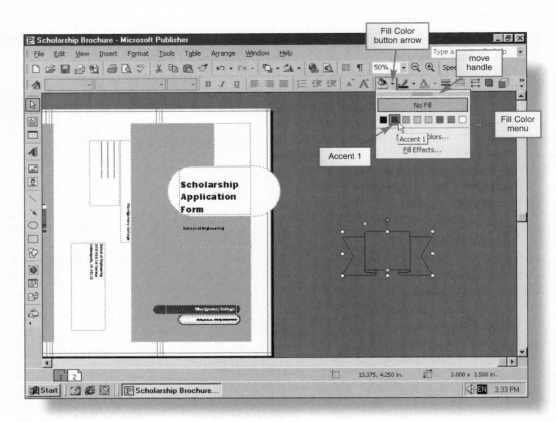

FIGURE 3-42

The Fill Color menu and other palette menus can be made floating toolbars by dragging the move handle at top of the menu (shown in Figure 3-42).

The workspace, also called the **scratch area**, can serve as a kind of drawing board to create new objects. Without disturbing any object already on the publications page, you can manipulate and edit objects in the workspace and then move them to the desired location. The rulers and status bar display the exact size of the new object. Moving objects off the page and into the workspace is sometimes advantageous as well. Small objects that are difficult to revise on the publication can be moved into the workspace, magnified and edited, and then moved back. As you place new objects in the workspace, more workspace room is allocated. Objects remaining in the workspace are saved with the file.

Creating an AutoFit, Transparent Text Box

The next step is to create a text box containing the letters M and C. The letters should fill the box. Recall that Publisher can adjust the size of text to fill a text box, by choosing the Best Fit option.

Because this text box will display on top of the Up Ribbon AutoShape, a **transparent** text box will allow the color of the AutoShape to show through. Black text on a dark background does not print as well as it displays on the monitor. On a color desktop printer, the darker black is applied over the top of the background color, which lends itself to streaking.

Perform the following steps to create a transparent text box, insert letters, choose the Best Fit option, and change the font color.

Steps To Create an AutoFit, Transparent Text Box for the Logo

1 **Click the Text Box button on the Objects toolbar. In a blank area of the workspace, near the Up Ribbon AutoShape, drag a text box approximately 1.500 × 1.000 in. Press CTRL+T.**

The text box displays in the workspace (Figure 3-43). Text boxes created in the workspace have no background and are therefore transparent; pressing CTRL+T, however, ensures no fill color in the text box.

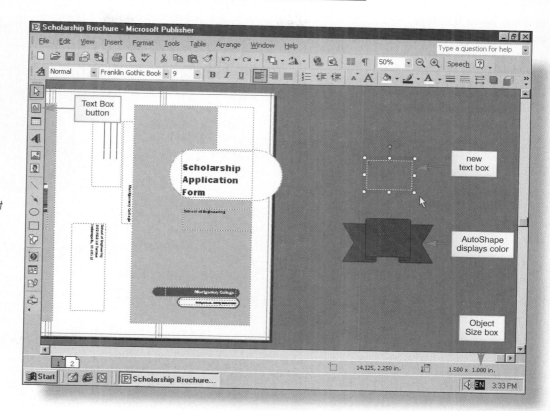

FIGURE 3-43

2 **Type MC in the text box and then press CTRL+A to select the text.**

The text is selected (Figure 3-44).

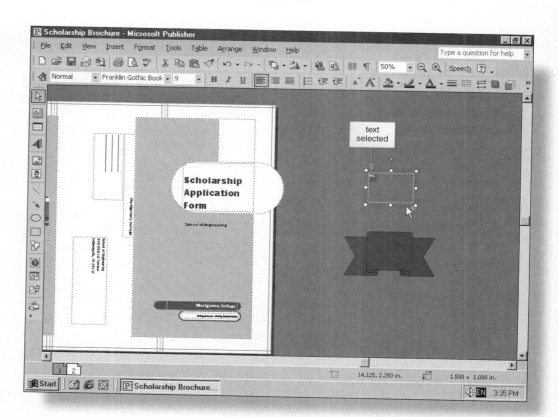

FIGURE 3-44

3 Right-click the text box. When the shortcut menu displays, point to Change Text, point to AutoFit Text, and then point to Best Fit on the AutoFit Text submenu (Figure 3-45).

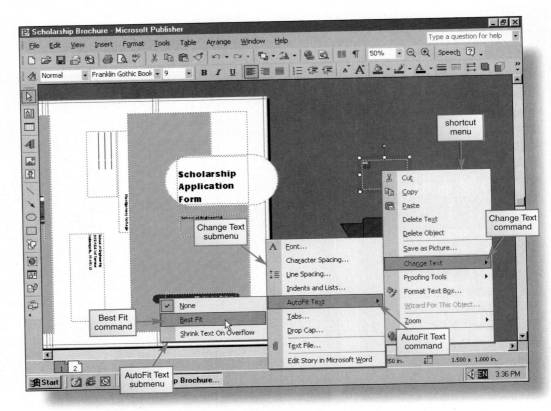

FIGURE 3-45

4 Click Best Fit on the AutoFit Text submenu. Press CTRL+E to center the text within the text box. Point to the Font Color button arrow on the Formatting toolbar.

The text in the text box displays in a larger font size (Figure 3-46). With the Best Fit command active on the AutoFit Text submenu, the font size is adjusted any time the text box is resized or moved.

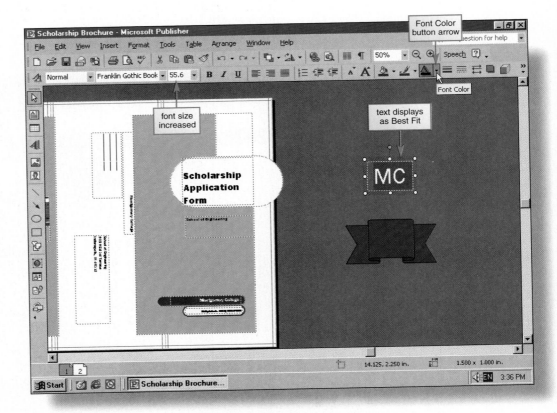

FIGURE 3-46

5 **Click the Font Color button arrow and then click Accent 5 on the menu. Click outside the text.**

The text now displays in white (Figure 3-47). The logo text is complete.

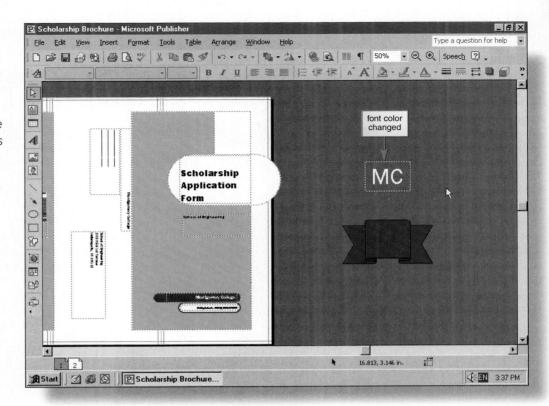

font color changed

FIGURE 3-47

Mixed colors of layered objects create challenges for commercial printing. Professional printers use a technique known as knocking out. **Knocking out** removes the background colors underneath foreground objects or text so the foreground colors print directly on the paper instead of on top of other colors. When colors print on top of each other on a commercial printer, they can mix to create an undesired color. For example, if a blue circle prints on top of a red rectangle, the overlapping colors can mix to create purple.

A cost saving alternative is to change the color as you did in the previous steps. Copy shops, printing services, and media design professionals all recommend white text on darker backgrounds. The white letters stand out and offer an appearance of distinction to the publication.

Grouping and Positioning the Logo Objects

The logo, when complete, is a composite object: a text box and a background shape. Repositioning and resizing objects independently can be tedious and prone to error. Placing objects on top of other objects, known as **layering,** can cause design errors if you are not careful. Moving the front objects to their final positions first can cause an **order error** with parts of objects obscured behind others.

When objects are grouped carefully, while adhering to the scheme colors and paying careful attention to the layering, objects can be moved, resized, formatted, and copied quite easily as a group.

Perform the steps on the next pages to format and group the logo.

Other Ways

1. On Format menu click AutoFit Text, click Best Fit
2. Right-click text box, click Format Text Box on shortcut menu, click Text Box tab, click Best Fit
3. In Voice Command mode, say "Format, AutoFit Text, Best Fit"

More *About*

The Workspace

Placing objects in the workspace is an easy way to move them from one page to the next. Simply drag the object into the blank scratch area of the workspace, click the new page icon in the Page Navigation control, and then drag the object onto the new page. Publisher allows you to save a publication with objects still in the scratch area of the workspace. Be sure to remove them, however, to avoid confusion before submitting a file to a commercial printer.

Steps | To Group and Position the Logo Objects

1 Drag the MC text box to a position on top of the Up Ribbon AutoShape.

The text box displays in front of the shape (Figure 3-48).

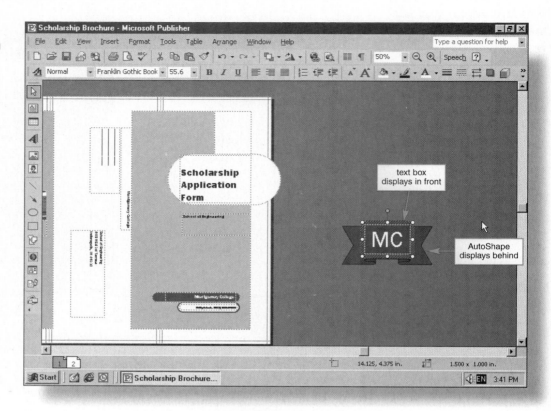

FIGURE 3-48

2 SHIFT-click a corner of the shape. Point to the Group Objects button that displays below the two objects.

Both objects are selected, each with its own set of sizing handles (Figure 3-49). The Group Objects button displays when multiple objects are selected.

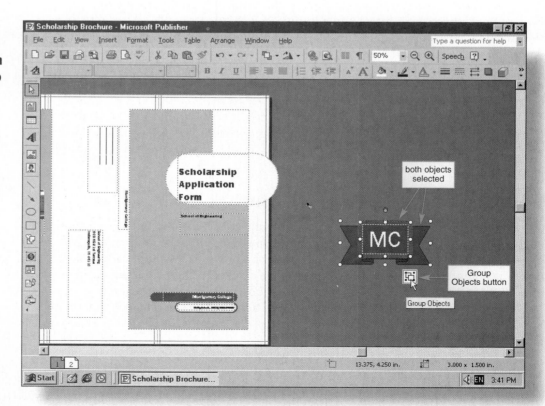

FIGURE 3-49

3 Click the Group Objects button. Drag the logo to the right panel, below the School of Engineering text box. Point to the Copy button on the Standard toolbar.

The two objects display as a grouped object with a single set of sizing handles (Figure 3-50). The Group Objects button becomes the Ungroup Objects button as indicated by the button's changed icon.

4 Click the Copy button. Click the page 2 icon on the status bar. If necessary, zoom to Whole Page and then click the Paste button. When the copied object displays, drag it to the lower portion of the center panel as shown in Figure 3-51 on the next page.

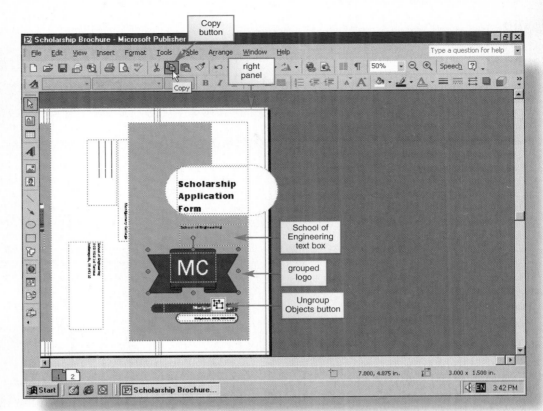

FIGURE 3-50

The final step is to resize the logo on page 2, so it does not overwhelm the page.

Resizing an Object

One way to resize an object is to use the sizing handles. Recall that sizing handles display as tiny circles at the corners and on the sides of an object. Dragging a corner sizing handle maintains the proportions of the graphic when you resize, whereas dragging a middle sizing handle may distort the proportion of the graphic. Proportionally resizing an object other than a graphic requires that you hold down the SHIFT key while dragging the corner sizing handle. To keep the center of an object in the same place as you resize it, hold down the CTRL key as you drag.

Perform the steps on the next page to resize the grouped logo on page 2 of the brochure.

Other Ways

1. On Arrange menu click Group
2. Press CTRL+SHIFT+G
3. In Voice Command mode, say "Arrange, Group"

More *About*

Symbols

If the character you are looking for is not on your keyboard, such as a trademark symbol or foreign language character, click Symbol on the Insert menu. A dialog box will display allowing you to choose from among many characters in many fonts and subsets. Click the character you want and then click the Insert button.

Steps **To Resize an Object**

1 **With the grouped logo on page 2 selected, point to a corner sizing handle of the logo.**

The copied logo displays (Figure 3-51). The Resize mouse pointer also displays.

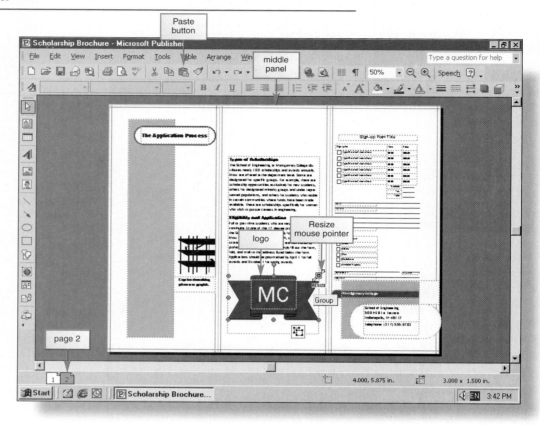

FIGURE 3-51

2 **Press and hold down the CTRL key while dragging the corner sizing handle toward the center of the logo, until the size is approximately 2.500 × 1.000 in. as shown in the Object Size box.**

The resized logo displays (Figure 3-52).

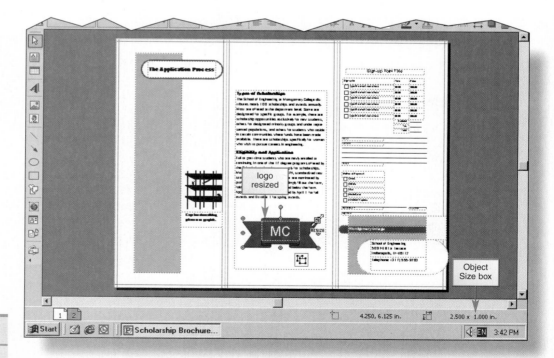

Other **Ways**

1. On Measurements toolbar type sizes
2. In Format dialog box, on Size tab, type sizes

FIGURE 3-52

Brochure Forms

Publisher provides three different forms to choose from when creating a brochure. The order form contains blank fields for entering items, quantities, and prices. The response form contains blanks for up to four multiple-choice questions and a comment section. The sign-up form displays options with times and prices, as well as payment information.

All three forms are meant to be detached and mailed in as **turnaround documents**. Each form contains blanks for the name and address of prospective customers or clients. The company not only verifies the marketing power of its brochure, but also is able to create a customer database with the information.

Editing the Sign-up Form

On page 2, Publisher's brochure options created a generic sign-up form in the right panel. The intent of the form is to make it easy for users to check options and fill in information. At the top of the form are several text boxes and rectangles to list sign-up options, times, and prices. The text must be edited to reflect appropriate topics for the scholarship brochure. The text in the Time text boxes must be deleted. To facilitate editing and resizing, you will drag a **selection rectangle** to select multiple objects in a large area.

Perform the following steps to move the article to the left panel and then edit the sign-up form.

Steps **To Edit a Sign-Up Form**

1 **Select the text box in the center panel. Press and hold the SHIFT key while dragging the border of the text box left to display in the left panel**

The text box now displays in the left panel (Figure 3-53). Holding down the SHIFT key while dragging keeps the text box in a straight line horizontally. The text automatically wraps around the graphic.

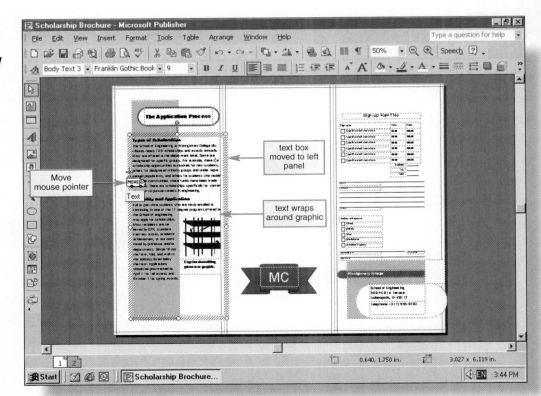

FIGURE 3-53

Microsoft **Publisher** 2002

2 **Point to the left and slightly above the sign-up form. Drag down and to the right so that the sign-up form displays completely within a drag rectangle.**

Dragging the mouse pointer creates a selection rectangle that easily selects multiple objects in a contiguous area (Figure 3-54). When no other button on the Objects toolbar is being used, the Select Objects button is selected by default.

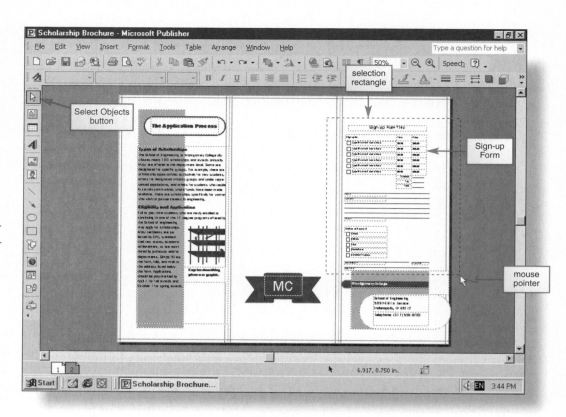

FIGURE 3-54

3 **Release the mouse button. Point to the Group button that displays below the objects.**

All of the objects within the selection rectangle are selected (Figure 3-55).

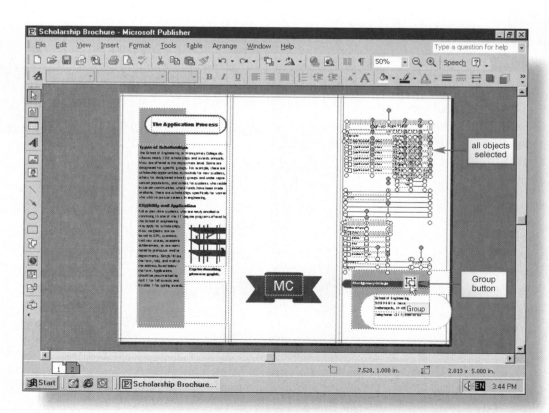

FIGURE 3-55

4 Click the Group button. Point to the left-middle sizing handle of the grouped object.

The objects in the sign-up form become a single grouped object, which is easier to manipulate (Figure 3-56). The Resize mouse pointer displays.

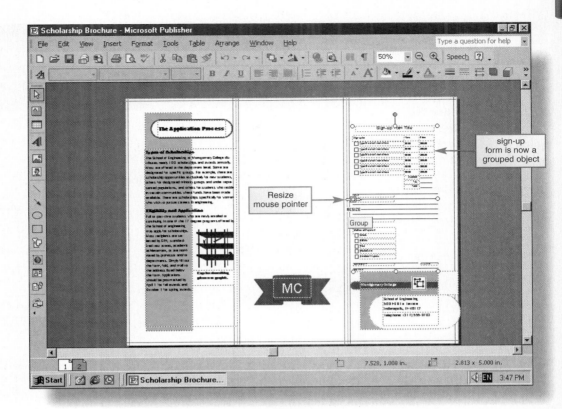

FIGURE 3-56

5 Resize the sign-up form to fit across both the center and right panels by dragging the left-middle sizing handle.

The form displays across both panels (Figure 3-57).

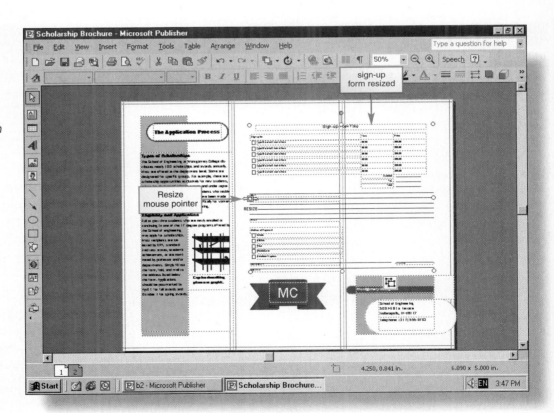

FIGURE 3-57

6 One at a time, click each text box using the F9 key as necessary to edit the text. In the upper portion of the form, replace the Publisher-supplied fields with the text from Figure 3-58.

The completed information displays. (Note: To make it easier to enter data, Figure 3-58 has been enlarged for readability.)

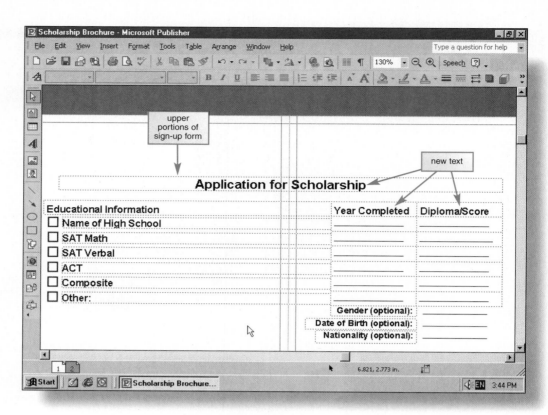

FIGURE 3-58

7 Scroll down to display the lower portion of the form. Edit each of the fields to match the text in Figure 3-59.

The completed information displays. (Note: To make it easier to enter data, Figure 3-59 has been enlarged for readability.)

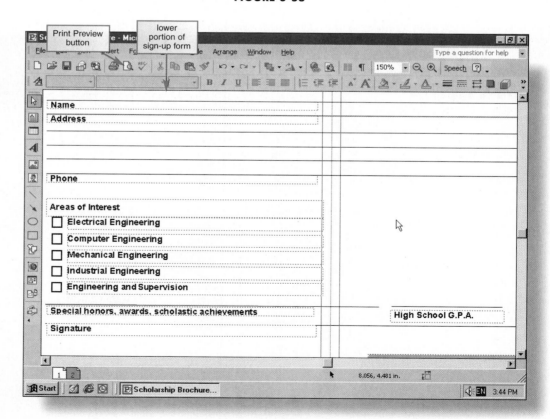

FIGURE 3-59

Checking Spelling and Saving Again

The publication is complete. After completing the publication, you should check the spelling of the document by clicking the Spelling command on the Tools menu. In addition, because you have performed several tasks since the last save, you should save the brochure again by clicking the Save button on the Standard toolbar.

TO CHECK SPELLING AND SAVE AGAIN

1 Click the Spelling button on the Standard toolbar. If Publisher flags any words that are misspelled, fix them.

2 When Publisher asks to check the entire document, click the Yes button.

3 When the spell check is finished, click the Save button on the Standard toolbar.

The checked document saves in the same location with the same file name.

Outside Printing

When they need mass quantities of publications, businesses generally **outsource**, or submit their publications to an outside printer, for duplicating. You must make special considerations when preparing a document for outside printing.

Previewing the Brochure before Printing

The first step in getting the publication ready for outside printing may be to look at a preview from your desktop. Publisher presents the entire printed page, proportionally correct, on the workspace. You can, however, perform a few steps to get the best representation of how the brochure will look by using the Print Preview button (Figure 3-59).

TO PREVIEW THE BROCHURE BEFORE PRINTING

1 Click the Print Preview button on the Standard toolbar.

The page 2 preview displays without the special characters and guides (Figure 3-60 on the next page). You also may preview page 1 by clicking the Page Up button on the Preview toolbar.

More *About*

Laser Printers

For details on laser printers, visit the Publisher 2002 More About Web page (scsite.com/pub2002/more.htm) and then click Discovering Laser Printers.

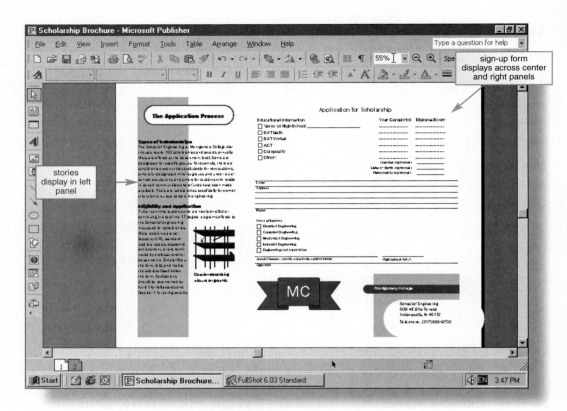

FIGURE 3-60

The next sequence of steps recommends publishing this brochure on a high grade of paper to obtain a professional look. A heavier stock paper helps the brochure to stand up better in display racks, although any paper will suffice. If you do use a special paper, be sure to click the Properties or Advanced Settings button in the Print dialog box for your printer, and then specify the paper you are using. Following your printer's specifications, print one side of the paper, turn it over, and then print the reverse side. The completed brochure prints as shown in Figure 3-1 on page PUB 3.05. You then can fold the brochure to display the title panel on the front.

Follow these steps to print a copy of the brochure.

More *About*

Printing in Color

Some printers do not have enough memory to print a wide variety of images and color. In these cases, the printer prints up to a certain point on a page and then cancels the print job automatically — resulting in only the top portion of the publication printing. Check with your instructor as to whether or not your printer has enough memory to work with colors.

TO PRINT THE BROCHURE

1 Ready the printer according to the printer instructions and insert paper.

2 Click the Close button on the Preview toolbar. With page 2 displaying in the workspace, click File on the menu bar and then click Print. Click Current page. If necessary, click the Properties button to choose a special paper. Click the OK button.

3 When page 2 finishes printing, turn the page over and reinsert it top first (or as your printer requires) into the paper feed mechanism on your printer.

4 Click the page 1 icon on the status bar. Click File on the menu bar and then click Print. When the Print dialog box displays, again click Current page and then click the OK button.

The brochure prints as shown in Figure 3-1 on page PUB 3.05.

Printing Considerations

If you start a publication from scratch, it is best to **set up** the publication for the type of printing you want before you place objects on the page. Otherwise you may be forced to make design changes at the last minute. You also may set up an existing publication for a printing service, however. In order to provide you with experience in setting up a publication for outside printing, this project takes you through the preparation steps — even if you are submitting this publication to only your instructor.

Printing options, such as whether or not to use a copy shop or commercial printer, have advantages and limitations. You may have to make some tradeoffs before deciding on the best printing option. Table 3-5 shows some of the questions you can ask yourself about printing.

Table 3-5	Choosing a Printing Option		
CONSIDERATION	QUESTIONS TO ASK	DESKTOP OPTION	PROFESSIONAL OPTIONS
Color	Is the quality of photographs and color a high priority?	Low- to medium-quality	High quality
Convenience	Do I want the easy way?	Very convenient and familiar	Time needed to explore different methods, unfamiliarity
Cost	How much do I want to pay?	Printer supplies and personal time	High-resolution color/high quality is expensive. The more you print, the less expensive the per copy price.
Quality	How formal is the purpose of my publication?	Local event Narrow, personal audience	Business marketing Professional services
Quantity	How many copies do I need?	1 to 10 copies	10 to 500 copies: copy shop 500+ copies: commercial printer
Turnaround	How soon do I need it?	Immediate	Rush outside printing, probably an extra cost

Paper Considerations

Professional brochures are printed on a high grade of paper to enhance the graphics and provide a longer lasting document. Grades of paper are based on weight. Desktop printers commonly use **20 lb. bond paper**, which means they use a lightweight paper intended for writing and printing. A commercial printer might use 60 lb. glossy or linen paper. The finishing options and their costs are important considerations that may take additional time to explore. **Glossy paper** is a coated paper, produced using a heat process with clay and titanium. **Linen paper**, with its mild texture or grain, can support high-quality graphics without the shine and slick feel of glossy paper. Users sometimes pick a special stock of paper such as cover stock, card stock, or text stock. This textbook is printed on 45 lb. blade coated paper. **Blade coated paper** is coated and then skimmed and smoothed to create the pages you see here.

These paper and finishing options may sound burdensome, but they are becoming conveniently available to desktop publishers. Local office supply stores have shelf after shelf of special computer paper especially designed for laser and ink-jet printers. Some of the paper you can purchase has been prescored for special folding.

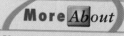

More About

Flipping Objects to Print on T-Shirts

You can use Publisher to create t-shirt designs with pictures, logos, words, or any of the Publisher objects. You need thermal t-shirt transfer paper that is widely available for most printers. Then create your design in Publisher. On the File menu, click Page Setup, click the Layout tab, and then click Full page. On the Printer & Paper tab, select Letter. If your design is a picture, clip art, or WordArt, flip it horizontally. If your design includes text, cut it from the text box, and insert it into a WordArt object; then flip it horizontally. Print your design on plain paper first to make sure it looks correct. After any adjustments, print it on the thermal t-shirt transfer paper.

Color Considerations

When printing colors, desktop printers commonly use a color scheme called **Composite RGB**. RGB stands for the three colors — red, green, and blue — that are used to print the combined colors of your publication. Professional printers, on the other hand, can print your publication using color scheme processes or **libraries**. These processes include black-and-white, spot-color, and process-color.

In **black-and-white printing**, the printer uses only one color of ink (usually black, but you can choose a different color if you want). You can add accent colors to your publication by using different shades of gray, or printing on colored paper. Your publication can have the same range of subtleties as a black-and-white photograph.

A **spot color** is used to accent a black and white publication. Newspapers, for example, may print their masthead in a bright, eye-catching color on page 1 but print the rest of the publication in black and white. In Publisher, you may apply up to two spot colors with a color matching system called **Pantone**. Spot-color printing uses semitransparent, premixed inks typically chosen from standard color-matching guides, such as Pantone. Choosing colors from a **color-matching library** helps ensure high-quality results because printing professionals who license the libraries agree to maintain the specifications, control, and quality.

In a spot-color publication, each spot color is **separated** to its own plate and printed on an offset printing press. The use of spot colors has become more creative in the last few years. Printing services use spot colors of metallic or florescent inks, as well as screen tints to obtain color variations without increasing the number of color separations and cost. If your publication includes a logo with one or two colors, or if you want to use color to emphasize line art or text, then consider using spot-color printing.

Process-color printing means your publication can include color photographs and any color or combination of colors. One of the process-color libraries, called **CMYK**, or **four-color printing**, is named for the four semitransparent process inks — cyan, magenta, yellow, and black. CMYK process-color printing can reproduce a full range of colors on a printed page. The CMYK color model defines color as it is absorbed and reflected on a printed page rather than in its liquid state.

Process-color is the most expensive proposition; black-and-white is the cheapest. Using color increases the cost and time it takes to process the publication. When using either the spot-color or process-color method, the printer first must output the publication to film on an **image setter**, which recreates the publication on film or photographic paper. The film then is used to create color **printing plates**. Each printing plate transfers one of the colors in the publication onto paper in an offset process. Publisher can print a preview of these individual sheets showing how the colors will separate before you take your publication to the printer.

A new printing technology called **digital printing** uses toner instead of ink to reproduce a full range of colors. Digital printing does not require separate printing plates. Digital printing is becoming cheaper than offset printing without sacrificing quality.

Publisher supports all three kinds of printing and provides the tools commercial printing services need to print the publication. You should ask your printing service which color-matching system it uses.

Choosing a Commercial Printing Tool

After making the decisions about printing services, paper, and color, you must prepare the brochure for outside printing. The first task is to assign a color library from the commercial printing tools, as illustrated in the following steps.

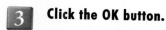 **To Choose a Commercial Printing Tool**

1 **Click Tools on the menu bar. Point to Commercial Printing Tools and then point to Color Printing on the Commercial Printing Tools submenu.**

The Commercial Printing Tools submenu displays (Figure 3-61).

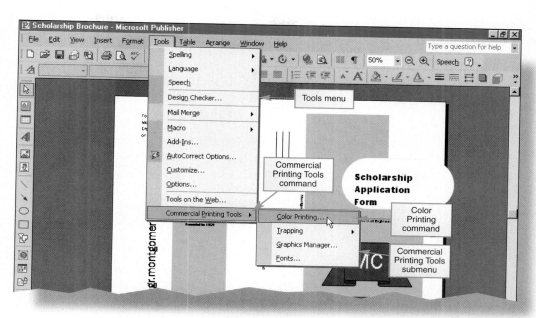

FIGURE 3-61

2 **Click Color Printing. When the Color Printing dialog box displays, click Process colors (CMYK) and then point to the OK button in the Color Printing dialog box.**

Publisher will convert all colors in text, graphics, and other objects to CMYK values and then internally create four plates, regardless of the color model originally used to create the colors (Figure 3-62).

3 **Click the OK button.**

Depending on your monitor colors and resolution, you may or may not see a noticeable difference.

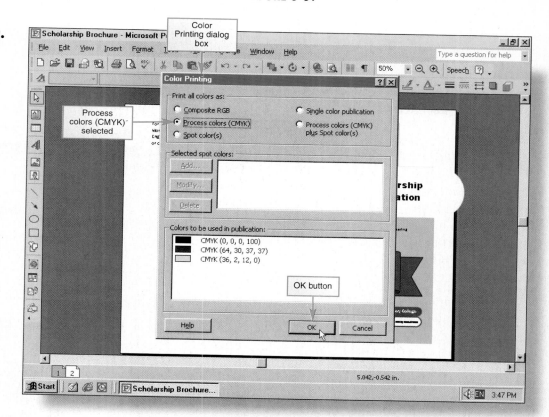

FIGURE 3-62

Other Ways

1. In Voice Command mode, say "Tools, Commercial Printing Tools"

More *About*

The Pack and Go Readme File

To look at a sample Pack and Go Readme file, visit the Publisher 2002 More About Web page (scsite.com/pub2002/more.htm) and then click Pack and Go.

Packaging the Publication for the Printing Service

The publication file can be packaged for the printing service in two ways. The first way is to give the printing service the Publisher file in Publisher format using the Pack and Go Wizard. The second way is to save the file in a format called Encapsulated PostScript. Both of these methods are discussed in the following sections.

Using the Pack and Go Wizard

The **Pack and Go Wizard** guides you through the steps to collect and pack all the files the printing service needs and then compress the files to fit on one or more disks. Publisher checks for and embeds the TrueType fonts used in the publication. **Embedding** ensures that the printing service can display and print the publication with the correct fonts. The Pack and Go Wizard adds a program called **Unpack.exe** to the disk that the printing service can use to unpack the files. At the end of Publisher's packing sequence, you are given the option of printing a composite color printout or color separation printouts on your desktop printer.

You need either sufficient space on a floppy disk or another formatted disk readily available when using the Pack and Go Wizard. Graphic files and fonts require a great deal of disk space. The Pack and Go Wizard also creates on disk a **Readme file** intended for the printing service. In the following steps, if you use a disk other than the one on which you previously saved the brochure, save it again on the new disk before beginning the process.

Perform the following steps to use the Pack and Go Wizard to ready the publication for submission to a commercial printing service.

Steps **To Use the Pack and Go Wizard**

1 **With a floppy disk in drive A, click File on the menu bar. Point to Pack and Go and then point to Take to a Commercial Printing Service on the Pack and Go submenu.**

The File menu and Pack and Go submenu display (Figure 3-63). Publisher also uses a Pack and Go Wizard to transport publications to other computers for printing and viewing purposes only.

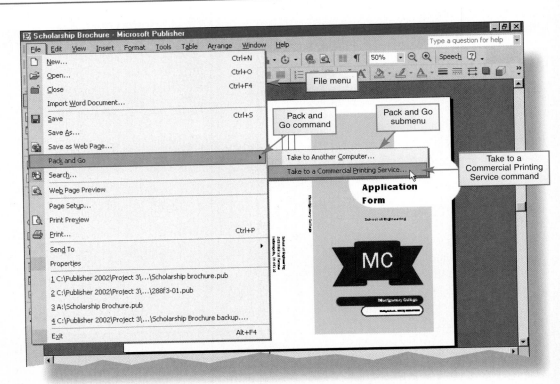

FIGURE 3-63

2 Click Take to a Commercial Printing Service. When the Pack and Go Wizard dialog box displays, point to the Next button.

The Pack and Go Wizard dialog box displays (Figure 3-64). This wizard guides you through each step of the packing process. Read each individual screen as you progress through the steps.

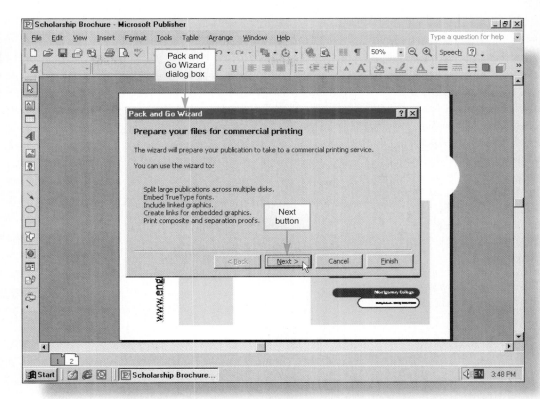

FIGURE 3-64

3 Click the Next button for each of the wizard steps, accepting the preset options. When the last step, Pack My Publication, displays, point to the Finish button in the Pack and Go Wizard dialog box.

The last dialog box of the Pack and Go Wizard displays (Figure 3-65).

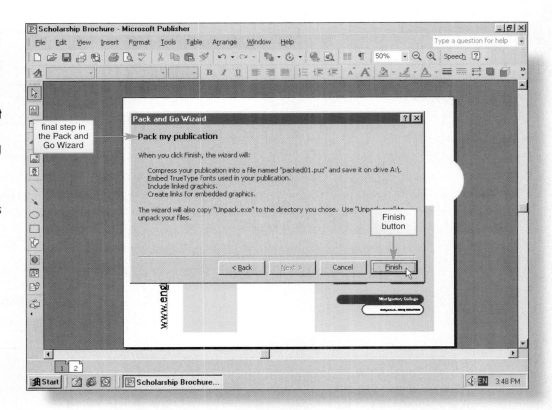

FIGURE 3-65

4 **Click the Finish button. If you used graphics from an external source, Publisher will ask you to insert the disk. If you used system fonts that cannot be embedded, Publisher will display a dialog box in which you may click the OK button for the purposes of this project. When the confirming dialog box displays, point to Print a composite.**

After Publisher finishes packing your publication, a confirming dialog box displays (Figure 3-66). Both print check boxes are selected.

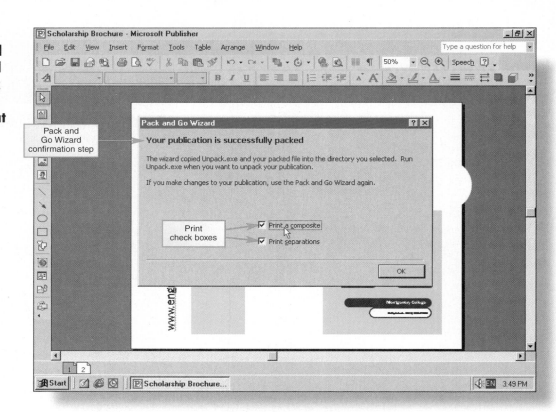

FIGURE 3-66

5 **If necessary, click both print check boxes so neither one is selected. Point to the OK button in the Pack and Go Wizard dialog box.**

The check boxes display without check marks (Figure 3-67). You already have printed the brochure and unless you are actually submitting this publication to a printing service, a separation print is unnecessary. If you want to see what the separations look like, you may print them.

6 **Click the OK button.**

Other Ways

1. In Voice Command mode, say "File, Pack and Go"

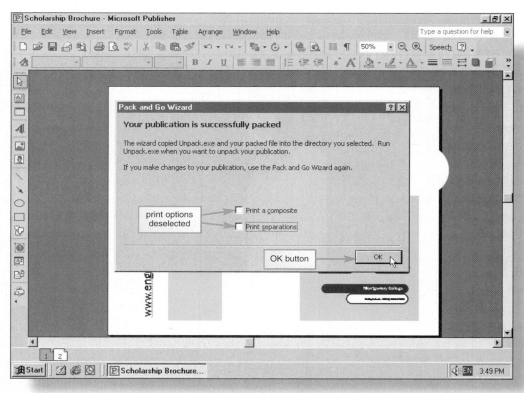

FIGURE 3-67

The files are saved on the disk in drive A. Publisher names and numbers the packed files and adds a .puz extension. For example, the first file will be named Packed01.puz, the second file will be named Packed02.puz, and so on. If you make changes to the publication after packing the files, be sure to run the Pack and Go Wizard again so the changes are part of the packed publication.

Using PostScript Files

If your printing service does not accept Publisher files, you can hand off, or submit, your files in PostScript format. **PostScript** is a page definition language that describes the document to be printed in language that the printer can understand. The PostScript printer driver includes a page definition language translator to interpret the instructions and print the document on a printer or a PostScript output device, such as an image setter. Because you cannot open or make changes directly to a PostScript file, everything in the publication must be complete before saving it.

Nearly all printing services can work with some type of PostScript file, either regular PostScript files, known as **PostScript dumps**, or **Encapsulated PostScript** (**EPS**) files, which are graphic pictures of each page. If you hand off a PostScript file, you are responsible for updating graphics, including the necessary fonts, and ensuring that you have all the files your printing service needs. Publisher includes several **PostScript printer drivers** (**PPD**s) and their description files to facilitate printing. You must install a PPD before saving in PostScript form. Because the most common installation of Publisher is for a single user in a desktop environment, this project will not take you through the steps involved to install a PostScript printer driver. That process would necessitate using original operating system disks and a more thorough knowledge of PostScript printers. Ask your printing service representative for the correct printer driver and see your Windows documentation for installing it. Then use the Save As command on the File menu to save the publication in PostScript format. Another question to ask your printing service is whether or not it performs the **prepress tasks** or a **preflight check**. You may be responsible for making color corrections, separations, setting the printing options, and other printing tasks.

Quitting Publisher

Perform the following steps to quit Publisher.

TO QUIT PUBLISHER

1 Click the Close button on the Publisher title bar.

2 If a dialog box displays reminding you to save the document, click its No button.

The Publisher window closes.

More *About*

Submitting PostScript Files

If you decide to hand off a PostScript *dump*, or file, to an outside printer or service bureau, include a copy of the original document as well — for backup purposes. Many shops are slowly changing over from Macintosh-based to cross-platform based operations. If something happens, the printer technician can correct the error from the original without another trip by you to the print shop.

More *About*

Opening Multiple Publications

In Office XP and Microsoft Publisher 2002, you now can open multiple publications from within the same running window. Simply click New on the File menu. To move among the publications, you can click the associated publication button that Publisher places on the taskbar, or click the publication name on the Windows menu.

CASE PERSPECTIVE SUMMARY

The School of Engineering likes the result of the brochure and is ready to take your files to the printing service. The logo on both the front and back panels enhances the brochure. The photograph of the college adds to the brochure's appeal. On the inside, the sign-up form can be filled in easily. You and the college made good choices about the printing service, the paper, and color. Montgomery College will have lots of scholarship applicants!

Project Summary

Project 3 introduced you to the brochure medium. You learned about the use of photographs versus images, and how to insert a photograph from a file. After entering new text and deleting unwanted objects, you created a logo from scratch using a custom shape and text grouped in the workspace. You also learned about design and printing considerations, such as overlapping, separations, color libraries, paper types, and costs. In anticipation of taking the brochure to a professional publisher, you previewed and printed your publication and then used the Pack and Go Wizard to create the necessary files.

What You Should Know

Having completed this project, you now should be able to perform the following tasks:

- Align Objects *(PUB 3.27)*
- Check Spelling and Save Again *(PUB 3.45)*
- Choose a Commercial Printing Tool *(PUB 3.48)*
- Choose Brochure Options *(PUB 3.08)*
- Create a Shape for the Logo *(PUB 3.32)*
- Create an AutoFit Transparent Text Box *(PUB 3.34)*
- Delete a Graphic *(PUB 3.31)*
- Delete Text Boxes *(PUB 3.19)*
- Edit a Sign-Up Form *(PUB 3.41)*
- Edit a Story in Microsoft Word *(PUB 3.14)*
- Edit Other Text Boxes *(PUB 3.13)*
- Edit Text in the Brochure Using Publisher *(PUB 3.11)*

- Group and Position the Logo Objects *(PUB 3.37)*
- Insert a Photograph from a File *(PUB 3.29)*
- Insert Text Boxes and Use the AutoCorrect Smart Tag *(PUB 3.21)*
- Preview the Brochure before Printing *(PUB 3.45)*
- Print the Brochure *(PUB 3.46)*
- Quit Publisher *(PUB 3.53)*
- Resize an Object *(PUB 3.39)*
- Rotate an Object *(PUB 3.25)*
- Save a Publication *(PUB 3.10)*
- Start Publisher *(PUB 3.07)*
- Use the Pack and Go Wizard *(PUB 3.50)*

More *About*

The Publisher Help System

The best way to become familiar with the Publisher Help system is to use it. Appendix A includes detailed information on the Publisher Help system and exercises that will help you gain confidence using it.

More *About*

Quick Reference

For a table that lists how to complete tasks covered in this book using the mouse, menu, shortcut menu, and keyboard, see the Quick Reference summary at the back of this book or visit the Shelly Cashman Series Office XP Web page (scsite.com/offxp/qr.htm), and then click Microsoft Publisher 2002.

More *About*

Microsoft Certification

The Microsoft Office User Specialist (MOUS) Certification program provides an opportunity for you to obtain a valuable industry credential — proof that you have the Office XP skills required by employers. For more information, see Appendix E or visit the Shelly Cashman Series MOUS Web page at scsite.com/offxp/cert.htm.

Learn It Online

Instructions: To complete the Learn It Online exercises, start your browser, click the Address bar, and then enter scsite.com/offxp/exs.htm. When the Office XP Learn It Online page displays, follow the instructions in the exercises below.

1 Project Reinforcement TF, MC, and SA

Below Publisher Project 3, click the Project Reinforcement link. Print the quiz by clicking Print on the File menu. Answer each question. Write your first and last name at the top of each page and then hand in the printout to your instructor.

2 Flash Cards

Below Publisher Project 3, click the Flash Cards link. When Flash Cards displays, read the instructions. Type 20 (or a number specified by your instructor) in the Number of Playing Cards text box, type your name in the Name text box, and then click the Flip Card button. When the flash card displays, read the question and then click the Answer box arrow to select an answer. Flip through Flash Cards. Click Print on the File menu to print the last flash card if your score is 15 (75%) correct or greater and then hand it in to your instructor. If your score is less than 15 (75%) correct, then redo this exercise by clicking the Replay button.

3 Practice Test

Below Publisher Project 3, click the Practice Test link. Answer each question, enter your first and last name at the bottom of the page, and then click the Grade Test button. When the graded practice test displays on your screen, click Print on the File menu to print a hard copy. Continue to take practice tests until you score 80% or better. Hand in a printout of the final practice test to your instructor.

4 Who Wants to Be a Computer Genius?

Below Publisher Project 3, click the Computer Genius link. Read the instructions, enter your first and last name at the bottom of the page, and then click the Play button. Hand in your score to your instructor.

5 Wheel of Terms

Below Publisher Project 3, click the Wheel of Terms link. Read the instructions, and then enter your first and last name and your school name. Click the Play button. Hand in your score to your instructor.

6 Crossword Puzzle Challenge

Below Publisher Project 3, click the Crossword Puzzle Challenge link. Read the instructions, and then enter your first and last name. Click the Play button. Work the crossword puzzle. When you are finished, click the Submit button. When the crossword puzzle redisplays, click the Print button. Hand in the printout.

7 Tips and Tricks

Below Publisher Project 3, click the Tips and Tricks link. Click a topic that pertains to Project 3. Right-click the information and then click Print on the shortcut menu. Construct a brief example of what the information relates to in Publisher to confirm you understand how to use the tip or trick. Hand in the example and printed information.

8 Newsgroups

Below Publisher Project 3, click the Newsgroups link. Click a topic that pertains to Project 3. Print three comments. Hand in the comments to your instructor.

9 Expanding Your Horizons

Below Publisher Project 3, click the Articles for Microsoft Publisher link. Click a topic that pertains to Project 3. Print the information. Construct a brief example of what the information relates to in Publisher to confirm you understand the contents of the article. Hand in the example and printed information to your instructor.

10 Search Sleuth

Below Publisher Project 3, click the Search Sleuth link. To search for a term that pertains to this project, select a term below the Project 3 title and then use the Google search engine at google.com (or any major search engine) to display and print two Web pages that present information on the term. Hand in the printouts to your instructor.

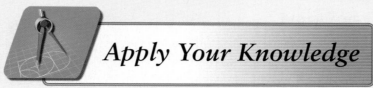

Apply Your Knowledge

1 Editing a Publication

Instructions: Start Publisher. Open the publication, Apply-3, from the Data Disk. See the inside back cover of this book for instructions for downloading the Data Disk or see your instructor for information on accessing the files required for this book. The edited publication is shown in Figures 3-68a and 3-68b.

FIGURE 3-68

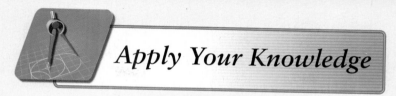

Apply Your Knowledge

Perform the following tasks.

1. With page 1 displayed, click Task Pane on the View menu. If necessary, click the Other Task Panes button and then click Brochure options. Click to include Customer Address. Close the task pane.

2. On page 1, make the following text changes, using the zoom features as necessary:
   a. Click the text, Seminar or Event Title. Type Spring Break Ski Trip to replace the text.
   b. Click the Address text box. Type Alpha Zeta Mu and then press the ENTER key. Type 1050 Greek Row and then press the ENTER key. Type P.O. Box 1050-3211 and then press the ENTER key. Type Kansas City, MO 64118 to finish the address.

3. Click the AutoShapes button on the Objects toolbar. Point to Stars and Banners, and when the list displays, click Wave. In the workspace area, draw a Wave AutoShape approximately 2 × 1.5 inches. Click the Fill Color button and then click Accent 1.

4. Click the Text Box button on the Objects toolbar. Draw a text box in the workspace approximately .7 × .7 inches. Type A in the text box. Right-click the text and point to Change text on the shortcut menu. Point to AutoFit text and then click Best Fit. Press CTRL+T to make it transparent.

5. With the text box still selected, click the Copy button on the Standard toolbar and then click the Paste button twice. Drag the copies away from the original to display in the Wave AutoShape as shown in Figure 3-68a. Replace the A with Z and M, respectively.

6. SHIFT+click each of the three letter text boxes and then SHIFT+click the Wave AutoShape. Click the Group Objects button. Drag the grouped object, now a logo, to display above the title.

7. Click the Copy button to copy the logo. Click the Paste button. Drag the copy into the workspace. Resize to make it smaller and then drag the rotation handle so that the logo displays sideways. Drag the rotated logo to display in the middle panel above the return address.

8. Click the page 2 icon on the task bar. Click the story in the middle panel. On the Edit menu, click Edit Story in Microsoft Word. Type the story from Table 3-6.

9. Run Check Spelling and Design Checker. Correct errors if necessary.

10. Click File on the menu bar and then click Save As. Use the file name, Ski Trip Brochure.

Table 3-6	Text for Middle Panel on Page 2
TEXT	
ALPHA ZETA MU SKI TRIP	
Alpha Zeta Mu Sorority is sponsoring a 4-day, 3-night ski trip to Colorado. Sorority members and their guests will fly from Kansas City International to Denver on JLM Airlines and then board a free shuttle to Sunset Mountain. All package option prices are based on Alpha Zeta Mu's ability to book at least 20 people, two to a room, with a maximum of 40. You may mix and match any of the options. You will receive a confirmation postcard in the mail.	
LODGING	
Sunset Mountain Lodge is the only bed and breakfast among the seven lodging experiences on Sunset Mountain. Nestled among the tall lodge pole pines, the lodge offers modern rooms with full baths. An optional dinner package is available at a modest cost. Other amenities include a game room, hot tub, meeting room, and of course the grand hearth — where the fireplace always is lit and the hot cinnamon cocoa always is ready!	

11. Click Tools on the menu bar, click Commercial Printing Tools, and then click Color Printing. When the Color Printing dialog box displays, click Process colors (CMYK) and then click the OK button.

12. With a floppy disk in drive A, click File on the menu bar. Click Pack and Go and then click Take to a Commercial Printing Service on the Pack and Go submenu. Click the Next button at each step.

13. When the wizard completes the packing process, if necessary click the Print a composite check box to select it. The brochure will print on two pages.

In the Lab

1 Creating an Event Brochure

Problem: You are the public relations assistant for the Dayton Symphonic Orchestra. Your supervisor has asked you to prepare an event brochure that will be mass-mailed to prospective attendees. The brochure should include articles about the upcoming Fall Concert Series, a form to order tickets, and appropriate graphics.

Instructions: Start Publisher and perform the following tasks to create the event brochure shown in Figures 3-69a and 3-69b.

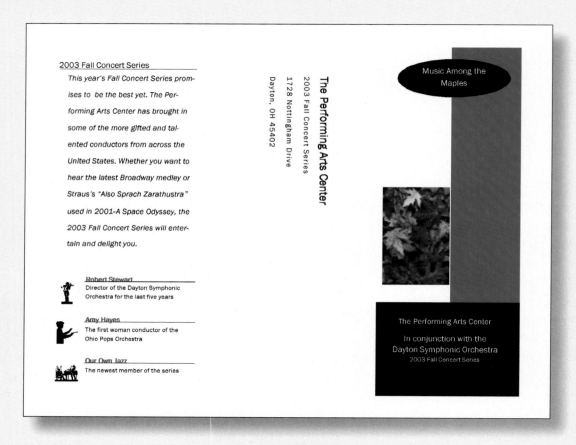

FIGURE 3-69a

1. Start Publisher. In the New Publication task pane, select the Floating Oval Event Brochure preview.
2. In the Brochure Options task pane, select a 3-panel Page size; include a Customer address and a Response form.
3. Click Color Schemes and then select Cranberry. Click Font Schemes and then select Perspective.
4. Edit the text boxes on page 1 as shown in Figure 3-69a. Right-click each text box. Point to Change Text on the shortcut menu, point to AutoFit Text, and then click Best Fit. Delete the text box for the mailing address in order to apply labels at a later date.

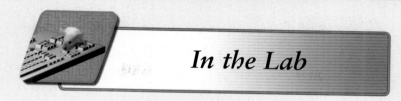

In the Lab

5. Double-click the graphic on the front panel. Insert a clip using the keyword, leaves. For the three small graphics in the left panel, search for a clip involving music, people, or instruments. Your graphics may differ.
6. Click the page 2 icon on the task bar. Delete the text box in the middle panel. Double-click the graphic and choose a picture with the keyword, music. Resize the graphic in the middle panel as necessary. Change the caption of the graphic to: For more information, visit our web site at www.arts.dayton.oh.org.
7. Delete the graphic in the left panel.
8. Click the story in the left panel. On the Edit menu, use the Edit a Story in Microsoft Word command to enter the text from Table 3-7.
9. On the right panel (shown in Figure 3-69b), edit the Response form's text boxes to match the figure. For each heading text box, click the text box, and then, on the Formatting toolbar, click the Fill Color button arrow. Choose an appropriate color from those displayed.
10. Edit the other text boxes on the right panel. Right-click each text box. Point to Change Text on the shortcut menu, point to AutoFit Text, and then click Best Fit.

Table 3-7 Text for Left Panel on Page 2
TEXT
The Classical Series: Performed by the Dayton Symphonic Orchestra, the Classical Series has been the mainstay of the summer repertoire since the series' inception in 1987. This 80-piece orchestra, made up of professional and semiprofessional musicians, has performed all over the northeast. This year's theme is music of the late nineteenth and twentieth century.
The Broadway Series: The Ohio Pops Orchestra is back by popular demand playing show tunes by famous duos. Performances of music by Rogers & Hammerstein and Lerner & Lowe highlight this family-oriented series.
The Jazz Series: The group, Our Own Jazz, brings its unique interpretation of jazz greats, Duke Ellington and Count Basie, to the Fall Concert Series. Don't miss this newest addition.
Friday and Saturday evening concerts begin at 8:00 p.m.; Sunday Matinees at 2:00 p.m.

Order Fall Concert Series Tickets

Enter the number of tickets you wish to purchase in the boxes. All orders are filled using best seating available.

Classical Series
- September 19
- September 28
- October 4

Broadway Series
- September 20
- September 26
- October 5

Jazz Series
- September 21
- September 27
- October 3

Season Tickets
- Friday Series
- Saturday Series
- Sunday Matinee Series

Name

Address

Telephone

Method of Payment
- Check
- Bill Me
- Visa
- MasterCard
- American Express

Credit Card #   Exp. date

Signature

FIGURE 3-69b

In the Lab

2 Creating a CD Liner

Instructions: Perform the following tasks to create the two-panel, two-sided CD liner as shown in Figures 3-70a and 3-70b.

1. Start Publisher. If the New Publication task pane does not display, click File on the menu bar and then click New.
2. In the Publication Types list, click Labels, and then click Compact Disc. Double-click the Compact Disc Case Liner preview.
3. Click Color Schemes in the task pane and then click Sienna in the list. Close the task pane.
4. Edit the text boxes in both panels as shown in Figure 3-70a.
5. Select the large rectangle border in the right panel. Press CTRL+T to make the rectangle transparent in preparation for the watermark.
6. Replace the small picture in the right panel using the Insert Clip Art task pane. Search using the keyword, music. Delete the old graphic if necessary.
7. Copy the new graphic using the Copy button on the Standard toolbar.
8. Insert a new blank page to follow page 1.
9. Paste the picture from page 1 onto page 2. Drag it to the left panel and then SHIFT-drag a corner sizing handle to enlarge the graphic.
10. Using the View menu, go to the Master Page.
11. Click the Clip Organizer Frame button on the Objects toolbar. Search for an appropriate line drawing graphic for the watermark effect using the keyword, CD. Resize the graphic to fill the right panel.
12. Go to the foreground of page 2 by pressing CTRL+M.
13. Create a large text box in the left panel. Make it transparent so the picture shows through. Choose a font color of white. Type the text as shown in Figure 3-70b. AutoFit the text using the Best Fit option.
14. Using the Design Gallery Object button, insert a Voyage Table of Contents. Use the Object position box to resize and place it approximately as follows: Width: 3.4; Height: 4.5, Horizontal: 5.4; and Vertical .1 in the right panel. Make it transparent. Edit the table of contents as shown in Figure 3-70b.
15. Save the publication on a floppy disk using the file name, Drums CD Liner.
16. Print a copy of the CD liner one page at a time. Use duplex printing. The default settings print the liner in the middle of an 8½-by-11-inch sheet of paper, with crop marks. Trim the printout.

In the Lab

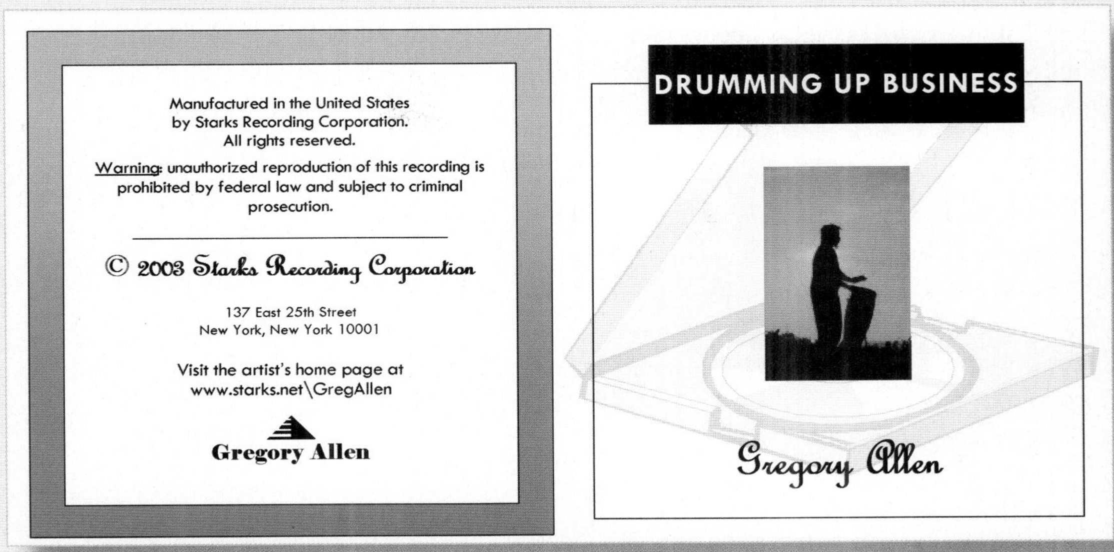

Manufactured in the United States
by Starks Recording Corporation.
All rights reserved.

<u>Warning</u>: unauthorized reproduction of this recording is
prohibited by federal law and subject to criminal
prosecution.

© 2003 Starks Recording Corporation

137 East 25th Street
New York, New York 10001

Visit the artist's home page at
www.starks.net\GregAllen

Gregory Allen

DRUMMING UP BUSINESS

Gregory Allen

(a)

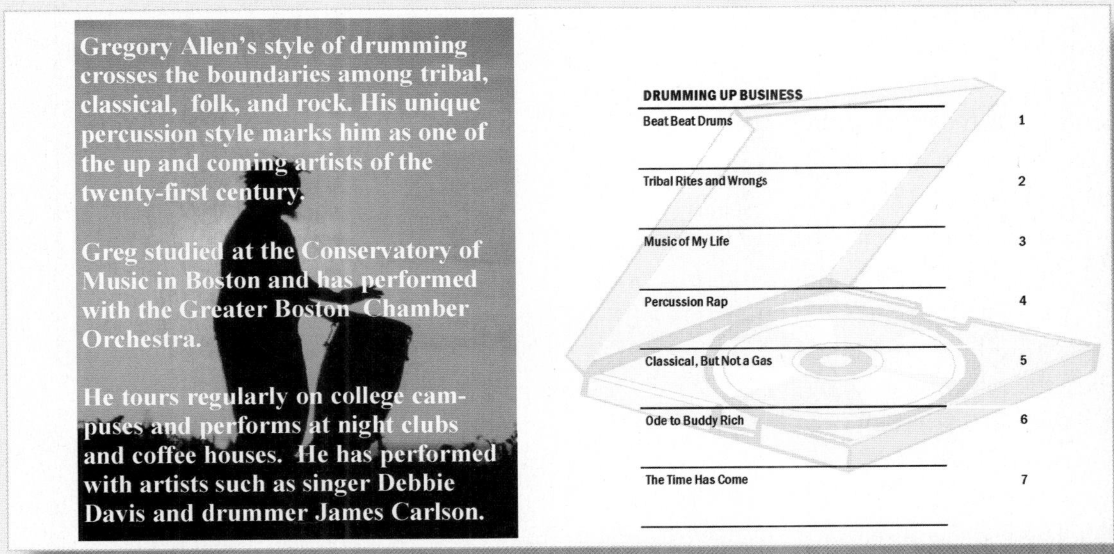

Gregory Allen's style of drumming
crosses the boundaries among tribal,
classical, folk, and rock. His unique
percussion style marks him as one of
the up and coming artists of the
twenty-first century.

Greg studied at the Conservatory of
Music in Boston and has performed
with the Greater Boston Chamber
Orchestra.

He tours regularly on college campuses and performs at night clubs
and coffee houses. He has performed
with artists such as singer Debbie
Davis and drummer James Carlson.

DRUMMING UP BUSINESS

Beat Beat Drums	1
Tribal Rites and Wrongs	2
Music of My Life	3
Percussion Rap	4
Classical, But Not a Gas	5
Ode to Buddy Rich	6
The Time Has Come	7

(b)

FIGURE 3-70

In the Lab

3 Creating an Emblem from Scratch

Problem: You volunteer at the Save-A-Pet mission on Saturdays. The office manager knows of your interest in desktop publishing and has asked you to design an emblem for the office to be used in signs, posters, letterhead, and logos. You decide to use a Publisher AutoShape along with an appropriate graphic to create the emblem shown in Figure 3-71.

Instructions: Start Publisher and perform the following tasks.

1. In the New Publication task pane, choose a Blank Publication.
2. Click the AutoShape button on the Objects toolbar. From the Stars and Banners list, choose a Vertical Scroll shape. Draw the shape to fill about one-fourth of the page. Use an appropriate fill color.
3. On the Insert menu, point to Picture, and then click Clip Art on the Picture submenu. When the Insert Clip Art task pane displays, type animal in the Search text box and then click the Search button. Drag the graphic to the lower right portion of the AutoShape. Resize as necessary.
4. Click the Text Box button on the Objects toolbar. Draw a text box on top of the AutoShape to fill the upper portion. Type Save-a-Pet Mission in the text box. Right-click the text, point to Change text on the shortcut menu. Point to AutoFit text and then click Best Fit.
5. SHIFT-click each of the three components and then click the Group Objects button.
6. Save the publication on a floppy disk with the file name, Mission Emblem. Print a copy.

FIGURE 3-71

Cases and Places

The difficulty of these case studies varies:
▶ are the least difficult; ▶▶ are more difficult; and ▶▶▶ are the most difficult.

1 ▶ Use the Blends Information brochure to create a brochure announcing the Youth Baseball League. Select an appropriate color and Font scheme. Type Spring Sign-Up as the brochure title. Type The Youth Baseball League as the Organization name. Type your address and telephone number in the appropriate text boxes. Delete the logo. Replace all graphics with sports-related clip art. Edit the captions to match. The league commissioner will send you content for the stories at a later date. Include a sign-up form on page 2. Edit the sign-up form event boxes as displayed in Table 3-8.

Table 3-8 Sign-up Form Check Box Content		
EVENT NAME	TIME	PRICE
Preschool T-Ball: ages 4 and 5	10:00	$25.00
Pee-Wee T-Ball: ages 6 and 7	11:00	$25.00
Instructional-Coach Pitched: ages 8 and 9	1:00	$40.00
Intermediate: ages 10 and 11	2:30	$40.00
Advanced: ages 12 and 13	4:00	$40.00
City Team: audition only	6:00	TBA

2 ▶ Recreate the Cases and Places logo at the top of this page. Use the flowchart rounded rectangle on the AutoShapes button menu. Use the Fill Color button to select an appropriate gradient effect. Type the words, Cases and Places, in a text box. Select clip art from the Clip Organizer or choose one from the data disk that accompanies this book. Layer and group the three objects.

3 ▶▶ You have recently joined Success America, Incorporated, as the new in-house desktop publisher. You are to design a tri-fold event brochure for their October 2003 training event in Orlando. The theme will be Every American Can Win. Featured speakers will include former U.S. Senator Charles Goolsby, television news anchor Leslie Schulke, and prominent businessperson Anita Louks. Your employer wants to mail the brochures to potential attendees. The company logo is a blue triangle with a white letter S in the center. Create a rough draft using an Event brochure that includes a sign-up form with a placeholder for the customer address. The technical writer will send you content for the stories at a later date.

4 ▶▶ Using the Blank Publication link on the New Publication task pane, recreate your school or company logo, as closely as possible, on a full-page publication. Use the AutoShapes button, fill and font colors, text boxes and symbols to match the elements in your logo. You may also use WordArt. Ask your instructor or employer for clip art files, if necessary. Use the scratch area to design portions of the logo and then layer and group them before dragging them onto the publication.

5 ▶▶▶ Bob Bert of Bert's Beanery has hired you to *spice up* and modernize the look of the restaurant's menu. You decide to use a menu wizard to create a full color menu for publication at a local copy shop. Bob wants special attention paid to his famous Atomic Chili, which is free if a diner can eat three spoonfuls without reaching for water. Bob serves salads, soups, and sandwiches a la carte. He has several family specials as well as combo meals.

Cases and Places

6 ▶▶▶ Visit or call several local copy shops or commercial printers in your area. Ask them the following questions: What kind of paper stock do your customers choose for brochures? What is the most commonly-used finish? Do you support all three color processes? Will you accept files saved with Microsoft Publisher Pack and Go, or EPS files? What prepress tasks do you perform? Use a blank publication in Publisher to create a table with the Table tool on the Objects toolbar. Insert the questions down the left side. Insert the names of the print shops across the top. Fill in the grid with the answers they provide.

Microsoft Publisher 2002

Creating Web Sites with Publisher 2002

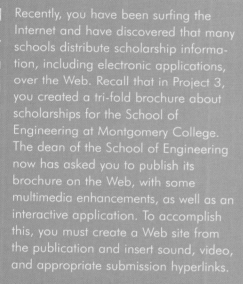

CASE PERSPECTIVE

Recently, you have been surfing the Internet and have discovered that many schools distribute scholarship information, including electronic applications, over the Web. Recall that in Project 3, you created a tri-fold brochure about scholarships for the School of Engineering at Montgomery College. The dean of the School of Engineering now has asked you to publish its brochure on the Web, with some multimedia enhancements, as well as an interactive application. To accomplish this, you must create a Web site from the publication and insert sound, video, and appropriate submission hyperlinks.

To complete this Web Feature, you will need the brochure created in Project 3 so you can convert it to a Web site and then edit the resulting Web pages. (If you did not create the brochure, see your instructor for a copy.)

Introduction

Publisher provides several techniques for creating Web pages and Web sites. You may save any Publisher publication as an HTML file so that it can be **posted**, or uploaded, to the Web and viewed by a Web browser, such as Internet Explorer. You also can start a new Web page by using a Publisher wizard. A **Web site** is a group of pages linked together with an interface called a **front page** or **home page**. The front page contains hyperlinks to other pages in the site.

If you have an existing Publisher publication, you can convert it quickly to a Web page using Publisher's conversion option. If you do not have an existing Publisher publication to convert, you can create a new Web page by using the **Web Page Wizard**, which opens a Web Site Options task pane. Publisher provides customized templates you can modify easily. In addition to these Web tools, Publisher has many other Web page authoring features. For example, you can insert hyperlinks, Web buttons and controls, sound, video, pictures, and HTML code fragments into your publications.

Once complete, you can **publish** or make the Web page or Web site available to others on your network, intranet, or the World Wide Web. Publisher will post the page(s) for you if you are connected to a **host**, which is a computer that stores Web pages. The host may be an **intranet**, which is a local network that uses Internet technologies, or it may be an **Internet service provider (ISP)**, that provides space for Web pages. Either way, you will need to know the exact address of the location, your user name, and your password to post the pages on the Web. You can complete this project and view it with a browser, however, even without an online connection.

If you decide to publish the Web site and have an online connection to your ISP or intranet, you may choose from three posting methods. First, if your ISP supports the concept of Web folders, you may save the publication directly to a Web folder. Second, Publisher can save the Web files in an FTP location on the host computer. **FTP (file transfer protocol)** is a program that sends copies of files, sounds, and graphics to the ISP. If supported by your ISP, FTP locations can be listed with other storage locations on your computer. Both Web folders and FTP are explained in detail in Appendix C. The third way to publish to the Web is to post the saved files yourself, using Microsoft's Web Publishing Wizard or the FTP program of your choice.

Using Publisher's Convert to Web Layout feature, the Scholarship Brochure created in Project 3 will be converted to an interactive Web site for online viewing and application. The following pages illustrate the steps to save your Web site in a folder on a floppy disk ready for posting. Then, check with your instructor for the best way to post your files to the Web. No matter which of the three posting methods you use to publish — or even if you do not plan to publish at all — you may preview your site using any standard Web browser.

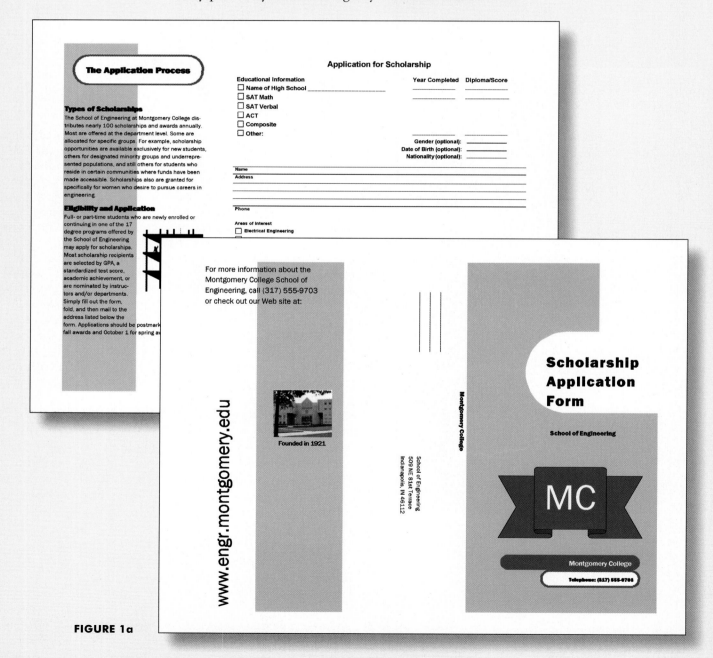

FIGURE 1a

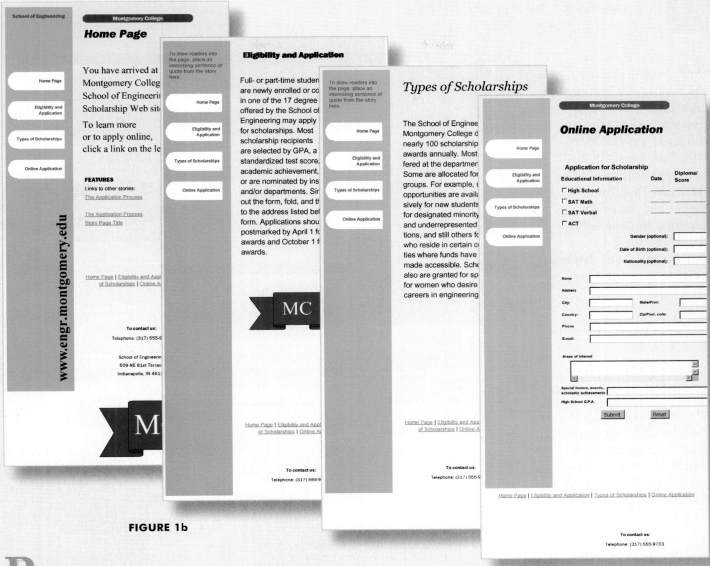

FIGURE 1b

Brochure to Web Site Conversion

A tri-fold brochure, such as the one created in Project 3, has two pages and a total of six panels (Figure 1a). In general, when converted to a Web site, the left fold-in panel from page 1 becomes the first page of the Web site (Figure 1b). The three panels from page 2 of the brochure become pages 2, 3, and 4 of the Web site. The color schemes, font schemes, and design set carry over; the extra graphic and text frames are either displayed for you to place precisely, or stored for optional insertion. The Web site pages are preset to 6-inches wide and 14-inches tall to display easily on most monitors.

Converting to Web Layout

Publisher provides the options of designing Web layouts yourself, using the Web Site Wizard and its pre-designed formats, or converting an existing publication. This Web Feature illustrates converting the tri-fold brochure, and then editing and customizing the layout. The Brochure Options task pane contains a **Convert to Web Layout button** that helps you through the conversion process. If you did not create the brochure from Project 3, see your instructor for a copy of the publication.

Perform the steps on the next page to convert the tri-fold brochure to a Web site.

Steps **To Convert a Brochure to a Web Site**

1 **Start Publisher and then open the scholarship brochure created in Project 3. If necessary, click View on the menu bar and then click Task Pane. On the task pane title bar, click the Other Task Panes button and then click Brochure Options in the list. When the Brochure Options task pane displays, point to the Convert to Web Layout button.**

The Brochure Options task pane displays (Figure 2).

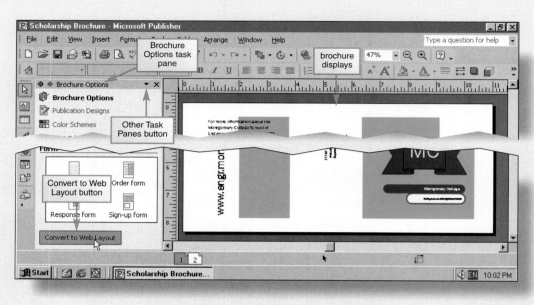

FIGURE 2

2 **Click the Convert to Web Layout button.**

After several seconds, Publisher displays page 1 of the Web site brochure (Figure 3). The Brochure Options task pane becomes the Web Site Options task pane. Your display may differ.

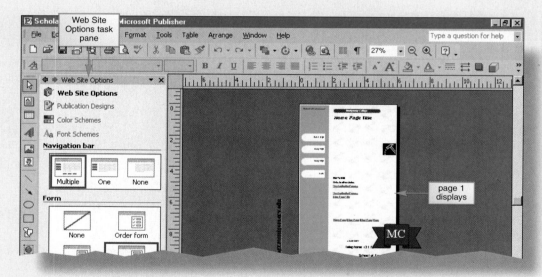

FIGURE 3

Publisher places its standard components in predetermined places on the Web pages; other objects, created especially for the brochure are displayed so that you can place them precisely.

Some objects on the Web site need to be moved, resized, edited, or deleted. The magnification in Figure 3 is 27% so that you can see the full page. Recall that you can use the F9 key to zoom selected objects to 100% as needed to facilitate editing. Perform the following steps to edit, move, and delete objects in the brochure.

TO EDIT, MOVE, AND DELETE OBJECTS ON PAGE 1

1 Right-click the Organization logo in the lower portion of page 1. On the shortcut menu, click Delete Object.

2 Drag the green ribbon logo with the capital MC to the location of the previous logo.

3 Click the Web address text box and point to its border. When the mouse pointer changes to the Move icon, drag the Web address text box from the workspace to the green rectangle on page 1 as shown in Figure 4.

4 Click the Zoom box arrow and then click 66% in the list. If necessary, scroll to the top of page 1.

5 Click the Text Box button on the Objects toolbar, and then, below the page title, drag a text box approximately 3 inches by 3 inches. Click the Font Size box arrow and click 18. Type You have arrived at the Montgomery College, School of Engineering Scholarship Web site. and then press the ENTER key. Type To learn more or to apply online, click a link on the left. and then press the ENTER key.

6 Double-click the graphic on the right. When the Insert Clip Art task pane displays, drag through any text in the Search text text box, type computer, and then press the ENTER key. Scroll and then point to the graphic shown in Figure 4. When a button displays beside the graphic, click it and then click Insert.

7 Edit the Home Page Title to delete the word Title.

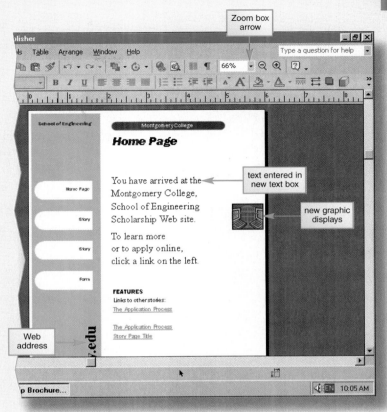

FIGURE 4

The objects display in their new positions (Figure 4). The graphic is an animated picture from the Clip Organizer.

Perform the following steps to edit objects on pages 2 and 3.

TO EDIT OBJECTS ON PAGES 2 AND 3

1 Click the page 3 icon in the Page Navigation control. When the page displays, right-click the graphic and then click Delete Object on the shortcut menu.

2 Click the text in the story. Press the F9 key. Scroll if necessary to view the first story. Drag through the first story heading and then press the DELETE key. Drag through the second story heading and then press the DELETE key.

3 Drag through the second story text. Click the Cut button on the Formatting toolbar. Press CTRL+A to select all of the remaining text. On the Formatting toolbar, click the Increase Font Size button three times.

4 Click the page 2 icon in the Page Navigation control. When page 2 displays, zoom to approximately 50%, and then click the Text Box button on the Objects toolbar. Drag a text box approximately 3 inches wide and 5 inches tall below the page title, as shown in Figure 5 on the next page. Click the Paste button on the Formatting toolbar. Press CTRL+A to select the text. On the Formatting toolbar, click the Increase Font Size button three times.

5 Right-click the graphic and then click Delete Object on the shortcut menu.

6 Drag the logo to the blank area below the text box.

The text displays in its new position with a larger font (Figure 5). The logo displays below the text box.

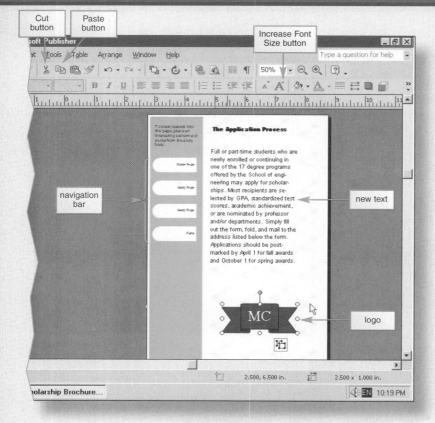

FIGURE 5

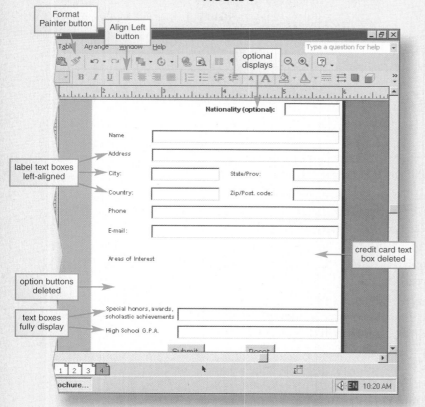

FIGURE 6

TO MOVE AND DELETE OBJECTS ON PAGE 4

1 Click the page 4 icon. Click toward the top of the application form and then press the F9 key. Click the Application for Scholarship text box and then click the Align Left button on the Formatting toolbar.

2 Click the word Time in the second column and then click the Bold button on the Formatting toolbar. Type Date to replace the text.

3 Click the Diploma/ text box and then, when the sizing handles display, drag the upper-middle sizing handle upward until the complete text displays. Drag through the words, Name of, in the Name of High School text box and then press the DELETE key.

4 Below the Date and Diploma columns, click the text box containing the word Gender and drag a left sizing handle until the word Optional displays. Scroll as necessary to repeat the process for the Date of Birth and Nationality text boxes.

5 Scroll to display the middle portion of the application, where the personal information labels and text boxes display. Click the Name text box label. Double-click the Format Painter button on the Standard toolbar. One at a time, click each of the text box labels in the personal information area.

6 One at a time, click each of the labels again and then click the Align Left button on the Formatting toolbar for each label.

7 Right-click the text box containing information about credit cards and then click Delete Object on the shortcut menu.

8 One at a time, right-click each of the option buttons under Areas of Interest and then click Delete Object on the shortcut menu.

9 Resize the text boxes that display the words Special honors and High School so they display all their text.

You will add a text area to replace the option buttons later in the project (Figure 6).

The final step in converting the brochure to a Web layout is to insert the picture of the school.

Using Extra Content

When Publisher converted the print layout to a Web layout, some objects in the print version could not be inserted directly into the Web layout. For instance, the picture of the school with its caption was not inserted. Publisher stores these objects for your later use.

Recall that the Design Gallery, accessible from the Objects toolbar, displays objects by category or design. You can insert these objects into any publication — print or Web versions. After converting from a print layout, an extra tab is added to the Design Gallery. The **Extra Content tab** displays objects that were unable to be inserted in the Web layout, such as the picture of the school and its caption.

Perform the following steps to display the Extra Content tab and insert the graphic.

Steps To Insert a Graphic from the Extra Content Tab

1 **Click the page 2 icon on the status bar. When page 2 displays zoom to 50% and then click the Design Gallery Object button on the Objects toolbar. When the Design Gallery window displays, click the Extra Content Tab. Scroll until you see the picture of the school as shown in Figure 7. Click the picture and then point to the Insert Object button.**

The Extra Content tab displays the objects Publisher was unable to insert automatically in the Web layout (Figure 7).

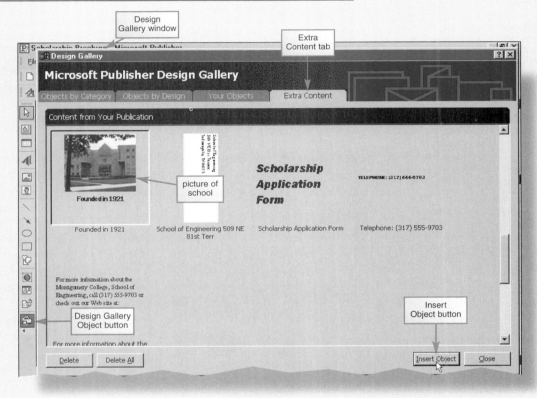

FIGURE 7

2 **Click the Insert Object button. When the picture displays on page 2, click the Bring to Front button on the Standard toolbar and then drag the picture to the right of the text.**

The text wraps around the picture and its caption (Figure 8).

1. To bring an object to front, on Arrange menu point to Order, click Bring to Front

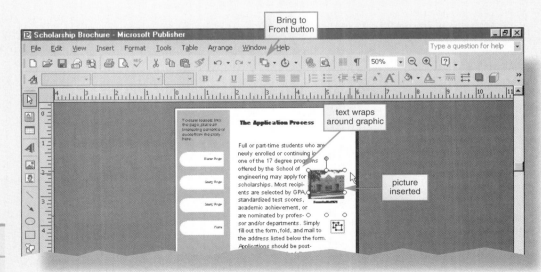

FIGURE 8

More *About*

Web Site Design

Publisher's Web site conversion process uses proven design strategies to create a well-designed Web site that is easy to navigate and view. Formatting not supported by HTML will display as plain text or graphics in your Web site. For example, you cannot emboss, shadow, or engrave characters; WordArt objects become graphics. You can display, however, bold, italic, and underline, and adjust font sizes of characters. For more information on designing Web sites, visit the Publisher 2002 More About Web page (scsite.com/pub2002/more.htm) and then click Web Design Text.

More *About*

Navigation

The major reason visitors leave Web sites is that they cannot find what they are looking for. Publisher's navigation bar provides a highly visible and easy way to navigate through the Web site. Other navigation tools can be imported or created from scratch. For more information on navigation, visit the Publisher 2002 More About Web page (scsite.com/pub2002/more.htm) and then click HTML Menu Bars.

More *About*

Search Engine Keywords

For more information about using keywords to attract search engines, and therefore visitors to your Web site, visit the Publisher 2002 More About Web page (scsite.com/pub2002/more.htm) and then click HTML Tags.

The **Bring to Front button** (Figure 8 on the previous page) helps you select objects that are layered on top of one another. The Bring to Front button menu displays options to Send to Back, Bring Forward, and Send Backward. Additionally, you can press SHIFT+TAB to move among and select objects on the page.

You now are ready to set Web properties and edit the form controls of the brochure.

Web Properties and Form Controls

Web sites and pages have several unique characteristics and components when published to the Web. Some of the special characteristics involve **Web properties**, such as naming conventions, search engine keywords, fills, and sound. **Form controls** are special Web components such as navigation bars, animated graphics, hyperlinks, hot spots, buttons, and boxes.

Editing Web Properties

One of the most marketable features of Web sites relates to Internet search engines. **Search engines** are programs that locate sites based on **keywords** entered by users. Registering your site with national search engines helps users locate your site quickly. Once located, search engines sometimes display a short description of the Web site for users to read before they click the hyperlink to jump to the site itself. The Web page itself usually displays a more descriptive, internally coded title on the browser title bar, however.

Publisher stores the keywords, description, and title in internal, HTML code called tags. Search engines use tags in the search process.

Finally, Publisher can provide background fill effects to emphasize your Web pages and background sounds or music. Publisher saves the linked fill effects and sound files with the pages and graphics of your Web site. Publisher also generates the internal HTML code and tags necessary to view and play your Web site. You may choose to have the sound or music play once or **loop** continually.

The Web Site Options task pane (Figure 3 on page PUBW 1.04) contains buttons to add navigation controls and forms to Web sites. It also contains links to insert new pages and to edit the background sound, fill effects, and Web properties of the Web site.

Perform the following steps to change the Web site's fill effect, edit Web properties, and insert background sound. The background sound is located on the Data Disk that accompanies this book. See the inside back cover for instructions for downloading the Data Disk or see your instructor for information about accessing the files required for this book. Alternately, you can use any sound on your computer system.

To Edit Web Properties

1 **Insert your Data Disk in drive A. Click the page 1 icon and zoom to Whole Page. In the Web Site Options task pane, click Background fill and sound. When the Background task pane displays, click the 30% tint of Accent 2 button in the Apply a background area. In the second column of the More colors area, point to the Gradient fill (horizontal) button and then click the button arrow that displays beside it. Point to the Apply to All Pages command.**

The gradient effect may be applied to one page or all pages (Figure 9).

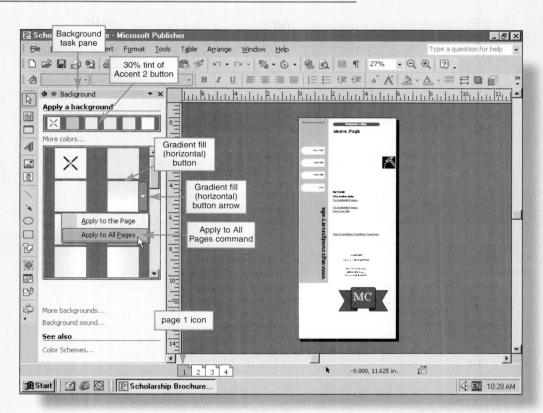

FIGURE 9

2 **Click the Apply to All Pages command. Point to Background sound in the lower portion of the Background task pane.**

The background displays on the page layout (Figure 10).

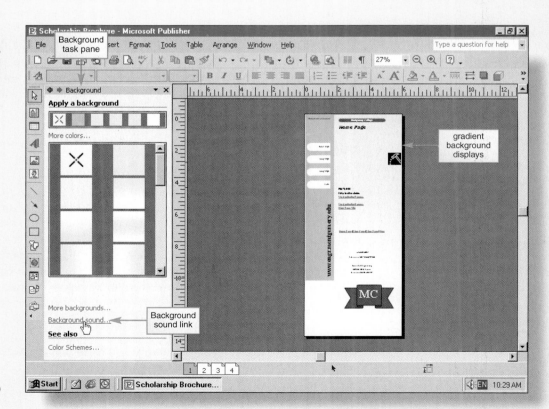

FIGURE 10

3 **Click Background sound. When the Web Options dialog box displays, if necessary, click the General tab, and then click the Keywords text box. Type** Montgomery College Engineering Scholarships **in the Keywords text box. Press the TAB key. Type** Scholarship Web site with application form **in the Description text box. Press the TAB key. Type** a:Schol_02 **in the File name text box for the Background sound. Point to the OK button.**

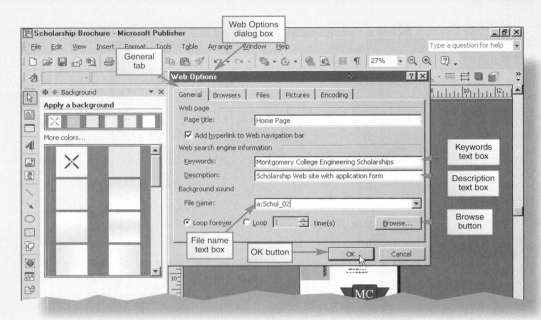

FIGURE 11

The Web Options dialog box fields display (Figure 11). You may click the Browse button to find a different background sound on your computer system.

4 **With your Data Disk in drive A, click the OK button.**

The address of your Web site itself is dependent on your ISP, but in general, the **address** is made up of the Web protocol prefix, the service provider domain name, and then your site name or path. It is common practice to use the site name as the Web folder name or FTP location name that holds all the files related to your Web site. For instance, if your Web site were called MySite, the address would include the usual prefixes (http://www.), then the name of your ISP, and then a slash followed by the word, MySite. Page 1 of your Web site would display automatically.

You now are ready to edit the form controls.

Editing Form Controls

Form controls are special objects that perform a function in Web pages. Typical form controls are navigation bars, command buttons, hot spots, and various kinds of boxes in which the user enters information or clicks to make a choice. A **navigation bar** is a form control that provides links to each page in the Web site. Publisher automatically creates a link for each page with default text. Replacing the default text creates user-friendly links and applies bold headings to each page. **Command buttons** perform specific functions on Web pages. Publisher supports a **Submit button** to send data via the Web and a **Reset button** to clear all data entry boxes. A special kind of hyperlink is a hot spot. When you position the mouse pointer over a **hot spot**, it changes to a hand with a pointing index finger. When you click a hot spot, it acts like any other link and transfers to the specified location. Hot spots are used to enliven graphics and other areas of the Web page. **Option buttons** and **list boxes** on Web pages allow users to click one of several choices; **check box buttons** allow users to click multiple choices. A **text box** or **text area** allows users to type in information.

Perform the following steps to edit the navigation bar, command buttons, and application form controls.

Steps **To Edit Form Controls**

1 **Close the task pane. Click the navigation bar in the upper-left corner of page 1. Press the F9 key. Click the text on the second button of the navigation bar. Type** Eligibility and Application **to replace the text. Click the third button's text. Type** Types of Scholarships **to replace the text. Click the fourth button's text. Type** Online Application **to replace the text.**

The navigation buttons now display the names of the pages (Figure 12). You may click each page of the Web site and see the page titles.

2 **Click the page 4 icon. Scroll to display the Areas of Interest text box, but do not select it. On the Objects toolbar, click the Form Control button and then point to the Text Area command.**

The Form Control button menu displays Publisher's available form controls (Figure 13).

3 **Click the Text Area command. When the text area displays on the page, resize it as shown in Figure 14.**

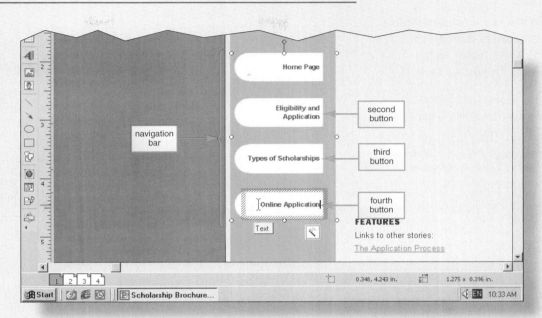

FIGURE 12

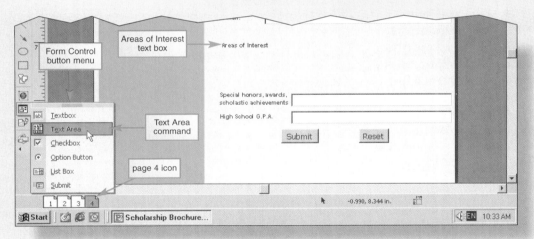

FIGURE 13

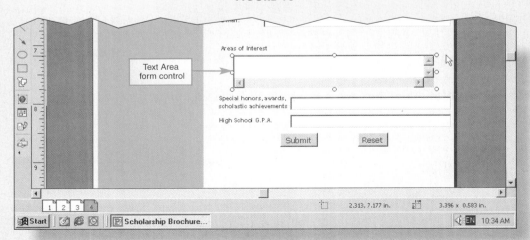

FIGURE 14

4 **Double-click the Submit button. When the Command Button Properties dialog box displays, point to the Form Properties button.**

The Command Button Properties dialog box allows you to choose the type of button as well as changing the button to a clickable image (Figure 15).

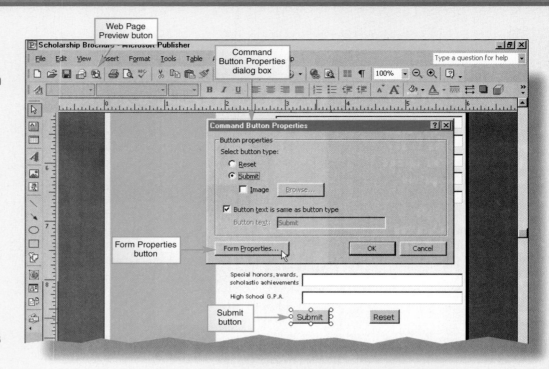

FIGURE 15

5 **Click the Form Properties button. When the Form Properties dialog box displays, click the Send data to me in e-mail option button. Press the TAB key. Type** scholarships@engr. montgomery.edu **and then point to the OK button.**

The Form Properties dialog box displays options to save the data from the Web site, send it via e-mail, or run a Web program script (Figure 16).

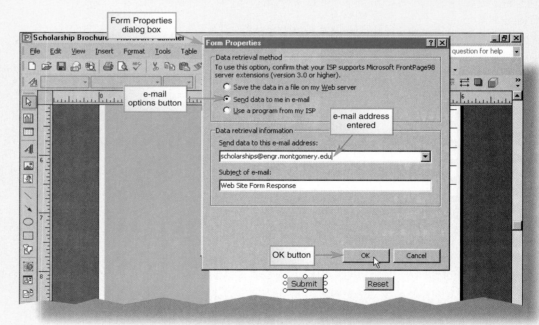

FIGURE 16

6 **Click the OK button. When the Command Button Properties dialog box again displays, click the OK button.**

The dialog boxes close.

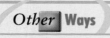

1 Right-click button, click Format Form Properties

Some ISP servers cannot send user data using a Publisher-supplied script, but most servers can accept user input and send it in an e-mail message. When the Web site user clicks the Submit button, form responses are sent to the e-mail address you supply. The Reset button automatically clears all input boxes on the form.

Viewing a Web Site

You may want to view the Web site in your default Web browser to see how it looks. When the brochure was converted to a Web site, Publisher added a **Web Page Preview button** to the Standard toolbar as shown in Figure 15. When working with Web files, the buttons on the toolbars change to provide additional Web authoring features.

Perform the following steps to view the Web site in your default browser.

Steps **To View a Web Site in a Browser**

1 **Click the Web Page Preview button on the Standard toolbar. When the Web Page Preview dialog box displays, click the OK button. When the browser window displays, if necessary double-click its title bar to maximize the window.**

Publisher opens your Web browser in a separate window and displays the first page of your Web site (Figure 17). The animation and sound play. You may click the links to check navigation.

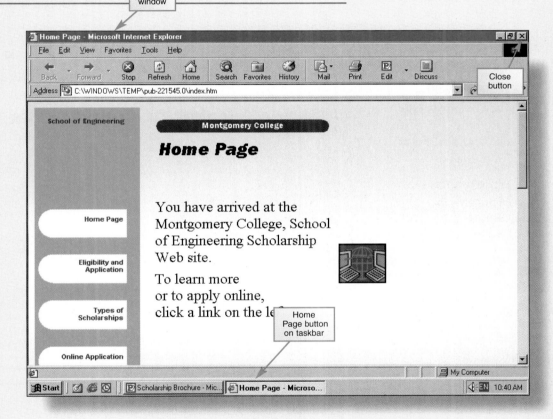
browser window

Home Page button on taskbar

Close button

FIGURE 17

 2 **Close the Web browser window by clicking the Close button.**

The browser window closes and the Publisher window redisplays.

Saving a Web Site

Recall that Publisher suggests saving Web pages and Web sites in separate folders. The folder for the brochure Web site will contain the linked pages, graphics, sounds, and motion clips. You also need to save the publication as a Publisher file for future editing. Perform the steps on the next page to save the Web site files and then save the Publisher file.

 **Other Ways**

1. On File menu click Web Page Preview
2. Press CTRL+SHIFT+B
3. In Voice command mode, say "Web Page Preview"

Steps **To Save the Web Site Files**

1 **If necessary, insert a floppy disk in** drive A. Click File on the menu bar and then click Save as Web Page. Select 3½ Floppy (A:) in the Save in list. Point to the Create New Folder button.

The Save as Web Page dialog box displays (Figure 18).

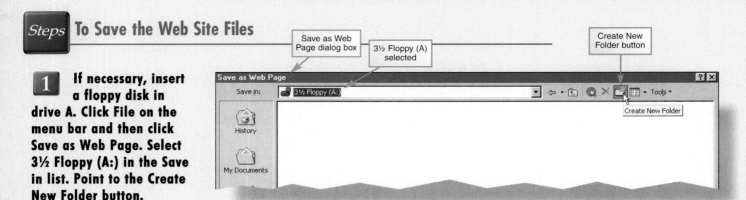

FIGURE 18

2 **Click the Create New Folder button.** When the New Folder dialog box displays, type Web Brochure Files **in the Name text box. Point to the OK button.**

The new folder name displays in the Name text box (Figure 19).

3 **Click the OK button. Click the Save button in the Save as Web Page dialog box.**

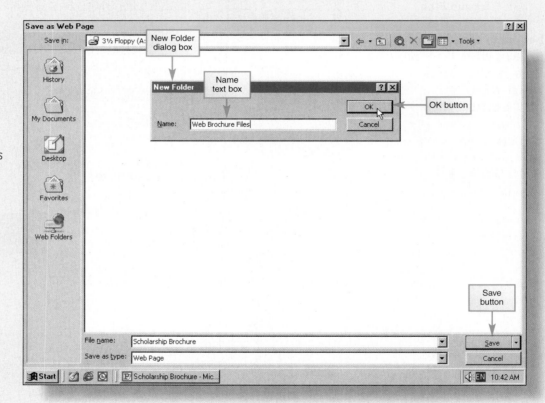

FIGURE 19

Other Ways

1. In Voice command mode, say "File, Save as Web Page"

Talk to your instructor about making this Web site available to others on your network, intranet, or the World Wide Web (see Appendix C). When you publish the site, do not forget to send all the files in your folder so the links, animation, and sound work correctly.

Saving the Publication

You should save the publication itself for future editing. The Web folder contains HTML files, which are not directly accessible in Publisher. It also is a good idea to give the Web version of the brochure a different file name than the print version. Follow these steps to save the publication and then quit Publisher.

TO SAVE THE PUBLICATION AND QUIT PUBLISHER

1 With a floppy disk still in drive A, click File on the menu bar and then click Save As.

2 When the Save As dialog box displays, select 3½ Floppy (A:) in the Save in list.

3 In the File name text box, type Scholarship Web Brochure to save the Web publication with a new name and then click the OK button.

4 Click the Close button on the Publisher title bar.

CASE PERSPECTIVE SUMMARY

The School of Engineering at Montgomery College is pleased with your work on its scholarship Web site. The site is easy to navigate, and the animation, fill effect, and sound create a multimedia enticement to attend the college. The dean verifies the electronic submission policy of the college's Internet service and then posts the pages to the host computer. The brochure looks great on the Web, and the college is eagerly awaiting electronic applications.

Web Feature Summary

This Web Feature introduced you to creating a Web site by saving an existing Publisher publication as a Web site or HTML files. You also edited the Web site properties, text frames, sounds, animation, hyperlinks, and command buttons in anticipation of publishing the brochure to the Web. Finally, you saved all the related files in a folder for later posting.

What You Should Know

Having completed this project, you now should be able to perform the following tasks:

▶ Convert a Brochure to a Web Site *(PUBW 1.04)*
▶ Edit Form Controls *(PUBW 1.11)*
▶ Edit, Move, and Delete Objects on Page 1 *(PUBW 1.04)*
▶ Edit Objects on Pages 2 and 3 *(PUBW 1.05)*
▶ Edit Web Properties *(PUBW 1.09)*
▶ Insert a Graphic from the Extra Content Tab *(PUBW 1.07)*
▶ Move and Delete Objects on Page 4 *(PUBW 1.06)*
▶ Save the Publication and Quit Publisher *(PUBW 1.14)*
▶ Save the Web Site Files *(PUBW 1.14)*
▶ View a Web Site in a Browser *(PUBW 1.13)*

In the Lab

1 Planning Web Sites

Instructions: Start Publisher. Open any existing publication or begin a new blank publication. In the Ask a Question box, type planning web sites and then press the ENTER key. When the list of topics displays, click Plan a Web Site. When the Microsoft Publisher Help window displays, click the Show All button in the top-right corner. Right-click the Help information and then click Print on the shortcut menu. If necessary, when the Print dialog box displays click the All option button, and then click the OK button. Read the information and turn in the printout to your instructor.

2 Creating a Web Site from a Price List Brochure

Problem: Small businesses maintain advertising Web sites, complete with product descriptions, links to manufacturers, price lists, and even maps to their location. Using the Axis Price List Brochure, create a Web site template to show a local company what might be involved in maintaining a Web site.

Instructions: Perform the following tasks.

1. Start Publisher and choose Brochures in the list of publication types. Click Price List under Brochures and then double-click the Axis Price List preview.
2. Print a copy of both pages of the brochure.
3. In the Brochure Options task pane, click the Convert to Web Layout button. When Publisher asks if you want to save the brochure, click the No button.
4. Click to include an Order form. Click the link for Background fill and sound in the task pane. When the Background task pane displays, click the Background sound link. On the General tab, use the Browse button to browse to and select a background sound for the Web site.
5. Enter appropriate keywords and a description.
6. Double-click the graphic on page 1. When the Insert Clip Art task pane displays, click the Clip Organizer link or the Clips Online link. Choose an appropriate animated graphic.
7. At the bottom of page 1, type your school's name and address.
8. On page 4, double-click the Submit button. When the Command Button Properties dialog box displays, click the Form Properties button. Choose to send data to yourself in an e-mail and then enter your e-mail address.
9. Save the file on your floppy disk with the name Web Price List Brochure.
10. Click File on the menu bar and then click Print. Print each page of the site. Compare the printouts of the brochure versus the Web site. Note extra Content items and story placement. Look for blank areas that could display a map. Mark those areas and turn the printout in to your instructor.

3 Creating a Web Page with Hyperlinks

Problem: You have decided to create your own personal Web site using Publisher.

Instructions: Perform the following tasks.

1. Start Publisher, click Web Sites in the list of publication types. Use the design preview of your choice.
2. Personalize the Web site by editing the text frames and graphics. If possible, insert a picture of yourself. Read the Publisher-supplied text in each text box for suggestions on content.
3. Use the Insert Hyperlink button on the Standard toolbar to create a link to your e-mail address, as well as a link to your school.
4. Edit the Web properties to add your name and interests as keywords for the search engines.
5. Add a background sound.
6. Save your publication for posting to the Web. Preview the site using a browser.
7. Ask your instructor for directions on posting your Web page so others may have access to it.

Microsoft Publisher 2002

Personalizing and Customizing Publications with Information Sets

You will have mastered the material in this project when you can:

O B J E C T I V E S

- Start Publisher with a blank publication
- Edit publication margins
- Use layout and ruler guides effectively
- Edit Personal Information Sets and components
- Discuss letterhead production techniques
- Create a letterhead
- Format an object with a gradient fill
- Differentiate among tints, shades, patterns, and textures
- Use the Measurement toolbar to position objects
- Explain character spacing techniques
- Format using the Format Painter
- Insert and edit a logo
- Recolor a graphic
- Describe the various graphic formatting options
- Create a business card
- Create a calendar
- Create an envelope
- Explain the merge process
- Create an address list
- Create a label
- Use field codes
- Merge an address list with a main document

Signs, Emblems, and Logos
Symbols of Success

Signs, emblems, and logos visually symbolize objects, ideas, groups, or features. They represent a language of images that direct, inform, and entertain. Logos are powerful symbols that help establish an identity for your company, organization, or product. Logos have an effect on you even if you are not consciously aware of it. A well-designed business logo can attract attention, reinforce a company's image, and provide a snapshot of a company's personality. Most businesses use their logos consistently on business cards, stationery, envelopes, and invoices.

A desktop publishing program such as Publisher 2002 can help you create business documents that are attractive, effective, and efficient. The complete capabilities of Publisher allow business or home users to create text frames as in word processing software; draw tables, perform mathematical and statistical operations, and embed charts as in spreadsheet software; and build databases for use with mass mailings, billings, and customer accounts as in database software. Merging these features and transferring objects between publications provides an efficient business tool.

Large corporations and small businesses alike realize that their most important assets are their customers, brands, logos, and slogans.

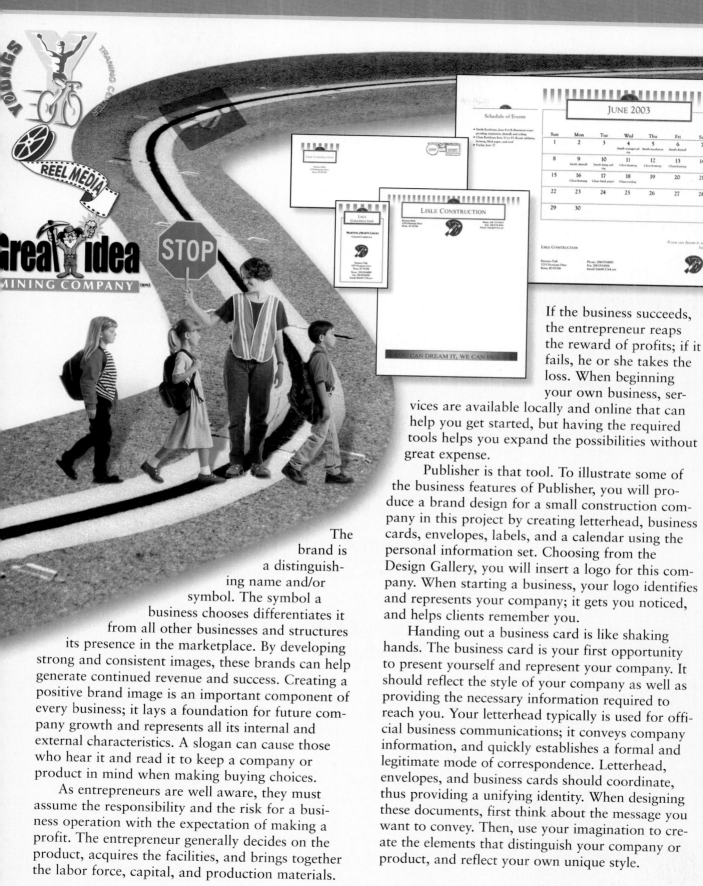

The brand is a distinguishing name and/or symbol. The symbol a business chooses differentiates it from all other businesses and structures its presence in the marketplace. By developing strong and consistent images, these brands can help generate continued revenue and success. Creating a positive brand image is an important component of every business; it lays a foundation for future company growth and represents all its internal and external characteristics. A slogan can cause those who hear it and read it to keep a company or product in mind when making buying choices.

As entrepreneurs are well aware, they must assume the responsibility and the risk for a business operation with the expectation of making a profit. The entrepreneur generally decides on the product, acquires the facilities, and brings together the labor force, capital, and production materials.

If the business succeeds, the entrepreneur reaps the reward of profits; if it fails, he or she takes the loss. When beginning your own business, services are available locally and online that can help you get started, but having the required tools helps you expand the possibilities without great expense.

Publisher is that tool. To illustrate some of the business features of Publisher, you will produce a brand design for a small construction company in this project by creating letterhead, business cards, envelopes, labels, and a calendar using the personal information set. Choosing from the Design Gallery, you will insert a logo for this company. When starting a business, your logo identifies and represents your company; it gets you noticed, and helps clients remember you.

Handing out a business card is like shaking hands. The business card is your first opportunity to present yourself and represent your company. It should reflect the style of your company as well as providing the necessary information required to reach you. Your letterhead typically is used for official business communications; it conveys company information, and quickly establishes a formal and legitimate mode of correspondence. Letterhead, envelopes, and business cards should coordinate, thus providing a unifying identity. When designing these documents, first think about the message you want to convey. Then, use your imagination to create the elements that distinguish your company or product, and reflect your own unique style.

Microsoft Publisher 2002

Personalizing and Customizing Publications with Information Sets

CASE PERSPECTIVE

Lisle Construction, located in Boise, Idaho, is a family owned construction company specializing in remodeling and room additions. In recent months, Lisle Construction has experienced a substantial increase in business as new residents move to this growing community. Marty Lisle, the owner of the company, has purchased several new computers for the office. He would like to publish his business documents in-house. Specifically, the company needs letterhead, business cards, envelopes, and mailing labels.

Because you have desktop publishing experience, you are hired to design the letterhead, business cards, and envelopes for Lisle Construction and then create a database of current customers. Marty also wants a calendar he can update with current construction projects and dates for outside contractors.

You decide to create a Personal Information Set, complete with color scheme and logo for Lisle Construction. You enter the data and address list, and then create the publications using items from the Design Gallery and Clip Organizer.

Introduction

Customizing desktop publications with personal information unique to the business, organization, or individual user expands the possibilities for using Publisher as a complete application product for small businesses. People create large text boxes and use Publisher like a word processor. Others create a table and perform mathematical and statistical operations or embed charts as they would with a spreadsheet. Still others create a database, using Publisher for mass mailings, billings, and customer accounts. Publisher's capability of merging these features and transferring objects between publications makes it an efficient tool in small business offices — without the cost and learning curve of some of the high-end dedicated application software.

Project Four — Creating Business Publications

To illustrate some of the business features of Microsoft Publisher, this project presents a series of steps to create a letterhead, business card, envelope, and calendar using a Personal Information Set for a construction company as shown in Figure 4-1. Additionally, it demonstrates the creation and use of a simple database, the sort a small business would use to keep track of its customers.

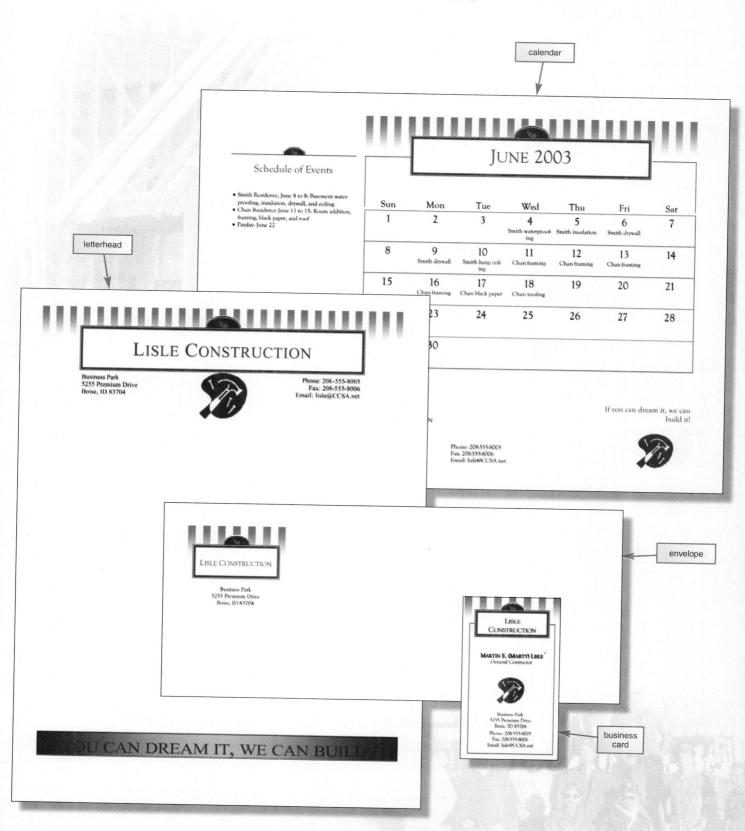

FIGURE 4-1

More About

Letterhead

To look at some samples of letterhead and for more information on content, visit the Publisher 2002 More About Web page (scsite.com/pub2002/more.htm) and then click Letterhead.

Creating Letterhead from Scratch

When you first start Publisher, the New Publication task pane displays. With its many wizards and templates, most users choose an item from the Publication Type list and then begin editing. It is not always the case, however, that a template will fit every situation. Sometimes you want to think through a publication while manipulating objects on a blank page, trying different shapes, colors, pictures, and effects. Other times you may have specific goals for a publication that do not match any of the wizards. In these cases, Publisher makes available a **blank publication** with no preset objects or design, allowing you to start from scratch.

Starting Publisher with a Blank Publication

The New Publication task pane displays a link you click to start with a blank publication; the Standard toolbar's **New button** also displays a blank publication. If you decide to start Publisher each time with a blank page, you can use the Options command on the Tools menu. The preset page options for a blank page include an 8½-by-11-inch publication with one-inch margins, although you can change the size of the paper by clicking Page Setup on the File menu. For the construction company's letterhead, you will use the standard size blank page.

Perform the following steps to start Publisher and choose a blank publication from the task pane.

More About

The Publisher Help System

The best way to become familiar with the Publisher Help system is to use it. Appendix A includes detailed information on the Publisher Help system and exercises that will help you gain confidence using it.

TO START PUBLISHER WITH A BLANK PUBLICATION

1 Click the Start button on the Windows taskbar and then click New Office Document.

2 When the New Office Document dialog box displays, if necessary, click the General tab and then double-click the Blank Publication icon.

3 If the Publisher window is not maximized, double-click its title bar to maximize it.

4 If the New Publication task pane does not display, click View on the menu bar and then click Task Pane.

5 If the Language bar displays, click its Minimize button.

6 Point to the Blank Publication link in the New Publication task pane (Figure 4-2).

7 Click the Blank Publication link. If the New Publication task pane does not close, click its Close button.

8 Zoom to Whole Page.

The blank full page displays in the workspace as shown in Figure 4-3 on page PUB 4.08.

Setting Publication Margins Using Layout and Ruler Guides

Publisher displays each publication with layout guides around the edge of the page as a sort of **margin** (Figure 4-3). This is not to say that you cannot position objects closer to the edge of the paper — if your printer is capable of printing close to the edge. The guides are there to help you edit object placement and alignment.

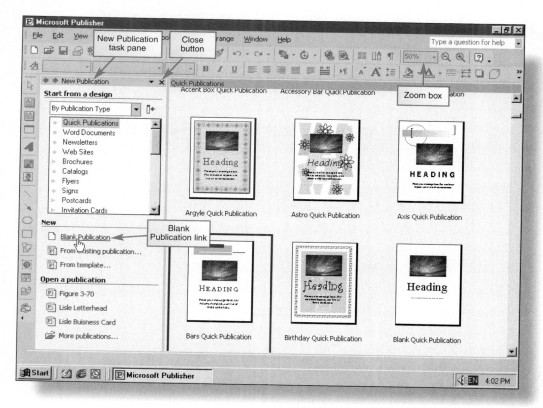

FIGURE 4-2

The size of the **printing area**, or printable region, varies among printers and depends on paper sizes. Most printers have a small area around the edge of the paper that they cannot use. On a desktop printer, the printable area can include the space up tothree-tenths of an inch from the edge; others can require five-tenths to seven-tenths of an inch. If you know your printer's nonprintable area, you can ensure that the printing area is large enough to include everything on each page. If your publication is destined for a commercial printer, you should consult the print professional about printable areas.

The size of the paper also makes a difference. Labels, envelopes, and business cards display a variety of different margins in Publisher depending on the number of copies per sheet and the size of the publication. Web pages, designed for electronic publication rather than print, display layout guides at the edge of the publication page.

Publisher's **boundaries** and **guides** help you align and position objects on the page. To help preview what your publication will look like when printed, the View menu allows you to hide these lines. During the creation/editing process, however, the lines are very helpful. Recall that **layout guides** are the nonprinting blue and pink dotted lines that display on the pages of a publication. These guides reside on the background and repeat on each page of a publication, serving as a template for uniformity in multipage publications. Additionally, when more than one person works on a publication, the final product has a consistent look. The layout guides organize text, pictures, and other objects into straight columns and rows. Green dotted lines are **ruler guides** used for alignment. Added to individual pages on an as-needed basis, ruler guides also help align objects.

Perform the steps on the next page to change the margins to one-half inch and set a ruler guide at two inches by editing the layout and ruler guides.

1 If the rulers do not display, click View on the menu bar and then click Rulers. If the layout guides do not display, click View on the menu bar and then click Boundaries and Guides. Click Arrange on the menu bar. Point to Layout Guides.

The Arrange menu displays (Figure 4-3).

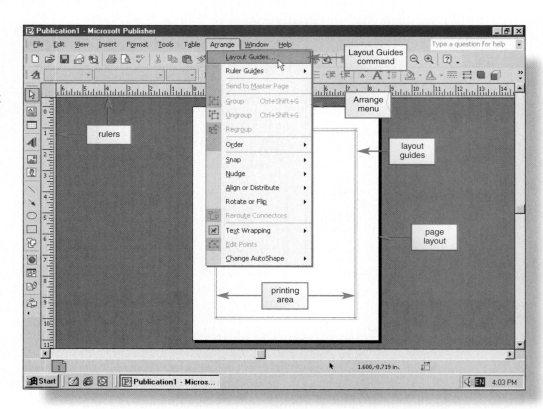

FIGURE 4-3

2 Click Layout Guides. When the Layout Guides dialog box displays, type .5 in the Left text box, and then press the TAB key. Repeat the process typing .5 in each of the other three Margin Guides text boxes and then point to the OK button.

The text boxes display .5 for a one-half inch margin (Figure 4-4).

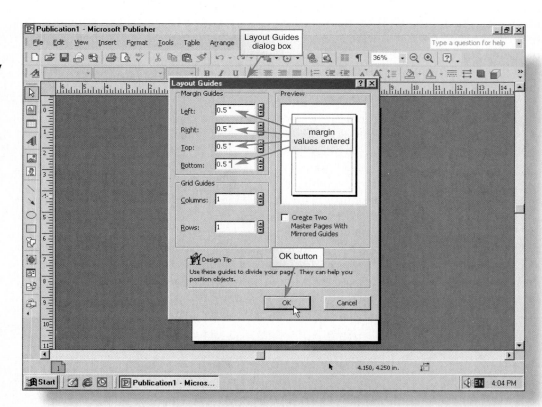

FIGURE 4-4

3 **Click the OK button. Point to the Horizontal Ruler at the top of the workspace.**

The publication displays with a .5-inch margin (Figure 4-5). The mouse pointer changes to a double-headed arrow when positioned on the Horizontal Ruler.

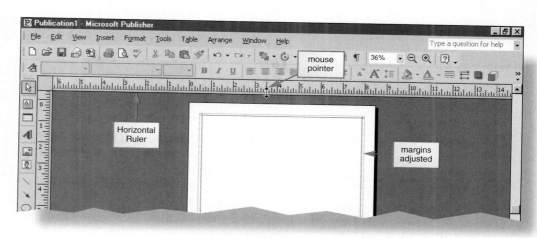

FIGURE 4-5

4 **SHIFT-drag the ruler guide down to the 2-inch mark on the Vertical Ruler and hold it there.**

The green dotted ruler guide displays horizontally two inches from the top of the page (Figure 4-6). The Adjust mouse pointer also displays.

5 **Release the mouse button.**

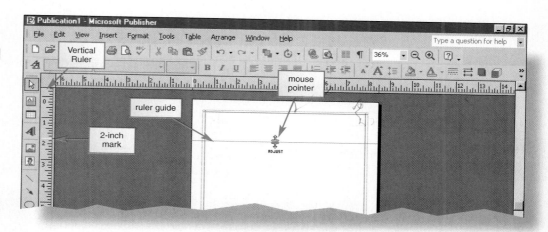

FIGURE 4-6

In addition to the page margins, each object on the page has its own individual boundary margins. For instance, text boxes are preset with a 0.04-inch margin, which means that text on all four sides begins 0.04 inches from the edge of the frame, and thus away from any other object snapped to the text box.

Other Ways

1. To insert ruler guide, on Arrange menu click Ruler Guides
2. In Voice Command mode, say "Arrange, Layout Guides"

Creating a Company Letterhead

In many businesses, **letterhead** is preprinted stationery with important facts about the company and blank space to display the purpose of the correspondence. Letterhead, typically used for official business communication, is an easy way to convey company information to the reader and quickly establish a formal and legitimate mode of correspondence. The company information displays in a variety of places — across the top, down the side, or split between the top and bottom. Although most business letterhead is 8½-by-11-inches, other sizes are becoming more popular, especially with small agencies and not-for-profit organizations.

More About

Online Paper Suppliers

For more information on where to obtain supplies for printing publications such as company letterhead, visit the Publisher 2002 More About Web page (scsite.com/ pub2002/more.htm) and then click Online Office Supplies.

Generally, it is cost effective for companies to outsource their letterhead. Designing the letterhead in-house and then sending the file to a commercial printer saves design consultation time, customization, and money. Large firms order thousands of copies at a time, as the data seldom changes. Black-and-white or spot-color letterhead is more common and less expensive than composite or process color.

Sometimes preprinted letterhead may not be purchased because of its expense, color, or limited quantity. In these cases, companies can design their own letterhead and save it in a file. Employees open the letterhead file, create the rest of their document, and then save the finished product with a new name — thus preserving the original letterhead file. Alternately, businesses can print multiple copies of their letterhead only; and then, using other application software, prepare documents to print on the letterhead paper. All of these types of letterhead production can be used in any combination to produce professional publications.

For the Lisle Construction company, the letterhead will consist of a masthead, personal information components, a logo, and a decorative rectangle across the bottom of the page as shown in Figure 4-1 on page PUB 4.05.

Creating the Letterhead Masthead

The company letterhead contains a masthead, positioned at the top of the page, with the company's color scheme. Perform the following steps to insert a masthead onto the blank page.

Steps **To Create the Letterhead Masthead**

1 **Click the Design Gallery Object button on the Objects toolbar. When the Design Gallery window displays, if necessary, click the Objects by Category tab, and then click Mastheads in the Categories pane. Scroll down to display the Marquee Masthead. Click the Marquee Masthead preview and then point to the Insert Object button in the Design Gallery window.**

The previews of mastheads display (Figure 4-7).

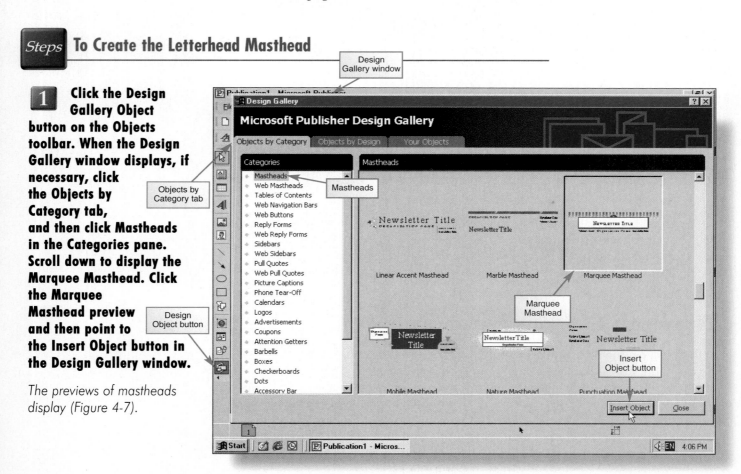

FIGURE 4-7

2 Click the Insert Object button. When the masthead displays in the publication, zoom to 66% and scroll as necessary to display the upper-third of the page layout, as shown in Figure 4-8.

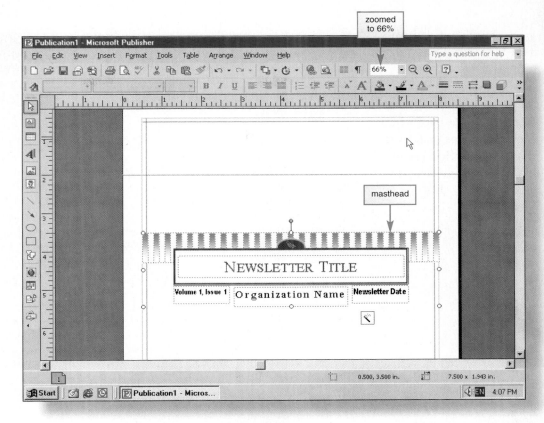

FIGURE 4-8

3 Press CTRL+SHIFT+G to ungroup the object. When the Microsoft Publisher dialog box displays, point to the Yes button.

You will edit the components of the masthead individually (Figure 4-9).

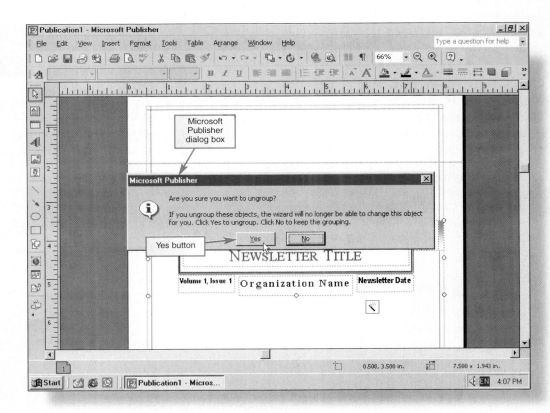

FIGURE 4-9

4 Click the Yes button, click Newsletter Title in the masthead, and then type Lisle Construction to replace the text. Delete each of the three text boxes under the title by right-clicking each one and then, on the shortcut menu, click Delete Object.

The new title displays (Figure 4-10). The masthead displays without the Volume, Organization Name, and Date text boxes.

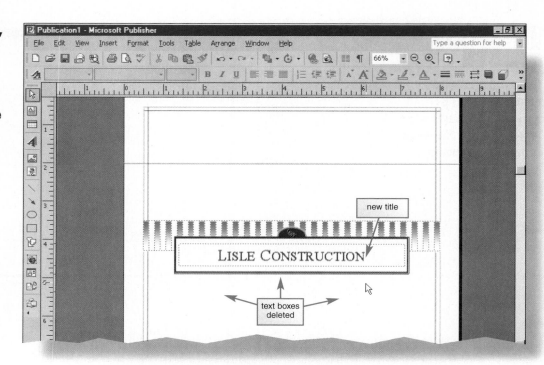

FIGURE 4-10

5 Click a blank part of the page layout and then press CTRL+A to select all of the remaining objects on the page. Press CTRL+SHIFT+G to group the objects. Drag the grouped object upward so that the bottom of the green rectangle displays at the green ruler guide.

The masthead displays snapped to the green ruler guide (Figure 4-11).

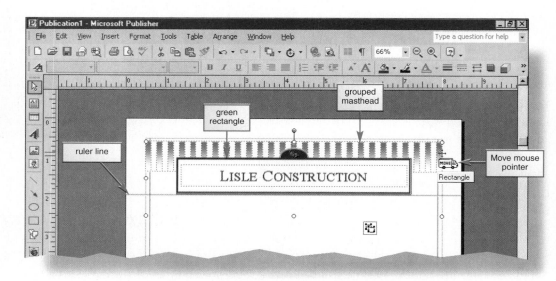

FIGURE 4-11

Other Ways

1. To insert masthead, on Insert menu click Design Gallery Object
2. To group, on Arrange menu click Group
3. To group, select objects, click Group button
4. To ungroup, click Ungroup on shortcut menu

Fill Effects

The next step is to create a rectangle and fill the inside. In Publisher, you can **fill**, or paint, the inside of a drawing object with a color or with an effect. **Fill effects** include gradient (two-toned) colors, textures, patterns, pictures, and tints/shades. Fill effects can be applied to text boxes, shapes, and even WordArt objects in Publisher. Fill effects add subtle contrast and create an illusion of texture and depth.

Publisher suggests using gradient fills to draw attention and heighten interest. A **gradient** is a gradual progression of colors and shades, usually from one color to another color, or from one shade to another shade of the same color. Gradient fills create a sense of movement and add dimension to a publication. A gradient uses tints or shades of one color to create a special pattern of increased shading with another color, usually white. Publisher displays more than 40 available gradients with patterns ranging from stars and swirls, to arrows, to three-dimensional abstractions.

Perform the following steps to draw a rectangle and fill it with a gradient fill effect.

More *About*

Fills

When a background fill is used, gradients, patterns, pictures, and textures are tiled, or repeated, to fill the page or object frame.

Steps **To Create a Gradient Fill**

1 **Zoom to Whole Page. Click the Rectangle button on the Objects toolbar and then drag a rectangle in the middle of the page. After releasing the mouse button, point to the Fill Color button arrow on the Formatting toolbar.**

The rectangle displays selected with its sizing handles (Figure 4-12).

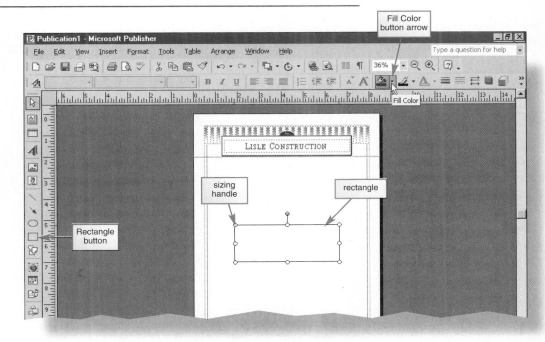

FIGURE 4-12

2 **Click the Fill Color button arrow and then point to Fill Effects in the palette.**

*The Fill Color button arrow displays a **palette** of color buttons and commands (Figure 4-13). Some palettes can become floating toolbars if you drag the move handle.*

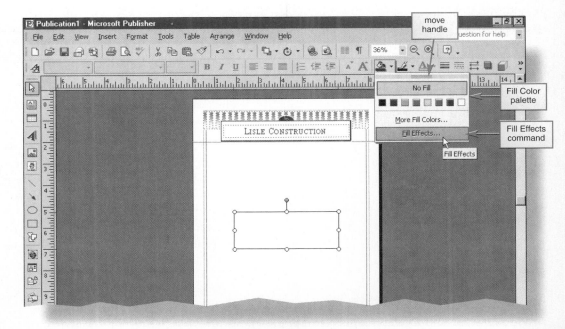

FIGURE 4-13

3 **Click Fill Effects. When the Fill Effects dialog box displays, if necessary click the Gradient tab. Click One color in the Colors area. When the Color 1 box displays, click the Color 1 box arrow and then point to Accent 1 in the Color 1 palette.**

The One color option button is selected (Figure 4-14). The available gradient colors display in the palette.

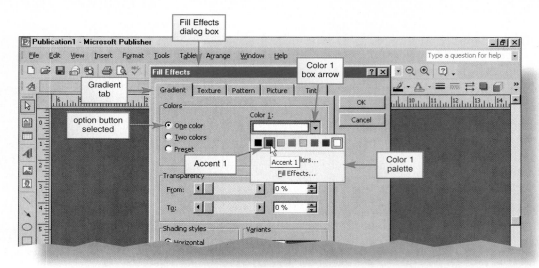

FIGURE 4-14

4 **Click Accent 1. Drag the Dark to Light scroll box all the way to the right. Type 50 in the From text box in the Transparency area. Click Vertical in the Shading styles area and then click the lower-left variant. Point to the OK button.**

The sample of the gradient background for the rectangle displays (Figure 4-15).

5 **Click the OK button.**

The rectangle displays with the gradient fill effect (shown in Figure 4-16 on page PUB 4.16).

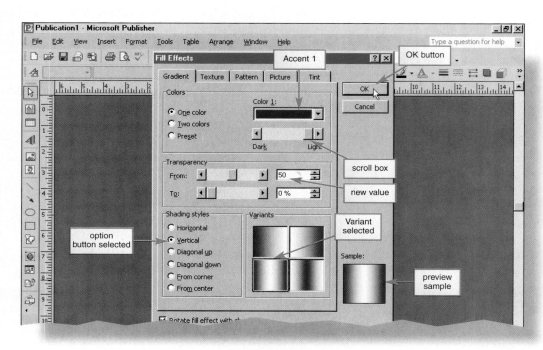

FIGURE 4-15

Other **Ways**

1. Double-click rectangle, click Colors and Line tab, choose settings
2. Right-click rectangle, click Format AutoShape, click Colors and Lines tab, choose settings
3. On Format menu click AutoShape, click Colors and Lines tab, choose settings
4. In Voice Command mode, say, "Format, Autoshape"

A **texture fill** is a combination of color and patterns without gradual shading. Publisher provides 24 different textures from which you may choose.

Patterns include variations of repeating designs such as lines, stripes, checks, and bricks. Publisher uses the base color and a second color to create the pattern. Patterns destined for commercial printing are usually more expensive than tints and shades, because they increase the time it takes to image the file to film.

You can use a **picture fill** to insert clip art or your own graphic to create a unique and personal texture in a Publisher object.

A **tint** is a gradation of a color with reference to its mixture with white. A **shade,** on the other hand, is a mixture of a base color and black. You use tints and shades to create a more sophisticated color scheme. Tints and shades are incremented in 10-percent intervals. For example, the first tint of red is nine parts red and 1 part white. Therefore, Publisher displays 10 tints and 10 shades of each basic color on the Tint sheet.

Using the Measurement Toolbar

To place the rectangle precisely, rather than drag and resize, you will use the Measurement toolbar to enter the exact values for width, height, left, and top of the rectangle. The **Measurement toolbar** not only sets the location and size of an object, but sets the angle of rotation, as well. If the object is text, the Measurement toolbar offers additional character spacing or typesetting options. Accessed either through the View menu or by double-clicking one of the Object boxes on the status bar, the Measurement toolbar is a floating toolbar with nine text boxes. Entries can be typed in each box or chosen by clicking the appropriate arrows. Table 4-1 lists the boxes available on the Measurement toolbar, their purpose, and their preset unit of measurement.

Table 4-1	Measurement Toolbar Boxes		
TOOLBAR SYMBOL	BOX NAME	PURPOSE	PRESET UNIT OF MEASUREMENT
x	Horizontal Position	Horizontal distance from the upper-left corner of the page to the upper-left corner of the object	Inches
y	Vertical Position	Vertical distance from the upper-left corner of the page to the upper-left corner of the object	Inches
(width icon)	Width	Width of object	Inches
(height icon)	Height	Height of object	Inches
(rotation icon)	Rotation	Rotate the object counterclockwise from the original orientation	Degrees
aaa	Text Scaling	Width of the text	Percent
A	Tracking	General space between characters	Percent
AW	Kerning	Subtle space between paired characters	Point size
A	Line Spacing	Vertical spacing between lines of selected text	Space (1 for single)

The lower four boxes on the Measurement toolbar, edit text only; however, they are very useful because they provide many possible combinations for spacing characters. Early typesetters were limited to just a few typefaces and sizes of type. The only way to change the spacing between characters was to insert or remove metal on each side of a piece of type. To stretch a title across the top of a page, they inserted several equally sized pieces of metal between each character. To position characters closer together, some typesetters actually used a knife to shave bits of lead from the sides of wide characters. The resulting overhang was called a **kern**.

In modern desktop publishing, the word, font, essentially has eliminated the word typeface, font size has replaced pitch and point in many instances; tracking and scaling have taken the place of proportional spacing; and kern has become a verb referring to both the subtraction and addition of subtle spacing.

Scaling, often called shrinking or stretching, is the process of changing the width of characters in text boxes. Recall that the WordArt toolbar has a button for scaling; however, scaling also is available for any text box using the Measurement toolbar or, alternately, using Character Spacing on the Format menu. **Tracking**, on the other hand, refers to the adjustment of the general spacing between characters. Tracking text compensates for the spacing irregularities caused when you make text much bigger or much smaller. For example, smaller type is easier to read when it has been tracked loosely. Tracking both maintains the original height of the font and overrides adjustments made by justification of the margins.

Kerning, or **track kerning**, is a special form of tracking related to pairs of characters that can appear too close together, even with standard tracking. For instance, certain letters such as T, V, W, and Y, often are kerned when they are preceded or followed by A, a, e, or o. Automatic kerning is applied to 14-point

Rotating

The Rotation text box on the Measurements toolbar allows you to enter any degree of rotation from -360 to +360. Positive numbers rotate counterclockwise. Negative numbers rotate clockwise and then are converted on the toolbar to their complemented angles. For example, an entry of -90 is converted to 270 (360 minus 90) and then the object is rotated 90 degrees clockwise. You can rotate any object or grouped objects, including text boxes, for special effects.

text and above. Text in smaller point size usually does not need to be kerned. With manual kerning Publisher lets you choose from normal, expanded, and condensed kerning for special effects. Kerning fine-tunes the amount of space between specific character pairs that would otherwise appear to be too close together or too far apart.

Perform the following steps to position the rectangle precisely using the Measurement toolbar. Later in this project, you will track text using the Measurement toolbar.

Steps To Position Objects Using the Measurement Toolbar

1 With the rectangle selected, double-click the Object Size box on the status bar. When the Measurement toolbar displays, point to the Horizontal Position text box.

The Measurement toolbar displays with five available text boxes (Figure 4-16). The Horizontal Position text box displays an x label.

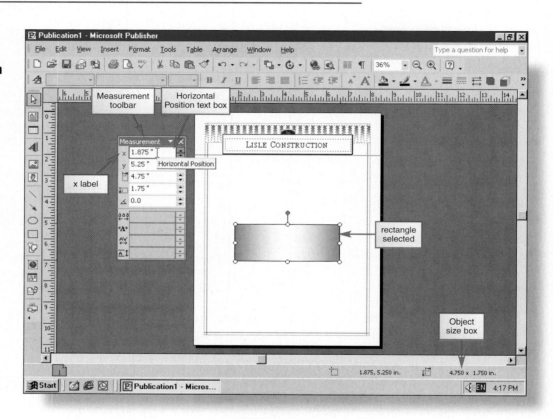

FIGURE 4-16

2 Type .5 and then press the TAB key.

The new value for the horizontal position displays (Figure 4-17). The rectangle moves to .5 inch from the left edge of the page layout. The Vertical Position text box is selected.

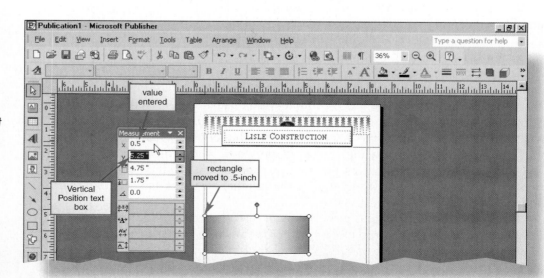

FIGURE 4-17

3 Type the values shown in Figure 4-18, pressing the TAB key to move from box to box. When finished, point to the Close button on the Measurement title bar.

The rectangle displays according to the entered locations (Figure 4-18).

4 Click the Close button on the Measurement title bar.

The Measurement toolbar closes.

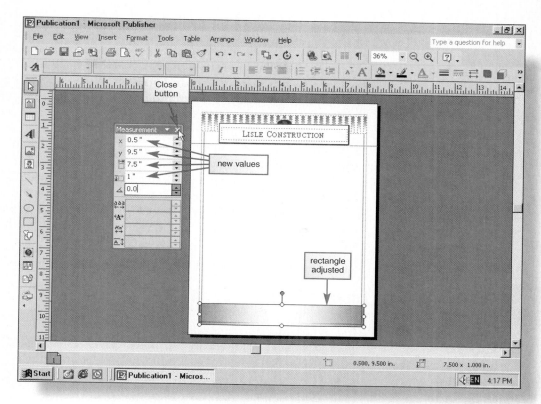

FIGURE 4-18

Now that the masthead and rectangle are complete, you will enter the Lisle Construction company information in Publisher.

Personal Information Sets

A **Personal Information Set** is a set of fields, or components, containing information about a person, a business, or an organization — components that Publisher maintains for use across publications. Many of the templates and wizards create personal information text boxes or components that incorporate the data from the Personal Information Set. Publications created from scratch also can integrate a Personal Information Set by including one or more of the components in the publication. For example, you can save your name, address, and telephone number in the Personal Information Set. It then automatically displays when inserted by you or by a wizard. Thus, a company could save its organizational data for use in a variety of publications.

Publisher provides four different, independent Personal Information Sets for use in business and home: Primary Business, Secondary Business, Other Organization, and Home/Family. Although every new publication has the Primary Business Personal Information Set selected by default, it is easy to apply a different Personal Information Set to the publication, as shown on the following pages.

Other Ways

1. On View menu point to Toolbars, then click Measurement
2. Right-click menu bar or toolbar, click Measurement
3. In Voice Command mode, say "View, Toolbars, Measurement"

More About

Personal Information Sets

If you want Publisher to update the Personal Information Set automatically from your publication, click Tools on the menu bar, and then click Options. Click the User Assistance tab and then click Update personal information when saving.

Editing the Personal Information Set

Each Personal Information Set contains eight components: Personal Name, Job Title, Address, Organization Name, Phone/fax/e-mail, Tag Line, Logo, and Color Scheme. When you first install Publisher, the personal information components contain preset, generic information for each of the four sets. If you edit a text box within a publication that contains personal information, you change that publication only. To affect changes for all future publications, you edit the components through the Edit menu. You can edit the information set at any time — before, during, or after performing other publication tasks.

Perform the following steps to edit the Secondary Business Personal Information Set. For purposes of this project, using the Secondary Business Personal Information Set will allow student labs and network installations to maintain their personal information. You will add text and a color scheme. The logo will be inserted later in the project.

 To Edit a Personal Information Set

1   **Click Edit on the menu bar and then point to Personal Information.**

The Edit menu displays (Figure 4-19).

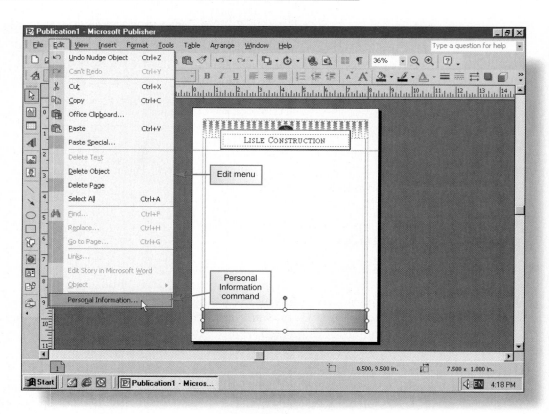

FIGURE 4-19

2 **Click Personal Information. When the Personal Information dialog box displays, if necessary, click Secondary Business and then press the TAB key.**

The Personal Information Set for the Secondary Business displays (Figure 4-20). The Name text box also is selected.

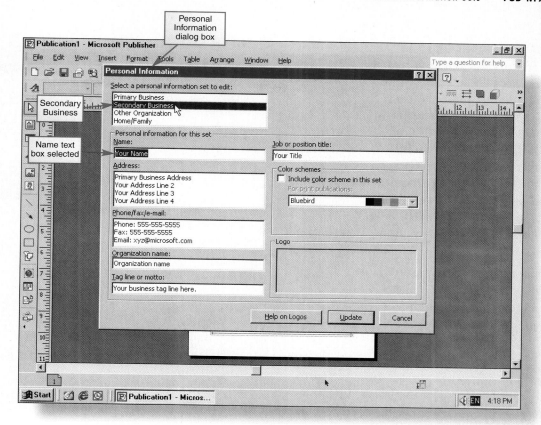

FIGURE 4-20

3 **Type** Martin E. (Marty) Lisle **in the Name text box and then press the TAB key.**

The new name displays in the Name text box (Figure 4-21). The Address text box is selected.

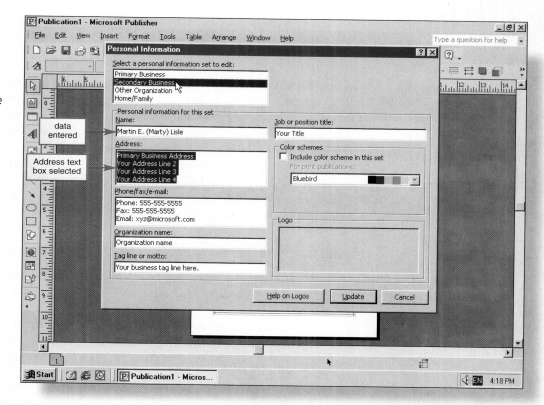

FIGURE 4-21

4 Repeat Step 3 to enter the data from Figure 4-22 in each of the text boxes. Press the TAB key to progress from one text box to the next. Click Include color scheme in this set to select it. Click the For print publications drop-down arrow and then click Lagoon in the list. Point to the Update button.

The completed text boxes display. The Lagoon color scheme will be included in the Secondary Business Personal Information Set.

5 Click the Update button.

The publication again displays.

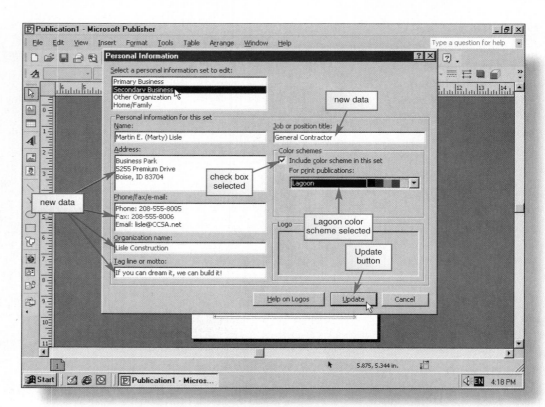

FIGURE 4-22

You can edit any of Publisher's four Personal Information Sets in the Personal Information dialog box. It is not necessary to save the publication in order to save the changes to the set. When you click the Update button, Publisher uses the displayed set in the current publication.

The four different Personal Information Sets allow you to maintain alternate information about your business; a second or related business, such as a major supplier or home business; an outside organization for which you maintain information, such as scouting or sports; and your personal home/family information.

To remove a personal information component in a single publication, you can delete it from the publication itself. To remove a personal information component permanently, you must delete its text from the Personal Information dialog box.

Inserting and Formatting Personal Information Components

The letterhead will contain three text box components from the Secondary Business Personal Information Set: the Address, the Phone/fax/e-mail, and the Tag Line. When you insert a component, Publisher places it in the center of the screen with a preset font and font size. Then, you may move it and format the text as necessary. Applied formatting affects the current publication only.

Perform the following steps to insert and format personal information components in the letterhead.

More *About*

The Workspace

If the buttons and toolbars on your screen are distracting to you, or if you merely want to increase the size of the workspace, you can hide the buttons and toolbars. On the View menu, point to Toolbars, and then click each toolbar name on the Toolbars submenu to turn it on or off. You also can hide the rulers using the View menu, thus increasing the size of the workspace.

Steps **To Insert and Format Personal Information Components**

1 **Zoom to Page Width. Click Insert on the menu bar, point to Personal Information, and then point to Address on the Personal Information submenu.**

The Insert menu and the Personal Information submenu display (Figure 4-23).

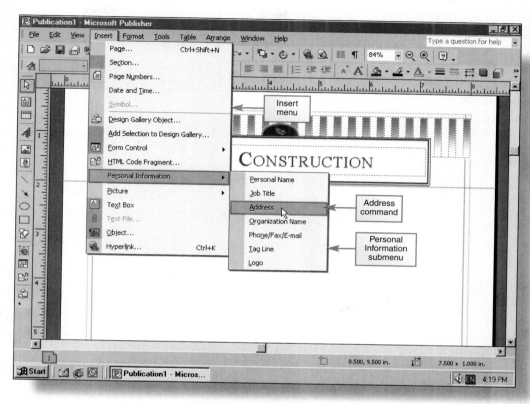

FIGURE 4-23

2 **Click Address. When the text box displays, drag it to the green ruler line as shown in Figure 4-24.**

The personal information data for Address displays (Figure 4-24).

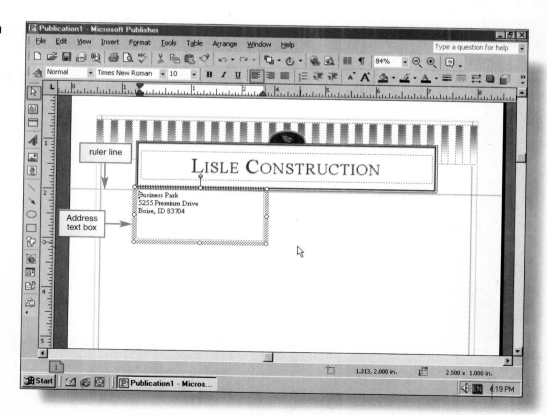

FIGURE 4-24

3 **Click Insert on the menu bar, point to Personal Information, and then click Phone/Fax/E-mail on the Personal Information submenu. When the text box displays, drag it upward to the green ruler line as shown in Figure 4-25.**

The personal information data for Phone/fax/e-mail displays (Figure 4-25).

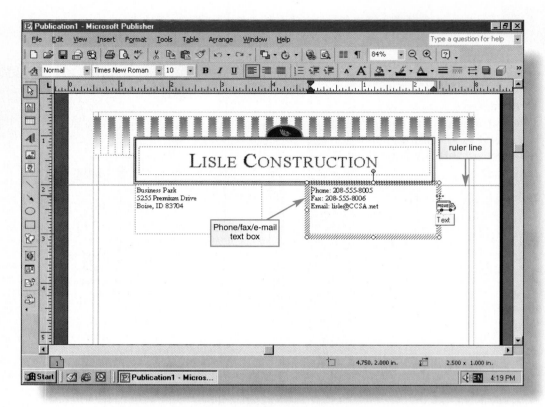

FIGURE 4-25

4 **Press CTRL+A to select all the text. Click the Align Right button on the Formatting toolbar.**

The text displays right-justified within the text box (Figure 4-26).

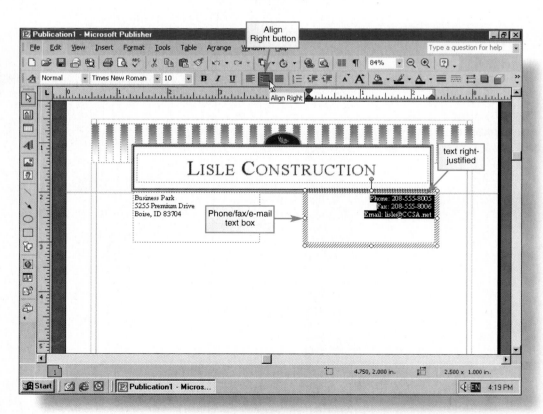

FIGURE 4-26

5 Click Insert on the menu bar, point to Personal Information, and then click Tag Line on the Personal Information submenu.

The personal information data for the company's tag line displays (Figure 4-27). The Text in Overflow button displays.

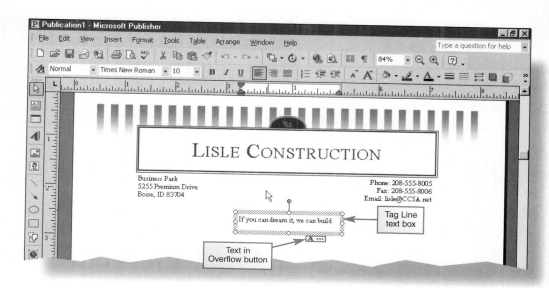

FIGURE 4-27

Formatting with the Format Painter

If you have a text box containing a font, size, and color that you would like to use in another text box, you can use the **Format Painter** to copy the format and apply it to the second text box. In the Lisle letterhead, you will copy the formatting from the letterhead title to the text box that contains the company's tag line.

Perform the following steps to change the text box to Best Fit and then insert and format the personal information tag line using the Format Painter.

Steps To Format the Tag Line with the Format Painter

1 Right-click the tag line text box. On the shortcut menu, point to Change Text, point to AutoFit Text, and then click Best Fit. Click the letterhead title, Lisle Construction, and then point to the Format Painter button on the Standard toolbar.

The Format Painter will copy the formatting of the letterhead title (Figure 4-28).

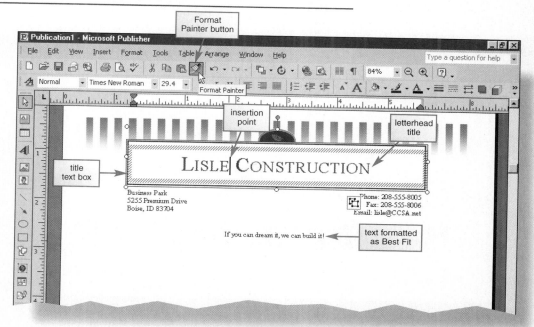

FIGURE 4-28

Microsoft **Publisher 2002**

2 **Click the Format Painter button and then drag through the text in the tag line.**

The tag line displays formatted the same as the letterhead title (Figure 4-29). Because the text box is formatted as Best Fit, the font size is reduced.

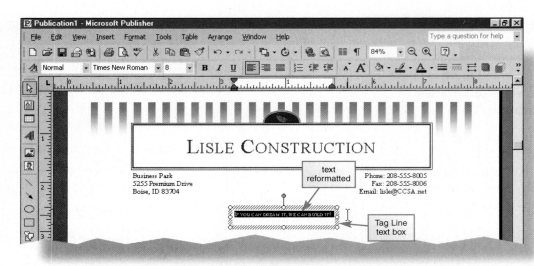

FIGURE 4-29

1. In Voice Command mode, say "Format Painter"

You can place a component many times in a publication, as long as you use separate text boxes each time. If you change the information in a personal information component, all components of that type will change or synchronize in the current publication. For example, if you edit the address in a personal information e-mail text box, all instances of that component will change. If you do not want all the components to change, after editing, click the Undo button on the Standard toolbar to cancel the synchronization.

To finish editing the tag line, perform the following steps to use the Measurement toolbar not only to place the text box in the correct location on the page and enlarge it, but also to scale and track the text.

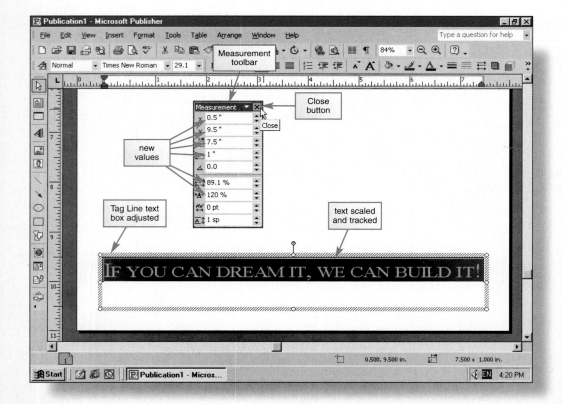

TO FINISH EDITING THE TAG LINE

1 With the text in the Tag Line text box still selected, double-click the Object Size box on the status bar.

2 When the Measurement toolbar displays, enter the values shown in Figure 4-30. Point to the Close button on the Measurement toolbar.

3 Click the Close button. Click outside the text box to remove the selection.

FIGURE 4-30

Editing any personal information component except the logo changes the current publication only. It does not change the data in the Personal Information dialog box, nor does it change other publications using the component. When you save a publication, Publisher asks whether to update the logo, as you will see in the next series of steps.

The Company Logo

The letterhead for Lisle Construction contains a logo of a hammer. The logo is placed in the center of the masthead between the two personal information components. You will insert a logo and then choose one with only a picture and no text. Objects such as logos, or objects from the Design Gallery typically have a wizard associated with them. These objects display a **smart object wizard button**, that when clicked, offers you more choices to format the object.

Perform the following steps to insert a logo in the publication and use its smart object wizard button.

More About

Logos in Information Sets

If you want to insert a logo into one of the four personal information sets, you should click Insert on the menu bar, point to Personal Information, and then click Logo. Once inserted, you can edit a logo's picture and text. When you save the publication, Publisher will ask if you want to save the logo to the Personal Information Set. Logos from the Design Gallery are not placed automatically into the information set.

Steps **To Insert a Logo**

1 **Zoom to Page Width. Click Insert on the menu bar. Point to Personal Information and then point to Logo on the Personal Information submenu.**

The Personal Information submenu displays (Figure 4-31).

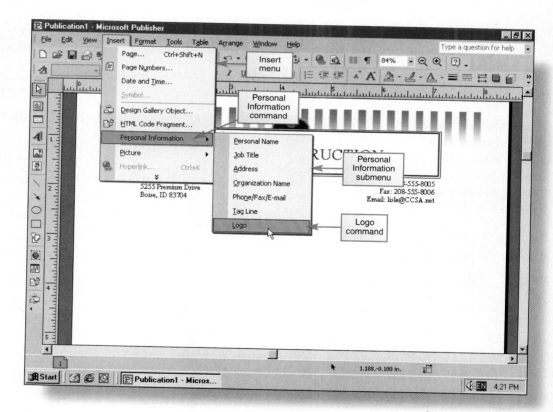

FIGURE 4-31

2 Click Logo. When the logo displays in the publication, point to the Wizard: Click to start button.

The logo placeholder displays in the publication (Figure 4-32). If the logo has been previously edited, it may display a different picture or different text. The smart object wizard button displays a wizard's wand. The ScreenTip displays instructions.

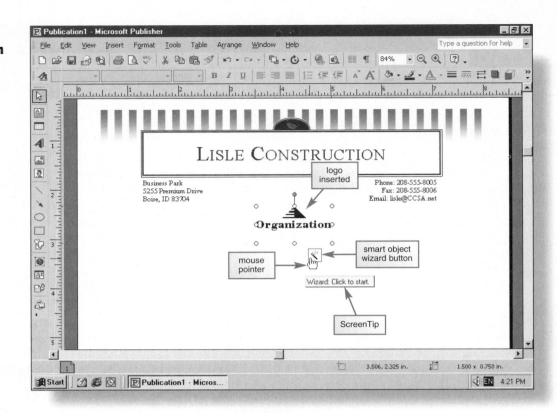

FIGURE 4-32

3 Click the smart object wizard button. When the Logo Designs task pane displays, point to the Logo Options link.

The Logo Designs task pane displays different logo designs (Figure 4-33).

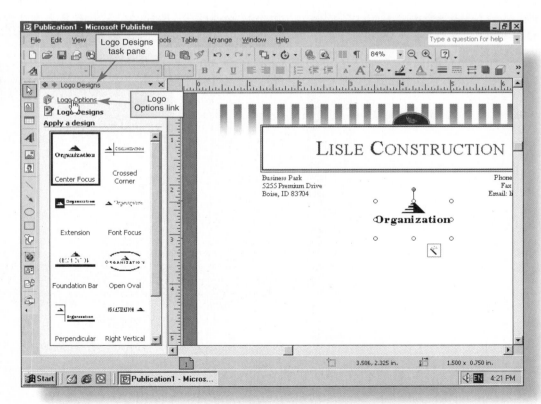

FIGURE 4-33

4 **Click Logo Options. When the options display, click Inserted Picture.**

The graphic changes to a picture without text (Figure 4-34).

5 **Click the Close button.**

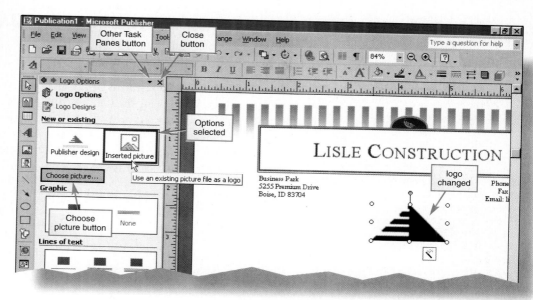

FIGURE 4-34

The Choose picture button (Figure 4-34) allows you to choose picture files saved on your storage devices. To choose a picture from the Clip Organizer, perform the following steps.

SELECTING A NEW GRAPHIC FOR THE LOGO

1 On the task pane title bar, click the Other Task Panes button (shown in Figure 4-34) and then click Insert Clip Art in the list. When the Insert Clip Art task pane displays, type `tools` in the Search text text box, and then click the Search button.

2 When the graphics display, find a black and white drawing of a tool similar to the one shown in Figure 4-35.

3 Point to the graphic, and then click its button. Click Insert on the button menu. If the old graphic still displays, right-click it and then click Delete Object on the shortcut menu.

4 Close the Insert Clip Art task pane by clicking its Close button.

5 Resize the graphic to approximately 1-inch square. Drag the graphic so it displays centered below the letterhead title.

The new graphic displays in the publication as shown in Figure 4-35.

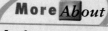

Deleting Logos

If you change your mind, Publisher will allow you to clear the logo from a publication but not delete it from the set. Logos in the information sets are stored in an application data folder for Microsoft Office with file names such as Biz1lgo7.jsp, Org1Lgo2.jsp, etc.

FIGURE 4-35

The next step is to recolor the graphic to match the Lagoon color scheme.

More About

Color Palettes

If your color palette contains fewer colors than shown in this book, then your system may be using a different color palette setting. The figures in this book were created using High Color (16 bit). To check your color palette setting, return to the desktop, right-click the desktop, click Properties on the shortcut menu, click the Settings tab, and locate the Colors drop-down box.

Recoloring Graphics

The graphic for Lisle Construction is a hammer colored green to match the color scheme of the letterhead. **Recoloring** means making a large-scale color change to the entire graphic. When chosen, the color applies to all parts of the graphic, with the option of leaving the black parts black. It is an easy way to convert a color graphic to a black and white line drawing in order to print more clearly. The reverse is also true; if you have a black and white graphic, you can convert it to any one color, as well as to a fill effect.

Perform the following steps to recolor the graphic.

 To Recolor a Graphic

1 **Right-click the graphic. On the shortcut menu, click Format Picture. When the Format Picture dialog box displays, if necessary click the Picture tab. Point to the Recolor button.**

The Format Picture dialog box displays (Figure 4-36).

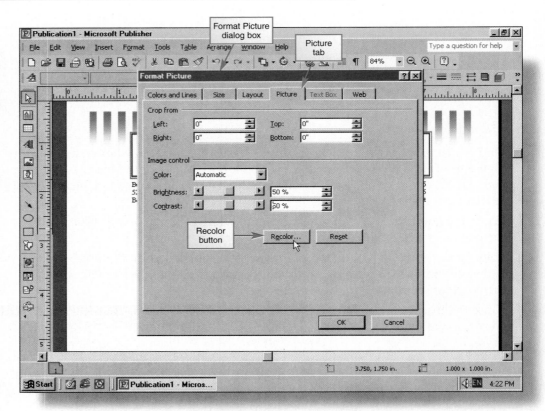

FIGURE 4-36

2 **Click the Recolor button. When the Recolor Picture dialog box displays, click the Color box arrow and then point to Accent 1 in the list.**

The green color from the color scheme will replace the black parts of the graphic (Figure 4-37).

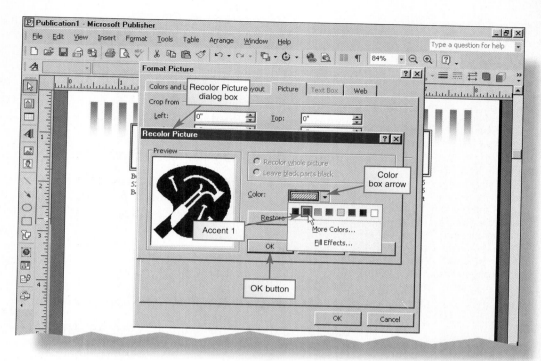

FIGURE 4-37

3 **Click Accent 1. Click the OK button in the Recolor Picture dialog box. Click the OK button in the Format Picture dialog box.**

The graphic displays green (Figure 4-38).

FIGURE 4-38

Other graphic effects you can apply to pictures include scaling, cropping, brightness, and contrast. **Scaling**, when it applies to graphics, means changing the vertical or horizontal size of the graphic by a percentage. Scaling can create interesting graphic effects. For example, a square graphic could become a long thin graphic suitable for use as a single border, if the scale height were increased to 200% and the scale width were reduced to 50%. Caricature drawings and intentionally distorted photographs routinely use scaling. Used for resizing, scaling is appropriate for subtle changes to make a graphic fit in tight places.

Cropping is cutting out part of a graphic. When cropping is chosen, Publisher changes the mouse pointer to the Scissor icon allowing you to cut from any of the

---

Other Ways

1. On Format menu click Picture
2. On Picture toolbar click Format Picture button
3. In Voice Command mode, say "Format, Picture"

Graphic Drawing Programs

Publisher supports the direct editing of objects drawn in Microsoft Paint, Microsoft PhotoDraw, Microsoft Photo Editor, MS Draw, Microsoft Picture It!, and others. Instead of inserting the object as a picture, you use the Paste Special command on the Edit menu. The object then can be linked or embedded to launch the drawing application when you edit the graphic. See the Integration Project for examples of object linking and embedding (OLE).

eight sizing handles. Additionally, cropping can cut down a large graphic in order to focus on a specific part, or eliminate a border or caption that came with the picture.

Using the Picture sheet (Figure 4-36 on page PUB 4.28), you can increase the contrast or brightness of a graphic. **Contrast** is the saturation or intensity of the color, the higher the contrast percentage, the more intense the color. **Brightness** is the amount of black or white added to the color. The higher the brightness percentage, the more white is added.

Saving and Printing the Letterhead

The Lisle Construction company letterhead is complete. In order for the logo to become part of the Personal Information Set you used a logo object from the Design Gallery and now must save the publication with the edited logo.

TO SAVE AND PRINT THE LETTERHEAD

1 Insert your floppy disk into drive A.

2 Click the Save button on the Standard toolbar.

3 When the Save As dialog box displays, type Lisle Letterhead in the File name text box. Do not press the ENTER key.

4 Click the Save in box arrow and then click 3½ Floppy (A:).

5 Click the Save button in the Save As dialog box.

6 When a message displays asking if you want to save the logo, click the Yes button.

7 Click the Print button on the Standard toolbar.

Publisher saves the publication on a floppy disk in drive A with the file name, Lisle Letterhead, and then prints a copy on the printer. The letterhead is shown in Figure 4-1 on page PUB 4.05.

The logo is saved with the publication and becomes part of the Personal Information Set for the Primary Business. Publisher creates a logo file named BIZ1LGO7.JSP, stores it in the default folder for Microsoft Office Applications, and associates it with the Personal Information Set, which means that the set will always look to that file for the logo. Each of the four Personal Information Sets can contain a different logo.

Finally, before you start the business card publication, close the letterhead file without quitting Publisher.

TO CLOSE A PUBLICATION WITHOUT QUITTING PUBLISHER

1 Click File on the menu bar and then click Close.

Publisher closes the letterhead but does not exit.

Printer Problems

If your printer stops short of printing the entire page, resulting in only the top portion of the publication printing, it may be a memory problem, sometimes called printer overrun. Some printers do not have enough memory to print a wide variety of images and color. Consider printing a single page at a time, changing the color scheme to black and white, printing the text and graphics separately on the same printed page, or optimizing the printer memory.

Business Cards

Another way companies are saving money on publishing costs is by designing their own business cards. A **business card** is a small publication, usually 3½-by-2-inches, printed on heavy stock paper. It usually contains the name, title, business, and address information for an employee, as well as a logo, distinguishing graphic, or color to draw attention to the card. Many employees want their telephone, pager, and fax numbers on their business cards in addition to their e-mail and Web page addresses, so that colleagues and customers can reach them quickly.

Business cards can be saved as files to send to commercial printers or printed by desktop color printers on special perforated paper.

The Business Card Wizard

Because the Personal Information Set contains information about Lisle Construction company, using a business card template is the quickest way to create a business card. Not only does the template set the size and shape of a typical business card, it also presets page and printing options for the easiest production.

The next sequence of steps uses the New Publication task pane to produce a business card for the owner at Lisle Construction company. The created template will automatically use information from the Personal Information Set edited earlier in this project.

TO CREATE A BUSINESS CARD

1 Click File on the menu bar and then click New.

2 When the New Publication task pane displays, scroll down in the By Publication Type list and then click Business Cards. If necessary, click Plain Paper.

3 Scroll down in the Plain Paper Business Cards preview pane and then double-click the Marquee Business Card preview.

4 If the Business Card Options task pane does not display, click Format on the menu bar and then click Business Card Options.

5 Click Edit on the menu bar, and then click Personal Information. When the Personal Information dialog box displays, click Secondary Business. Click the Update button and then close the Personal Information dialog box.

The Personal Information components display in the business card, as does the Lisle logo (Figure 4-39).

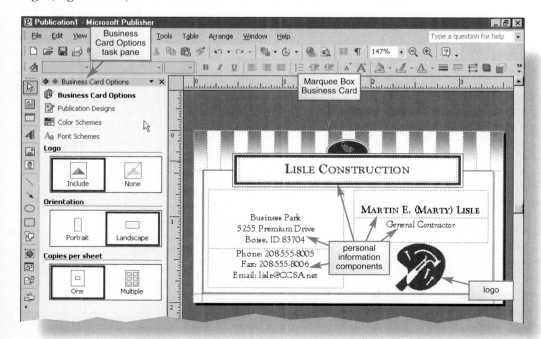

FIGURE 4-39

Editing the Business Card

The template created from the New Publication task pane uses information from the Secondary Business Personal Information Set. The wizard places typical business card fields in appropriate places in the publication. Editing the layout customizes the business card even further. The term **layout** refers to both the process and the result of planning and arranging objects in a publication. Sending objects behind other objects, layering, and aligning objects are part of editing the layout.

The **Business Card Options task pane** displays choices for logo, orientation, and copies. The following steps edit the orientation of the business card and change the number of copies per sheet.

Steps **To Edit the Business Card Orientation**

1 In the Orientation area of the Business Card Options task pane, click Portrait. Click Multiple in the Copies per sheet area.

The orientation change is made in the workspace (Figure 4-40). The Copies per sheet change will take effect when you print.

2 Click the Close button on the Business Card Options task pane title bar.

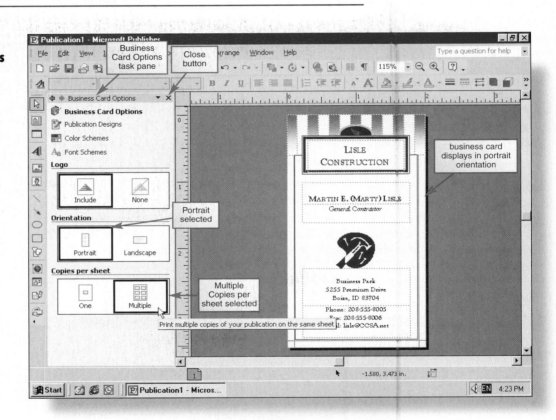

FIGURE 4-40

Other **Ways**

1. On Format menu click Business Card Options
2. In Voice Command mode, say "Format, Business Card Options"

Saving, Printing, and Closing the Business Card

The business card is complete, and you are ready to save and print it. If you have perforated paper available, the Page Options button in the Print dialog box contains option buttons to customize the number of cards per sheet.

Follow these steps to save, print, and then close the business card publication.

TO SAVE, PRINT, AND CLOSE THE BUSINESS CARD

1 Insert your floppy disk into drive A.

2 Click the Save button on the Standard toolbar.

3 When the Save As dialog box displays, type `Lisle Business Card` in the File name text box. Do not press the ENTER key.

4 If necessary, click the Save in box arrow and then click 3½ Floppy (A:).

5 Click the Save button in the Save As dialog box.

6 Click the Print button on the Standard toolbar.

7 Click File on the menu bar and then click Close.

Publisher saves the publication on a floppy disk in drive A with the file name, Lisle Business Card, and then prints a copy on the printer. The business card is shown in Figure 4-1 on page PUB 4.05.

Calendars

Publisher includes Calendars in its list of publication types and in the Design Gallery, as objects that can be added to other publications. **Calendars** are a popular way for businesses to keep track of events and schedules. Calendars are used in all kinds of businesses including such applications as a work schedules, school lunch calendars, sporting events, and appointments. Publisher has more than 20 different styles of calendars from which you can choose. Calendars are a special kind of table object in Publisher. A **table** uses rows and columns, similarly to a spreadsheet, to display organized data. Calendars represent the weeks of the month in rows, and the days of the week in columns. The intersection of a row and a column is called a **cell**, which displays the numeric day of the month. You can add other objects, such as text or graphics, to a cell.

Creating a Custom Calendar

The Lisle Construction company calendar will display scheduled remodeling jobs. The calendar will include the days of the month of June, the jobs, and the job sites.

Perform the steps on the next page to create the calendar.

Microsoft **Publisher 2002**

Steps **To Create a Calendar**

1 **Click File on the menu bar and then click New. When the New Publication task pane displays, scroll down to click Calendars. Click Full Page. Scroll down in the preview pane and then double-click the Marquee Calendar preview.**

The calendar displays in the workspace (Figure 4-41). Your date may differ.

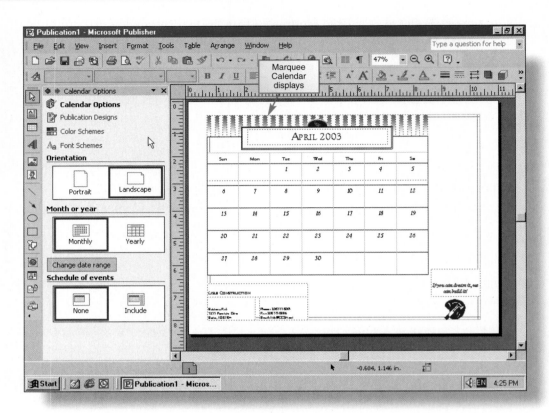

FIGURE 4-41

2 **If the Calendar Options task pane does not display, click Format on the menu bar and then click Calendar Options. In the Calendar Options task pane, click Include in the Schedule of events area, and then point to the Change date range button.**

The Calendar Options task pane displays choices for orientation, month or year, and schedule of events (Figure 4-42).

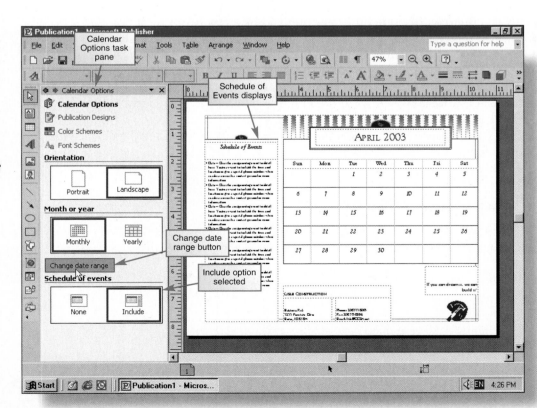

FIGURE 4-42

3 Click the Change date range button. When the Change Calendar Dates dialog box displays, click the arrows to display June and 2003, for both the Start and End dates. Point to the OK button.

The calendar will include one month only (Figure 4-43). If you had chosen a different end date, the publication would contain more than one page.

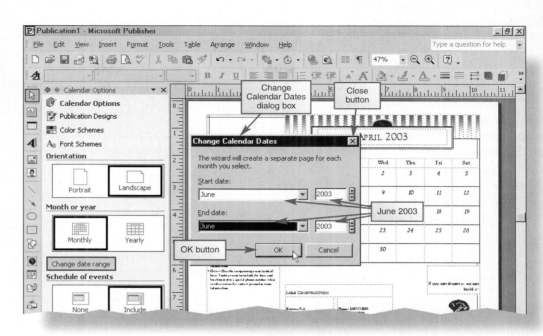

FIGURE 4-43

4 Click the OK button. Click the Close button in the Calendar Options task pane.

The calendar changes to the appropriate month (Figure 4-44).

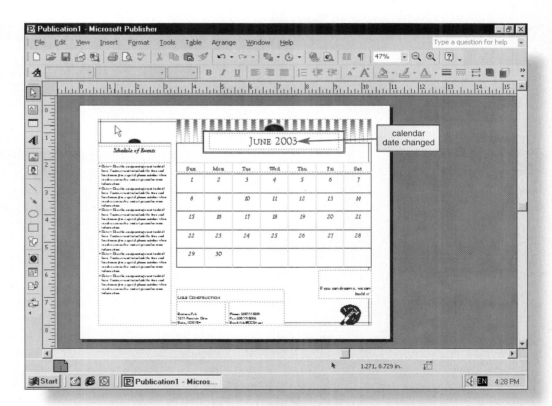

FIGURE 4-44

Perform the steps on the next page to customize the calendar further by editing the Schedule of Events and inserting specific data into cells.

Other Ways

1. In Voice Command mode, say "Format, Calendar Options"

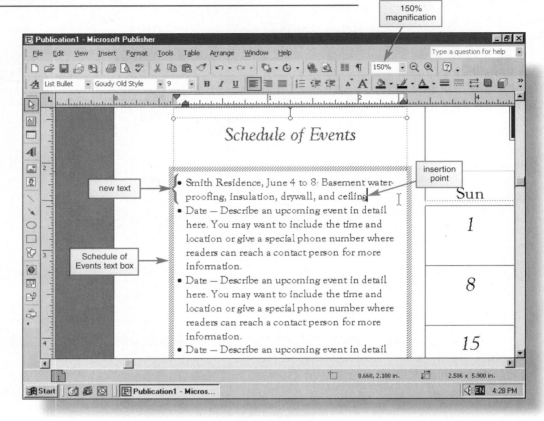

Steps To Customize the Calendar

1 Click the first bulleted item in the Schedule of Events text box in the upper-left corner of the calendar. Zoom to 150%. Type the text as shown in Figure 4-45. Do not press the ENTER key.

FIGURE 4-45

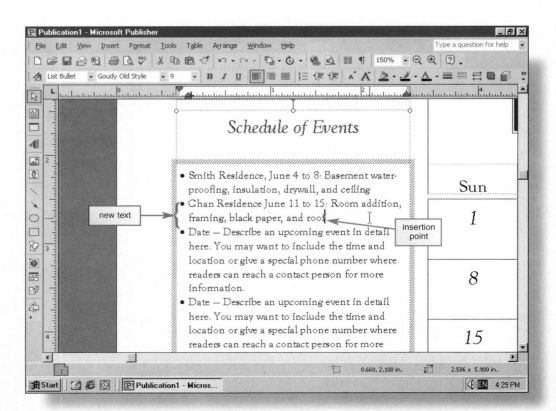

2 Repeat Step 1 for the second bulleted item, replacing text as shown in Figure 4-46.

FIGURE 4-46

3 **Click any remaining bulleted item. Replace the text as shown in Figure 4-47.**

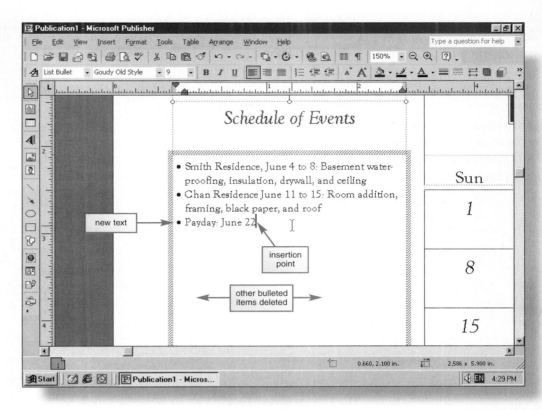

FIGURE 4-47

4 **Zoom to Whole Page. Click the June 4 cell, just to the right of the number, 4. Zoom to 150%. Click the Special Characters button on the Standard toolbar. Press SHIFT+ENTER to create a manual line break. Click the Font Size box and type 9 as the font size. Click the Italic button on the Formatting toolbar, so it is not selected. Type** Smith waterproofing **as the entry.**

The new text displays in the cell (Figure 4-48).

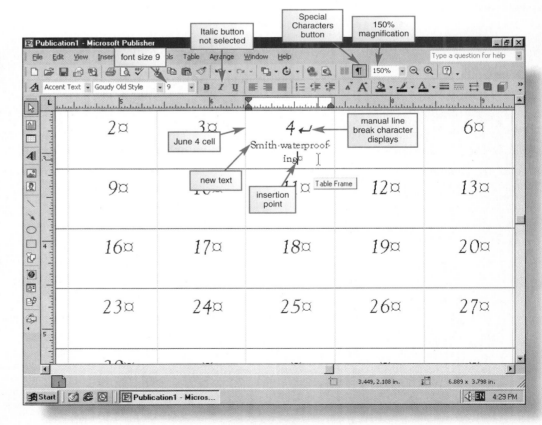

FIGURE 4-48

5 Repeat the process for each of the weekday cells from June 5 through June 18, as shown in Figure 4-49. Use SHIFT + ENTER to create manual line breaks. Use a font size of 9 and turn off italic formatting before typing in each cell.

The completed cells display (Figure 4-49).

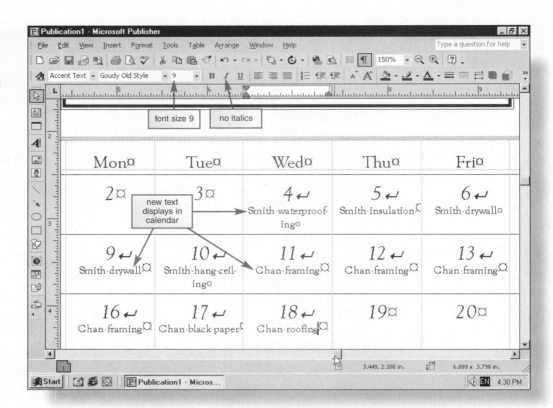

FIGURE 4-49

If you have more text than will fit in a cell, you can click Grow to Fit Text on the Table menu. The cells for that week in the Calendar table will grow or enlarge to fit the text. If you want to insert a tab within a cell in a calendar, press CTRL+TAB.

Saving, Printing, and Closing the Calendar

The Lisle Construction company calendar is complete. Follow these steps to save, print, and then close the calendar publication.

TO SAVE, PRINT, AND CLOSE THE CALENDAR

1 Insert your floppy disk into drive A.

2 Click the Save button on the Standard toolbar.

3 In the Save As dialog box, type Lisle Calendar in the File name text box. Do not press the ENTER key.

4 If necessary, click the Save in box arrow and then click 3½ Floppy (A:).

5 Click the Save button in the Save As dialog box.

6 Click the Print button on the Standard toolbar.

7 Click File on the menu bar and then click Close.

Publisher saves the publication on a floppy disk in drive A with the file name, Lisle Calendar and then prints a copy on the printer. The calendar is shown in Figure 4-1 on page PUB 4.05.

Envelopes

Envelopes come in a variety of sizes and shapes. The most common sizes are #6 personal envelopes that measure 3⅝-by-6½-inches, and #10 business envelopes that measure 4⅛-by-9½-inches. Publisher also can print envelopes for invitations, cards, and mailers by customizing the page layout.

Although the majority of businesses outsource their preprinted envelopes, most desktop printers have an envelope feeding mechanism that works especially well for business envelopes. Check your printer documentation for any limitations on the size and shape of envelopes. You can print the envelope for this project on 8½-by-11-inch paper, if necessary.

Creating an Envelope

Perform the following steps to create an envelope for Lisle Construction Company. You will create mailing labels later in this project. Therefore, you will delete the Mailing Address text box on the envelope.

TO CREATE AN ENVELOPE

1 Click File on the menu bar and then click New.

2 When the New Publication task pane displays, click Envelopes.

3 If necessary, scroll to view the Marquee Envelope preview.

4 Double-click the Marquee Envelope preview.

5 When the Envelope Options task pane displays, click None in the Logo area and then click #10 in the Size area.

6 Right-click the Mailing Address text box. Click Delete Object on the shortcut menu.

The envelope displays in the workspace (Figure 4-50).

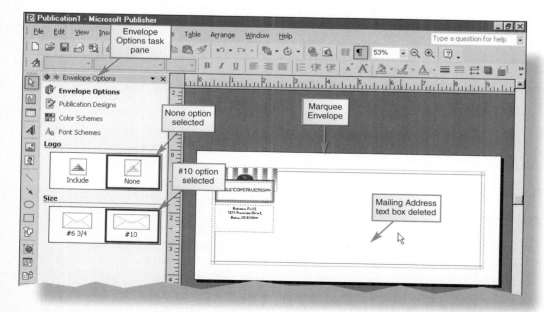

FIGURE 4-50

Printing a Custom Size Publication

If you are working on a network printer, choosing a custom size publication may cause the printer to pause, waiting for custom size paper. Many labs have a hands-off policy on loading printer paper yourself. Check with your instructor on the best way to print custom sizes.

Follow these steps to save, print, and then close the envelope publication.

TO SAVE, PRINT, AND CLOSE THE ENVELOPE

1 Insert your floppy disk into drive A.

2 Click the Save button on the Standard toolbar.

3 In the Save As dialog box, type `Lisle Envelope` in the File name text box. Do not press the ENTER key.

4 If necessary, click the Save in box arrow and then click 3½ Floppy (A:).

5 Click the Save button in the Save As dialog box.

6 Click the Print button on the Standard toolbar.

7 Click File on the menu bar and then click Close.

Publisher saves the envelope on the floppy disk in drive A and then prints it on the printer. If you are using standard size paper in your printer, the envelope will print landscape on a single sheet. The envelope is shown in Figure 4-1 on page PUB 4.05.

If you have an unusual sized envelope, do the following. On the File menu, click Page Setup, and then click the Layout tab. In the Publication type area, click Envelopes. In the Page size area, click Custom Size. Finally, enter the width and height of your envelope.

Using the Mail Merge Feature

More About

Main Publications

When you open a main publication, Publisher attempts to open the associated data source file, too. If the data source is not in exactly the same location (i.e., drive and folder) as when it originally was merged and saved, Publisher displays a dialog box indicating that it cannot find the data source. When this occurs, click the Find Data Source button to display the Open Data Source dialog box, where you can locate the data source file.

Whether you want individual letters sent to everyone on a **mailing list**, personalized envelopes, an invoice sent to all customers, or a printed set of mailing labels to apply to your brochures, you can use Publisher to maintain your names and addresses and make the task of mass mailing easier.

Readers expect documents such as these to be timely and professional looking, yet at the same time, individualized and personal. Take, for example, a form letter. Used regularly in both business and personal correspondence, a **form letter** has the same basic content no matter to whom it is sent; however, items such as name, address, city, state, and zip code change from one letter to the next. Thus, form letters are personalized to the addressee. An individual is more likely to open and read a personalized letter than a standard Dear Sir or Dear Madam letter. With word processing and database techniques, it is easy to generate individual, personalized documents even for a large group. Publisher extends that capability to any type of publication.

The process of generating an individualized publication for mass mailing involves creating a main publication and a data source. The two then are merged or blended into a series of publications ready for printing or saving. **Merging** is the process of combining the contents of a data source with a main publication. The **main publication** contains the constant or unchanging text, punctuation, space, and graphics. Conversely, the data source contains the variable or changing values in each publication. A **data source** or database is a file where you store all addresses or other information for customers, friends and family, or merchants with whom you do business. The term **database** generically describes a collection of data, organized in a manner that allows access, retrieval, and use of that data.

Microsoft Publisher allows users to create data sources internally, which means using Publisher as the creation and editing tool. Publisher creates a special database that can be edited independently by using Microsoft Access; however, you do not need to have Microsoft Access, or any database program, installed on your computer to create and use a database in Publisher.

If you plan to **import**, or bring in data from another application, Publisher can accept data from a variety of other formats, as shown in Table 4-2.

Creating a Publisher Address List

The internally created data sources are called **Publisher address lists**. Each customer or client is an entry in Publisher's address list. Similar to a record in other database applications, an **entry** represents all the information about one person or one business. In Table 4-3, an entry is equivalent to a row of information. Entries are broken down into pieces of information called **fields**. The preset fields in a typical Publisher address list include Title, First Name, Last Name, Company Name, Address Line 1, Address Line 2, City, State, ZIP Code, Country, Home Phone, Work Phone, and E-mail Address. In Table 4-3, a field is equivalent to a column. Each field contains a piece of **data** about a customer. In Table 4-3, the data is located in the intersection of the row and column where one piece of information displays.

Perform the following steps to create a Publisher address list containing information about the customers at Lisle Construction company and then save it on a floppy disk. Notice in Table 4-3 that some customers have no Address Line 2. You will leave that field blank. Publisher will adjust the printing automatically so blank lines will not print. You can create or edit address lists at any time, from any publication, just as you did with Personal Information Sets.

Table 4-2 Data Formats		
DATA-CREATION PROGRAM	**VERSION**	**FILE EXTENSION**
ASCII text files	Text delimited	.txt
dBase	III, IV, and V	.dbf
Microsoft Access	All versions	.mdb
Microsoft Excel	3.0, 4.0, 5.0, 7.0, and 8.0	.xls
Microsoft FoxPro	2.0, 2.5, and 2.6	.fxd
Microsoft Outlook	All versions	.pst
Microsoft Word tables or merge data documents	All versions	.doc
Microsoft Works (no formulas)	All Windows versions and MS-DOS 3.0	.wdb

Table 4-3 Customer Address List Data							
TITLE	**FIRST NAME**	**LAST NAME**	**ADDRESS LINE 1**	**ADDRESS LINE 2**	**CITY**	**STATE**	**ZIP**
Dr.	Elias	Coser	1400 Mall Drive	Suite B	Boise	ID	83704
Mr.	Javier	Nunez	8006 Howard		Boise	ID	83704
Mr.	Ali	Nassir	150 Grant Building	Office 24 East	Boise	ID	83704
Rev.	Brian	Smith	Eastwood Church	247 Antioch Ave.	Nearby	ID	83706
Ms.	Rose	Chan	942 Main		Boise	ID	83704
Dr.	Jean	Tingler	1400 Mall Drive	Suite K	Boise	ID	83704
Ms.	Anna	VanKrimpen	1135 Calumet		Nearby	ID	83706

To Create the Address List

1 **If necessary, close the New Publication task pane. Click Tools on the menu bar, point to Mail Merge, and then point to Create Address List.**

The Mail Merge submenu displays (Figure 4-51).

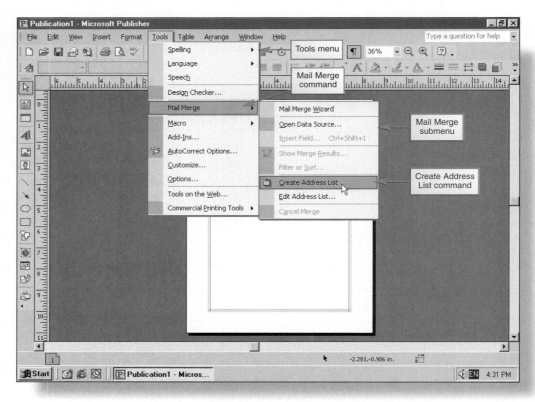

FIGURE 4-51

2 **Click Create Address List. When the New Address List dialog box displays, type Dr. in the Title text box and then press the TAB key. Type Elias in the First Name text box and then press the TAB key.**

The data displays (Figure 4-52). The insertion point displays in the Last Name text box.

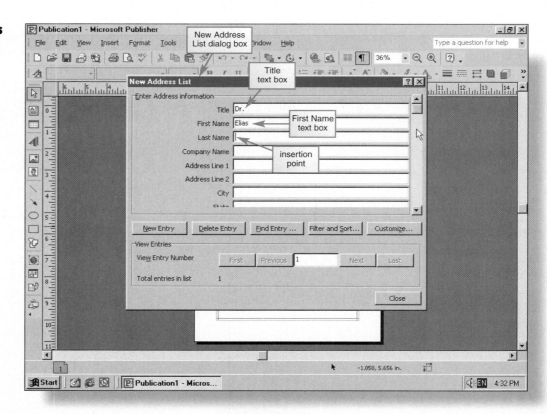

FIGURE 4-52

3 Type `Coser` in the Last Name text box and then press the TAB key twice to skip the Company Name. Continue to enter data from the first row in Table 4-3 on page PUB 4.41. Press the TAB key to progress to each new text box. When you finish typing the ZIP Code, point to the New Entry button.

The first record is complete (Figure 4-53). The data entry fields automatically scroll as you enter each field. This entry number is 1.

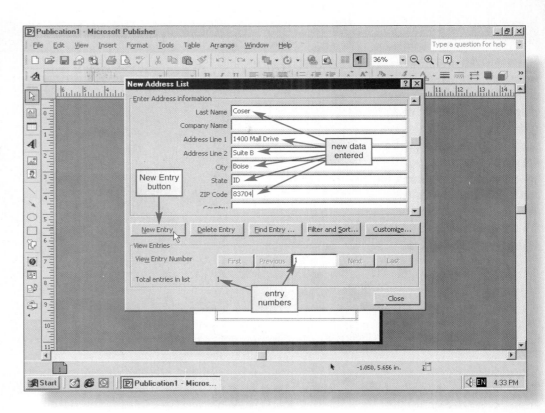

FIGURE 4-53

4 Click the New Entry button. Continue to add all the entries from Table 4-3, clicking the New Entry button after each row of information in the table is complete. Press the TAB key twice to skip an empty field. When you finish the last entry, do not click the New Entry button, but point to the Close button in the New Address List dialog box.

The last fields display for entry number 7 (Figure 4-54).

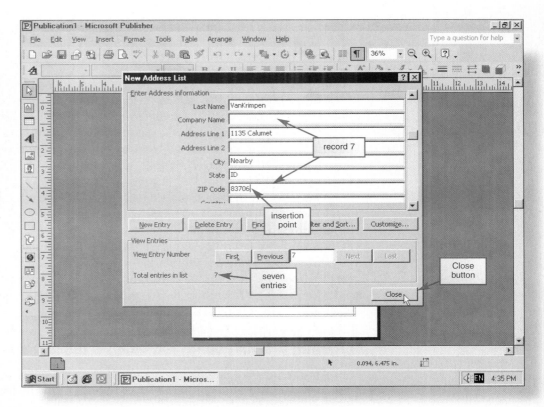

FIGURE 4-54

5 Click the Close button in the New Address List dialog box. When the Save Address List dialog box displays, insert a floppy disk into drive A. Type `Lisle Customers` in the File name text box. Do not press the ENTER key. If necessary, click the Look in box arrow and then click 3½ Floppy (A:). Point to the Save button in the Save Address List dialog box.

The file name Lisle Customers displays in the File name text box (Figure 4-55). The database file will be saved on the floppy disk in drive A.

6 Click the Save button in the Save As dialog box.

The address list file is saved.

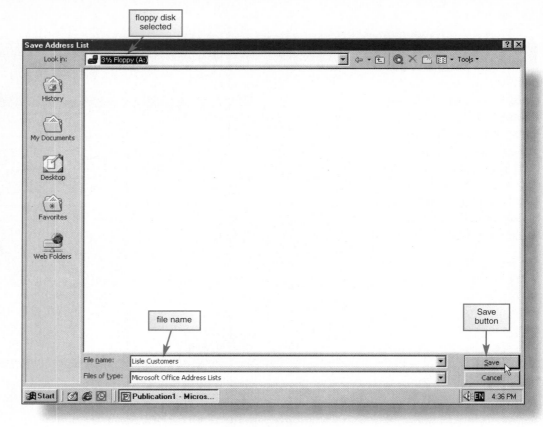

FIGURE 4-55

Other Ways

1. Click Type a new list in Mail Merge task pane, click Create
2. In Voice Command mode, say "Tools, Mail Merge, Create Address List"

You can use Publisher address lists for additional, non-address information, as Publisher does not test the data entered into the address list in any way. If you want to keep track of other information, such as charges, rates, prices, or time, you still can use Publisher to maintain the data. The Customize button in the New Address List dialog box (Figure 4-52 on page PUB 4.42) allows you to add, delete, and rename fields in your data source.

You also can maintain multiple address lists for data sources such as customers, employees, or vendors, if you create and name the lists with different names. The Edit Address List command on the Mail Merge submenu (Figure 4-51 on page PUB 4.42) permits you to specify to which data source you want to connect.

When you create an address list in Publisher, you can edit its entries without needing to close the current publication. If you are using a data source from another program, such as Microsoft Excel or Microsoft Word, you cannot edit the data source without closing the Publisher publication.

Creating a Main Publication Using a Label Wizard

Another application for merging involves the use of mailing labels. For documents that are not available electronically and for large quantities that have been mass-produced, a mailing label is sometimes the most economical method of addressing. Several paper supply companies produce labels for desktop printers in a variety of sizes and configurations.

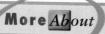

Perform the following steps to create a main publication using the Label Wizard to merge with the address list.

TO USE THE LABEL WIZARD

1. With a blank publication still displaying, click View on the menu bar and then click Task Pane.
2. In the New Publication task pane list, click Labels and then double-click Medium (Avery 5161) in the Labels pane.

The label displays in the workspace (Figure 4-56).

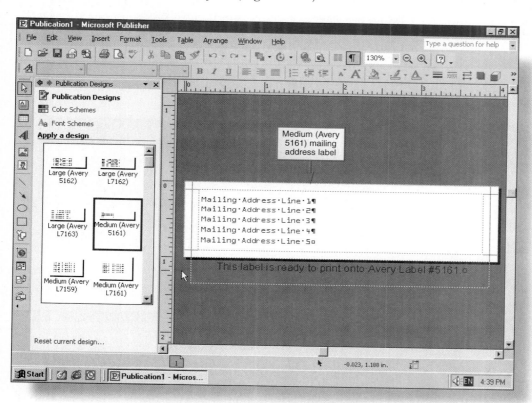

FIGURE 4-56

Inserting Field Codes

A publication designed for merging not only must be connected to its data source, but it also must contain field codes. A **field code** is placeholder text in the publication that shows Publisher where to insert the information from the data source. You can format, copy, move, or delete a field code just as you would regular text. Field codes need to be spaced and punctuated appropriately.

Publisher supplies some grouped field codes. A **grouped field code** is a set of standard fields, such as typical address fields or salutation fields, preformatted and spaced with appropriate words and punctuation. For example, instead of entering the field codes for Title, First Name, Last Name, Company Name, Address Line 1, etc., you can choose an Address Block that includes all the fields displayed correctly.

With the floppy disk containing the customer database in drive A, perform the steps on the next page to insert the field codes from the address list using the Mail Merge Wizard. The **Mail Merge Wizard** displays a task pane to guide you step-by-step through the merging process.

More About

Filter and Sort

The Filter and Sort button (shown in Figure 4-53 on page PUB 4.43) allows you either to merge a subset of records from your total data source or to merge your data in a particular order. The filter and sort orders do not permanently change your data source or mail merge.

More About

Zooming

To facilitate editing, you may enter any number between 10 and 400 in the Zoom box. If you click the Zoom box arrow, you may choose one of the standard magnifications or a specialty magnification. Whole Page displays the entire page at the largest magnification possible for your monitor. Page Width displays the page to fill the workspace left to right. Selected Objects displays the selected objects as large as possible.

Steps **To Insert Field Codes and Merge**

1 If necessary, insert the floppy disk containing the data source file Lisle Customers. With the label still displayed in the workspace, click Tools on the menu bar, point to Mail Merge, and then point to Mail Merge Wizard.

The placeholder text is selected and the Mail Merge submenu displays (Figure 4-57).

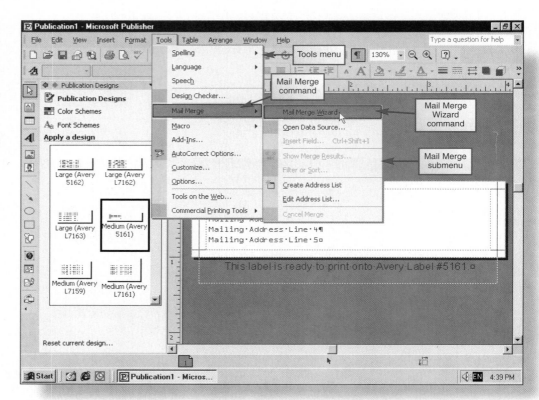

FIGURE 4-57

2 Click Mail Merge Wizard. When the Mail Merge Wizard task pane displays, if necessary, click Use an existing list, and then point to Browse.

Step 1 of 4 displays in the Mail Merge Wizard Task Pane (Figure 4-58). This step allows you to select recipients.

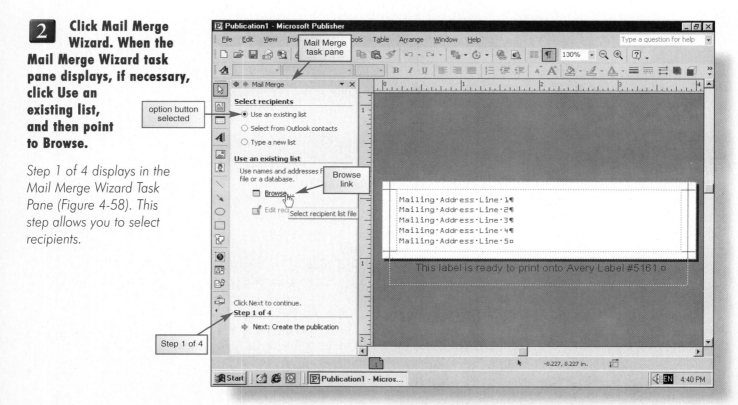

FIGURE 4-58

3 Click Browse. When the Select Data Source dialog box displays, point to Lisle Customers in the file list. If the file name does not display, check to make sure your floppy disk is inserted properly and that the Look in box displays 3½ Floppy (A:).

The list of files on the floppy disk displays (Figure 4-59).

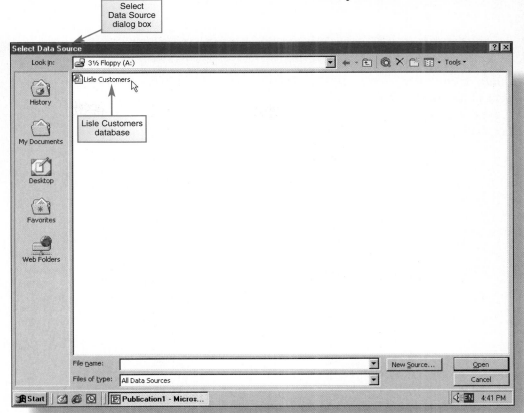

Select Data Source dialog box

Lisle Customers database

FIGURE 4-59

4 Double-click Lisle Customers. When the Mail Merge Recipients dialog box displays, point to the OK button.

The Mail Merge Recipients *dialog box* displays ways to sort, select, and edit the fields in the address list (Figure 4-60).

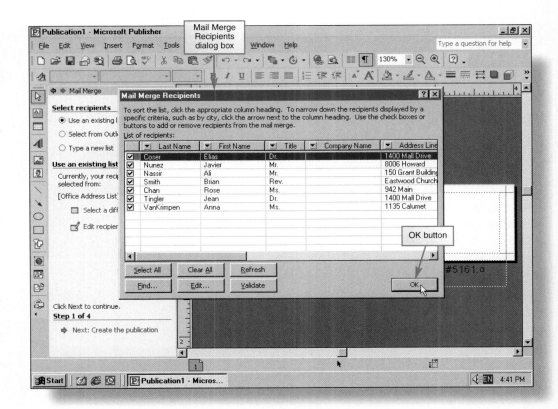

Mail Merge Recipients dialog box

OK button

FIGURE 4-60

5 **Click the OK button. Point to Next wizard step link in the lower portion of the Mail Merge task pane, as shown in Figure 4-61.**

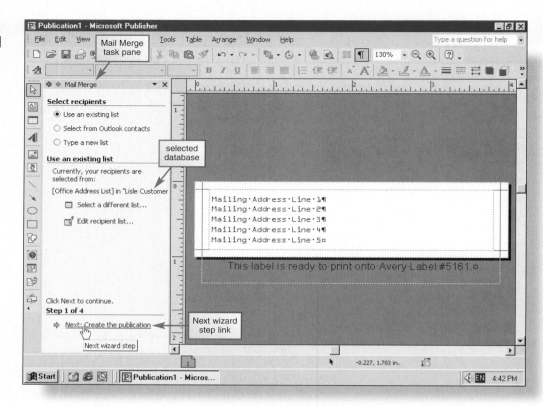

FIGURE 4-61

6 **Click the Next wizard step link. Click the Mailing Address text box in the publication to select it. When Step 2 of 4 displays, point to Address block.**

Step 2 of 4 displays in the Mail Merge task pane (Figure 4-62). This step will create the publication, if users already have not done so. In addition, it allows you to choose fields or groups of fields to merge into the publication. The Mailing Address text box displays selected.

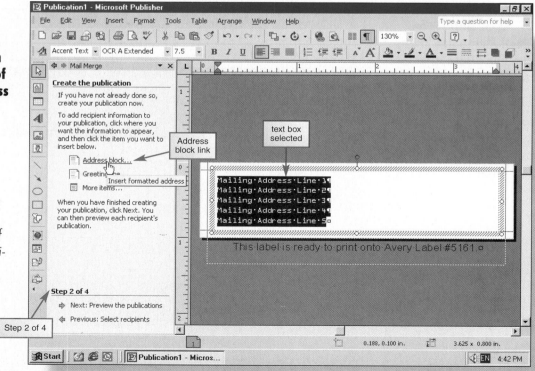

FIGURE 4-62

7 **Click Address block. When the Insert Address Block dialog box displays, point to the OK button.**

The *Insert Address Block dialog box* specifies address elements you can include in the publication (Figure 4-63).

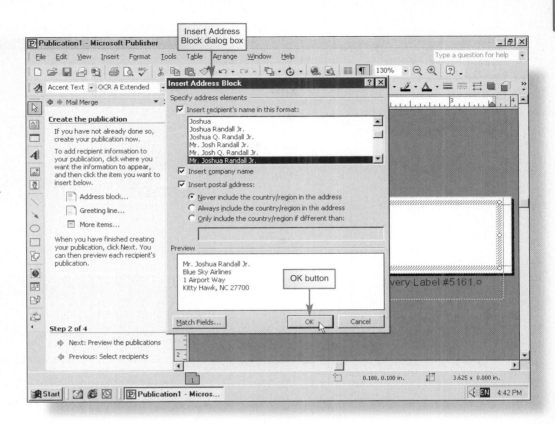

FIGURE 4-63

8 **Click the OK button. Point to Next wizard step link in the Mail Merge task pane.**

The *Mailing Address text box* displays the field code for the address block (Figure 4-64).

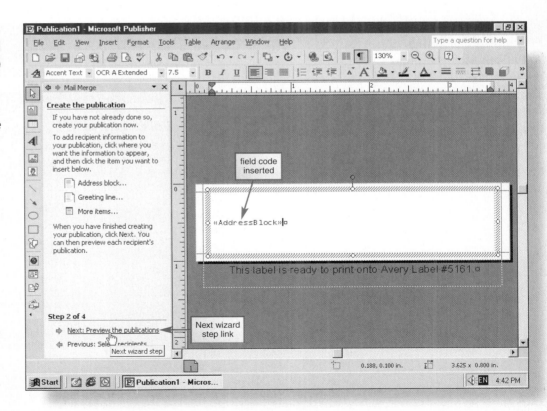

FIGURE 4-64

Microsoft **Publisher 2002**

9 Click the Next wizard step link. When Step 3 of 4 displays in the task pane, point to the Next wizard step link.

Step 3 of 4 displays in the Mail Merge task pane (Figure 4-65). You can click the previous and next arrows to traverse and display the records in the Address List.

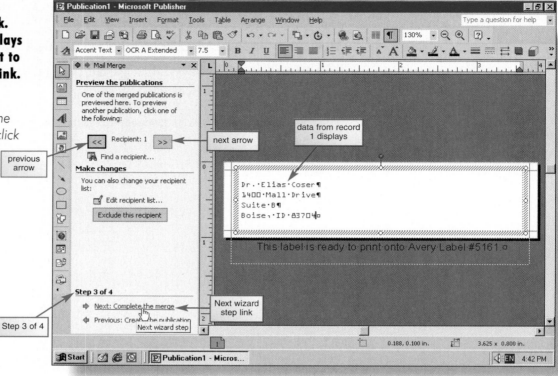

FIGURE 4-65

10 Click the Next wizard step link. When Step 4 of 4 displays in the task pane, click the Print link. When the Print Merge dialog box displays, point to the OK button.

The Print Merge dialog box contains options for printing merged documents (Figure 4-66).

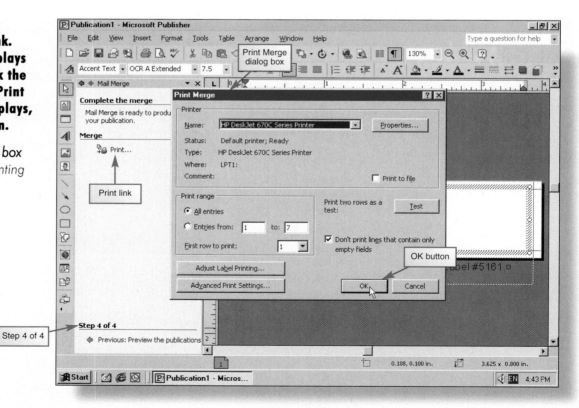

FIGURE 4-66

11 **Click the OK button.**

The mailing labels print as shown in Figure 4-67. The preset label layout is two per row and 10 per column for a total of 20 labels per sheet.

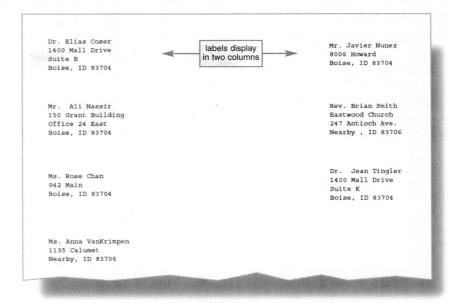

Dr. Elias Coser
1400 Mall Drive
Suite B
Boise, ID 83704

Mr. Javier Nunez
8006 Howard
Boise, ID 83704

Mr. Ali Nassir
150 Grant Building
Office 24 East
Boise, ID 83704

Rev. Brian Smith
Eastwood Church
247 Antioch Ave.
Nearby , ID 83706

Ms. Rose Chan
942 Main
Boise, ID 83704

Dr. Jean Tingler
1400 Mall Drive
Suite K
Boise, ID 83704

Ms. Anna VanKrimpen
1135 Calumet
Nearby, ID 83706

labels display in two columns

FIGURE 4-67

If you have blank fields in your data source, Publisher will omit the field when the publication is merged. For instance, if no second address line exists, Publisher will move the other fields up during the print process, to fill the gap.

You can edit the fonts for field codes that will affect the way they print after merging. The preset font for field codes is OCR A Extended. **OCR** stands for optical character recognition, which means that the post office can scan the address easily with electronic equipment, thereby speeding up the process.

Publisher can save the merged files as one large file on the disk, and if you are planning to print labels many times, it might be beneficial to do so. It requires a large amount of disk space, and the data is **static**, which means that updates to the data source are not reflected. It is easy to merge the label and address list again if you need to print at a future time, and you can include any updates to the address list.

The final step is to quit Publisher without saving the merged file.

TO QUIT PUBLISHER WITHOUT SAVING

1 Click the Close button on the Publisher title bar.

2 When Publisher asks if you want to save the changes, click the No button.

Publisher closes and the desktop displays.

More About

Printer's Marks

When you print a publication that is smaller than a piece of paper, your printer may add marks outside the printable area to help you or your commercial printing service trim, align, and control color in your publication. In Publisher, you can choose which printer's marks you want to print in the Print dialog box. Printer's marks include crop marks (to trim), registration marks (to align color separations), color bars (to monitor color separations), and bleed marks (to show where images extend beyond the trim). You also may print job information such as the name of the publication, page number, date, time, and plate name.

C A S E   P E R S P E C T I V E   S U M M A R Y

Lisle Construction is very happy with its letterhead, business cards, envelopes, and calendar. The owner was impressed with the logo and stylistic masthead. The database of customers will be easy to update and expand as the construction company adds jobs to its schedule. You print several sets of labels for them to use in mailing the next set of statements and an upcoming promotional publication. Lisle Construction now wants to use Publisher for all of its business forms. You decide to use the letterhead as a template and begin to investigate Publisher's many business form objects and tables.

Project Summary

Project 4 introduced you to generating business publications from the desktop. First, you created the Personal Information Set with its many components; then you used the information, along with a graphic background, to create a letterhead complete with a logo. Next, you applied the same components to a business card using a wizard to help you get started. You created a calendar and envelope for mass mailing. Finally, you designed and created a database of customers and merged it with the mailing label publication.

What You Should Know

Having completed this project, you now should be able to perform the following tasks:

▶ Close a Publication without Quitting Publisher *(PUB 4.30)*

▶ Create a Business Card *(PUB 4.31)*

▶ Create a Calendar *(PUB 4.34)*

▶ Create a Gradient Fill *(PUB 4.13)*

▶ Create an Envelope *(PUB 4.39)*

▶ Create the Address List *(PUB 4.42)*

▶ Create the Letterhead Masthead *(PUB 4.10)*

▶ Customize the Calendar *(PUB 4.36)*

▶ Edit a Personal Information Set *(PUB 4.18)*

▶ Edit the Business Card Orientation *(PUB 4.32)*

▶ Edit the Layout and Ruler Guides *(PUB 4.08)*

▶ Finish Editing the Tag Line *(PUB 4.24)*

▶ Format the Tag Line with the Format Painter *(PUB 4.23)*

▶ Insert a Logo *(PUB 4.25)*

▶ Insert and Format Personal Information Components *(PUB 4.21)*

▶ Insert Field Codes and Merge *(PUB 4.46)*

▶ Position Objects Using the Measurement Toolbar *(PUB 4.16)*

▶ Quit Publisher without Saving *(PUB 4.51)*

▶ Recolor a Graphic *(PUB 4.28)*

▶ Save, Print, and Close the Business Card *(PUB 4.33)*

▶ Save, Print, and Close the Calendar *(PUB 4.38)*

▶ Save, Print, and Close the Envelope *(PUB 4.40)*

▶ Save and Print the Letterhead *(PUB 4.30)*

▶ Selecting a New Graphic for the Logo *(PUB 4.27)*

▶ Start Publisher with a Blank Publication *(PUB 4.06)*

▶ Use the Label Wizard *(PUB 4.45)*

More About

Quick Reference

For a table that lists how to complete tasks covered in this book using the mouse, menu, shortcut menu, and keyboard, see the Quick Reference Summary at the back of this book or visit the Shelly Cashman Series Office XP Web page (scsite.com/offxp/qr.htm) and then click Microsoft Publisher 2002.

More About

Microsoft Certification

The Microsoft Office User Specialist (MOUS) Certification program provides an opportunity for you to obtain a valuable industry credential — proof that you have the Office XP skills required by employers. For more information, see Appendix E or visit the Shelly Cashman Series MOUS Web page at scsite.com/offxp/cert.htm.

Learn It Online

Instructions: To complete the Learn It Online exercises, start your browser, click the Address bar, and then enter scsite.com/offxp/exs.htm. When the Office XP Learn It Online page displays, follow the instructions in the exercises below.

1 Project Reinforcement TF, MC, and SA

Below Publisher Project 4, click the Project Reinforcement link. Print the quiz by clicking Print on the File menu. Answer each question. Write your first and last name at the top of each page and then hand in the printout to your instructor.

2 Flash Cards

Below Publisher Project 4, click the Flash Cards link. When Flash Cards displays, read the instructions. Type 20 (or a number specified by your instructor) in the Number of Playing Cards text box, type your name in the Name text box, and then click the Flip Card button. When the flash card displays, read the question and then click the Answer box arrow to select an answer. Flip through Flash Cards. Click Print on the File menu to print the last flash card if your score is 15 (75%) correct or greater and then hand it in to your instructor. If your score is less than 15 (75%) correct, then redo this exercise by clicking the Replay button.

3 Practice Test

Below Publisher Project 4, click the Practice Test link. Answer each question, enter your first and last name at the bottom of the page, and then click the Grade Test button. When the graded practice test displays on your screen, click Print on the File menu to print a hard copy. Continue to take practice tests until you score 80% or better. Hand in a printout of the final practice test to your instructor.

4 Who Wants to Be a Computer Genius?

Below Publisher Project 4, click the Computer Genius link. Read the instructions, enter your first and last name at the bottom of the page, and then click the Play button. Hand in your score to your instructor.

5 Wheel of Terms

Below Publisher Project 4, click the Wheel of Terms link. Read the instructions, and then enter your first and last name and your school name. Click the Play button. Hand in your score to your instructor.

6 Crossword Puzzle Challenge

Below Publisher Project 4, click the Crossword Puzzle Challenge link. Read the instructions, and then enter your first and last name. Click the Play button. Work the crossword puzzle. When you are finished, click the Submit button. When the crossword puzzle redisplays, click the Print button. Hand in the printout.

7 Tips and Tricks

Below Publisher Project 4, click the Tips and Tricks link. Click a topic that pertains to Project 4. Right-click the information and then click Print on the shortcut menu. Construct a brief example of what the information relates to in Publisher to confirm you understand how to use the tip or trick. Hand in the example and printed information.

8 Newsgroups

Below Publisher Project 4, click the Newsgroups link. Click a topic that pertains to Project 4. Print three comments. Hand in the comments to your instructor.

9 Expanding Your Horizons

Below Publisher Project 4, click the Articles for Microsoft Publisher link. Click a topic that pertains to Project 4. Print the information. Construct a brief example of what the information relates to in Publisher to confirm you understand the contents of the article. Hand in the example and printed information to your instructor.

10 Search Sleuth

Below Publisher Project 4, click the Search Sleuth link. To search for a term that pertains to this project, select a term below the Project 4 title and then use the Google search engine at google.com (or any major search engine) to display and print two Web pages that present information on the term. Hand in the printouts to your instructor.

online

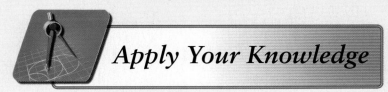

Apply Your Knowledge

1 Working with a Form Letter

Instructions: Start Publisher. Open the publication, Apply-4a from the Data Disk. See the inside back cover for instructions for downloading the Data Disk or see your instructor for information about accessing the files required for this book. The publication is a main document for Prairie University (Figure 4-68). The Data Disk also contains an address list for prospective graduate students in a file named, Apply-4b. You will edit the address list to insert your own personal information into the database, insert the date and field codes, and then merge the main publication with the data source. Perform the following tasks.

1. Start Publisher. Open the existing Apply-4a file from the Data Disk. When the publication displays, click Tools on the menu bar, point to Mail Merge, and then click Mail Merge Wizard.
2. When the Mail Merge task pane displays, click the Browse link. When the Select Data Source dialog box displays, click the Look in box arrow, and then click 3½ Floppy (A:) in the list. When the files display, double-click the Apply-4b file name.
3. When the Mail Merge Recipients dialog box displays, click the Edit button. When the Apply-4b dialog box displays, click the New Entry button. Enter your name and address into the appropriate fields and then click the Close button. When the Mail Merge Recipients dialog box again displays, click the OK button.
4. In the publication, click the Enter date here text box and then press the F9 key. Press CTRL+A to select the text and then on the Insert menu, click Date and Time. In the Date and Time dialog box, choose an appropriate style from the Available formats list. Click the Update Automatically check box to display its check mark. Click the OK button.
5. In the publication, click the Enter address block here text box. Press CTRL+A to select the text. At the bottom of the Mail Merge task pane, click the Next wizard step link. When the Create the publication step displays in the task pane, click the Address block link. When the Insert Address Block dialog box displays, click the OK button.
6. In the publication, click the Enter greeting line here text box. Press CTRL+A to select the text. In the Mail Merge task pane, click the Greeting line link. When the Greeting Line dialog box displays, click the OK button.
7. Click File on the menu bar and then click Save As. Use the file name, Prairie Form Letter, then save the publication on your floppy disk.
8. At the bottom of the Mail Merge task pane, click the Next wizard step link. When the Preview the publications step displays in the task pane, click the next recipient arrows until the letter with your name displays.
9. At the bottom of the Mail Merge task pane, click the Next wizard step link. When the Complete the merge step displays in the task pane, click the Print link. Click the OK button in the Print Merge dialog box to print the letters.
10. Close the file. Turn in the printouts to your instructor.

Apply Your Knowledge

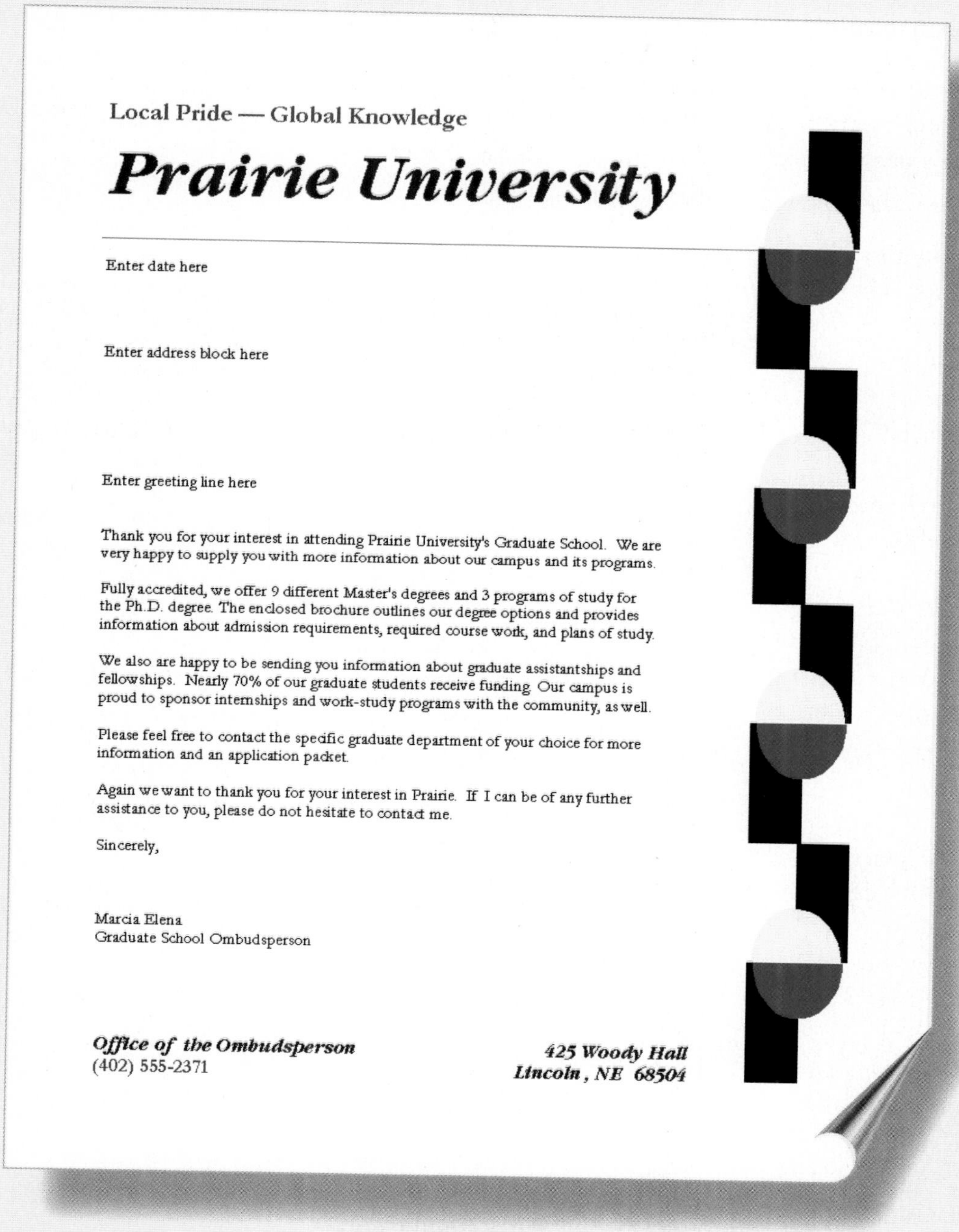

Local Pride — Global Knowledge

Prairie University

Enter date here

Enter address block here

Enter greeting line here

Thank you for your interest in attending Prairie University's Graduate School. We are very happy to supply you with more information about our campus and its programs.

Fully accredited, we offer 9 different Master's degrees and 3 programs of study for the Ph.D. degree. The enclosed brochure outlines our degree options and provides information about admission requirements, required course work, and plans of study.

We also are happy to be sending you information about graduate assistantships and fellowships. Nearly 70% of our graduate students receive funding. Our campus is proud to sponsor internships and work-study programs with the community, as well.

Please feel free to contact the specific graduate department of your choice for more information and an application packet.

Again we want to thank you for your interest in Prairie. If I can be of any further assistance to you, please do not hesitate to contact me.

Sincerely,

Marcia Elena
Graduate School Ombudsperson

Office of the Ombudsperson
(402) 555-2371

425 Woody Hall
Lincoln , NE 68504

FIGURE 4-68

In the Lab

1 Creating Stationery

Problem: Your uncle is the volunteer commissioner for the local children's baseball league. Because he is responsible for organizing the teams, ordering equipment, and scheduling games, fields, and umpires, he has asked you to create some stationery for his correspondences (Figure 4-69).

Instructions: Perform the following tasks using a computer.

1. Start Publisher with a blank publication. On the Arrange menu, click Layout Guides and then set the margins to .5 inches.

2. At the bottom of the page, insert a graphic relating to baseball. Resize and move it as necessary. Insert a text box next to the graphic. Change the font size to 20 and then type the name and address as shown in Figure 4-69.

3. Click the AutoShapes button on the Objects toolbar. Click Basic Shapes and then click Bevel. Draw a bevel shape at the top of the page. Use the Measurement toolbar to adjust the size of the bevel: 7.5 inches wide, 1.5 inches tall, .5 from the top and left margins.

From the desk of the commissioner...

Paul Cooper
454 Royal Avenue
Kansas City, MO 64118
(816) 555-5179

FIGURE 4-69

In the Lab

4. On the Fill Color menu, click Fill Effects. Choose a gradient fill effect with a color that compliments the graphic. Drag the Dark to Light scroll box all the way to the right.

5. Click the Line Color button. On the Line Color palette, choose a red color.

6. In front of the bevel, insert a text box for the heading. Use a script font that resembles handwriting and a font size of at least 24. Type From the desk of the commissioner… in the text box. Click the Line Color button to make the text box line color red, as well.

7. Select all the text in the heading and then use the Measurement toolbar to change the text scaling to 150%. If necessary, adjust the size and position of the text box as shown in Figure 4-69. Autofit the text box.

8. Save the publication on a floppy disk in drive A with the file name, Baseball Stationery, and then print a copy.

9. Click the graphic at the bottom of the page and then SHIFT-click the address frame. Click the Copy button on the Standard toolbar to copy both objects to the Clipboard.

10. Click the New button on the Standard toolbar. If the New Publication task pane displays, click Blank Publication. When the blank publication displays, click Page Setup on the File menu. Choose the #10 envelope. When the envelope displays in the workspace, click the Paste button to paste from the Clipboard onto the envelope. Use the Measurement toolbar and the Best Fit option to reposition as necessary for an appropriate return address.

11. Save the publication on a floppy disk in drive A with the file name, Baseball Envelope, and then print a copy.

2 Creating a Data Source and Form Letter

Problem: Hope Fishers, the owner of Café of Hope, has asked you to prepare a form letter to announce the cafe's new hours. Customers have recently filled out a satisfaction survey and Hope wants to start a Publisher Address list. You decide to create the form letter shown in Figure 4-70 on the next page.

Instructions: Perform the following tasks using a computer.

1. Start Publisher with a blank publication.

2. Using the Mail Merge feature, create a Publisher address list using data from Table 4-4 on page PUB 4.59. Click the New Entry button after each customer except the last. Close the New Address List dialog box and, when prompted, save the file as Hope Address List on your floppy disk.

3. Using the Design Gallery Object button on the Objects toolbar, choose the Arcs masthead. Choose the Sunrise color scheme and the Breve Font Scheme.

4. Drag the masthead to the top of the page. Edit the text boxes in the masthead as shown in Figure 4-70.

5. Insert text boxes underneath the masthead for the address and greeting line blocks. Use the Measurement toolbar to position the name of the shop and adjust the tracking, scaling, and/or kerning.

6. Create a large text box and enter the remainder of the letter text shown in Figure 4-70.

7. Click the Address block text box. SHIFT-click the greeting line text box. SHIFT-click the text box containing the body of the letter. Use the Arrange menu, to align the three text boxes on the left.

8. Save the publication on a floppy disk with the file name, Hope Form Letter.

9. Merge the letter with the address list.

10. Print all the pages of the merged file.

(continued)

In the Lab

Creating a Data Source and Form Letter *(continued)*

Café of Hope

9500 Mall Avenue

November 12, 2003

Joliet, IL

<<address block>>

<<greeting line>>

With the holiday season quickly approaching, you may find more and more demands on your time. We can help by offering you a quick, healthy lunch or by catering your holiday parties. Our new menu includes the latest in heart-healthy dishes and diabetic entrees. Visit our Hope Gift Shop for most of your holiday shopping needs. In addition to a huge selection of boxed and individual cards, we have ornaments, crafts, collectibles, stuffed animals, candy, and many other gifts for the entire family!

Beginning November 15 through December 23, we will open at 9:00 a.m. and close at 10:00 p.m. every day of the week. We accept personal checks and all major credit cards. We look forward to serving you.

Sincerely,

Hope Fishers

Owner

FIGURE 4-70

In the Lab

	FIRST NAME	LAST NAME	ORGANIZATION	ADDRESS LINE 1	ADDRESS LINE 2	CITY	STATE	ZIP
Table 4-4	**Hope Address List Data**							
TITLE								
Mr.	Ian	Peters	Carr & Associates, CPAs	P. O. Box 19		Orland Park	IL	60462
Ms.	Charlotte	Winters		44 River Road		Joliet	IL	60435
Mrs.	Karen	Bissell		105 Lake Street	Apt. 3D	New Lenox	IL	60451
Dr.	John	Groves	Medical Associates	P. O. Box 67		Mokena	IL	60448
Mr.	Samuel	Easton		123 Michigan	Apt. 5A	Joliet	IL	60435

3 Creating a Custom Calendar

Problem: Your friend runs a maid service and has asked you to produce a calendar he can use to schedule house cleanings for the month of August 2003. He already has booked the first five days. He wants the homeowner's name and location of the home in the schedule of events and then the homeowner's name in the cell with the date. You decide to use an Axis calendar with a graphic (Figure 4-71).

FIGURE 4-71

(continued)

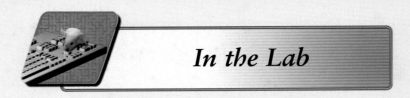

In the Lab

Creating a Custom Calendar *(continued)*

Instructions: Perform the following tasks using a computer.

1. Start Publisher. In the New Publication task pane, choose Calendars. Double-click the Axis calendar preview. Choose landscape orientation and include a schedule of events. Click the Change date range button and then choose August 2003.
2. Find a suitable graphic from the Clip Gallery. Using the Measurement toolbar, change the width of the graphic to 1" and the height of the graphic to 2".
3. Delete the text boxes and shapes to the right of the calendar. Delete any personal information components or logos.
4. Click the calendar table itself and then drag the right-middle sizing handle to enlarge the table.
5. Use the data from Table 4-5 to complete the Schedule of Events.

Table 4-5	Data for Calendar	
DATE	**NAME**	**ADDRESS**
August 4	Starks	10050 N. 800
August 5	Harvey	1404 Ironton
August 6	Baxter	1265 Buchanan Blvd.
August 7	Vermaat	741 Adams
August 8	Kosmatka	8 Mockingbird Lane

6. Include the homeowner name for the appropriate days in the cells of the calendar table.
7. Add your name to one other date in August.
8. Save the publication on a floppy disk using the file name, Work Calendar.
9. Print the calendar and turn in a copy to your instructor.

Cases and Places

1 ▶ Copy Cat Creations has asked you to create a new corporate letterhead. They would like an arrow shape with a gradient fill to serve as a background for the words, Copy Cat Creations. Use a blank page publication and insert an arrow from the AutoShapes button on the Objects toolbar. Position the arrow in the upper-left corner of the page. Use a text box for the corporation name. Insert a text box at the bottom of the page and type 1350 Ridgeway Avenue, Mesa, AZ 85211, (480) 555-3770 as the address and telephone number.

2 ▶ Enter new data into the Other Organization Personal Information Set. Use the information in Table 4-6. Use the concepts and techniques presented in this project to create a business card using personal information components and a suitable logo.

Table 4-6 Personal Information Data	
Name:	Bernita Montgomery
Address:	Winding River Council 9817 Ridge Plaza Tulsa, OK 74112
Phone/fax/e-mail:	Telephone: (918) 555-8606 Fax: (918) 555-8607 E-mail: Bernita_Montgomery@wrc.org
Organization name:	Boy Scouts of America
Tag line or motto:	Be Prepared
Job or position title:	Committee Chair
Color scheme:	Prairie

3 ▶▶ Start Publisher and choose any of the Business Card Templates from the list. Choose the preset values for each option in the task pane. Edit the Personal Information Set for Home/Family. Use your own name and the title, Student Extraordinaire. Enter the name and address of your school or workplace as the organization. Choose a color scheme. In the Personal Information dialog box, click Update. Print the business card with the Home/Family information components.

4 ▶▶ Using a blank publication, create your own personal stationery. Edit the page setup to use a special size of 5½-by-7-inches. Insert a graphic or a background shape with a fill effect. Include your name, address, and telephone number in text boxes. If your first or last name begins with the letter, A, T, V, W, Y, M, or Z, kern that letter and the following letter. Save the file as My Letterhead on a floppy disk. Create a matching #6 envelope using the concepts and techniques present in this project. Print a copy of the stationery and the envelope to use in your own correspondence.

Cases and Places

5 ▶▶ Create a large mailing label using the New Publication task pane. Choose an appropriate font scheme. Use the Mail Merge Wizard to create an address list of the students in your class. Insert data into the fields for first name, and e-mail address. Create a new field called Year in School in which you will enter freshman, sophomore, junior, or senior. If your instructors permit you to do so, go from one computer station to the next, inserting your personal data. On your computer, in the label's address text box, delete the text. Use the More Items link in the task pane to insert the four fields. Print multiple labels on the page.

6 ▶▶▶ You currently are seeking employment in your field of study. You already have prepared a resume and would like to send it to a group of potential employers. You decide to design a cover letter to send with the resume. Obtain a recent newspaper and cut out five classified advertisements pertaining to your field of study. Create the cover letter for your resume as a main publication to merge with a data source. Be sure the cover letter has an attractive letterhead containing your name, address, and telephone number, as well as a logo from the Design Gallery. Use the information in the classified ads for the address list. Insert the personal information components as the inside mailing address underneath the letterhead. Create a large text box for the body of your letter. Merge the letter with the address list and print all five copies. Turn in the want ads with your printouts.

7 ▶▶▶ If Microsoft Access is installed on your system, you can use it to create a data source and then merge that file with a publication. Start Access and then create the table in Project 4 on page PUB 4.41 as an Access database table. You may need to use Help in Access to assist you in the procedure for creating and saving a database that contains a table. Quit Access. Start Publisher. Open an envelope wizard of your choice. Begin the mail merge process as discussed in this project. When specifying the data source, change the file type to MS Access Database and then click the database name of the file you created in Access. Insert the fields from the data source in the Mailing Address text box. Print the merged envelopes.

Microsoft Publisher 2002

PROJECT

5

Creating Business Forms and Tables

You will have mastered the material in this project when you can:

OBJECTIVES

- List common business forms
- Create an invoice template
- Use styles
- Create a font effect
- Insert a graphic from the Web collections
- Format drop caps
- Identify tools on the ruler
- Set a tab stop
- Define the difference between tab and indent
- Insert the system date
- Create a border
- Create and format tables
- Navigate through table cells to enter data
- Merge cells and insert a cell diagonal
- Attach a publication to an e-mail message
- Understand electronic forms
- Identify form controls
- Insert a hot spot
- Insert form controls
- Align objects

Attention Shoppers

Internet Retailers Connect People and Products

At-home shopping has a whole new meaning in today's virtual world of e-commerce. From the comfort of your home you can shop for everything from a new car to a new set of golf clubs. Improvements in e-commerce software have made shopping on the Internet easier and more convenient than ever.

Things can be a bit more complicated, however, when it comes to buying clothes on the Net. After all, you cannot try on a pair of jeans or see if a green sweater clashes with your red hair when you are shopping online. This logistical problem can be frustrating to shoppers who are expected to spend $13 billion online for apparel by 2003.

Lands' End has come up with a solution to these virtual shopping woes. This Wisconsin-based direct merchant of traditional, casual clothes has developed Your Personal Model, a personalized 3-D representation of female customers that selects the most flattering clothes for their figures, suggests specific outfits for various occasions, and provides an online dressing room to try on the garments.

Shoppers begin their Your Personal Model shopping adventure by answering several questions regarding their physical features. For example, they select specific skin tones, face shapes, hairstyles, and hair colors. They then give their models a name, save their profiles for future shopping sprees, and proceed to the Welcome Page.

At this point, their models appear along with custom outfits designed for their bodies and for their lifestyles. The site might suggest women with broad shoulders and hips wear gray Chinos and a beige sweater set for a casual workplace and a simple black knit dress for an informal weekend party.

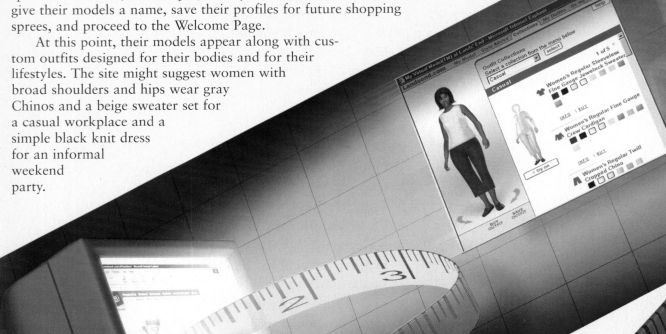

The next step is to take these garments to The Dressing Room. There, the shoppers can view the particular clothes on their models. They even can mix and match outfits and change colors. The site gives advice on choosing the proper size and then places the items in the customers' virtual shopping carts.

Ordering is easy. If they use Your Personal Model, the contents of their shopping carts display automatically in an order form. Otherwise, they can use the table found in the Lands' End Intelligent Order Blank and input an item number in each table row and then indicate size, color, quantity, and the desire for a monogram or a gift box.

Likewise, you will create a form in this Publisher project that allows instructors to order books and supplies online. The reorder form contains text boxes, check boxes, and list boxes to facilitate ordering. In addition, you will create the Web page where clients can use the automated ordering process. Then, you will publish the page to the World Wide Web.

Gary C. Comer, an avid sailor and advertising copywriter, founded Lands' End in 1961 in Chicago to sell sailing equipment and hardware via a catalog. In the 1970s, the company's focus switched to clothing. Today, Lands' End features apparel for men, women, and children, along with luggage and home furnishings. It is the second largest apparel mail-order company with sales of more than $1.37 billion to its 6.1 million customers. The Lands' End Web site (www.landsend.com) was unveiled in 1995 and receives 15 million visitors yearly.

As retail companies such as Lands' End *dress up* their Web sites with features that make online shopping efficient and fun, more and more shoppers will discover the ease and convenience of making their purchases on the Internet.

Microsoft Publisher 2002

Creating Business Forms and Tables

PROJECT

5

Jason Perry, owner of Perry's Bookstore, just came back from a student services seminar where he learned about using Microsoft Publisher to create interactive order forms. He saw demonstrations of instructors submitting their textbook order forms online. Perry's Bookstore, located just off-campus, has been relying on paper forms and e-mails for ordering books and supplies — a time consuming and labor-intensive process. Jason knows of your interest in desktop publishing and has asked you to design an order form he can post to the Web. He hopes instructors will find it easy to fill in the title, author, date, and ISBNs of textbooks they need for their fall classes. At the bottom of the form, he wants to include an *Other* box for instructors to order additional required supplies, such as templates, graphing calculators, and disks.

Perry's Bookstore recently purchased a copy of Office XP Professional Special Edition. Jason intends to use Publisher to create an invoice, a book order form, and a coupon for $5 off student purchases of $75 or more. You will need to work swiftly; the fall registration is approaching quickly.

Introduction

Computers commonly are used to produce modern business forms, such as invoices, statements, purchase orders, expense reports, fax covers, time records, and inventory lists. Not only do computers make it easy to maintain a consistent look and style for business forms, but they update and manipulate the forms more quickly and inexpensively than manual processing. Some of Publisher's forms typical to business applications are defined below.

An **invoice** is an itemized list of goods or services, stating quantities, prices, fees, and other charges with a request for payment. Invoices usually accompany delivered orders; occasionally they are mailed to customers. A **statement** is a form sent to customers at regular intervals, displaying a compilation of invoices, charges, and payments. A formal request to buy a product from a vendor and bill it to a business account is called a **purchase order**. When employees travel or entertain for business purposes they prepare an **expense report** as a means of itemizing incurred business expenses for reimbursement. A **fax cover** is a cover sheet for a facsimile transmission to send images over telephone lines. Companies use **timecards** or time records to keep track of the exact time employees begin and end their workdays for payroll purposes. An **inventory list** may take any of several different forms, but usually includes fields for quantities, serial numbers, descriptions, warranties, and values.

Project Five — Creating Business Forms and Tables for Perry's Bookstore

Project 5 illustrates the generation of several business forms for a college bookstore including an invoice, a coupon, and order forms as shown in Figure 5-1.

(a) Invoice Template

Perry's Bookstore

8355 Hillcrest Drive Telephone: 214-555-BOOK
Dallas, TX 75202 Fax: 214-555-0533

Invoice

Invoice #
Invoice Date:
Customer ID:

Bill To: **Ship To:**

Mailing Address Line 1 Shipping Address Line 1
Mailing Address Line 2 Shipping Address Line 2
Mailing Address Line 3 Shipping Address Line 3
Mailing Address Line 4 Shipping Address Line 4
Mailing Address Line 5

Date	Your Order #	Our Order #	Sales Rep.	FOB	Ship Via	Terms	Tax ID

Quantity	Item	Units	Description	Discount %	Taxable	Unit Price	Total
						Subtotal	
						Tax	
						Shipping	
						Miscellaneous	
						Balance Due	

REMITTANCE
Customer ID:
Date:
Amount Due:
Amount Enclosed:

*T*hank you for your business!

(b) Coupon

Perry's Bookstore

$5.00 off

On purchases of $75 or more

Just off-campus in Liberty Mall

Coupon expires August 1, 2004

Telephone: 888-BOOK

Online at www.perrysbookstore.com

(d) Web Book Order Form

Perry's Bookstore
Your Textbook Connection

We are currently accepting textbook orders for Fall 2004.
Please enter the textbook and personal information below.

Course Number	Book Title	Author	ISBN	Req.	Rcv.

Enter other supplies for your courses here.

Please enter your name, department, and telephone number.

Page Title Page 2 of 2

Submit Reset

(c) Book Order Form

Perry's Bookstore Order Form

Book Information	Author	Title	Edition or Date	Publisher	ISBN
Course and Section Number					

FIGURE 5-1

The invoice for Perry's Bookstore will become a reusable template with fields for individualizing customer data and charges. The coupon is a special-sized publication with text boxes and a page border. The print version of the book order form includes a formatted table that instructors will complete when ordering textbooks. The electronic version of the book order form contains form controls, allowing user input via the Web.

Business Forms

Publisher contains 35 templates for each of 10 different business forms. If you cannot find the exact form you want, you also can visit the Microsoft Publisher Web site for additional forms. If you want to use the format of a current paper form, simply scan it into Publisher by clicking Insert on the menu bar, pointing to Picture, and then clicking From Scanner or Camera.

Starting Publisher

To start Publisher, Windows must be running. Perform the following steps to start Publisher.

TO START PUBLISHER

1 Click the Start button on the Windows taskbar and then click New Office Document.

2 When the New Office Document dialog box displays, if necessary, click the General tab and then double-click the Blank Publication icon.

3 If the Publisher window is not maximized, double-click its title bar to maximize it.

4 If the New Publication task pane does not display, click View on the menu bar and then click Task Pane.

5 If the Language bar displays, click its Minimize button.

You now are ready to use Publisher's New Publication task pane to create an invoice and statement.

Creating an Invoice Template

Invoices come in a variety of styles and sizes. Some invoices are handwritten on generic invoice pads, while others may be multipart carbonless forms sold commercially. Most invoices have several things in common. First, they display the name of the company, its location, and contact information. Invoices generally include the creation date, an invoice number, and the name of the customer to whom the invoice is presented. Invoices may contain different addresses for billing and shipping. Finally, invoices display quantities, descriptions, prices, taxes, and totals.

While larger businesses may use accounting programs, point-of-sale terminals, or transaction processing systems to create invoices automatically from inventory databases or work records, smaller businesses that use a computer to keep track of billing and customers usually generate invoices on an as-issued basis. That means that when a customer orders an item, an employee accesses an **invoice template** on the computer, filling in the parts of the invoice that change. Once saved, this data-enriched template becomes an **instance** of the invoice.

Invoice Template

Using one of the invoice templates provided by Publisher, you will create an invoice template for Perry's Bookstore employees to complete on the screen. Perform the following steps to choose an appropriate invoice preview.

Imposition

Imposition means inserting an entire printed page as an object in another publication. This book uses imposition to display output from the printer. Even though Publisher does not support full-page imposition, several ways exist to work around the problem. You can select all of the objects from a publication page, group and copy, and then in a new publication, create a white rectangle with a shadow. Paste the objects on top of the rectangle and then resize as necessary.

Steps To Create an Invoice Template

1 In the New Publication task pane, scroll down in the publications list and click Business Forms. Click Invoice in the Business Forms list. Point to Accent Box Invoice in the Invoice Business Forms pane.

Previews of the Invoice Business Forms display (Figure 5-2). Your previews of business forms may vary.

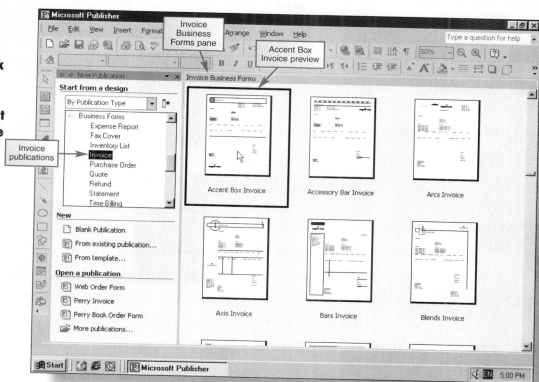

FIGURE 5-2

2 Double-click Accent Box Invoice. When the Business Form Options task pane displays, click None in the Logo area and then point to Color Schemes.

The invoice will not include a logo from the Personal Information Set (Figure 5-3).

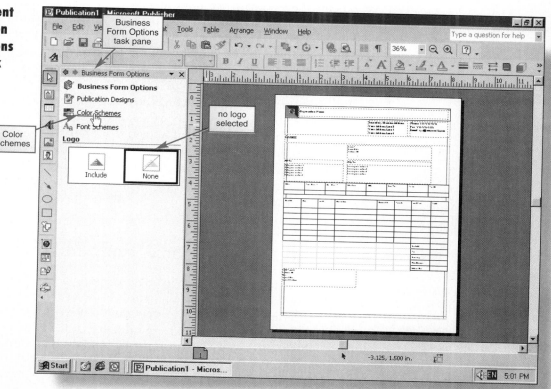

FIGURE 5-3

3 Click Color Schemes and then click Citrus in the Apply a color scheme list. Click Font Schemes and then click Capital in the Apply a font scheme list. Point to the Close button in the Font Schemes task pane.

The color scheme changes and the Capital font scheme displays in the invoice (Figure 5-4).

4 Click the Close button.

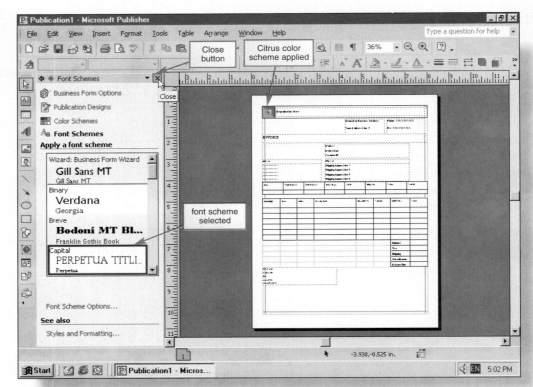

FIGURE 5-4

Automating business forms such as invoices, statements, and purchase orders can be expedited even further in Publisher by cutting and pasting the input portion of the form onto pre-designed letterhead, like that you created in Project 4. To use letterhead open a business form preview and then select all of the objects below the name and address. Click the Group button and then click the Copy button. Then, open the letterhead file, click the Paste button, and then drag the pasted objects below the letterhead masthead.

Business forms also can be completed using merged data sources. As you learned in Project 4, Publisher's capability of using an external data source can facilitate the processing of standard forms and letters. If a company uses a database such as Microsoft Access to store charges, they can merge the business form with the data source. Field codes corresponding to those in the database can be inserted into the appropriate text boxes, and then all the forms will be updated, computerizing the process even more.

Formatting the Invoice Template

Formatting the invoice template involves creating a style for the company name and then applying the style to make the word, Invoice, more prominent. Second, you will insert the location and contact information for Perry's Bookstore. Additionally, you will create a large dropped initial capital letter called a drop cap. Finally, you will create a tab stop to position a formatted date field that automatically updates each time employees open the publication.

Using Styles

The owner of Perry's Bookstore wants to use a special font, font size, and font color for his business. He would like this style of formatting to be used across all of the publications he creates. If you want to save formatting for use in future publications, Publisher uses a concept called styles, as do many word processing applications. A **style** is a set of formatting characteristics that you apply to text to change its appearance quickly. A style contains all text formatting information: font and font size, font color, indents, character and line spacing, tabs, and special formatting, such as numbered lists. When you apply a style, you apply a whole group of formats in one step. For example, you may want to format the Web page address of a company to make it stand out. Instead of taking four separate steps to format the address as underlined, blue, 16-point, and center-aligned, you can achieve the same result in one step by applying a saved style. The formatting changes affect the entire paragraph.

Publisher installs a predefined Normal style as 10-point Times New Roman, flush-left. Other text styles can come from a variety of sources. You can define your own styles in Publisher, import text styles from other publications, or use text styles you have saved. For example, styles from Microsoft Word documents can be imported into Publisher.

Creating a New Style

The organization name located in the letterhead has specific formatting that the company would like to become part of its unique identity. Once created, you can import the style from the invoice to the book order form and the coupon.

The style used for Perry's Bookstore will include a font effect. A **font effect** is similar to a WordArt text effect in that it applies a special embossed, engraved, outlined, or shadowed formatting to text.

Perform the following steps to create a new text style from the Organization Name text box and name it Perry.

Font Effects

Depending on the effect you want, you can shadow or emboss text in one of three different ways. First, you can add a shadow or embossed effect directly to the text. Using this method, you cannot change shadow features such as offset or color. Also, the border of the text does not display when the effect is added, so that you can see the full effect. If you remove the effect, the border again displays. Second, you can add a shadow or embossed effect to an unfilled object that contains text. With this method, the text takes on the same shadow options as the object, and you can control and change shadow features. Finally, you can use WordArt to draw an object that contains special text effects such as shadowing and perspective.

Steps **To Create a New Text Style**

1 **Click the Organization Name text box at the top of the invoice. Press the F9 key. If necessary, press CTRL+A to select all of the text.**

The text is selected (Figure 5-5). Depending on which Personal Information Set is selected and previous changes to personal information data, your organization name may differ.

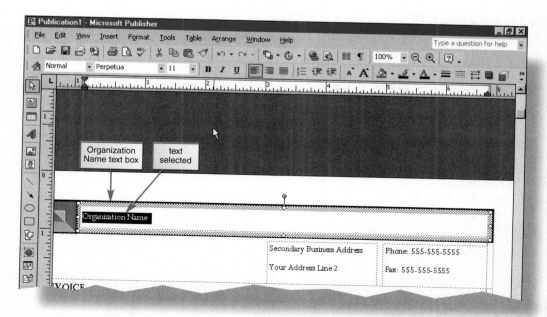

FIGURE 5-5

2 **Type** Perry's Bookstore **to replace the text. Press CTRL+A to select the text. Click Format on the menu bar and then point to Font.**

Figure 5-6 displays the page layout scrolled to the right in order to display both the selected text and the Format menu. Your Format menu may display in front of the selected text.

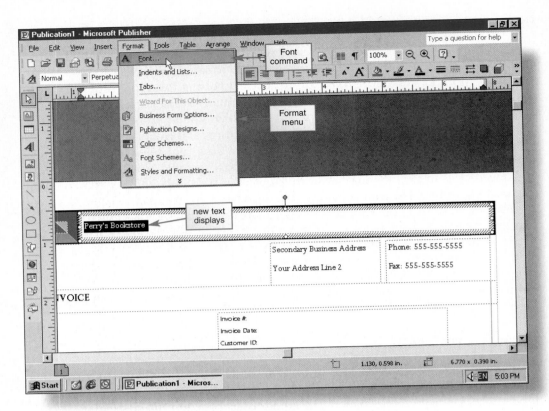

FIGURE 5-6

3 **Click the Font command. When the Font dialog box displays, click the Font box arrow and then select Baskerville Old Face or a similar font on the computer. Click the Font style box arrow and then click Italic. Click the Size box arrow and then click 26. Click the Color box arrow and then click Accent 2. In the Effects area, click only the Emboss check box to display its check mark. Point to the OK button.**

The new font settings display in the preview (Figure 5-7). Your preview may differ. The color, Accent 2, from the Citrus color scheme is a light ... Embossing makes ... text appear as ... off the page

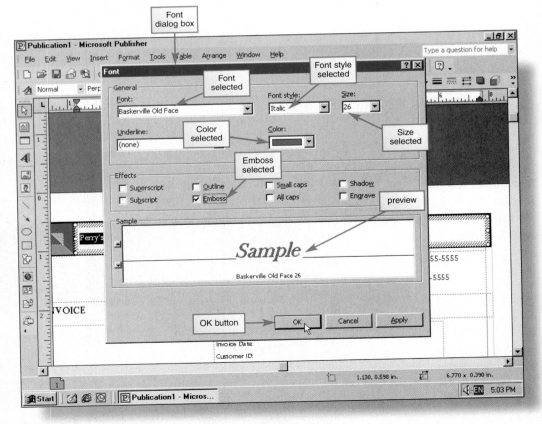

FIGURE 5-7

4 Click the OK button. With the text still selected, point to the Styles and Formatting button on the Formatting toolbar.

The new formatting is applied to the company name (Figure 5-8).

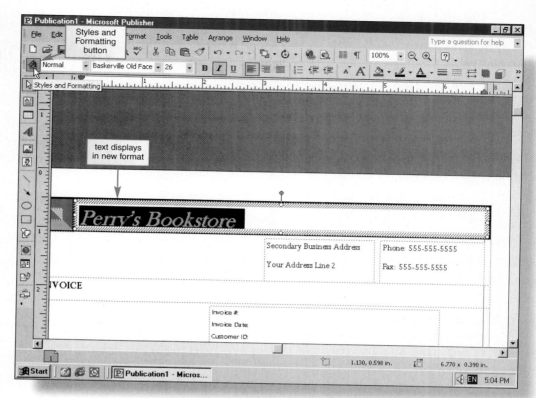

FIGURE 5-8

5 Click the Styles and Formatting button. When the Styles and Formatting task pane displays, point to the Create new style button.

The Styles and Formatting task pane contains a list of standard styles from which you may choose as well as buttons to import and create new styles (Figure 5-9).

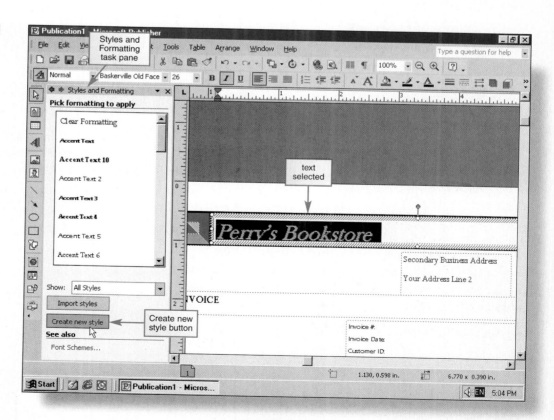

FIGURE 5-9

Click the Create new style button. When the Create New Style dialog box displays, type Perry **in the Enter new style name text box. Point to the OK button.**

The Create New Style dialog box displays a description of the new style and a sample (Figure 5-10). Your preview may differ. The buttons in the Click to change area allow you to customize the new style even further.

 **Click the OK button. Close the Styles and Formatting task pane by clicking its Close button.**

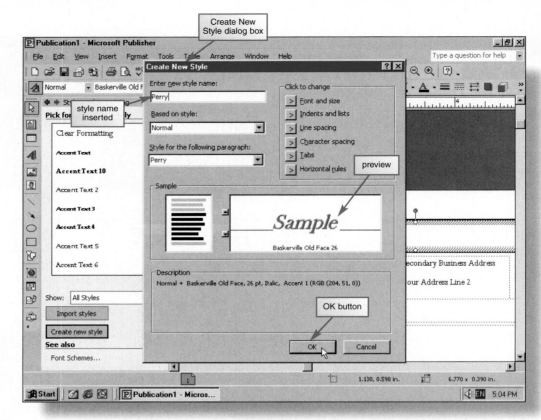

FIGURE 5-10

Embedding Fonts

When you take your Publisher file to a commercial printing service, the printing service needs to have the fonts you used in order to print your publication correctly. To embed the fonts, click Tools on the menu bar, point to Commercial Printing Tools, and then click Fonts. In the Fonts dialog box, you will see options for embedding the entire font set, or a subset. You also will see a list of the necessary fonts and their legal restrictions, if any. Publisher supplied fonts have no license restrictions; however, if you use outside fonts, your printing service may need to purchase a copy.

Styles are saved when the publication is saved. The next step is to apply the new style to more text.

Applying a Style

When you want to use a previously created style or a style from Publisher's standard list, you select the text, click the Style box arrow, and then click the Style you wish to use as shown in the following steps.

More *About*

Importing Styles from Microsoft Word

Publisher fully supports importing styles from documents created in Word, Works, Excel, and other applications. For example, if you have created a style to use a font unique to your printer, or perhaps a font for a multinational character set, instead of recreating the style, in the Import Styles dialog box, click the Files of type box arrow and then choose the appropriate application.

Steps **To Apply a Style**

1 **Double-click the word Invoice. On the Formatting toolbar, click the Style box arrow, and then point to Perry in the list.**

The styles display (Figure 5-11). For illustration purposes, the page layout in Figure 5-11 is scrolled to the right. Your display will differ.

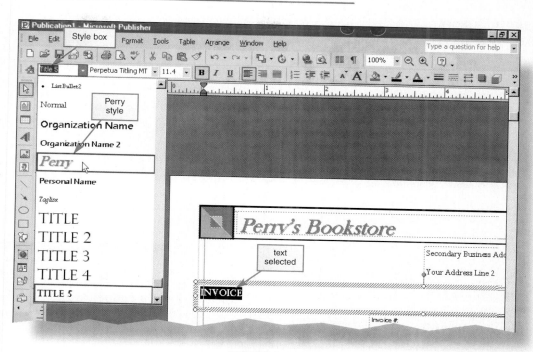

FIGURE 5-11

2 **Click Perry. Click the text box to remove the selection highlight.**

The word, Invoice, displays using the new Perry style (Figure 5-12).

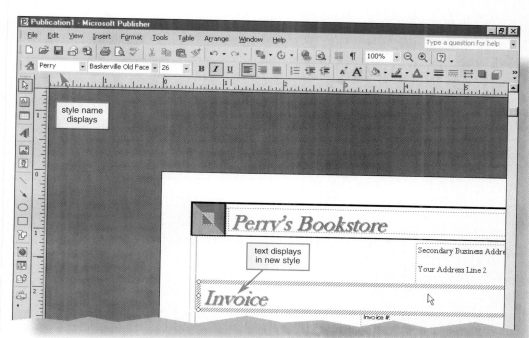

FIGURE 5-12

Using a style is easier than using the Format Painter when you have multiple pages or multiple documents. You do not have to search for the text with the formatting you like, click the Format Painter, and then return to new text. Rather, you can choose the preferred style from the Formatting toolbar.

1. Click Styles and Formatting button on Formatting toolbar, select style from list
2. In Voice Command mode, say "Style [select from list]"

AutoCorrect

On the Tools menu, you can set AutoCorrect to capitalize the first letter in a sentence and the first letter of the days of the week automatically. You also can correct automatically two initial capital letters, initial capital letters in table cells, as well as accidental use of the CAPS LOCK key. AutoCorrect's most powerful feature, however, allows you to insert your own typical errors for automatic correction.

The AutoCorrect Smart Tag

The AutoCorrect Options button displays after an automatic correction or change, such as a lowercased letter that was changed to a capital or text that has been converted to a hyperlink. If you do not want the correction, point to the correction, click the AutoCorrect Options button, and then use the options on the menu to undo it, turn off this type of correction for good, or connect to the AutoCorrect dialog box to adjust settings.

The Paste Smart Tag

The Paste Options button gives you more control and flexibility in choosing the format for a pasted item. The button displays just below a pasted item, such as a text box or a table frame. When clicked, the Paste Options button allows you to choose to retain the original text formatting or match the destination formatting.

The next step is to insert the address and contact information for Perry's Bookstore.

TO INSERT TEXT

1 Zoom to Page Width. Click the Address text box below Perry's Bookstore. If necessary, press CTRL+A to select all the text.

2 Type 8355 Hillcrest Drive and then press SHIFT+ENTER. Type Dallas, TX 75202 to complete the address.

3 Click the Phone/fax/e-mail text box to the right of the Address text box. If necessary, press CTRL+A to select all the text.

4 Type Telephone: 214-555-BOOK and then press SHIFT+ENTER. Type Fax: 214-555-0533 and then press SHIFT+ENTER. Type E-mail: pbs@bkstore.com to complete the text box.

The new text displays (Figure 5-13).

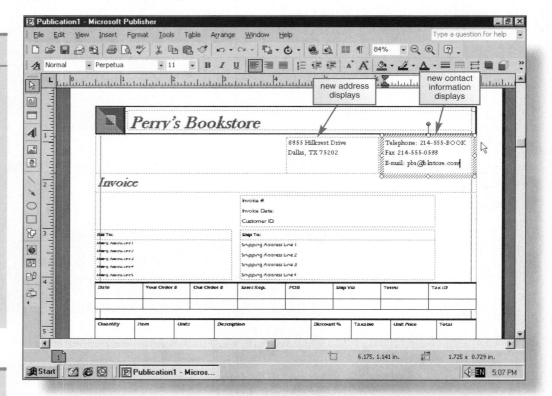

FIGURE 5-13

The next step is to create a text box for a thank you message that contains a drop cap.

Using a Drop Cap

A dropped capital letter, or **drop cap**, is a decorative large initial capital letter extending down below the other letters in the line. A drop cap displays larger than the rest of the characters in the line or paragraph and commonly is used to mark the beginning of an article or text box. If the text wraps to more than one line, the paragraph typically wraps around the dropped capital letter. You can format up to 15 contiguous letters and spaces as drop caps at the beginning of each paragraph.

Perform the following steps to create a dropped capital letter T as you create a thank you message text box in the lower-right portion of the invoice.

To Format with a Drop Cap

1 **Zoom to Page Width and then scroll to display the lower portion of the invoice. Click the Text Box button on the Objects toolbar. Drag a text box approximately 3.75 by 1.75 inches as displayed on the status bar. Move the text box to the position shown in Figure 5-14.**

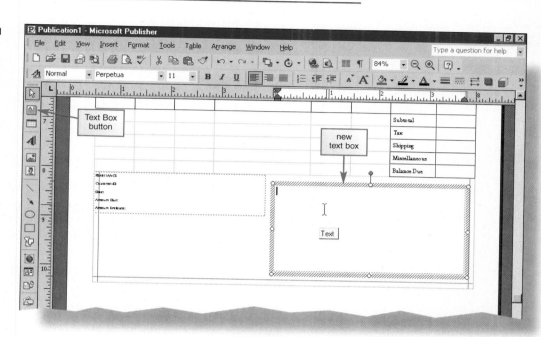

FIGURE 5-14

2 **Click the Style box arrow on the Formatting toolbar and then select Perry from the list. Type** Thank you for your **and then press the ENTER key. Type** business! **to finish the text. If Publisher capitalizes the b of business, point to the b. When the AutoCorrect Options button displays, click its button arrow, and then click Undo Automatic Capitalization on the menu.**

The thank you message displays in the Perry style (Figure 5-15).

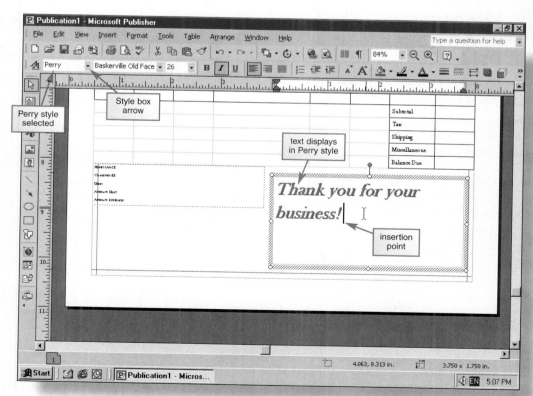

FIGURE 5-15

3 **Click to the left of the letter T in Thank you. Click Format on the menu bar and then point to Drop Cap.**

The Format menu displays (Figure 5-16).

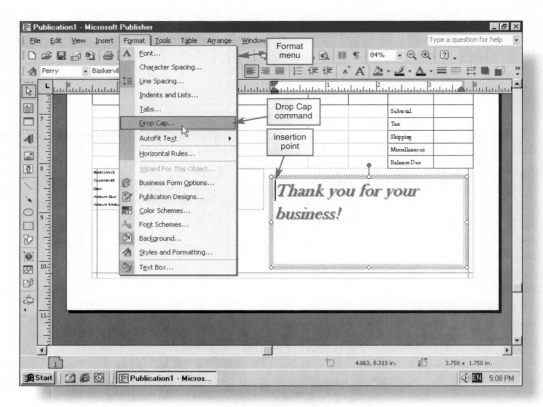

FIGURE 5-16

4 **Click Drop Cap. When the Drop Cap dialog box displays, if necessary, click the Drop Cap tab. In the Available drop caps area, click a preview that is similar to the one shown in Figure 5-17. Point to the Custom Drop Cap tab.**

The Available drop caps list displays using colors from the color scheme of the publication (Figure 5-17). Your list may vary.

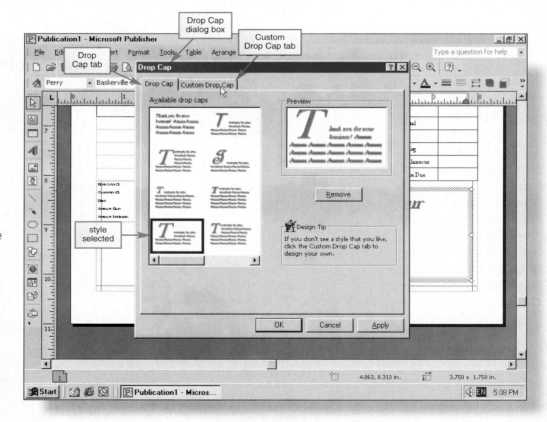

FIGURE 5-17

5 **Click the Custom Drop Cap tab. In the Select letter position and size area, click the Dropped preview. Drag through any number in the Size of letters text box, and then type 2 to replace it. Point to the OK button.**

The Custom Drop Cap sheet allows you to customize the drop cap further (Figure 5-18).

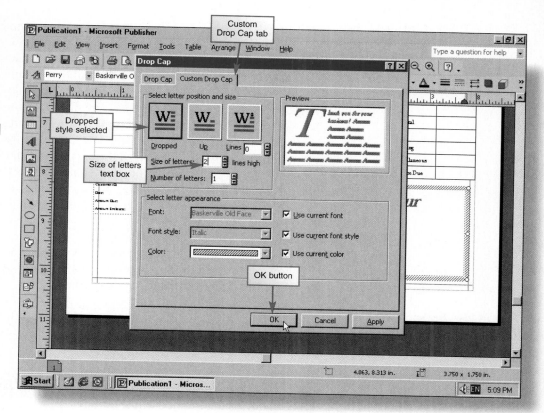

FIGURE 5-18

6 **Click the OK button.**

The drop cap letter displays in the text box (Figure 5-19).

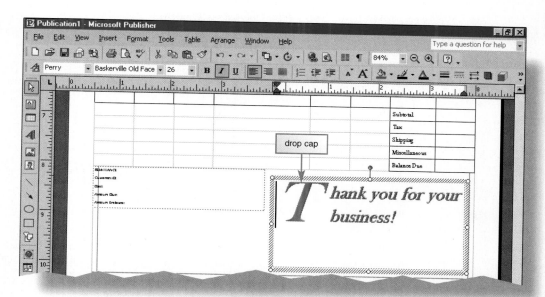

FIGURE 5-19

When you create a custom drop cap, the custom style is added to the Available drop caps list in the Drop Cap sheet. You can use this style to create other drop caps in the current publication. Another option is to use an **Up cap**, which extends above the paragraph, rather than sinking into the first few lines of the text.

Other Ways

1. In Voice Command mode, say "Format, Drop Cap"

Drop caps deserve special consideration if you are sending the file to a commercial printer. A file prepared for commercial submission includes all fonts from the publication. If you use only a small number of characters from a font, as in drop caps or for headlines, you can have Publisher embed only the characters you used from the font. Embedding only part of a font is called **subsetting**. The advantage of font subsetting is that it decreases the overall size of the file. The disadvantage is that it limits the ability to make corrections at the printing service. If the printing service does not have the full font installed on its computer, corrections can be made using only the characters included in the subset. Using the Fonts command on the Format menu, you are able to turn on font subsetting so that all the fonts you use in the publication will be subsetted when you embed them.

Working with Tabs and Markers

To make the invoice template as user-friendly as possible, it is important to help the user enter data in the correct places as much as you can. Text boxes with exact margin settings help the user identify where to place the text as well as the typical length of the entry. One way to position the insertion point inside the text box, at the correct spot, is with **tabs**. The ruler contains several tools to help you set text box margins, indents, and tabs. Table 5-1 explains the functions of the tools displayed in the figures on the following pages and how to modify them.

Table 5-1 Ruler Tools			
TOOL NAME	*DESCRIPTION*	*HOW TO CHANGE*	*OTHER WAYS*
First-line indent marker	The position at which paragraphs begin	Drag to desired location	On Format menu click Indents and Lists
Left and first-line indent marker	A small rectangle used to move both markers at once	Drag to desired location	On Format menu click Indents and Lists
Left indent marker in a paragraph	The left position at which text will align	Drag to desired location	On Format menu click Indents and Lists
Object margins	Gray indicates the area outside the object margin; white indicates the area inside the object margin	Resize object	On Format menu click Text box properties
Right indent marker	The right position at which text wraps to the next line	Drag to desired location	On Format menu click Indents and Lists
Move Both Rulers button (tab alignment button)	Displays the current alignment setting: left, right, center, or leader	Click to toggle choice	Double-click tab stop marker
Tab stop marker	Displays the location of a tab stop	Click to create; drag to move	On Format menu click Tabs
Zero point	A ruler setting commonly used to measure distances from the upper-left corner of a page or object	SHIFT+right-click ruler at desired location	SHIFT+right-drag to move both horizontal and vertical zero points

The triangles and rectangles on the ruler are called **markers**. You drag markers to any place on the ruler within the object margin. You can click a marker to display a dotted line through the publication to see in advance where the marker is set. Markers are paragraph-specific, which means that the tabs and indents apply to the whole paragraph. If you are typing a long passage of text, pressing the ENTER key carries forward the paragraph formatting.

Recall that the Special Characters button (Figure 5-20) on the Standard toolbar makes visible special nonprinting characters to help you format text passages, including tab characters, paragraph marks, and end-of-frame marks.

Perform the following steps to add a tab stop to the text box that contains the Invoice #, Invoice Date, and Customer ID. A **tab stop** will ensure that the data is properly aligned when entered by the user.

More *About*

Tabs

For an illustration of the many tools available within the Publisher rulers including tab markers, visit the Publisher 2002 More About Web page (scsite.com/pub2002/more .htm) and then click Rulers.

Steps **To Insert a Tab Stop for the Date**

1 **Zoom to Page Width. Click the text box that contains Invoice #, Invoice Date, and Customer ID. Press the F9 key. Click the Special Characters button on the Standard toolbar. Point to the 1" position on the Horizontal Ruler.**

*The **paragraph marks** display in the text box (Figure 5-20). Each line of this text box is a paragraph. The **end-of-frame markers** display as embellished circles.*

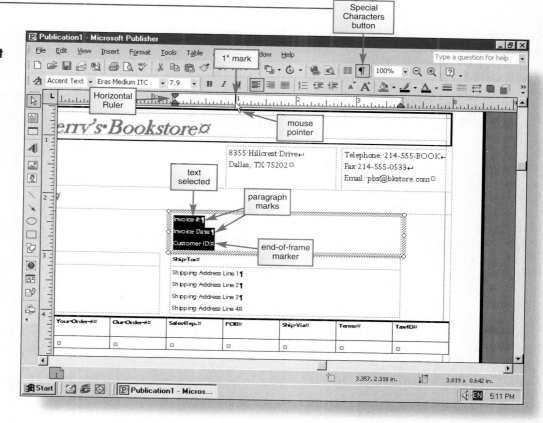

FIGURE 5-20

2 Click the Horizontal Ruler at the 1" position. Type `Invoice #`, press the TAB key, and then press the ENTER key. Type `Invoice Date`, press the TAB key, and then press the ENTER key. Type `Customer ID` and then press the TAB key.

The *tab stop marker* displays on the Horizontal Ruler, and the *nonprinting tab characters* display in each line to indicate the position of the tab stop (Figure 5-21).

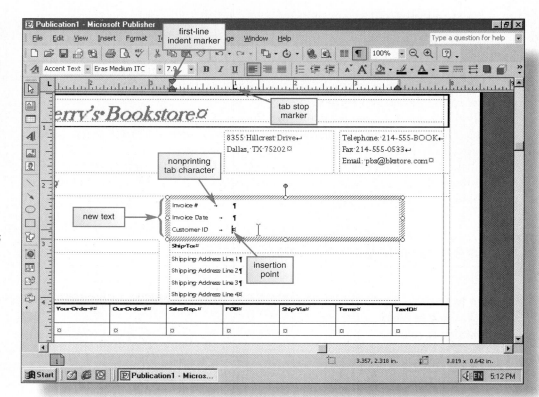

FIGURE 5-21

Hanging Indents

A first-line indent placed to the left of the left margin sometimes is called a hanging indent or exdent. Exdents typically are found in bibliographies and alphabetized listings. Creating an exdent saves keystrokes and formatting time.

Sometimes it is difficult to determine whether to use tab stops or indents. Use **tab stops** when you want to indent paragraphs as you go or when you want a simple column. You may want to tab the first line in a single paragraph, or add leaders (dots or dashes), as in a table of contents. Using the TAB key to indent the first line of each paragraph in a long passage of text is inefficient, however, because you must press it each time you begin a new paragraph. In those cases, it is better to use an **indent** because it automatically carries forward when you press the ENTER key. Use indents when you want the lines in a paragraph to be automatically adjusted for you, or when you want to indent all the lines in a paragraph without inserting tab stops at the beginning of each line.

The final step to format the Invoice template is to add a date that updates automatically each time you open the template.

Inserting the System Date

When creating an invoice, the date is an important piece of information. To print the correct date always, and to save time and keystrokes each time you create an instance of the invoice, you will create a field that Publisher will update from the computer's operating system. As part of its system administration functions, Windows keeps track of the date and time using a battery inside the processing unit. Besides the internal needs of the operating system to monitor performance, this date and time can be used by application software, to not only track the date and time of file creation and modification, but as an accessible field of information. Most Windows application software packages, including Publisher, can access the **system date and time** in order to display the current data as fixed text or to create an automatically updating field. That way, each time you access the file, the date will be correct.

Steps To Insert a System Date

1 Click just to the left of the paragraph mark on the Invoice Date line. Click Insert on the menu bar and then point to Date and Time.

The Insert menu displays (Figure 5-22). The publication has been scrolled to the right in the figure to display both the text box and the menu. Your display will differ.

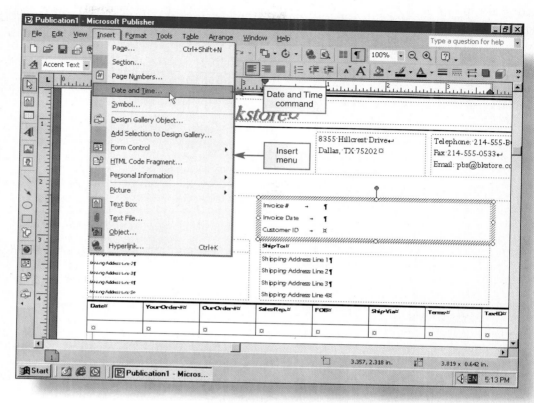

FIGURE 5-22

2 Click Date and Time. When the Date and Time dialog box displays, click the format, January 24, 2004 (or the current date on your screen). If necessary, click Update automatically to select the check box. Point to the OK button.

The Date and Time dialog box displays (Figure 5-23). Your screen most likely will not show January 24, 2004; instead, it will display the current system date stored in your computer according to the highlighted format.

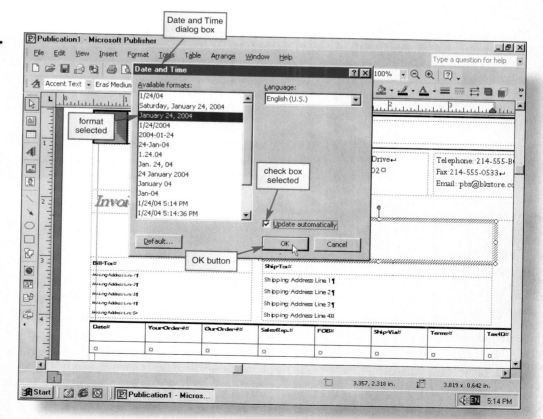

FIGURE 5-23

3 Click the OK button. Click the Special Characters button so it is not selected.

Publisher displays the current system date (Figure 5-24).

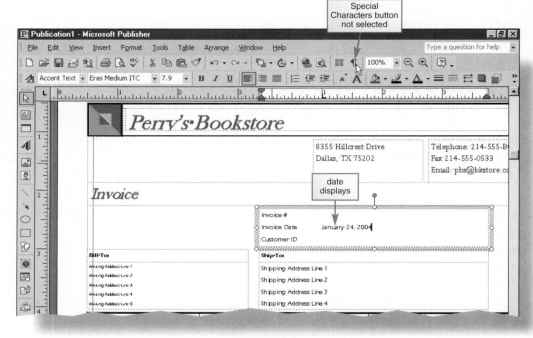

FIGURE 5-24

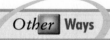
You may insert a system date, a system time, or both in a text box or table cell. In addition, you can determine the language and format you want. When you open or print the publication, Publisher will update the date or time you inserted to reflect the current date or time.

Now that the invoice template is complete, the file can be used to generate instances on an as-needed basis. Complete the following steps to save and print the invoice template.

TO SAVE AND PRINT THE INVOICE TEMPLATE

1 Insert a floppy disk into drive A.

2 Click the Save button on the Standard toolbar.

3 When the Save As dialog box displays, type `Perry Invoice Template` in the File name text box. Do not press the ENTER key.

4 If necessary, click the Save in box arrow and then click 3½ Floppy (A:).

5 Click the Save button in the Save As dialog box.

6 Click the Print button on the Standard toolbar.

Publisher saves the publication on a floppy disk in drive A with the file name, Perry Invoice Template, and then prints a copy on the printer. The completed invoice template is shown in Figure 5-1 on page PUB 5.05.

You can protect this template file from accidental deletion, forcing users to save instances with a different name, by changing the **read-only attribute**. The Windows operating system provides a Properties command on every file's shortcut menu. If you want to protect the file, click the Read-only check box in the General sheet.

Perform the following step to close the file without quitting Publisher.

TO CLOSE THE FILE WITHOUT QUITTING PUBLISHER

1 On the File menu, click Close. If a Microsoft Publisher dialog box displays asking if you want to save, click the No button.

A blank page displays to start the next business publication.

Creating a Special-Sized Coupon with a Border

Coupons are a popular way for businesses to attract customers to a product or to a store. A coupon also is a valued advertising tool. Because many coupons are never used, they are an inexpensive investment in advertising, to remind the customer of a product or service. Businesses may use coupons as a promotion, to offer a special deal to move merchandise, or to gain advantage over a competitor.

Creating a Custom Size Publication

Perry's Bookstore wants to provide coupons at the college registration for $5 off purchases of $75 or more. The coupon should be 7 inches by 5 inches and include the name of the bookstore, the amount, the location of the store, the expiration date, the telephone number, and the Web site address.

Steps **To Create a Custom Size Publication**

1 If a blank publication does not display, click the New button on the Standard toolbar. Click File on the menu bar and then point to Page Setup.

The File menu displays (Figure 5-25).

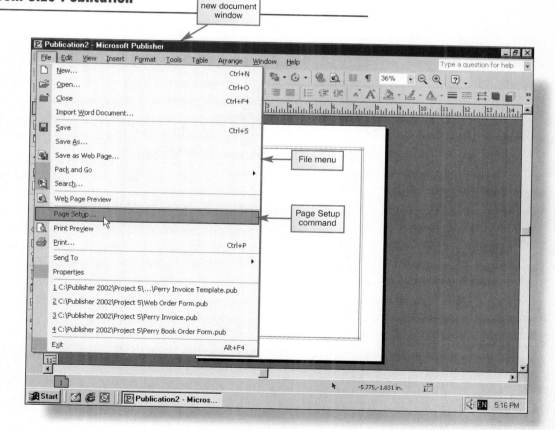

FIGURE 5-25

Click Page Setup. When the Page Setup Dialog box displays, if necessary, click the Layout tab. In the Publication type list, click Custom and then press the TAB key. Type 7 in the Width text box and then press the TAB key. Type 5 in the Height text box. Click Landscape and then point to the OK button.

The coupon will use landscape orientation and be 7 inches wide and 5 inches tall (Figure 5-26).

Click the OK button.

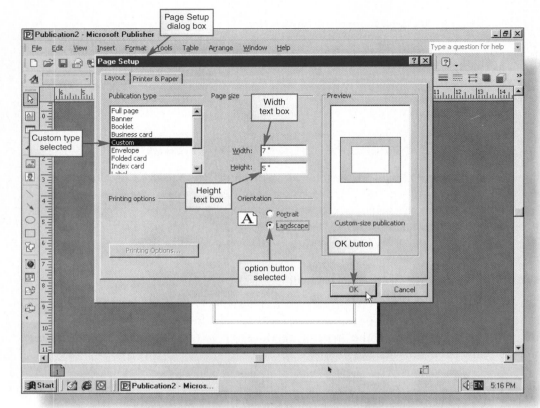

FIGURE 5-26

Other Ways

1. In Voice Command mode, say "File, Page Setup"

More *About*

Fonts

If you use TrueType fonts, Publisher uses the same font to display text on the screen and on the printout. TrueType font names are preceded by TT in the Font box on the Formatting toolbar. TrueType fonts are installed automatically when you set up Windows. If you use non-TrueType fonts, try to use a screen font that matches your printer font. If a matching font is not available or if your printer driver does not provide screen font information, Windows chooses the screen font that most closely resembles the printer font.

Perry's Bookstore wants to maintain the color and font schemes from the invoice to the coupon. Perform the following steps to choose the Citrus color scheme and the Capital font scheme.

TO SELECT A COLOR AND FONT SCHEME

1 Click Format on the menu bar and then click Color Schemes.

2 When the Color Schemes task pane displays, click Citrus in the list.

3 Click Font Schemes and then click Capital in the list.

4 Close the Font Schemes task pane.

The next step is to create text boxes for the coupon. You will import the Perry style from the Perry Invoice for the first two text boxes. You will format the other text boxes individually. Table 5-2 displays the text of each text box and the formatting and placement.

Table 5-2 Text Boxes for the Coupon

TEXT	LOCATION	SIZE	FONT	FONT SIZE	FORMATTING
Perry's Bookstore	1.0, .50	5.0 x .50	Perry		
$5.00 off	2.0, 1.2	3.7 x 1.0	Perry		
On purchases of $75 or more	1.0, 2.25	5.0 x .50	Rockwell Condensed	28	Bold, Centered
Just off-campus in Liberty Mall	1.2, 2.9	4.5 x .25	Rockwell	14	Centered
Coupon expires August 1, 2004	1.8, 3.4	3.0 x .25	Times New Roman	10	Centered
Telephone: 555-BOOK	1.8, 3.9	3.0 x .25	Rockwell	12	Centered
Online at www.perrysbookstore.com	1.9, 4.3	3.0 x .30	Times New Roman	11	Centered

Steps **To Create Text Boxes and Import a Style**

1 **Click the Text Box button on the Objects toolbar. Draw a text box in the upper portion of the coupon. Double-click the Object Size box. When the Measurement toolbar displays, enter the amounts from the first row in Table 5-2.**

The new dimensions and location of the text box display (Figure 5-27).

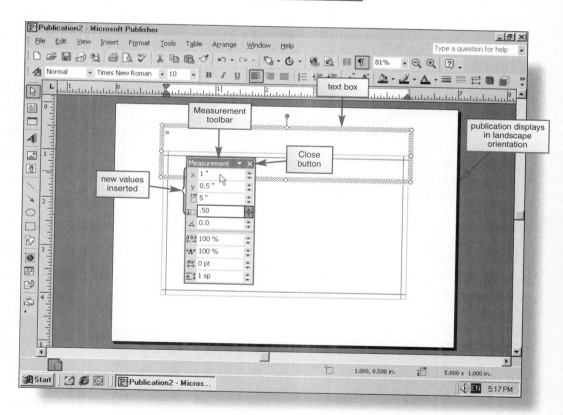

FIGURE 5-27

2 Close the Measurement toolbar. Click the Styles and Formatting button on the Formatting toolbar. When the Styles and Formatting task pane displays, point to the Import styles button as shown in Figure 5-28.

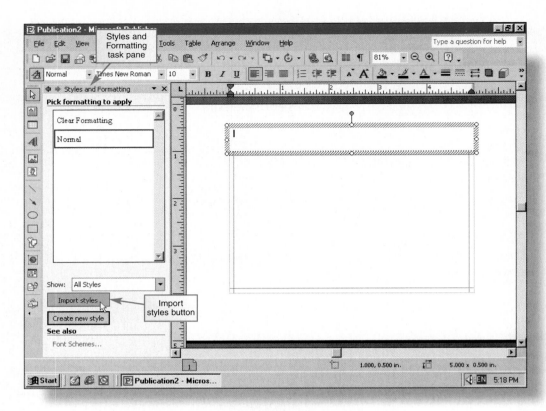

FIGURE 5-28

3 Click the Import styles button. When the Import Styles dialog box displays, click 3½ Floppy (A:) in the Look in list. When the list displays, point to Perry Invoice Template.

The list of files on the floppy disk in drive A display (Figure 5-29). Styles from the Perry Invoice will be imported into the coupon.

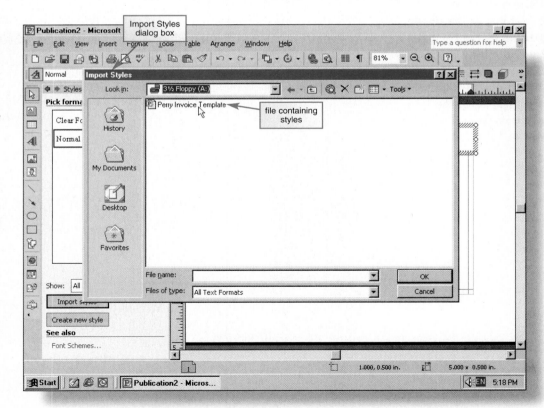

FIGURE 5-29

4 Double-click Perry Invoice. When a dialog box displays asking if you want to import the normal style, click the Yes button. In the Styles and Formatting task pane, scroll down in the list. When the Perry style displays in the task pane, click it, and then type `Perry's Bookstore` in the text box.

The formatted text displays (Figure 5-30).

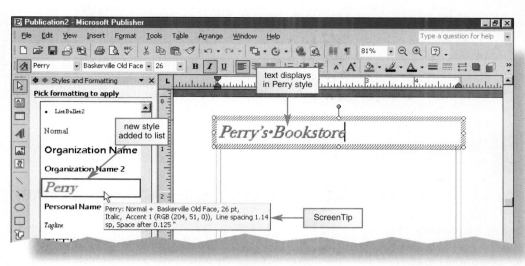

FIGURE 5-30

5 Close the Styles and Formatting task pane. Repeat Step 1 for the second text box, selecting Perry from the Style drop-down list on the Formatting toolbar. Then create the other text boxes listed in Table 5-2. For each text box, select the font, the font size, and the formatting before you type the text.

The completed text boxes display (Figure 5-31).

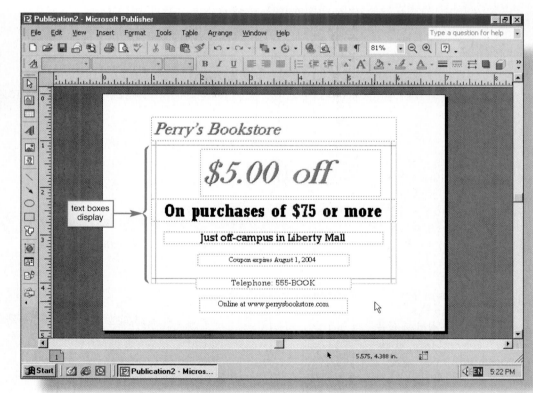

FIGURE 5-31

If you want to align text boxes with each other, the Align or Distribute command on the Arrange menu, displays choices for left, center, right, top, middle, or bottom. Simply SHIFT-click the boxes and then make a selection from the menu.

Other Ways

1. In Voice Command mode, say "Styles and Formatting, Import Styles"

Adding a Border to the Coupon

The final steps to complete the coupon involve adding a border and then saving the coupon. A **border** is a visible line or design around the edge of an object. Borders may be as simple as a single black line or as complex as repeated pictures from a graphics file. Borders can add interest and emphasis to publications.

Steps **To Add a Border**

1 **Click the Text Box button on the Objects toolbar and then draw a text box that fills the entire page layout. Right-click the text box and then point to Format Text Box on the shortcut menu.**

The shortcut menu for text boxes displays (Figure 5-32).

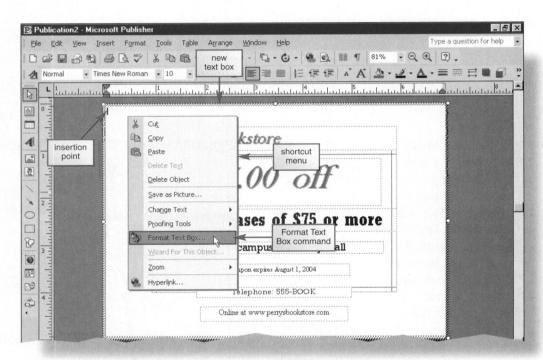

FIGURE 5-32

2 **Click Format Text Box. When the Format Text Box dialog box displays, if necessary, click the Colors and Lines tab. Point to the BorderArt button as shown in Figure 5-33.**

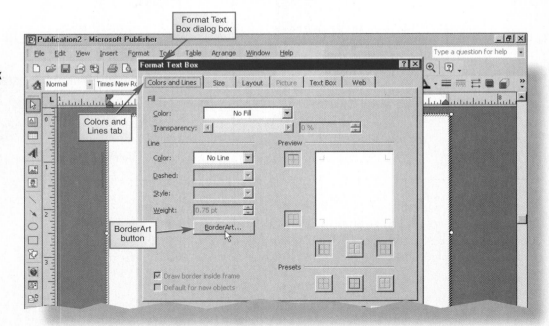

FIGURE 5-33

3 Click the BorderArt button. When the BorderArt dialog box displays, scroll to and then click Packages in the Available Borders list. Point to the OK button.

The Available Borders list displays decorative borders (Figure 5-34).

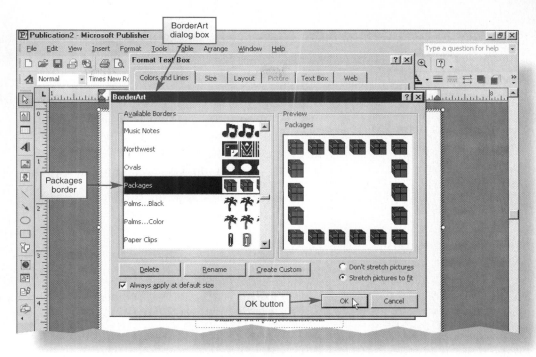

FIGURE 5-34

4 Click the OK button. When the Format Text Box dialog box again displays, click the OK button.

The border around the edge of the text box, and the coupon, displays (Figure 5-35).

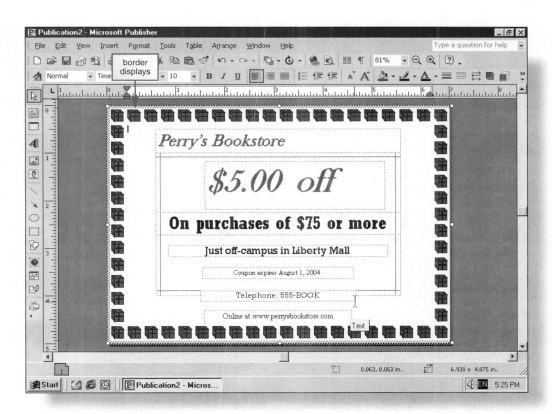

FIGURE 5-35

Other **Ways**

1. In Voice Command mode, say "Format, Text Box, BorderArt"

More About

Commercial Printing Tools

On the Tools menu, the Commercial Printing Tools submenu gives you four commands to assist you in preparing your publication for outside printing. Color Printing allows you to select a color-printing scheme such as RGB or spot color. Graphics Manager gives commercial printers comprehensive information about every graphical component in a publication. You can change the status of an image from embedded to linked, allowing the printer to enhance images while retaining the integrity of the original graphic. Trapping allows you to set the percentages and color thresholds for trapping objects. You can choose general settings for the publication or Per Object Trapping. Fonts can be completely embedded or subsetted for the commercial printer.

Perform the following steps to save, print, and then close the coupon.

TO SAVE, PRINT, AND CLOSE THE COUPON

1 Insert a floppy disk into drive A. Click the Save button on the Standard toolbar.

2 When the Save As dialog box displays, type Perry Coupon in the File name text box. Do not press the ENTER key.

3 If necessary, click the Save in box arrow and then click 3½ Floppy (A:).

4 Click the Save button in the Save As dialog box.

5 Click the Print button on the Standard toolbar.

6 Click File on the menu bar and then click Close.

Publisher saves the publication on a floppy disk in drive A with the file name, Perry Coupon, and then prints a copy on the printer. The completed coupon is shown in Figure 5-1 on page PUB 5.05. The file is closed without quitting Publisher.

U sing Tables

You may recall that a Publisher table is a collection of rows and columns and that the intersection of a row and column is called a cell. Cells are filled with data. Within a table, you easily can rearrange rows and columns, change column widths and row heights, and insert diagonal lines, pictures, and text. You can format the cells to give the table a professional appearance. You can add a border to the entire table as well. For these reasons, many Publisher users create tables rather than using large text boxes with tabs. Tables allow you to input data in columns as you would for a schedule, price list, a resume, or a table of contents.

Creating a Book Order Form

Perform the following steps to draw the table for the book order form for Perry's Bookstore. You will format it using the Create Table dialog box. The first step is to set up the publication. Then, you will draw an empty table in a blank publication with the **Insert Table button** on the Objects toolbar. Finally, you will add a **shadow** to the table to give it a three-dimensional look.

More About

Page Setup

In Publisher, page size refers to the size of your publication, not to the paper. Page orientation refers to the portrait (vertical) or landscape (horizontal) layout of the publication. The publication layout you choose includes the page size and orientation most often used for that particular type of publication. ...u can change page size, ...ge orientation, and pre-...our changes using the ...tup dialog box.

Steps To Create a Formatted Table

1 If a blank publication does not display, click the New button on the Standard toolbar. Click File on the menu bar and then click Page Setup. When the Page Setup dialog box displays, if necessary, click the Layout tab. Click Landscape and then point to the OK button.

The book order form will be a full page in Landscape orientation (Figure 5-36).

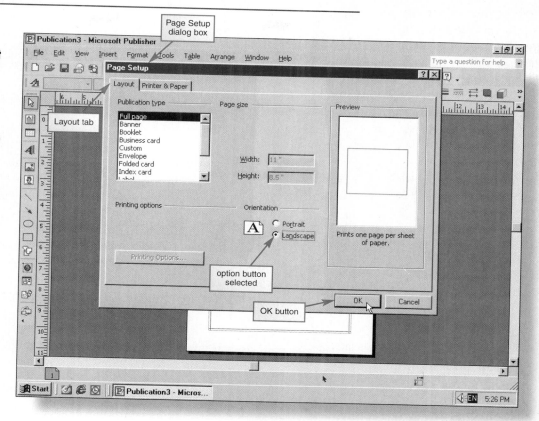

FIGURE 5-36

2 Click the OK button. Click the Insert Table button on the Objects toolbar. Drag the cross hair mouse pointer from the upper-left portion of the publication downward and to the right until the created frame is approximately 9 inches by 6 inches.

The frame of the table displays before you release the mouse button (Figure 5-37).

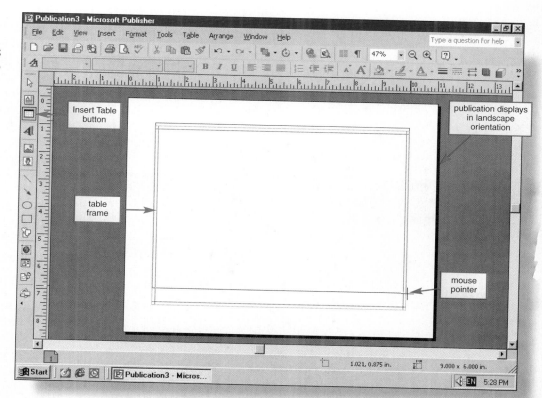

FIGURE 5-37

3 Release the mouse button. When the Create Table dialog box displays, type 6 in the Number of rows box. Press the TAB key. Type 6 in the Number of columns box. Click the down scroll arrow in the Table format list box until List with Title 2 displays in the Table format list. Click List with Title 2 and then point to the OK button.

The Create Table dialog box displays (Figure 5-38). The Table format list includes formats with and without titles.

4 Click the OK button. Click Format on the menu bar and then click Color Schemes. When the Colors Schemes task pane displays, click Citrus in the list and then close the task pane.

The formatted table displays in the workspace (shown in Figure 5-39).

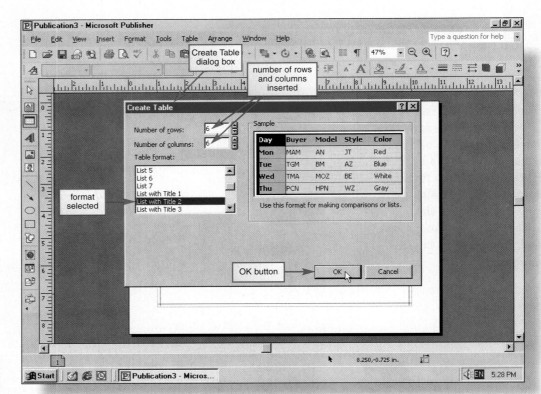

FIGURE 5-38

A non-formatted table looks different from a text box. When selected, Publisher tables display vertical and horizontal gray gridlines. The nonprinting gridlines display in the frame so you can see the rows and columns. Cell heights automatically increase as inserted text wraps to the next line.

To customize a table or data within a table, first you must select the cell(s) and then apply the appropriate formats. Table 5-3 describes techniques to select items in a table.

Merging Cells and Inserting a Cell Diagonal

The first row of the table will hold the title of the table. Publisher uses the **Merge Cells command** to create one large cell instead of several smaller ones.

Table 5-3 Selecting Items in a Table	
ITEMS TO SELECT	**ACTION**
Cell	Triple-click the cell or drag through the text.
Column	Point to the top of the column. When the mouse pointer becomes a black, down arrow, click.
Contiguous cells, rows, or columns	Drag through the cells, rows, or columns.
Entire table	On the Table menu, point to Select, and then click Table.
Row	Point to the left of the row. When the mouse pointer becomes a black, right arrow, click.
Text in next cell	Press the TAB key.
Text in previous cell	Press SHIFT+TAB.

The first cell in the second row will hold both the column heading and the row heading. Publisher uses the **Cell Diagonals command** to split the cell in half diagonally. Perform the following steps to merge cells and create a cell diagonal.

 Steps **To Merge Cells and Create a Cell Diagonal**

1 **Point to the left of the first row. When the mouse pointer displays a black, right arrow, click it.**

The first row is selected (Figure 5-39).

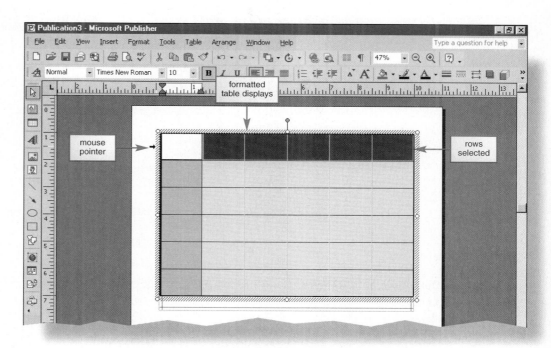

FIGURE 5-39

2 **Click Table on the menu bar and then point to Merge Cells.**

The Table menu displays, and the first row is selected (Figure 5-40).

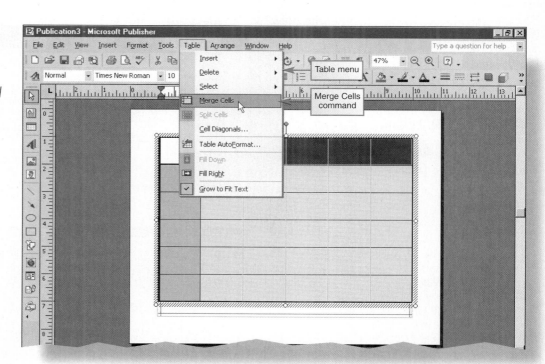

FIGURE 5-40

3 Click Merge Cells. Click the first cell in the second row. Click Table on the menu bar and then point to Cell Diagonals.

The first row displays as a single, large cell (Figure 5-41). The insertion point displays in the second row.

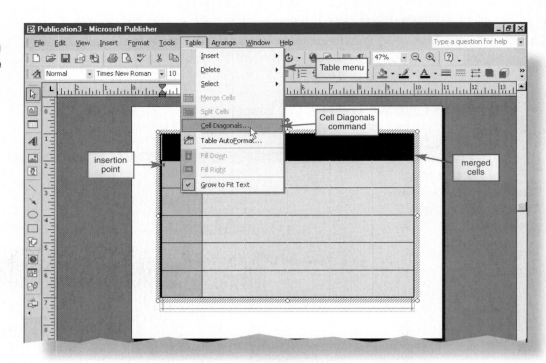

FIGURE 5-41

4 Click Cell Diagonals. When the Cell Diagonals dialog box displays, click Divide down, and then point to the OK button.

The Cell Diagonals dialog box displays (Figure 5-42). The Divide down option button is selected.

5 Click the OK button.

The cell is split into two cells with a diagonal line (shown in Figure 5-43).

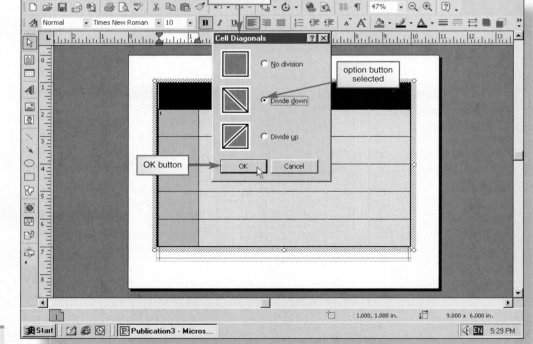

FIGURE 5-42

Other Ways

1. To merge cells, in Voice Command mode, say "Table, Merge Cells"

2. To create cell diagonals, in Voice Command mode, say "Table, Cell Diagonals"

Entering Data into the Table

Efficiently navigating cells is an important skill when entering data into a table. To advance from one cell to the next, press the TAB key. To advance from one column to the next, also press the TAB key; do not press the ENTER key. The ENTER key is used to begin new paragraphs within a cell. To advance from one row to the next, press the DOWN ARROW key. Perform the following steps to enter the data into the table.

TO ENTER DATA INTO A TABLE

1 Zoom to Page Width. Click the top title cell of the table. Press CTRL+E to center the text. Click the Font Size box arrow and then click 36 in the list. Type Perry's Book Order Form and then press the TAB key.

2 Type Course and Section Number and then press the TAB key. Type Book Information and then press the TAB key.

3 Continue to enter data as shown in Figure 5-43, zooming as necessary.

The title, column headings, and row headings display in the table (Figure 5-43).

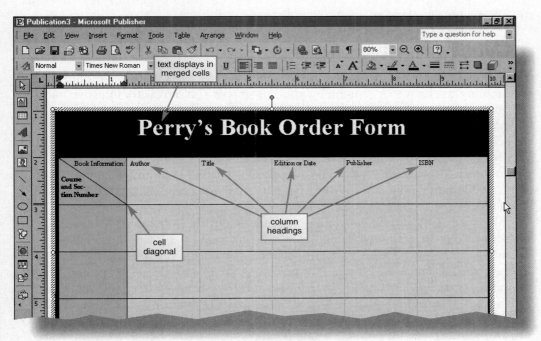

FIGURE 5-43

The Table menu contains a command called **Grow to Fit Text** (Figure 5-40 on page PUB 5.34) that displays a check mark when turned on. Table cells, except those diagonally split, automatically display all entered text if Grow to Fit Text is enabled. If you turn off the command, the table is locked and the extra text is stored in the cell's overflow area.

To resize manually the height of a row or the width of a column, you may point to a border of any cell. When the Adjust mouse pointer displays, you may drag the column or row to the desired size.

More About

The Ruler

When the insertion point is in a table, the ruler shows the boundaries of the selected cell in the table, both horizontally and vertically.

More About

Filling a Table

Publisher uses the Fill command to copy cell data quickly. Similar to the Fill command in spreadsheet applications, the Fill command in Publisher examines the contents of the first selected cell, and then copies the data to all other selected cells. You may Fill Down or Fill Right, depending upon the situation. Publisher's Fill command does not adjust the cells, create a series, or update relative references, as do most electronic spreadsheet programs; it simply is an extended copy command.

Saving the Table

The next step is to save and print the book order form.

TO SAVE AND PRINT THE BOOK ORDER FORM

1 Insert a floppy disk into drive A. Click the Save button on the Standard toolbar.

2 When the Save As dialog box displays, type `Perry Book Order Form` in the File name text box. Do not press the ENTER key.

3 Click the Save in box arrow and then click 3½ Floppy (A:).

4 Click the Save button in the Save As dialog box.

5 Click the Print button on the Standard toolbar.

Publisher saves the publication on a floppy disk in drive A with the file name, Perry Book Order Form, and then prints a copy on the printer. The completed order form is shown in Figure 5-1 on page PUB 5.05.

The final step is to send a copy of the book order form to Jason Perry attached to an e-mail message.

Microsoft Outlook

Outlook and Outlook Express are both popular e-mail handlers with Windows 2000. For more information about these applications, visit the Publisher 2002 More About Web page (scsite.com/pub2002/more.htm) and then click Outlook.

Attaching a Publication to an E-mail Message

E-mail messages by themselves have limited graphic capabilities, although that is beginning to change. As communication protocols and hardware improve, more and more formatting will be included in e-mail messages. Sending e-mail with attachments, however, is still the standard way to send documents and publications electronically with formatting and graphics. An **attachment** is a separate file electronically sent with a message to and from other computer users. A Publisher publication may be sent as an attachment for consultation purposes or when multiple employees work on the same publication. Many times publications are sent as attachments when forwarded to outside printing services.

Publisher's **Send To command** automatically opens the system's preset e-mail software and creates an attachment of the current saved publication. Because Publisher is part of the Microsoft Office Suite of application software, the Send To command usually activates an Outlook message. **Microsoft Outlook** is a **personal information management (PIM)** software package, integrated with Microsoft Office, which not only handles e-mail, but also automates the desktop and communication, with tools for maintaining the appointment calendar, contacts, tasks, and notes. Some other examples of popular **e-mail handlers**, or electronic mail software packages, are **Microsoft Mail**, **Lotus cc:Mail**, and **Eudora**.

Most e-mail handlers — even on **intranets**, or internal networks — can send attachments. A few of the packages limit the file size of the attachments.

Sending a Publisher File via E-mail

The following steps direct you to send a message and attachment. You may substitute your instructor's e-mail address if you actually want to send the message. Ask your instructor or network administrator for directions to complete these steps properly for your computer. You can perform these steps, however, even if you have no Internet connection.

Steps **To Send a Publisher File via E-Mail**

1 **Click File on the menu bar, point to Send To, and then point to Mail Recipient (as Attachment).**

The File menu displays (Figure 5-44).

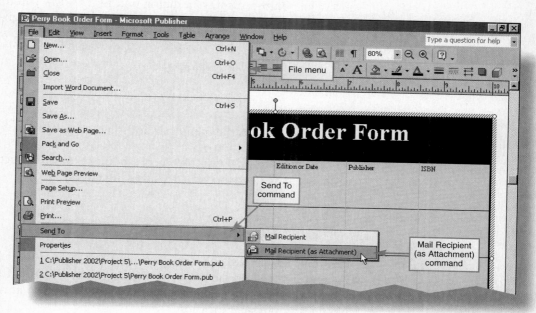

FIGURE 5-44

2 **Click Mail Recipient (as Attachment). If your computer does not connect automatically to the Internet, a Choose Profile dialog box may display. If your computer connects automatically to an intranet or the Internet, a password or login dialog box may display. Enter the required To, Subject, and Message data as shown in Figure 5-45. Point to the Send button.**

The Book Order Form message window displays (Figure 5-45). You can use your instructor's e-mail address, if permitted. If a From text box displays, type your name or e-mail address in the text box.

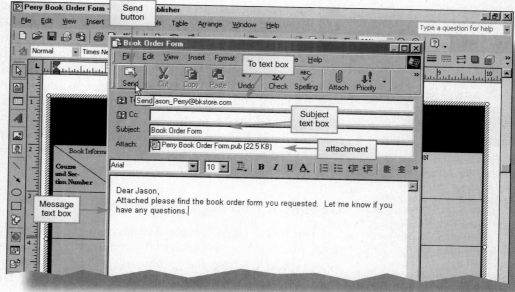

FIGURE 5-45

5 **Click the Send button.**

The message is sent with the attachment, and the publication again displays. If you were not connected to the Internet, the message is stored in Outlook's Outbox.

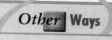

Other Ways

1. In Voice Command mode, say "File, Send To, Mail Recipient as Attachment"

Multiple files can be attached to e-mail messages. Microsoft Office message windows contain an **Insert File button** on the Standard toolbar. When clicked, the Insert File button displays a dialog box that allows you to browse and select the file you want to attach. Additionally, Microsoft Office gives you the choice of either creating a file and then sending a message, or beginning with a message and then attaching a file.

You now can close the file.

TO CLOSE THE FILE

1   Click File on the menu bar and then click Close.

The final publication for Perry's Bookstore is the electronic version of the book order form as described in the following pages.

Web Pages with Electronic Forms

Electronic commerce, or **e-commerce**, has established itself in the business world as an inexpensive and efficient way to increase visibility and, therefore, sales. Customers visit, browse, make purchases, and ask for assistance at a Web site, just as they would at a physical location.

An electronic form is used on a Web page to collect data from visitors. **Electronic forms** are used to request and collect information, comments, or survey data, and to conduct business transactions. An electronic form is made up of a collection of **form controls**, which are the individual buttons, boxes, and hyperlinks that let Web site visitors communicate with Web site owners. Electronic forms must include a submit button; otherwise Web site visitors cannot return their form data.

As e-commerce becomes more popular, desktop publishing theory must include electronic as well as print publishing concepts. Publisher's Design Gallery contains many electronic mastheads, navigation bars, Web buttons, and forms, designed to look good and load quickly on the Web. Additionally, the Form Object menu contains many features to assist in designing forms from scratch. Most desktop publishers use a combination of rapid form development techniques to tailor their Web site to suit their needs.

Creating a Web Page from Scratch

You will create a sample Web form in an effort to automate the company's book order process. You will insert text and appropriate electronic form controls, as well as a graphic. Clicking the graphic in the Web site will allow visitors to e-mail Perry's Bookstore. After running the publication through the Design Checker, you will save both the publication and the Web files on a floppy disk.

Creating a Blank Web Page

Publisher provides a blank Web page for users who wish to start from scratch. The New Publication task pane has a design set of blank publications with examples of business cards, greeting cards, Web pages, among others. Perform the following steps to display a blank Web page.

More About

Testing Electronic Forms

It is a good practice to test your electronic form to make sure it functions as you intended, and returns the form data to you. Test your form in one or more of the following ways. Connect your system to the Web and then use a browser to locate your form. Complete the electronic form yourself and record your responses. As you use the form, make sure the controls work as you intended. Try submitting your form. Verify that you received the data you entered. Finally, check the data to make sure you understand the format in which the responses were returned to you.

Steps To Create a Blank Web Page

1 Click File on the menu bar and then click New. When the New Publication task pane displays, click the By Publication Type box arrow and then point to By Blank Publications.

Three different sets of designs are available (Figure 5-46).

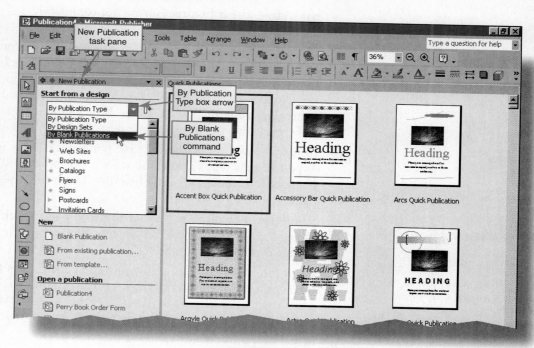

FIGURE 5-46

2 Click By Blank Publications. When the Blank Full Page pane displays, point to Web Page.

The Blank Full Page pane displays previews of many types of blank publications (Figure 5-47).

3 Double-click Web Page. Click Format on the menu bar and then click Color Schemes. Click Citrus in the list. Click Font Schemes and then click Capital in the list. Close the task pane. Zoom to Page Width.

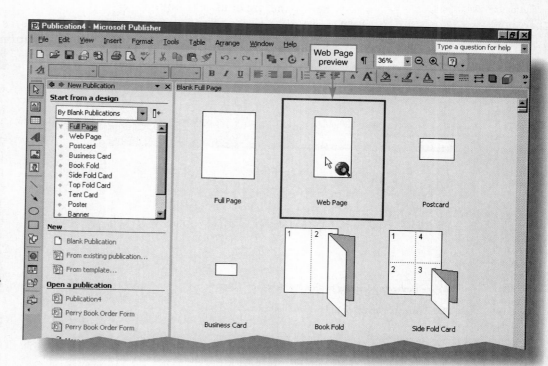

FIGURE 5-47

The next step is to insert text boxes and a table in the publication.

TO INSERT OBJECTS ON THE WEB PAGE

1 Click the Text Box button on the Objects toolbar. One inch from the top of the page, drag a text box measuring approximately 5.3 inches by 1.5 inches, across the top of the page.

2 Click the Styles and Formatting button on the Formatting toolbar. When the Styles and Formatting task pane displays, click the Import styles button. When the Import Styles dialog box displays, select 3½ Floppy (A:) from the Look in list. Double-click the Perry Invoice Template file to import the Perry style. When Publisher displays a dialog box asking if you want to change the Normal style, click the Yes button.

3 In the Styles and Formatting task pane, click Perry in the list of available styles. Type Perry's Bookstore and then press the ENTER key. Type Your Textbook Connection to complete the heading. Close the Styles and Formatting task pane.

4 Scroll down to display more of the Web page. Click the Text Box button on the Objects toolbar and then drag a text box below the previous one, approximately 5 inches by 1 inch.

5 Click the Font Size box arrow and then click 14 in the list. Type We are currently accepting textbook orders for Fall 2004. and then press the ENTER key. Type Please enter the textbook and personal information below. to complete the instructions.

6 Scroll down to display more of the Web page. Click the Insert Table button on the Objects toolbar and then drag a table approximately 5 inches by .5 inch, below the previous text box.

7 When the Create Table dialog box displays, type 1 as the entry press the TAB key, and then type 6 as the entry. Click the OK button.

8 Type Course Number and then press the TAB key. Type Book Title and then press the TAB key. Type Author and then press the TAB key. Type ISBN and then press the TAB key. Type Req. and then press the TAB key. Type Rec. and then press the TAB key.

The objects display in the Web publication (Figure 5-48).

An instruction text box will display approximately halfway down the page, telling users to enter the name, department and telephone number. Perform the following step to create one more text box.

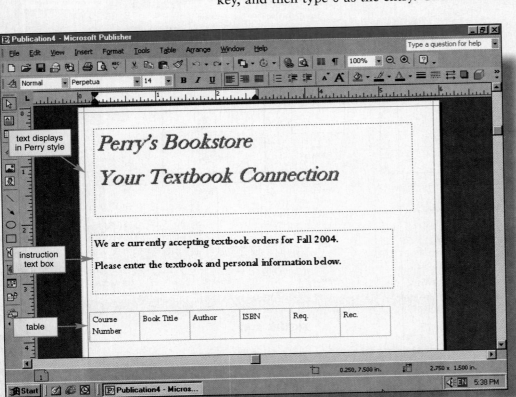

FIGURE 5-48

TO CREATE ANOTHER TEXT BOX

1 Scroll to approximately 7.5 inches down the page. On the left side of the page, create a text box approximately 2.75 by 1.0 inches. Click the Font Size box arrow and then click 14 in the list. In the text box, type `Please enter your name, department, and telephone number,` to insert the instructions.

The text box displays (Figure 5-49).

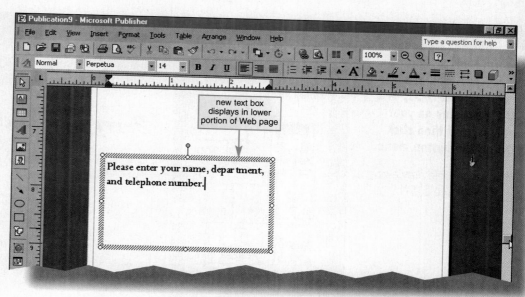

FIGURE 5-49

Inserting an Animated Graphic

Perform the following steps to insert an animated graphic in the publication. You will specify to search for only graphics from the Web collection on your computer. If you are connected to the Internet, the Insert Clip Art task pane will search for Web collection graphics from the Design Gallery Live Web site as well. The graphic displayed in the following figures also is available on the Data Disk that accompanies this book. See the inside back cover for instructions for downloading the Data Disk or see your instructor for information about accessing the files required for this book.

Steps — To Insert an Animated Graphic from the Web Collection

1 **Zoom to Page Width. Click the Clip Organizer Frame button on the Objects toolbar. When the Insert Clip Art task pane displays, drag through any text in the Search text text box, and then type** books **as the text. Click the Search in box arrow. Click the check marks next to My Collections and Office Collections so they do not display. Point to the Search button.**

Publisher will search for Web collection graphics associated with the term, books (Figure 5-50).

FIGURE 5-50

2 **Click the Search button. When the graphics display, click the button beside the graphic shown in Figure 5-51, or a suitable graphic on your computer, and then click Insert on the button menu.**

Your list of graphic previews may differ (Figure 5-51).

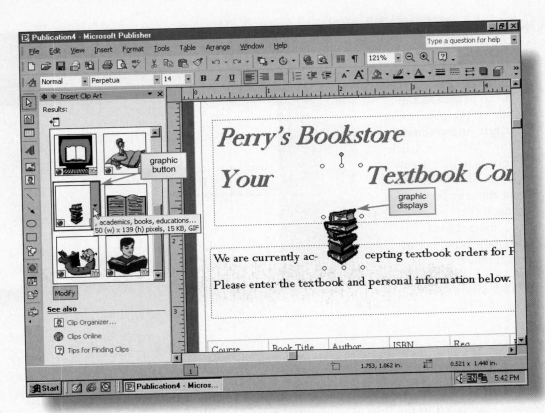

FIGURE 5-51

3 **When the graphic displays in the publication, drag it to the upper-right corner of the page. Close the Insert Clip Art task pane. Resize the graphic as necessary.**

The graphic displays in its new location (Figure 5-52).

FIGURE 5-52

Other Ways

1. In Voice Command mode, say, "Clip Organizer Frame"

Hot Spots

To facilitate communication, electronic forms also may contain hyperlinks and hot spots. Recall that hyperlinks are colored and underlined text that you click to go to a file, an address, or another HTML page on the Web. A **hot spot** is a specific area or object containing a hyperlink, typically a graphic. An entire object can be a single hot spot, or an object can contain multiple hot spots. Users may click the hot spot in the same way they click text hyperlinks.

When viewing a Web page with a browser, the mouse pointer changes to a hand when positioned on a hot spot. The change in the mouse pointer icon is called a **mouse over event. Events** are an integral part of the object-oriented concepts used in Web technology. Even the click of a hyperlink or button is considered an event.

Creating a Hot Spot

Perform the following steps to create a hot spot over the graphic in the Web order form.

Steps **To Insert a Hot Spot**

1 **Click the Hot Spot button on the Objects toolbar. When the Insert Hyperlink dialog box displays, type** Jason_Perry@bkstore .com **in the e-mail address text box and then point to the OK button.**

The hot spot directs users to the e-mail address of the company (Figure 5-53).

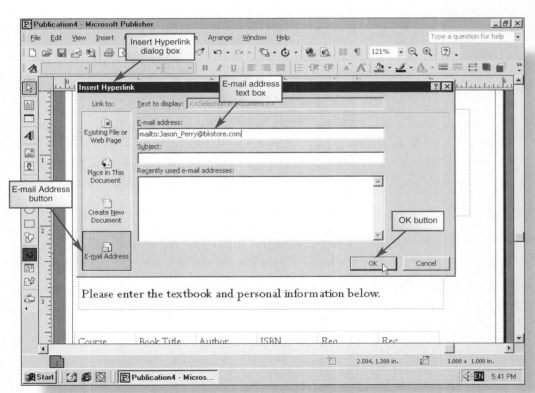

FIGURE 5-53

2 **Click the OK button. Drag the hot spot frame so it displays over the top of the graphic as shown in Figure 5-54.**

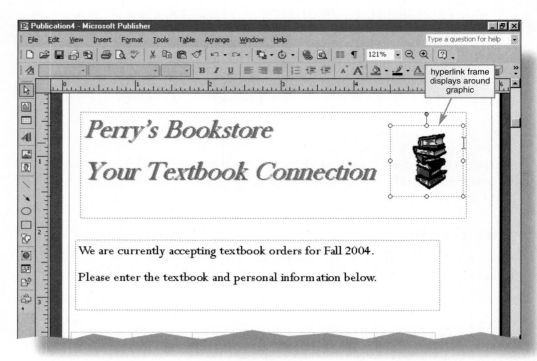

FIGURE 5-54

The graphic now is a hot spot that, when clicked, opens the user's e-mail message window. Pointing to the hot spot, even during editing, now will display a hand mouse pointer and an e-mail ScreenTip with the e-mail address.

Using Form Controls

Form controls are the individual boxes and buttons used by Web site visitors to enter data. The data from a form control is transmitted from the visitor to the site owner via a **submit button**. Publisher supports six types of form controls.

A **Checkbox** is a square box that presents a yes/no choice. Selected, it displays a check mark or X. Several Checkboxes function as a group of related but independent choices. An **Option Button** is a round radio button that presents one choice. Selected, an option button circle displays filled in. When grouped, option buttons function like multiple-choice questions. The difference between an option button and a check box is that users can select only one option button within a group, but any number of check boxes. Checkboxes and Option Buttons both display a label you can edit. Furthermore, you can choose to display either control selected or not selected at startup.

A **List Box** presents a group of items in a list. Visitors can scroll to select from one or any number of choices in the List Box. You determine the available choices and the number that may be selected when you set List Box properties.

If you want Web visitors to type information in a text box, you insert a form control called a **Textbox**. Sensitive information, such as credit card information or passwords, can display with asterisks. A **Text Area**, or multiline text box, provides a means of entering information by making available to the visitor a larger text box with multiple blank lines. Next to Textbox and Text Area form controls, it is advisable to include regular text boxes as instruction labels, to assist visitors in entering the correct information.

You must include a **Submit command button** on every form. This button allows visitors to send you their form data. A **Reset command button** is optional, but provides a way to clear form data and allow the Web visitor to start over. Command buttons can display any words in their visible labels, such as Send or Clear. Form controls each have a logical, or **internal data label**, as well. This data label references and identifies the visitor-supplied information when submitted to the Web site owner. For instance, the label words, Course1, would accompany the user-supplied course number in the e-mail submission. You may assign these internal data labels as well as other settings by double-clicking the control and then clicking the **Form Properties button**.

Inserting Form Controls on the Web Book Order Form

For each book, the Web order form contains four Textbox form controls and two Checkbox form controls. Below that, a Text Area displays in which users enter other supplies requested for their classes. A second Text Area form control allows users to enter their name, department, and telephone number. Perform the following steps to add form controls to the Web book order form.

Steps **To Insert Textbox Form Controls**

1 **Scroll to display the middle portion of the Web page. Click the Form Control button on the Objects toolbar and then point to Textbox on the Form Control menu.**

The six choices on the Form Control menu display (Figure 5-55).

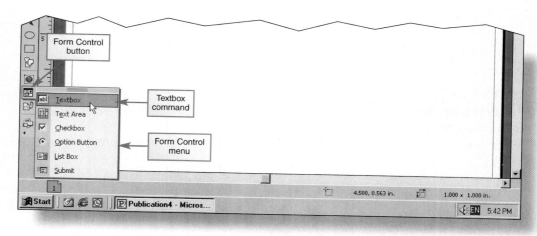

FIGURE 5-55

2 **Click Textbox. Drag the Textbox under the first cell of the table, below the words, Course Number. Resize the Textbox to match the width of the cell.**

The Textbox displays in the publication (Figure 5-56). Your screen need not match the figure exactly; you will align the objects later in the project.

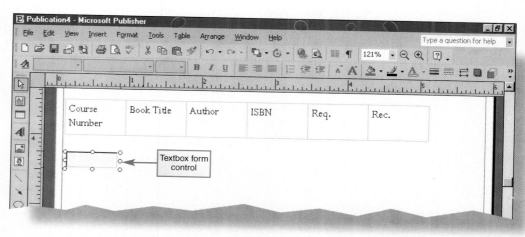

FIGURE 5-56

3 Double-click the Textbox. When the Single-Line Text Box Properties dialog box displays, enter the data as shown in Figure 5-57 and then point to the Form Properties button.

The Single-Line Text Box Properties dialog box displays internal labels and allows you to customize how the data will return to you (Figure 5-57).

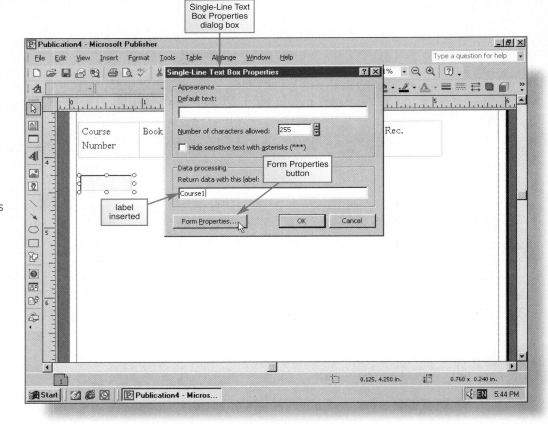

FIGURE 5-57

4 Click the Form Properties button. Click the Send data to me in e-mail option button. Type `Jason_Perry@bkstore.com` in the Send data to this e-mail address text box. Point to the OK button.

The data from the electronic form will be sent via e-mail (Figure 5-58).

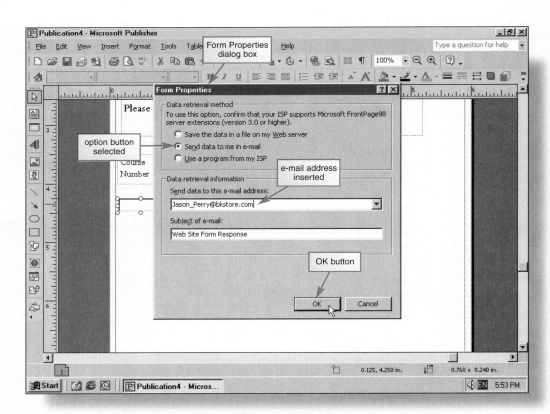

FIGURE 5-58

5 Click the OK button and then click the OK button in the Single Line Text Box Properties dialog box. With the Textbox selected, click the Copy button on the Standard toolbar. Click the Paste button on the Standard toolbar and then drag the new Textbox below the previous one. Double-click the text box form control. When the Single-Line Text Box Properties dialog box displays, enter the data as shown in Figure 5-59 and then point to the OK button.

The Single-Line Text Box Properties dialog box for the second Course Number text box displays (Figure 5-59).

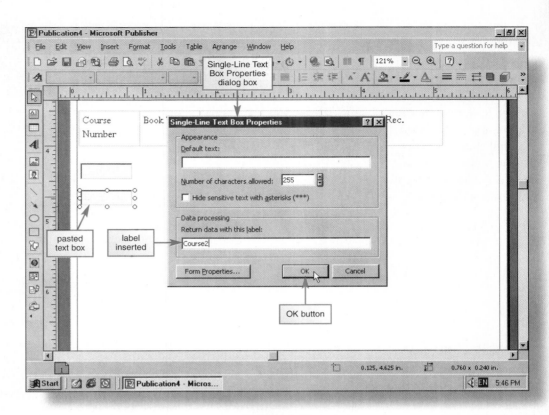

FIGURE 5-59

6 Repeat Step 5 twice, to create two more text boxes named Course3 and Course4. Repeat Step 5 in a similar manner to create four text boxes for Book Title, named Title1 through Title4. Repeat for Author1 through Author4, and ISBN1 through ISBN4. Position the controls as shown in Figure 5-60.

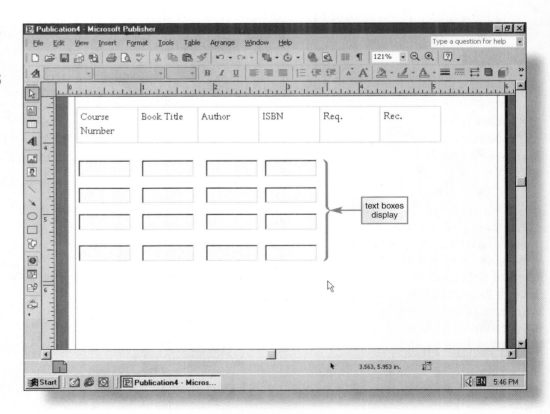

FIGURE 5-60

Microsoft **Publisher** 2002

7 **Click the Form Control button on the Objects toolbar and then click Checkbox. When the Checkbox form control displays in the publication, click the text, Type label here, and then press the DELETE key. Drag the check box to a position below the word Req. in the table.**

The check box displays without a caption (Figure 5-61).

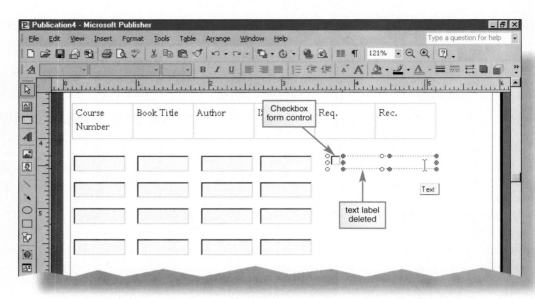

FIGURE 5-61

8 **Double-click the check box and then, when the Checkbox Properties dialog box displays, type** Required1 **in the Return data with this label text box. Point to the OK button.**

The Checkbox Properties dialog box displays (Figure 5-62).

9 **Click the OK button to close the Checkbox Properties dialog box.**

10 **Repeat Steps 7 through 9 to create a total of seven more check boxes with internal data labels of Required2 through Required4 and Rec1 through Rec4. Position the controls to the right of the Textbox form controls, below the appropriate column headings in the table.**

The Checkbox form control displays in the publication as shown in Figure 5-63 on the next page. Your check boxes may overlap.

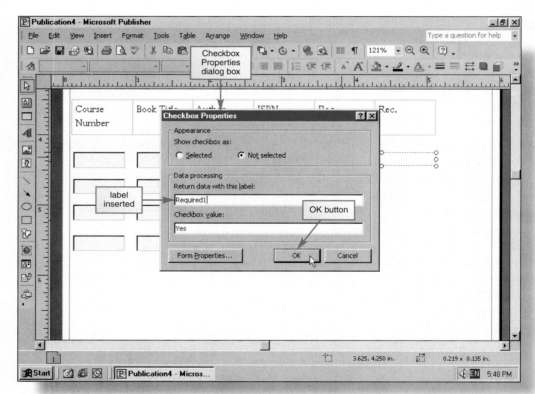

FIGURE 5-62

Other Ways

1. On Insert menu point to Form Control, click Textbox
2. In Voice Command mode, say "Form Control, Textbox"
3. In Voice Command mode, say "Insert, Form Control, Textbox"

Inserting Text Areas

Perry's Web book order form will contain two text areas, one for other supplies and another for instructors to enter their contact information. Perform the following steps to insert two text areas.

 To Insert Text Areas

1 **Click the Form Control button on the Objects toolbar and then point to Text Area as shown in Figure 5-63.**

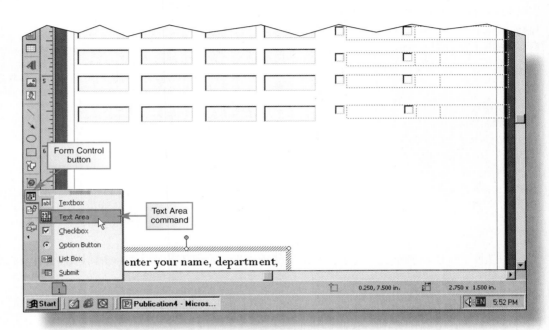

FIGURE 5-63

2 **Click Text Area. When the Text Area form control displays in the publication, drag it to a location just below the Textbox form controls. Resize the text area by dragging a corner sizing handle until it is approximately the size shown in Figure 5-64.**

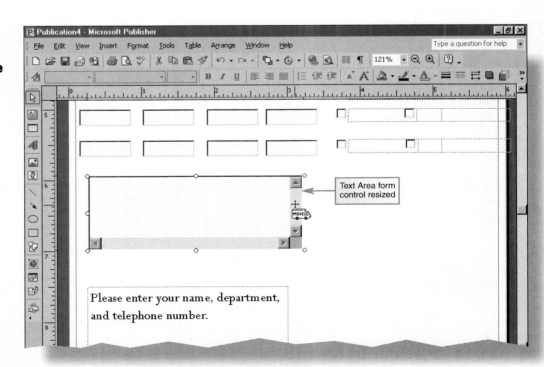

FIGURE 5-64

3 **Double-click the text area. When the Multiline Text Box Properties dialog box displays, type** Enter other supplies for your courses here. **in the Default text text box. Press the TAB key and then type** Other **in the Return data with this label text box. Point to the OK button.**

The Multiline Text Box Properties dialog box displays properties similar to the Single-Line Text Box Properties and Checkbox Properties dialog boxes (Figure 5-65).

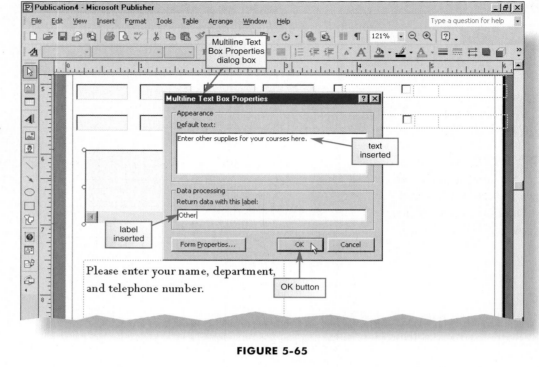

FIGURE 5-65

4 **Click the OK button. Click the Form Control button on the Objects toolbar, again. When the text area displays, drag it to the right of the instruction message text box and resize it as shown in Figure 5-66.**

5 **Double-click the new text area. When the Multiline Text Box Properties dialog box displays, press the TAB key, and then type** Instructor **in the Return data with this label text box.**

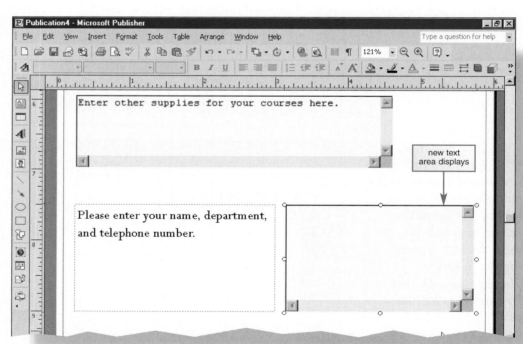

FIGURE 5-66

1. On Insert menu point to Form Control, click Text Area
2. In Voice Command mode, say "Form Controls, Text Area"

The last controls to add to the Web book order form are the command buttons.

Inserting Command Buttons on the Web Book Order Form

You will insert a submit button and a reset button in the same manner you inserted the other controls.

TO INSERT COMMAND BUTTONS

1 Scroll down to display the lower portion of the Web page. Click the Form Control button on the Objects toolbar and then click Submit on the Form Control menu.

2 When the Command Button Properties dialog box displays, click the OK button.

3 Drag the button below the other objects on the page.

4 Click the Copy button on the Standard toolbar and then click the Paste button on the Standard toolbar to create another copy of the command button.

5 Drag the copy to the right of the original button and then double-click the button.

6 When the Command Button Properties dialog box displays, click Reset to select it.

7 Click the OK button. When the publication displays, click outside the Reset button to remove the selection.

The command buttons display in the publication (Figure 5-67).

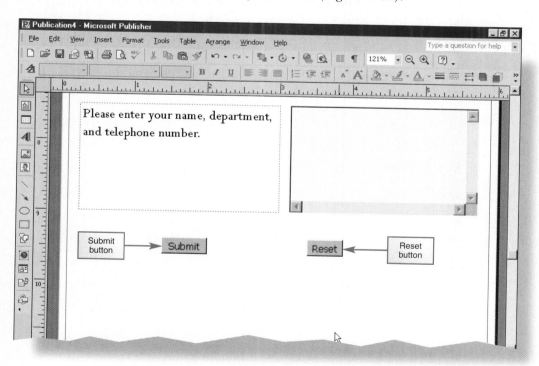

FIGURE 5-67

Aligning Objects

To align the Textbox and Checkbox form controls on the Web book order form, you will use the Align or Distribute command on the Arrange menu. The **Align or Distribute command** offers left to right and top to bottom alignment choices. The Align or Distribute command works only when more than one object is selected.

Aligning Objects in the Web Book Order Form

Perform the following steps to top-align each row of text boxes and check boxes on the Web book order form. You also will left-align the columns of form controls vertically.

TO ALIGN OBJECTS

1 Scroll to display the middle of the publication. If necessary, click the Pointer Tool button on the Objects toolbar. Drag a selection box around the first row of form controls.

2 Click Arrange on the menu bar, point to Align or Distribute, and then click the Align Top command. Click outside the selected objects.

3 Repeat Steps 1 and 2 for each row of form controls.

4 Repeat Steps 1 and 2 for each column, choosing Alight Left on the Align or Distribute submenu.

The form controls align along their top and left edges (Figure 5-68).

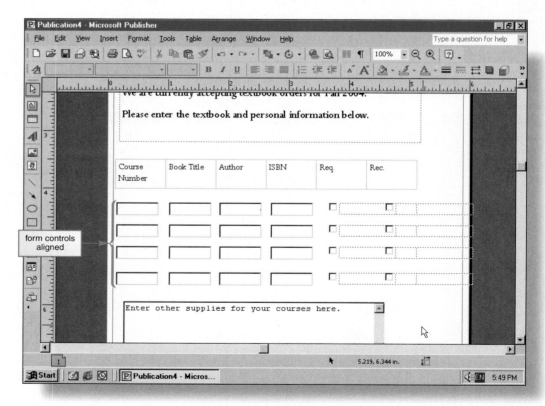

FIGURE 5-68

Checking and Saving the Publication

To complete the Web book order form, you will run it through the Design Checker, save the Web files in a folder, and save the publication itself for future editing.

Running the Design Checker

Recall that Publisher's Design Checker scans the publication for overlapping errors and large graphics that may prevent the page from loading quickly on the Web.

Perform the following steps to run the Design Checker.

TO RUN THE DESIGN CHECKER

1 Click Tools on the menu bar and then click Design Checker. When the Design Checker dialog box displays, click the OK button.

2 If a dialog box displays warning you of the logo frame overlapping the edge, click the Ignore button. If other errors occur, click the Explain button and then follow the instructions to fix the error. If necessary, click the Continue button.

3 If a dialog box displays asking you to check the publication for its ability to download quickly, click the Yes button.

4 After a few moments, Publisher's Design Checker indicates that the Design Check is complete. Click the OK button.

The Design Checker terminates.

Saving the Web Files

Saving the Web book order form involves creating a folder to hold the page and associated graphics for possible uploading to the Web.

TO SAVE THE WEB FILES

1 Make sure you have a floppy disk with adequate free space in drive A. Click File on the menu bar and then click Save as Web Page.

2 Click 3½ Floppy (A:) in the Save in list.

3 Type Web Book Order Form in the File name text box.

4 Click the Save button in the Save as Web Page dialog box.

The saved files are ready to post to the Web.

You may preview the Web site with a browser by clicking the Web Page Preview button on the Standard toolbar.

Talk to your instructor about making this Web site available to others on your network, intranet, or the World Wide Web (see Appendix C). When you publish the site, do not forget to send all the files in your folder so the links and animation work correctly.

The business forms for Perry's Bookstore are complete.

More About

Quick Reference

For a table that lists how to complete tasks covered in this book using the mouse, menu, shortcut menu, and keyboard, see the Quick Reference Summary at the back of this book or visit the Shelly Cashman Series Office XP Web page (scsite.com/offxp/qr.htm) and then click Microsoft Publisher 2002.

More About

Microsoft Certification

The Microsoft Office User Specialist (MOUS) Certification program provides an opportunity for you to obtain a valuable industry credential — proof that you have the Excel 2002 skills required by employers. For more information, see Appendix E or visit the Shelly Cashman Series MOUS Web page at scsite.com/offxp/cert.htm.

CASE PERSPECTIVE SUMMARY

Jason Perry received your e-mail with the attachment, Perry Book Order Form. The Perry Invoice should automate the invoice process. Workers will load the file, fill it out, and then print it for each order. Speaking of automation, the whole staff loved your presentation of the Web book order form with its animated graphic and form controls. Mr. Perry directed you to upload the files and get them posted so customers can fill out their orders over the Web. Guess who gets to check the e-mail submissions every day?

Project Summary

Project 5 introduced you to generating business forms. First, you created an invoice and a coupon using styles, tabs, and an automatic date. Next, you created a table to display a book order form. You learned how to edit by merging cells and creating a diagonal. Finally, you created an electronic form for Web ordering. You learned how to edit and align the various form controls and set their properties.

What You Should Know

Having completed this project, you now should be able to perform the following tasks:

▶ Add a Border *(PUB 5.28)*
▶ Align Objects *(PUB 5.53)*
▶ Apply a Style *(PUB 5.13)*
▶ Close the File *(PUB 5.38)*
▶ Close the File without Quitting Publisher *(PUB 5.23)*
▶ Create a Blank Web Page (PUB 5.39)
▶ Create a Custom Size Publication *(PUB 5.23)*
▶ Create a Formatted Table *(PUB 5.31)*
▶ Create a New Text Style *(PUB 5.09)*
▶ Create an Invoice Template *(PUB 5.07)*
▶ Create Another Text Box *(PUB 5.41)*
▶ Create Text Boxes and Import a Style *(PUB 5.25)*
▶ Enter Data into a Table *(PUB 5.35)*
▶ Format with a Drop Cap *(PUB 5.15)*
▶ Insert a Hot Spot *(PUB 5.44)*
▶ Insert a System Date *(PUB 5.21)*
▶ Insert a Tab Stop for the Date *(PUB 5.19)*

▶ Insert an Animated Graphic from the Web Collection *(PUB 5.42)*
▶ Insert Command Buttons *(PUB 5.52)*
▶ Insert Textbox Form Controls *(PUB 5.46)*
▶ Insert Objects on the Web Page *(PUB 5.40)*
▶ Insert Text *(PUB 5.14)*
▶ Insert Text Areas *(PUB 5.50)*
▶ Merge Cells and Create a Cell Diagonal *(PUB 5.33)*
▶ Run the Design Checker *(PUB 5.54)*
▶ Save and Print the Book Order Form *(PUB 5.36)*
▶ Save and Print the Invoice Template *(PUB 5.22)*
▶ Save the Web Files *(PUB 5.54)*
▶ Save, Print, and Close the Coupon *(PUB 5.30)*
▶ Select a Color and Font Scheme *(PUB 5.24)*
▶ Send a Publisher File via E-Mail *(PUB 5.37)*
▶ Start Publisher *(PUB 5.06)*

Learn It Online

Instructions: To complete the Learn It Online exercises, start your browser, click the Address bar, and then enter scsite.com/offxp/exs.htm. When the Office XP Learn It Online page displays, follow the instructions in the exercises below.

1 Project Reinforcement TF, MC, and SA

Below Publisher Project 5, click the Project Reinforcement link. Print the quiz by clicking Print on the File menu. Answer each question. Write your first and last name at the top of each page and then hand in the printout to your instructor.

2 Flash Cards

Below Publisher Project 5, click the Flash Cards link. When Flash Cards displays, read the instructions. Type 20 (or a number specified by your instructor) in the Number of Playing Cards text box, type your name in the Name text box, and then click the Flip Card button. When the flash card displays, read the question and then click the Answer box arrow to select an answer. Flip through Flash Cards. Click Print on the File menu to print the last flash card if your score is 15 (75%) correct or greater and then hand it in to your instructor. If your score is less than 15 (75%) correct, then redo this exercise by clicking the Replay button.

3 Practice Test

Below Publisher Project 5, click the Practice Test link. Answer each question, enter your first and last name at the bottom of the page, and then click the Grade Test button. When the graded practice test displays on your screen, click Print on the File menu to print a hard copy. Continue to take practice tests until you score 80% or better. Hand in a printout of the final practice test to your instructor.

4 Who Wants to Be a Computer Genius?

Below Publisher Project 5, click the Computer Genius link. Read the instructions, enter your first and last name at the bottom of the page, and then click the Play button. Hand in your score to your instructor.

5 Wheel of Terms

Below Publisher Project 5, click the Wheel of Terms link. Read the instructions, and then enter your first and last name and your school name. Click the Play button. Hand in your score to your instructor.

6 Crossword Puzzle Challenge

Below Publisher Project 5, click the Crossword Puzzle Challenge link. Read the instructions, and then enter your first and last name. Click the Play button. Work the crossword puzzle. When you are finished, click the Submit button. When the crossword puzzle redisplays, click the Print button. Hand in the printout.

7 Tips and Tricks

Below Publisher Project 5, click the Tips and Tricks link. Click a topic that pertains to Project 5. Right-click the information and then click Print on the shortcut menu. Construct a brief example of what the information relates to in Publisher to confirm you understand how to use the tip or trick. Hand in the example and printed information.

8 Newsgroups

Below Publisher Project 5, click the Newsgroups link. Click a topic that pertains to Project 5. Print three comments. Hand in the comments to your instructor.

9 Expanding Your Horizons

Below Publisher Project 5, click the Articles for Microsoft Publisher link. Click a topic that pertains to Project 5. Print the information. Construct a brief example of what the information relates to in Publisher to confirm you understand the contents of the article. Hand in the example and printed information to your instructor.

10 Search Sleuth

Below Publisher Project 5, click the Search Sleuth link. To search for a term that pertains to this project, select a term below the Project 5 title and then use the Google search engine at google.com (or any major search engine) to display and print two Web pages that present information on the term. Hand in the printouts to your instructor.

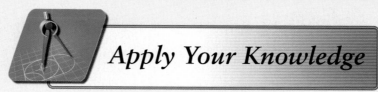

Apply Your Knowledge

1 **Working with Form Controls**

Instructions: Start Publisher. Open the publication, Apply-5, on the Data Disk. See the inside back cover for instructions for downloading the Data Disk or see your instructor for information about accessing the files required for this book. The publication is a Web page order form for a swimming pool store. You are to insert a masthead, a drop cap, graphics, hot spot, and form controls as described below to create an electronic form. You also need to edit the properties of the credit card information form controls. The completed form is shown in Figure 5-69. Perform the following tasks.

1. Click the Design Gallery button on the Objects toolbar. Click Web Mastheads in the Categories list and then insert the Bubbles Masthead at the top of the publication. Triple-click each text box in the masthead individually, and edit the text to match Figure 5-69.

2. Ungroup the masthead by pressing CTRL+SHIFT+G. Delete the graphic. Use the Insert Clip Art task pane to insert a new animated graphic similar to the one in Figure 5-69. Insert another graphic of your choice lower on the page.

3. Click the Got a question? text box and then, on the Format menu, click Drop Cap. Choose a style from those available in your list.

4. Click the Hot Spot button on the Objects toolbar and make the Got a question text box a hot spot to send e-mail to the pool store, at webmaster@coolpools.com.

5. Use the Align or Distribute command on the Arrange menu to align the Zip code form control with the form control directly above it. Align any other controls that seem out of place.

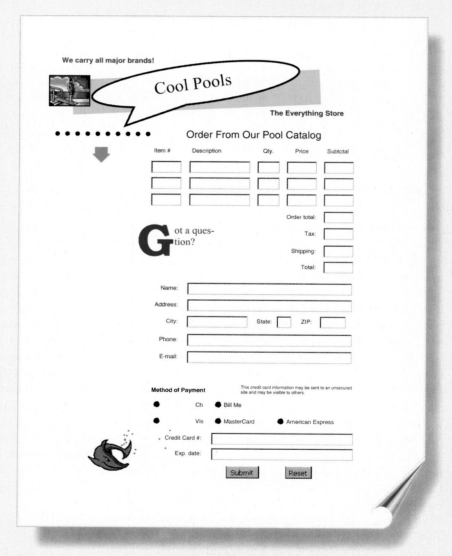

FIGURE 5-69

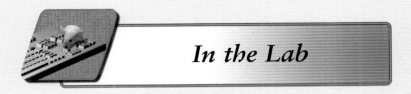

Apply Your Knowledge

6. Click the Credit Card # text box. Ungroup the label from the Textbox form control. Double-click the form control. When the Properties dialog box displays, click to select the check box that hides sensitive text with asterisks. Do the same for the expiration date.

7. Use the Form Control button on the Objects toolbar to insert a Submit button and a Reset button at the bottom of the page. Use the Align or Distribute command on the Arrange menu to align the two command buttons along their top edges. Double-click the Submit button and have the data sent to webmaster@coolpools.com.

8. Run the Design Checker.

9. If errors occur, click the Explain button and follow the instructions to fix the error. If a dialog box displays asking you to check the publication for its ability to download quickly, click the Yes button.

10. Make sure you have a floppy disk with adequate free space in drive A.

11. On the File menu, click Save as Web Page, and then click 3½ Floppy (A:) in the Save in list.

12. Type Pool Order Form in the File name text box and then click the Save button in the Save as Web Page dialog box.

In the Lab

1 Creating a Monthly Statement

Problem: Ray Lykins owns and operates a candy store named, The Fudge Factory. He has asked you to create a monthly statement he can use to send to retail outlets who order from his store. You decide to use a statement business form (Figure 5-70 on the next page).

Instructions: Perform the following tasks using a computer.

1. Start Publisher. From the New Publication task pane, click Business Forms and then click Statement. Double-click the Radial Statement.

2. When the Business Form Options task pane displays, click None in the Logo area.

3. Use the Mistletoe color scheme and the Economy font scheme.

4. Click the top text box, press the F9 key, and then type The Fudge Factory in the text box.

5. Insert an appropriate graphic using the Clip Organizer Frame button on the Objects toolbar. Resize the graphic to fit to the right of the address text boxes.

6. Click the word, Statement, to select the text box. Click Format on the menu bar and then click Drop Cap on the Format menu. Choose an appropriate style from the Available Drop Caps list. If necessary, enlarge the text box.

7. Click the text box for Statement #, Date, and Customer ID. Press CTRL+A to select the entire frame. Press the DELETE key.

(continued)

In the Lab

Creating a Monthly Statement *(continued)*

8. Click the .75" mark on the Horizontal Ruler to set a tab. Type Statement #: and then press the TAB key. Press the ENTER key. Type Date: and then press the TAB key. Enter a system date and then press the ENTER key. Type Customer ID: and then press the TAB key.

9. Click the Mailing Address text box and then type in your name and address.

10. Save the publication with the file name, Cool Pool Statement, on your floppy disk. Print a copy.

2 Creating an Origami Box

Problem: A local youth organization has asked you to create party favors for their annual Blue and Gold Banquet. You would like to include foil-covered chocolates (in blue and gold, of course) at each place setting. Because you are on a tight budget, you decide to try your hand at designing a do-it-yourself gift box to hold the candies. Printing on heavy card stock paper, you use the ancient art of Origami paper folding to create two boxes, one slightly larger than the other for a top and bottom box set.

Instructions: Perform the following tasks using a computer.

1. Start Publisher. From the New Publications task pane, click Blank Publications and then zoom to Full page. Close the task pane.

2. Use the Insert Table button on the Objects toolbar to draw a table, 6-inches square. When the Create Table dialog box displays, create four rows and four columns, using the Default table format. Close the Create Table dialog box by clicking its OK button.

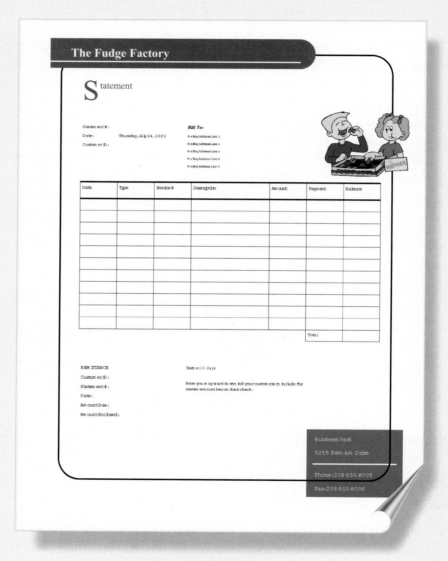

FIGURE 5-70

In the Lab

3. Click Table on the menu bar, point to Select, and then click Table. On the Formatting toolbar, click the Line/Border Style button, and then click More Lines on the menu.

4. When the Format Table dialog box displays, if necessary, click the Colors and Lines tab. In the Presets area, click the third button (full grid), and then click the OK button.

5. Click Table on the menu bar and then click Cell Diagonals. When the Cell Diagonals dialog box displays, click Divide up. Click the OK button in the Cell Diagonals dialog box. Click outside the table to remove the highlight.

6. Using the Line button on the Objects toolbar, draw seven lines to dissect the table cells the opposite way from the diagonals. Holding down the SHIFT key while drawing the line ensures a straight 45-degree line.

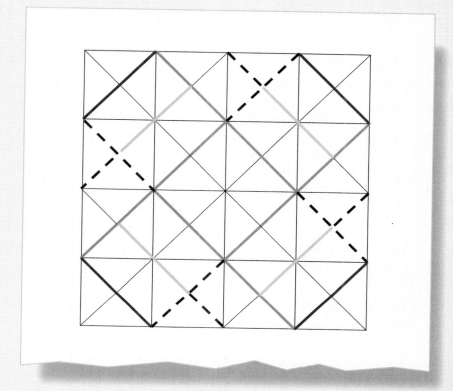

FIGURE 5-71

7. If desired you may draw colored and dotted lines over the other lines in the figure or simply use the figure as a reference for folding and trimming in Step 8.

   a. To draw the colored lines, click the Line button on the Objects toolbar and then click the Line Color button on the Formatting toolbar. Choose the appropriate color from the Line Color menu. Hold down the SHIFT key and draw the colored lines over the top of the black lines in the table as shown in Figure 5-71.

   b. To draw the dotted lines, click the Line button on the Objects toolbar and then click the Dash Style button on the Formatting toolbar. Choose an appropriate dotted line from the Dash Style menu. Hold down the SHIFT key and draw the dotted lines over the top of the black lines in the table as shown in Figure 5-71.

8. Save the publication as Origami box on your floppy disk. Print the publication, and then using Figure 5-71 as a guide, trim the printout, and fold the bottom of the box set as follows:

   a. Cut around the edge of the table and on the dotted lines.

   b. Fold the orange lines first to form a box shell, keeping the tabs on the inside.

   c. Fold the blue lines inward.

   d. Fold the yellow lines third, working around from one corner of the box to the next.

9. On the Edit menu, click Select All. Click the Group Objects button and then SHIFT-drag a corner sizing handle until the box is approximately 1/5-inch larger. Print and assemble the top of the box set. (**Hint:** You may cheat and use a small piece of tape to hold down the "blue" fold if you like.)

In the Lab

3 Creating a Table with Graphics

Problem: As an office automation specialist at the college, you have been asked to create a flyer to send out to prospective dormitory residents. The flyer should contain a table showing some of the features that are available in each dorm. A sample displays in Figure 5-72.

Instructions: Perform the following tasks using a computer:

1. Start Publisher with a blank publication. Use the Page Setup command on the File menu to specify landscape orientation. On the View menu, click Task Pane, and then click the Other Task Panes button and choose Color Schemes. Click the Black and Gray color scheme. Close the task pane.

2. Use the Layout Guides command on the Arrange menu to change each of the margins to 0.5 inches.

3. Create a table beginning in the upper-left corner of the page, approximately seven-inches tall by nine-inches wide. Use four rows and five columns. Select the checkbook register format.

4. Click the Line/Border Style button, and then click More Styles. On the BorderArt tab, choose a border similar to the Weaving Strips border shown in Figure 5-72. Use a Border Size of 24.

5. Enter the names of the dorms in the first column, beginning with the second row. Drag through all four cells. On the Format menu, point to Align Text Vertically, and then click Center. Increase the font size to 14. If necessary, drag the border between columns one and two to the right, approximately one-half inch, so that the dorm names display on single lines.

6. Merge the cells across row one, and insert the heading shown in Figure 5-72. Center the heading and make it bold, if necessary. Increase the font size to 36.

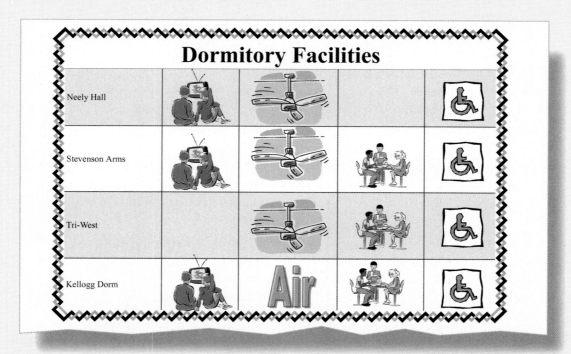

FIGURE 5-72

In the Lab

7. If necessary, drag the table to center it on the page. Click outside the table.
8. Locate a graphic of a television. Position and size the graphic to fit in a single cell. Use the copy and paste technique to paste copies of the graphic in the cells as shown in Figure 5-72. SHIFT-click each of the three graphics and then click Align Objects on the Arrange menu. Choose to align their left edges.
9. Repeat Step 8 for graphics of fans, cafeterias, and handicap accessibility. When all graphics have been aligned on their corresponding left edges, align their top edges with the other graphics in each row.
10. Save the publication on your floppy disk with the file name, Dorm Facilities Table. Print a copy.

Cases and Places

The difficulty of these case studies varies:
▶ are the least difficult; ▶▶ are more difficult; and ▶▶▶ are the most difficult.

1 ▶ The owner of Copy Cat Creations, located at 905 Rodd Street, Carterville, IL, 60431, conducted an inventory and found himself short several items. Use the Bars Purchase Order to order materials from We Are The Office Place, whose logo is a picture of pens and papers. They are located at 1525 E. Huron, Chicago, IL, 60609. Copy Cat Creations needs 50 reams of paper at $20.00 each, 60 cartons of pens at $3.50 each, 10 rolls of bubble wrap at $14.00 each, and 12 bags of rubber bands at $1.50 each. Fill in the Taxable column with Xs, as all the materials are taxable. Copy Cat Creations receives no discount and will pick up the order. The tax is 7.5%.

2 ▶ You are a private investigator named Colonel Ketchup who needs an expense report for his client, Miss Pink. You include your daily charges of $200 for four days work, plus itemized expenses for a knife, a lead pipe, and a candlestick. Over dinner, you interviewed an expert witness named Professor Banana. Prepare an expense report using a Business Form Wizard. Itemize expenses and entertainment in the report. Include a logo of a magnifying glass.

3 ▶▶ Research laboratories at major teaching hospitals usually are funded not only by their research grants, but also by providing services to the hospital and associated physicians. The Flow Cytometry Lab at University Hospital faxes results to pathologists and transplant surgeons at the hospital, and to blood banks all over the city. They need a standardized fax cover sheet for their multi-page lab reports. Using a wizard, create a fax cover template they will print on pre-printed Lab stationary. Leave two inches at the top of the page to accommodate their masthead and format the objects with the tools you learned in this project. Use a system date, a drop cap, and tab stops in each data entry field so the lab assistants can position text easily.

Cases and Places

4 ▶▶ The Tire Garage needs a time card. The owner has just hired two extra mechanics and an office manager because business is booming. Using a Weekly Record business form, draw a box around the time card table, and then paste it into a blank publication. In the lower-left corner of the table, merge the gray cells in the penultimate row and type Name: and then merge the gray cells in the bottom row and type Date: to create room for the employees to sign and date the time card. Print multiple copies for The Tire Garage's employees.

5 ▶▶▶ As director of the sales force at a regional real estate company, you are responsible for providing each sales person with a company car. Each year you must submit a proposal to the CEO for approval. You would like some feedback from your sales associates all across the state and decide that a Web electronic form is the best way to reach them. Create a feedback form with check boxes, option buttons, list boxes, and text boxes. Collect information about makes of car, options, mileage, satisfaction ratings, and/or suggestions for improvement. Include a Submit button linked to your e-mail address.

6 ▶▶▶ Research four or five Internet service providers (ISPs) in your area. Ask friends and consult ISP advertisements. Use your school or work Internet provider as one of the examples. Look for information on monthly charges, type of Internet connection provided, rate of speed, and the e-mail handler programs they recommend or support. Create a table with a merged title cell and formatting to display your findings. Send the table publication to your instructor as an e-mail attachment.

7 ▶▶▶ Microsoft Publisher is a popular solution to desktop publishing needs. Other software is available, however, for preparing everything from greeting cards to book publication film. Several products exist for desktop publishing such as QuarkXPress, Adobe Acrobat, and Print Shop; and products such as Microsoft FrontPage and Macromedia Director create interactive kiosks and Web pages. Surf the net looking for pages that display a creation product logo. Compare Publisher's Web form controls to those of some other popular Web creation products and use Publisher to write a report about your findings. Include a table listing popular controls as columns and products as rows.

Microsoft Publisher 2002

Linking a Publisher Publication to an Excel Worksheet

CASE PERSPECTIVE

Fredrick Russell, director of sales and marketing for Digital Cameras International, sends out a memo to all sales staff showing the most recent quarterly report of sales and returns for the company. He currently uses Publisher to produce the memo and then attaches a table of the quarterly figures that he creates in Excel. The wording in the memo remains constant while the table of quarterly sales and returns changes each quarter.

Fredrick recently heard of the Object Linking and Embedding (OLE) capabilities of Microsoft Office XP. He wants to use it to create the basic memo, using Publisher (Figure 1a on the next page), and then link the quarterly earnings from an Excel worksheet (Figure 1b). Each quarter he envisions sending out the publication with the updated worksheet (Figure 1c). Once the link is established, he can update the worksheet each quarter, then print and distribute the report or send it electronically as an attachment.

As Fredrick's technical assistant, he has asked you to handle the details of linking the Excel quarterly report to the Publisher sales memo.

Introduction

With Microsoft Office XP, you can incorporate parts of files or entire files called objects from one application into another application. In Project 2, you learned how to import a text file from Microsoft Word into Publisher. Now, you will copy a worksheet created in Excel into a publication created in Publisher. In this case, the worksheet in Excel is called the **source publication** (copied from) and the publication in Publisher is called the **destination publication** (copied to). Copying specific objects between applications can be accomplished in one of three ways: (1) copy and paste; (2) copy and embed; or (3) copy and link.

All of the Microsoft Office XP applications allow you to use these three methods to copy objects between applications. The first method uses the Copy and Paste buttons. The latter two use the Paste Special command on the Edit menu with **Object Linking and Embedding (OLE)**.

You would use **copy and paste** when you want a static or non-changing copy of an object in two different documents. For example, a pie chart of last year's sales probably is not going to change; thus, if you paste it into a Publisher brochure about the company's sales history, it will look the same each time you open the publication. Copy and paste is easy to do across publications.

You would use the **copy and embed** method when you want the ability to edit the object in its destination location. For example, if someone sends you a table of figures that you would like to use in a Publisher expense report, you can paste it into Publisher, but retain the ability to edit some of the numbers and recalculate the totals. When you edit an embedded object, the source application software actually opens and allows you to use its features; however, when you save the file, the changes are reflected in the destination publication only.

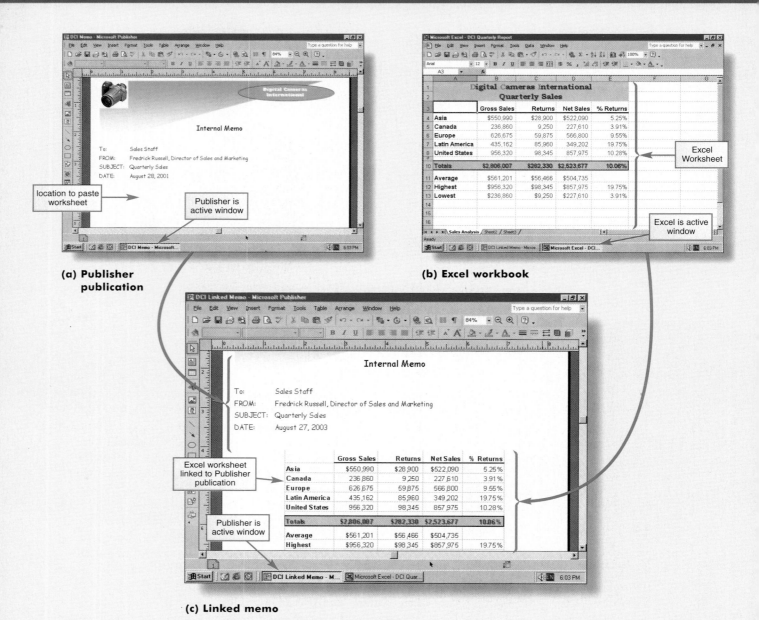

(a) Publisher publication

(b) Excel workbook

(c) Linked memo

FIGURE 1

You would use the **copy and link** method over the other two methods when an object is likely to change and you want to make sure the object reflects the changes in both the source and destination documents. For example, if you link a portion or all of an Excel worksheet to a Publisher investment statement and update the worksheet quarterly in Excel, anytime you open the investment statement in Publisher, the latest update of the worksheet will display as part of the investment statement; in other words, you always have the latest data. You also might use the copy and link method when the copied object is large, such as a video clip or sound clip, because only one copy of the object is stored on disk when you link.

Table 1 summarizes the differences between the three methods.

METHOD	CHARACTERISTICS
Table 1	**Copying Between Applications**
Copy and paste	Source object becomes part of the destination document. Object can be edited, but the editing features are limited to those in the destination application. An Excel worksheet becomes a Publisher table. If changes are made to values in the Publisher table, any original Excel formulas are not recalculated. Publisher objects become pictures when pasted into Excel worksheets.
Copy and embed	Source object becomes part of the destination document. Object can be edited in destination application using source-editing features. Excel worksheet remains a worksheet in Publisher. If changes are made to values on the worksheet within Publisher, Excel formulas will be recalculated, but the changes are not updated in the Excel worksheet in the workbook on disk. If you use Excel to change values on the worksheet, the changes will not show in the Publisher publication the next time you open it.
Copy and link	Source object does not become part of the destination document even though it displays. Rather, a link is established between the two documents so that when you open the Publisher publication, the worksheet displays as part of it. When you attempt to edit a linked worksheet in Publisher, the system activates Excel. If you change the worksheet in Excel, the changes will show in the Publisher publication the next time you open it. When copying from Publisher to Excel, a link becomes an icon on the worksheet.

Moving objects from Publisher into other applications deserves special consideration. Text boxes paste, embed, and link in a similar manner as Microsoft Word documents; that is, as text. Tables paste, embed, and link in a similar manner as Microsoft Excel worksheets. Other objects paste as pictures, or link as icons. The embed option is not typically available when moving non-text or non-chart objects from Publisher into another application.

Most Office XP applications also provide a method for copying the entire files from one application to another. On the Insert menu, the Object command gives you the same linking or embedding options as discussed above, but extends the connection to a wider array of file types.

Linking an Excel Worksheet to a Publisher Publication

The following pages discuss how to link an Excel worksheet to a Publisher publication so that the publication updates automatically after the worksheet is edited. Both of the files you will use in this project, the Publisher publication (DCI Memo.pub) and the Excel workbook (DCI Quarterly Report.xls), are on the Data Disk. If you did not download the Data Disk, see the inside back cover for instructions for downloading the Data Disk or see your instructor.

Starting Publisher and Excel

The first step in linking the Excel worksheet to the Publisher publication is to open both the publication in Publisher and the workbook in Excel as shown in the steps on the next page.

More About

Office XP

Because you can use OLE among Word, Excel, Access, PowerPoint, Publisher, FrontPage, and Outlook, Office XP can be viewed as one large integrated software package, rather than separate applications. Files that display as icons in any window can be dragged into an open application creating an automatic embedded object. This drag-drop functionality creates many ways to integrate and share data among users.

Steps To Open a Publisher Publication and an Excel Workbook

1 **Insert the Data Disk in drive A. Click the Start button on the Windows taskbar. Click Open Office Document on the Start menu. Click 3½ Floppy (A :) in the Look in list. Double-click the file name, DCI Memo.**

Publisher becomes active and the DCI Memo displays in Whole Page View (Figure 2).

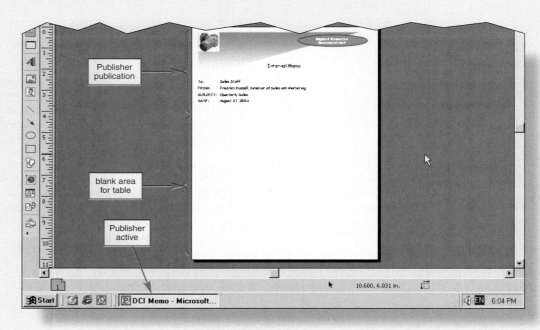

FIGURE 2

2 **Click the Start button on the Windows taskbar. Click Open Office Document on the Start menu. If necessary, click 3½ Floppy (A :) in the Look in list. Double-click the file name, DCI Quarterly Report.**

Excel becomes active and the DCI Quarterly Report workbook displays (Figure 3). At this point, Publisher is inactive, but is still in main memory. Excel is the active window as shown on the taskbar.

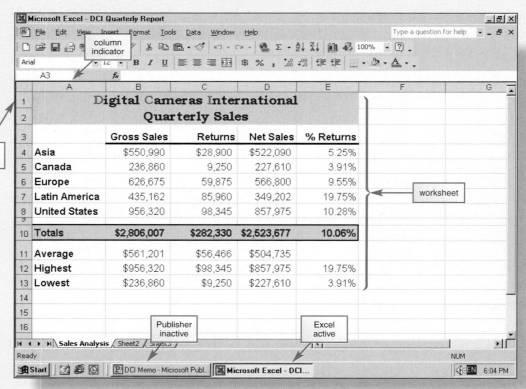

FIGURE 3

Other Ways

1. To start Publisher, click Start button on Windows taskbar, point to Programs, click Microsoft Publisher

2. To start Excel, click Start button, point to Programs, click Microsoft Excel

With both Publisher and Excel in main memory, you can switch between the applications by clicking the appropriate button on the taskbar.

Linking an Excel Worksheet to a Publisher Publication

With both applications running, the next step is to link the Excel worksheet to the Publisher publication. The Excel cell references in the following steps represent the intersection of the column (indicated by a capital letter) and the row (indicated by a number).

Steps | **To Link an Excel Worksheet to a Publisher Publication**

---

1 **With the Excel window active, drag through the range from cell A3 through cell E13. Click the Copy button to place the selected range on the Office Clipboard.**

Excel displays a marquee around the range A3:E13 (Figure 4). You need not copy the heading because the Publisher publication text boxes will explain the table.

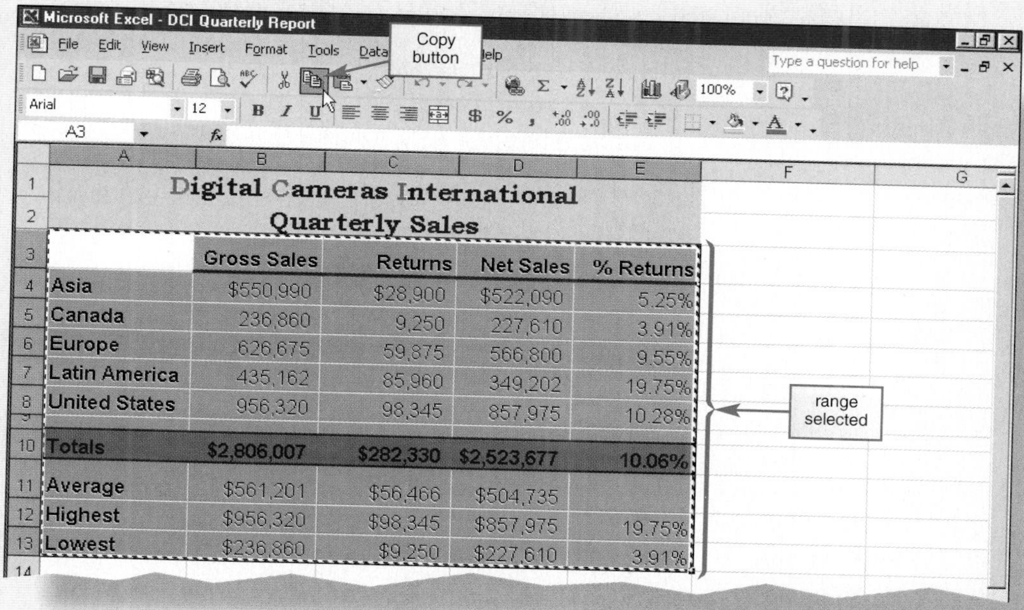

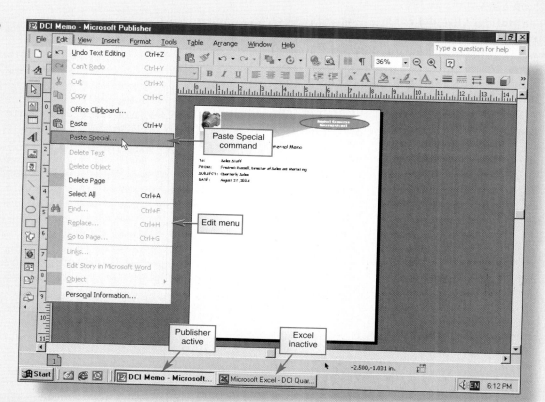

FIGURE 4

---

2 **Click the DCI Memo button on the taskbar to activate the Publisher window. Click Edit on the menu bar and then point to the Paste Special command.**

The DCI Memo publication and the Edit menu display on the screen (Figure 5).

FIGURE 5

3 **Click Paste Special. When the Paste Special dialog box displays, click Paste Link. If necessary, click Microsoft Excel Worksheet Object Link in the As box. Point to the OK button in the Paste Special dialog box.**

The Paste Special dialog box displays (Figure 6). An explanation of the purpose of Paste Link also displays.

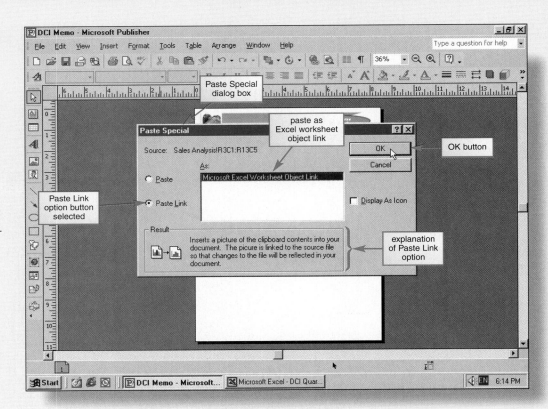

FIGURE 6

4 **Click the OK button. If necessary, when the table displays, drag it to an open space in the publication. Click the Zoom In button to increase the magnification.**

The range A3:E12 of the worksheet displays in the Publisher publication (Figure 7).

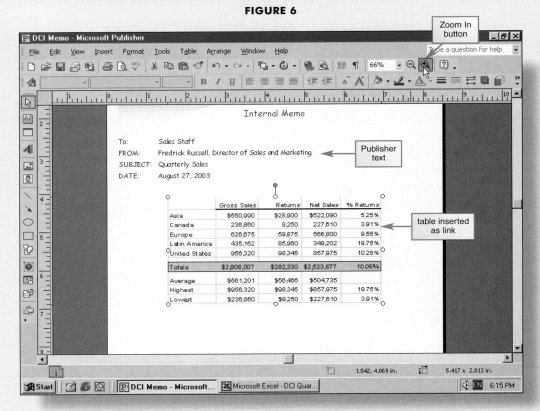

FIGURE 7

The Excel worksheet now is linked to the Publisher publication. If you save the Publisher publication and reopen it, the worksheet will display just as it does in Figure 7. If you want to delete the linked worksheet in Publisher, select it and then press the DELETE key. The next section shows how to print and save the publication with the linked worksheet.

Printing and Saving the Publisher Publication with the Linked Worksheet

The following steps print and then save the Publisher publication with the linked worksheet.

Steps To Print and Save the Publisher Publication with the Linked Worksheet

1 With the Publisher window active, click the Print button on the Standard toolbar.

The statement and the worksheet print as one publication (Figure 8).

2 With your floppy disk in drive A, click File on the menu bar and then click Save As. Type the file name DCI Linked Memo **in the File name text box. Click the OK button.**

Publisher saves the publication on your floppy disk with the file name, DCI Linked Memo.

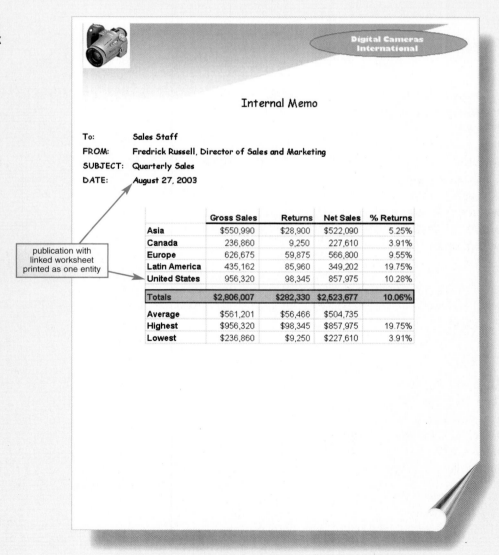

publication with linked worksheet printed as one entity

Internal Memo

To: Sales Staff
FROM: Fredrick Russell, Director of Sales and Marketing
SUBJECT: Quarterly Sales
DATE: August 27, 2003

	Gross Sales	Returns	Net Sales	% Returns
Asia	$550,990	$28,900	$522,090	5.25%
Canada	236,860	9,250	227,610	3.91%
Europe	626,675	59,875	566,800	9.55%
Latin America	435,162	85,960	349,202	19.75%
United States	956,320	98,345	857,975	10.28%
Totals	$2,806,007	$282,330	$2,523,677	10.06%
Average	$561,201	$56,466	$504,735	
Highest	$956,320	$98,345	$857,975	19.75%
Lowest	$236,860	$9,250	$227,610	3.91%

Digital Cameras International

FIGURE 8

If you exit both applications and re-open DCI Linked Memo, the worksheet will display in the publication even though Excel is not running. Because Publisher supports Object Linking and Embedding (OLE), it can display the linked portion of the Excel worksheet without opening Excel.

The next section illustrates what happens when you attempt to edit the linked worksheet while Publisher is active.

Editing the Linked Worksheet

You can edit any of the cells on the worksheet while it displays as part of the Publisher publication. To edit the worksheet in Publisher, double-click it. If Excel is running in main memory, the system will switch to Excel and display the linked workbook and its worksheet. If Excel is not running, the system will start Excel automatically and display the linked workbook. The following steps show how to edit the sales from Europe (cell B6) from 626,657 to 684,123.

To Edit the Linked Worksheet

1 **With the Publisher window and the DCI Linked Memo publication active, double-click the worksheet table. When the Excel window becomes active, double-click the worksheet title bar to maximize the screen.**

Windows switches from Publisher to Excel and displays the original workbook, DCI Quarterly Report.

2 **Click cell B6 and then type** 684123 **as the new value for European sales. Click the green check mark ENTER button on the Formula bar.**

Excel recalculates all formulas on the worksheet (Figure 9).

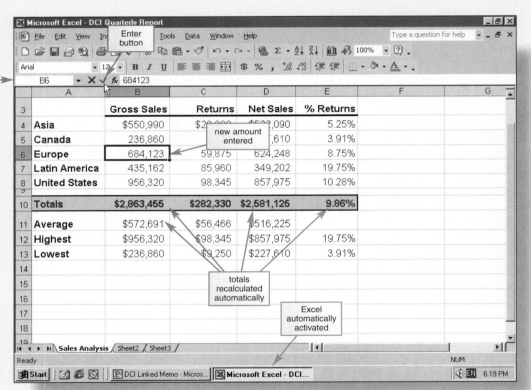

FIGURE 9

3 **Click the DCI Linked Memo button on the taskbar.**

The Publisher window becomes active (Figure 10). The amount for European sales, which was 626,657, is now 684,123. New totals for Gross Sales, Net Sales, and Average display.

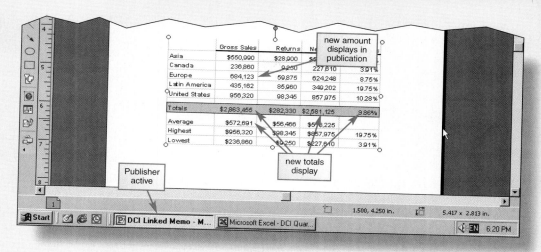

FIGURE 10

As you can see from the previous steps, you double-click a linked object when you want to edit it. Windows will activate the application and display the workbook or publication from which the object came. You then can edit the object and return to the destination application. Any changes made to the object will display in the destination publication.

If you want the edited changes to the linked worksheet to be permanent, you must save the DCI Quarterly report.xls file, before quitting Excel.

CASE PERSPECTIVE SUMMARY

As the sales figures for the previous quarter come in, Fredrick updates the Excel worksheet. He then opens the Publisher sales memo from the previous quarter. He is happy to see that the updated figures display automatically. Fredrick saves the Publisher publication, prints it, and distributes it to the appropriate employees.

Integration Feature Summary

This Integration Feature introduced you to Object Linking and Embedding (OLE). OLE allows you to bring together data and information that has been created using different applications. When you link an object to a publication and save it, only a link to the object is saved with the publication. You edit a linked object by double-clicking it. The system activates the application and opens the file in which the object was created. If you change any part of the object and then return to the destination publication, the updated object will display.

What You Should Know

Having completed this project, you now should be able to perform the following tasks:

▶ Edit the Linked Worksheet *(PUBI 1.08)*
▶ Link an Excel Worksheet to a Publisher Publication *(PUBI 1.05)*
▶ Open a Publisher Publication and an Excel Workbook *(PUBI 1.04)*
▶ Print and Save the Publisher Publication with the Linked Worksheet *(PUBI 1.07)*

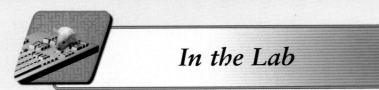

In the Lab

1 Linking an Investment Statement to a Report

Problem: Stanley Bennet is director of human resources for Green Assembly Division. He sends out a report (Figure 11a) to all employees in the retirement program and attaches a statement of investment earnings for the previous quarter. You have been asked to simplify his task by linking the investment worksheet (Figure 11b) to the quarterly report.

Instructions: Perform the following tasks.

1. One at a time, open the publication, Investment Report, and the workbook, Quarterly Earnings, from the Data Disk. If you did not download the Data Disk, see the inside back cover for instructions for downloading the Data Disk or see your instructor.
2. With the Excel workbook active, copy the range A3 through F26 from the Excel workbook.
3. Click the Publisher publication button on the taskbar. Use the Paste Special command to link the copied range to the Investment Report publication. If necessary, drag the table to the open space in the publication.
4. Print and then save the publication as Quarterly Earnings Report.
5. Double-click the linked worksheet and use the keyboard to increase the James Worldwide stock value from 98,661 to 99,500.
6. Activate the Publisher window again, and print it with the new values. Close the publication and the workbook without saving them.

2 Pasting a Publication into a Workbook

Problem: Stanley Bennet now has asked you to paste the Publisher publication into the Excel workbook, rather than linking the Excel workbook to the Publisher publication as was done in Exercise 1.

Instructions: Perform the following tasks.

1. One at a time, open the publication, Investment Report, and the workbook, Quarterly Earnings, from the Data Disk. If you did not download the Data Disk, see the inside back cover for instructions for downloading the Data Disk or see your instructor.
2. With the Excel window active, drag through the row numbers 1 through 20 on the left border of the worksheet. Click Insert on the menu bar and then click Rows. When the blank rows display, click cell A1.
3. Click the Publisher publication button on the taskbar. Click Select All on the Edit menu. Click the Copy button on Publisher's Standard toolbar to copy the selected objects.
4. Click the Excel workbook button on the taskbar. On the Edit menu, click Paste Special. When the Paste Special dialog box displays, click Picture (Enhanced Metafile), and then click the OK button.
5. When the publication object displays, drag the picture to the top left corner of the worksheet and resize as necessary.
6. Save the workbook as Quarterly Earnings with Memo. Print a copy. Quit Excel. Quit Publisher without saving the publication.

In the Lab

Green Assembly Division

TO: All Benefited Employees, West Assembly Division
FROM: Stanley Bennet, Director of Human Resources
SUBJECT: Self-Managed Plan Asset Allocation Quarterly Statement
DATE: April 27, 2003

We are pleased to present your group retirement investment earnings for the first quarter of 2003. Please note that individual accounts are not represented in these figures.

ICMA Growth Portfolio is the default fund for members who have selected have not yet selected individual mutual/variable annuity funds.

publication

Self-Managed Plan Asset Allocation
April 27, 2003

	U.S. Stocks	Non U.S. Stocks	Fixed Income	Balanced	Total
Crawford Funds					
Bond Fund			5,666		5,666
Growth & Income Fund	3,846				3,846
MFS Mass Investors	13,402				13,402
Index Plus Fund	14,564				14,564
James Worldwide		98,661			98,661
Subtotal	31,812	98,661	5,666		136,139
ICMA Funds					
ICMA Bond Index			1,561		1,561
ICMA Growth Portfolio				740,706	740,706
ICMA International Fund		888			888
Subtotal		888	1,561	740,706	743,155
W.A.D. - O.F. Funds					
Money Market			17,997		17,997
Traditional Annuity			20,027		20,027
Bond Market					
Stock Account	91,981				91,981
Global Equities		40,579			40,579
Subtotal	91,981	40,579	38,024		170,584
FUND	123,793	140,128	45,251	740,706	1,049,878

worksheet

(a) Publisher publication

FIGURE 11

(b) Excel workbook

In the Lab

3 Embedding a Worksheet

Problem: Stanley Bennet now has asked you to embeds the Excel workbook into the Publisher publication, rather than linking it as you did before.

Instructions: Perform the following tasks.

1. One at a time, open the publication, Investment Report, and the workbook, Quarterly Earnings, from the Data Disk. If you did not download the Data Disk, see the inside back cover for instructions for downloading the Data Disk or see your instructor.
2. With the Excel workbook active, copy the range A3 through F26 from the Excel workbook. Close the Excel window by clicking its Close button.
3. Click the Publisher publication button on the taskbar. On the Edit menu, click Paste Special. When the Paste Special dialog box displays, click the Paste option button to embed the worksheet rather than link it. Click Microsoft Excel Worksheet Object in the As box. Click the OK button.
4. When the worksheet range displays as a table in the publication, double-click it. Notice that Excel is not linked or activated. Rather, row and column borders display around the table.
5. Look at the toolbars. The Standard toolbar now displays some buttons unique to Excel. Below the Standard toolbar is an Excel Formula bar. Point to each button on the toolbars and, as their ScreenTips display, make a list of their names on a piece of paper. Turn the list in to your instructor.

More About

Quick Reference

For a table that lists how to complete tasks covered in this book using the mouse, menu, shortcut menu, and keyboard, see the Quick Reference Summary at the back of this book or visit the Shelly Cashman Series Office XP Web page (scsite.com/ offxp/qr.htm) and then click Microsoft Publisher 2002.

More About

Microsoft Certification

The Microsoft Office User Specialist (MOUS) Certification program provides an opportunity for you to obtain a valuable industry credential — proof that you have the Office XP skills required by employers. For more information, see Appendix E or visit the Shelly Cashman Series MOUS Web page at scsite.com/ offxp/cert.htm.

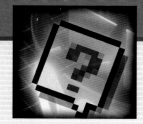

APPENDIX A
Microsoft Publisher Help System

Using the Publisher Help System

This appendix shows you how to use the Publisher Help system. At anytime while you are using Publisher, you can interact with its Help system and display information on any Publisher topic. It is a complete reference manual at your fingertips.

As shown in Figure A-1, you can access Publisher's Help system in four primary ways:

1. Ask a Question box on the menu bar
2. Function key F1 on the keyboard
3. Microsoft Publisher Help command on the Help menu
4. Microsoft Publisher Help button on the Standard toolbar

If you use the Ask a Question box on the menu bar, Publisher responds by opening the Microsoft Publisher Help window, which gives you direct access to its Help system. If you use one of the other three ways to access Publisher's Help system, Publisher responds in one of two ways:

1. If the Office Assistant is turned on, then the Office Assistant displays with a **balloon** (lower-right side in Figure A-1).
2. If the Office Assistant is turned off, then the Microsoft Publisher Help window opens (lower-left side in Figure A-1).

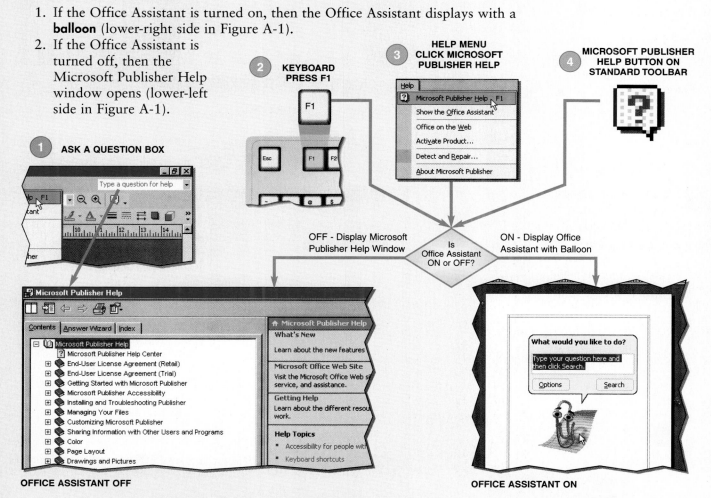

FIGURE A-1

Microsoft **Publisher 2002**

The best way to familiarize yourself with the Publisher Help system is to use it. The next several pages show examples of how to use the Help system. Following the examples are a set of exercises titled Use Help that will sharpen your Publisher Help system skills.

Ask a Question Box

The **Ask a Question box** on the right side of the menu bar lets you type questions in your own words, or you can type terms, such as border, rotate, or change margins. Publisher responds by displaying a list of topics related to the term(s) you entered. The following steps show how to use the Ask a Question box to obtain information on borders.

Steps **To Obtain Help Using the Ask a Question Box**

1 **Click the Ask a Question box on the right side of the menu bar, type** borders**, and then press the ENTER key. When the Ask a Question list displays, point to the Add or change a border link.**

The Ask a Question list displays (Figure A-2). Clicking the See more link displays additional links.

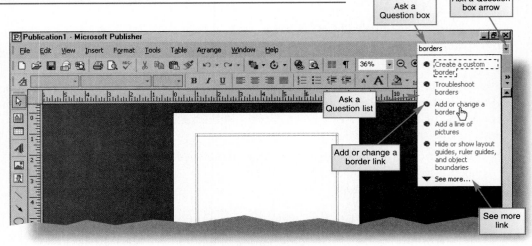

FIGURE A-2

2 **Click Add or change a border. Point to the Microsoft Publisher Help window title bar.**

The Microsoft Publisher Help window displays (Figure A-3).

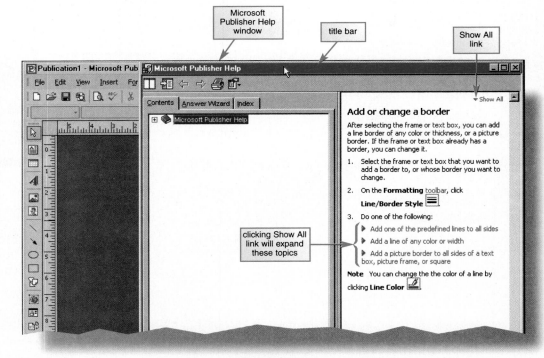

FIGURE A-3

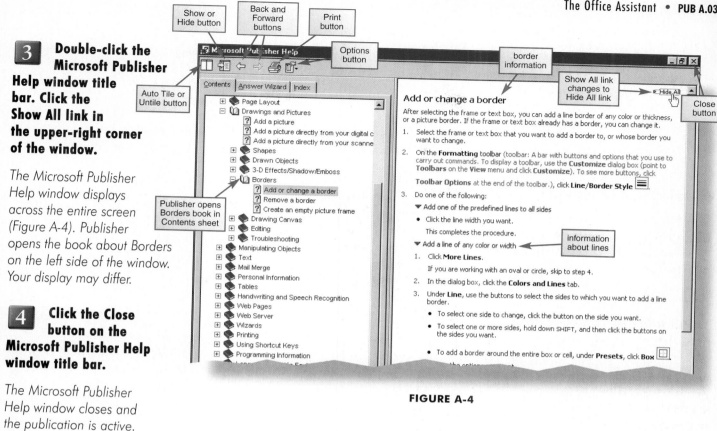

3 Double-click the Microsoft Publisher Help window title bar. Click the Show All link in the upper-right corner of the window.

The Microsoft Publisher Help window displays across the entire screen (Figure A-4). Publisher opens the book about Borders on the left side of the window. Your display may differ.

4 Click the Close button on the Microsoft Publisher Help window title bar.

The Microsoft Publisher Help window closes and the publication is active.

FIGURE A-4

As you enter questions and terms in the Ask a Question box, Publisher adds them to its list. Thus, if you click the Ask a Question box arrow (shown in Figure A-2), a list of previously asked questions and terms will display.

Use the six buttons in the upper-left corner of the Microsoft Publisher Help window (Figure A-4) to navigate through the Help system, change the display, and print the contents of the window. Table A-1 lists the function of each of these buttons.

The Office Assistant

The **Office Assistant** is an icon (lower-right side of Figure A-1 on page PUB A.01) that displays in the Publisher window when it is turned on and not hidden. It has dual functions. First, it will respond in the same way the Ask a Question box does with a list of topics that relate to the entry you make in the text box at the bottom of the balloon. The entry can be in the form of a word, phrase, or question, written as if you were talking to a human being. For example, if you want to learn more about saving a file, in the balloon text box, you can type any of the following terms or phrases: save, save a file, how do i save a file, or anything similar. The Office Assistant responds by displaying a list of topics from which you can choose. Once you choose a topic, it displays the corresponding information.

Table A-1	Microsoft Publisher Help Toolbar Buttons	
BUTTON	**NAME**	**FUNCTION**
▢▢ or ▢	Auto Tile or Untile	Tiles or untiles the Microsoft Publisher Help window and Microsoft Publisher window when the Microsoft Publisher Help window is maximized
◄▢ or ▢►	Show or Hide	Displays or hides the Contents, Answer Wizard, and Index tabs
◄	Back	Displays the previous Help topic
►	Forward	Displays the next Help topic
🖶	Print	Prints the current Help topic
▢▾	Options	Displays a list of commands

Second, the Office Assistant monitors your work and accumulates tips during a session on how you might increase your productivity and efficiency. You can view the tips at any time. The accumulated tips display when you activate the Office Assistant balloon. Also, if at anytime you see a light bulb above the Office Assistant, click it to display the most recent tip.

You may or may not want the Office Assistant to display on the screen at all times. You can hide it and then show it later. You may prefer not to use the Office Assistant at all. Thus, not only do you need to know how to show and hide the Office Assistant, but you also need to know how to turn the Office Assistant on and off.

Showing and Hiding the Office Assistant

When Publisher initially is installed, the Office Assistant may be off. You turn it on by invoking the **Show the Office Assistant command** on the Help menu. If the Office Assistant is on the screen and you want to hide it, you click the **Hide the Office Assistant command** on the Help menu. You also can right-click the Office Assistant to display its shortcut menu and then click the **Hide command** to hide it. You can move it to any location on the screen. You can click it to display the Office Assistant balloon, which allows you to request Help.

Turning the Office Assistant On and Off

The fact that the Office Assistant is hidden does not mean it is turned off. To turn the Office Assistant off, it first must be displaying in the Publisher window. You right-click the Office Assistant to display its shortcut menu (right side of Figure A-5). Next, click Options on the shortcut menu. Invoking the **Options command** causes the **Office Assistant dialog box** to display (left side of Figure A-5).

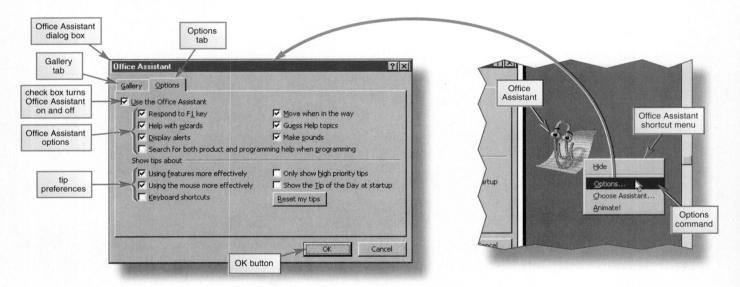

FIGURE A-5

The top check box on the **Options sheet** determines whether the Office Assistant is on or off. To turn the Office Assistant off, remove the check mark from the **Use the Office Assistant check box** and then click the OK button. As shown in Figure A-1 on page PUB A.01, if the Office Assistant is off when you invoke Help, then Publisher opens the Microsoft Publisher Help window instead of displaying the Office Assistant. To turn the Office Assistant on at a later date, click the Show the Office Assistant command on the Help menu.

Through the Options command on the Office Assistant shortcut menu, you can change the look and feel of the Office Assistant. For example, you can hide the Office Assistant, turn the Office Assistant off, change the way it works, choose a different Office Assistant icon, or view an animation of the current one. These options also are available by clicking the **Options button** that displays in the Office Assistant balloon (Figure A-6).

The **Gallery sheet** in the Office Assistant dialog box (Figure A-5) allows you to change the appearance of the Office Assistant. The default is the paper clip (Clippit). You can change it to a bouncing red happy face (The Dot), a robot (F1), the Microsoft Office logo (Office Logo), a wizard (Merlin), the earth (Mother Nature), a cat (Links), or a dog (Rocky).

Using the Office Assistant

As indicated earlier, the Office Assistant allows you to enter a word, phrase, or question and then responds by displaying a list of topics from which you can choose to display Help. The following steps show how to use the Office Assistant to obtain Help on searching for files.

Steps **To Use the Office Assistant**

1 **If the Office Assistant is not on the screen, click Help on the menu bar and then click Show the Office Assistant. Click the Office Assistant. When the Office Assistant balloon displays, type** i can't find my file **in the text box immediately above the Options button. Point to the Search button.**

The Office Assistant balloon displays as shown in Figure A-6.

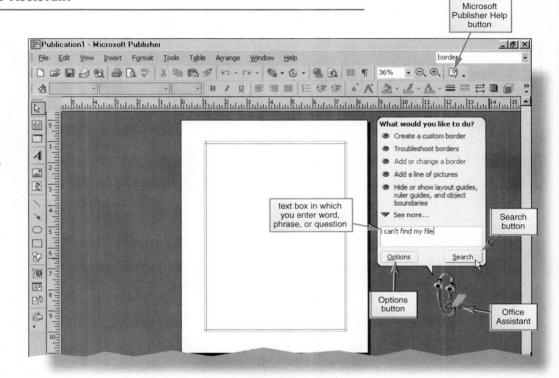

FIGURE A-6

2 **Click the Search button. When the Office Assistant balloon redisplays, point to the topic, About finding files.**

A new list of links display in the Office Assistant's balloon (Figure A-7).

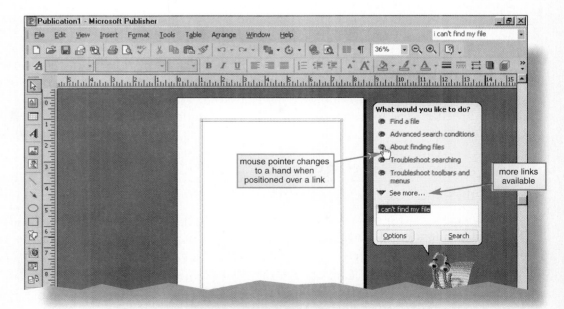

FIGURE A-7

3 **Click the topic About finding files. If necessary, move or hide the Office Assistant so you can view all of the text in the Microsoft Publisher Help window.**

The Microsoft Publisher Help window displays the information about finding files (Figure A-8).

4 **Click the Close button on the Microsoft Publisher Help window title bar.**

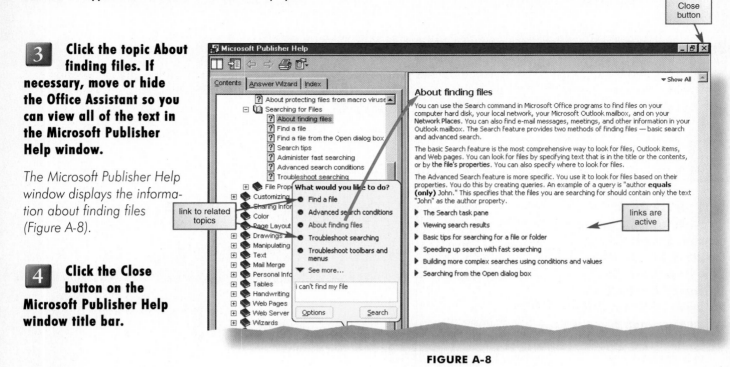

FIGURE A-8

The Microsoft Publisher Help Window

If the Office Assistant is turned off and you click the Microsoft Publisher Help button on the Standard toolbar, the Microsoft Publisher Help window opens (shown in Figure A-9). The left side of this window contains three tabs: Contents, Answer Wizard, and Index. Each tab displays a sheet with powerful look-up capabilities.

Use the Contents sheet as you would a table of contents at the front of a book to look up Help. The Answer Wizard sheet answers your queries the same as the Office Assistant. You use the Index sheet in the same fashion as an index in a book to look up Help. Click the tabs to move from sheet to sheet.

Besides clicking the Microsoft Publisher Help button on the Standard toolbar, you also can click the Microsoft Publisher Help command on the Help menu, or press the F1 key to display the Microsoft Publisher Help window to gain access to the three sheets.

Using the Contents Sheet

The **Contents sheet** is useful for displaying Help when you know the general category of the topic in question, but not the specifics. The following steps show how to use the Contents sheet to obtain information on using mail merge in Publisher.

TO OBTAIN HELP USING THE CONTENTS SHEET

1 With the Office Assistant turned off, click the Microsoft Publisher Help button on the Standard toolbar.

2 When the Microsoft Publisher Help window opens, double-click the title bar to maximize the window. If necessary, click the Show button (see Table A-1 on page PUB A.03) to display the tabs.

3 Click the Contents tab. If necessary double-click Microsoft Publisher Help on the left side of the window, to displays the Help books. Double-click the Mail Merge book. Double-click the Data Sources book.

4 Click the subtopic Create an address list for mail merge below the Data Sources book.

Publisher displays Help on the subtopic of address lists (Figure A-9).

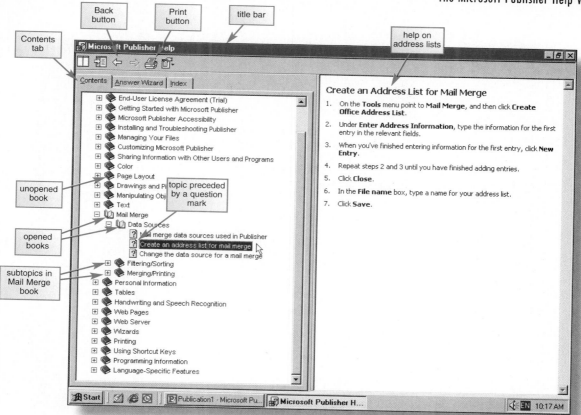

FIGURE A-9

Once the information on the subtopic displays, you can scroll through and read it or you can click the Print button to obtain a printed copy. If you decide to click another subtopic on the left or a link on the right, you can get back to the Help page shown in Figure A-9 by clicking the Back button.

Each topic in the Contents sheet is preceded by a book icon or question mark icon. A **book icon** indicates subtopics are available. A **question mark icon** means information on the topic will display if you double-click the title. The book icon opens when you double-click the book (or its title) or click the plus sign (+) to the left of the book icon. Right-clicking the Contents sheet displays a shortcut menu with choices to close all the books, open all the books, or print selected topics.

Using the Answer Wizard Sheet

The **Answer Wizard sheet** works like the Office Assistant in that you enter a word, phrase, or question and it responds by listing topics from which you can choose to display Help. The following steps show how to use the Answer Wizard sheet to obtain Help on adding text to an AutoShape.

TO OBTAIN HELP USING THE ANSWER WIZARD SHEET

1 With the Office Assistant turned off, click the Microsoft Publisher Help button on the Standard toolbar (see Figure A-6 on page PUB A.05).

2 When the Microsoft Publisher Help window opens, double-click the title bar to maximize the window. If necessary, click the Show button to display the tabs.

3 Click the Answer Wizard tab. Type add text to an autoshape in the What would you like to do? text box on the left side of the window. Click the Search button.

4 When a list of topics displays in the Select topic to display list, click the Add text to a shape link. Click Autoshape link on the right side of the Microsoft Publisher Help window. Click the bulleted How? link.

Publisher displays Help on adding text to AutoShapes (Figure A-10 on the next page).

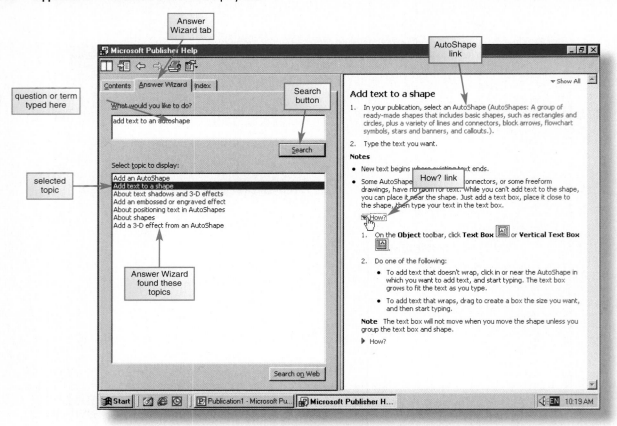

FIGURE A-10

Clicking bulleted blue text, such as How?, in the right side of the Microsoft Publisher Help window displays more information about the topic. Clicking non-bulleted blue text, such as AutoShape displays definitions in a green font. Both kinds of links display in Figure A-10.

If the topic, Add text to a shape, does not include the information you are seeking, click another topic in the list. Continue to click topics until you find the desired information.

Using the Index Sheet

The third sheet in the Microsoft Publisher Help window is the Index sheet. Use the **Index sheet** to display Help when you know the keyword or the first few letters of the keyword you want to look up. The following steps show how to use the Index sheet to obtain Help on using Web forms in a publication.

TO OBTAIN HELP USING THE INDEX SHEET

1. With the Office Assistant turned off, click the Microsoft Publisher Help button on the Standard toolbar.

2. When the Microsoft Publisher Help window opens, double-click the title bar to maximize the window. If necessary, click the Show button to display the tabs.

3. Click the Index tab. Type `form control` in the Type keywords text box on the left side of the window. Click the Search button.

4. When a list of topics displays in the Choose a topic list, click What form controls should I use?.

Publisher displays Help on Web form controls (Figure A-11). When you click the Search button, Publisher automatically appends a semicolon to the keyword in the Type keywords text box.

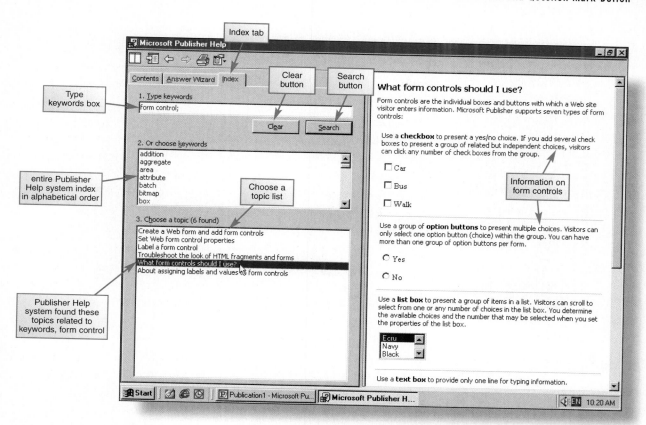

FIGURE A-11

An alternative to typing a keyword in the Type keywords text box is to scroll through the Or choose keywords list (the middle list on the left side of the window). When you locate the keyword you are searching for, double-click it to display Help on the topic. Also in the Or choose keywords list, the Publisher Help system displays other topics that relate to the new keyword. As you begin typing a new keyword in the Type keywords text box, Publisher jumps to that point in the middle list box. To begin a new search, click the Clear button.

The How? link (shown in Figure A-10) is used throughout the Help system to offer step by step instructions on how to do a specific task in Publisher.

What's This? Command and Question Mark Button

Use the What's This? command or the Question Mark button in a dialog box when you are not sure what an object on the screen is or what it does.

What's This? Command

You use the **What's This? command** on dialog box shortcut menus to display a detailed ScreenTip. When you invoke this command, a detailed description displays in a ScreenTip. For example, right-clicking Columns in the Layout Guides dialog box displays the What's This? command on the shortcut menu. Clicking the What's This? command then displays a description of how to divide a page into columns (Figure A-12 on the next page). You can print the ScreenTip by right-clicking it and then clicking Print Topic on the shortcut menu.

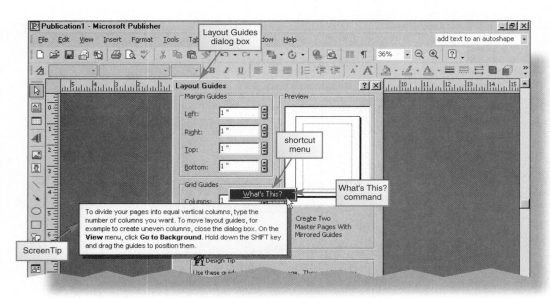

FIGURE A-12

Question Mark Button

In a fashion similar to the What's This? command, the **Question Mark button** displays a ScreenTip. You use the Question Mark button with dialog boxes. It is located in the upper-right corner on the title bar of dialog boxes, next to the Close button. For example, in Figure A-13, the Insert Object dialog box displays on the screen. If you click the Question Mark button and then click one of the options

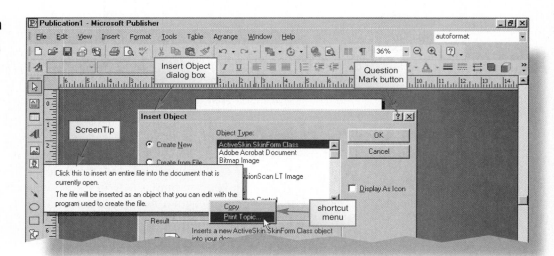

FIGURE A-13

buttons in the Insert Object dialog box, an explanation displays. You can print the ScreenTip by right-clicking it and then clicking Print Topic on the shortcut menu.

If a dialog box does not include a Question Mark button, press SHIFT+F1. This combination of keys displays an explanation or displays the Microsoft Publisher Help window.

Office on the Web Command

The **Office on the Web command** on the Help menu displays a Microsoft Web page containing up-to-date information on a variety of Office-related topics (Figure A-14). To use this command, you must be connected to the Internet. Once the Microsoft Office Assistance Center displays, scroll down to click the Publisher link in the lower portion of the window. The Publisher Help Articles page displays links to Help articles, to the Design Gallery and to the Download Center among others. The Product Updates page contains Publisher software updates. The Design Gallery Live page offers free clip art and photos.

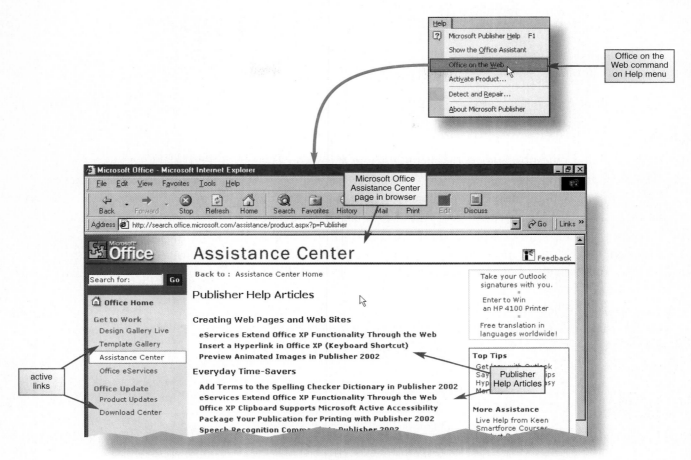

FIGURE A-14

Other Help Commands

Three additional commands available on the Help menu are Activate Product, Detect and Repair, and About Microsoft Publisher.

Activate Product Command

The **Activate Product command** on the Help menu lets you activate Publisher if it has not already been activated.

Detect and Repair Command

Use the **Detect and Repair command** on the Help menu if Publisher is not running properly or if it is generating errors. When you invoke this command, the Detect and Repair dialog box displays. Click the Start button in the dialog box to initiate the detect and repair process.

About Microsoft Publisher Command

The **About Microsoft Publisher command** on the Help menu displays the **About Microsoft Publisher dialog box**. The dialog box lists the owner of the software and the product identification. You need to know the product identification if you call Microsoft for assistance. The three buttons below the OK button are the System Info button, the Tech Support button, and the Disabled Items button. The **System Info button** displays system information, including hardware resources, components, software environment, and applications. The **Tech Support button** displays technical assistance information. The **Disabled Items button** displays a dialog box with any Publisher features that were disabled because Publisher was not functioning properly.

Use Help

1 Using the Ask a Question Box

Instructions: Perform the following tasks using the Publisher Help system.

1. Click the Ask a Question box on the menu bar, and then type shortcuts. Press the ENTER key.
2. Click Keyboard shortcuts for Microsoft Publisher in the Ask a Question list. Double-click the Microsoft Publisher Help window title bar. Read and print the information. One at a time, click two of the links on the right side of the window to learn about shortcuts. Print the information. Hand in the printouts to your instructor. Use the Back and Forward buttons to return to the original page.
3. If necessary, click the Show button to display the tabs. Click the Contents tab to prepare for the next step. Click the Close button in the Microsoft Publisher Help window.
4. Click the Ask a Question box and press the ENTER key. Click Customize a shortcut menu in the Ask a Question box. When the Microsoft Publisher Help window displays, maximize the window. Read and print the information. Click the two bulleted items on the right side of the window. Print the information for each. Close the Microsoft Publisher Help window.

2 Expanding on the Publisher Help System Basics

Instructions: Use the Publisher Help system to understand the topics better and perform the tasks listed below.

1. Right-click the Office Assistant. If it is not turned on, click Show the Office Assistant on the Help menu. When the shortcut menu displays, click Options. Click Use the Office Assistant to remove the check mark, and then click the OK button.
2. Click the Microsoft Publisher Help button on the Standard toolbar. Maximize the Microsoft Publisher Help window. If the tabs are hidden on the left side, click the Show button. Click the Index tab. Type undo in the Type keywords text box. Click the Search button. Click Restore original settings for buttons, commands, or toolbars. Print the information. Click the Hide and then Show buttons. Click the Show All link. Read and print the information. Close the Microsoft Publisher Help window. Hand in the printouts to your instructor.
3. Press the F1 key. Click the Answer Wizard tab. Type help in the What would you like to do? text box, and then click the Search button. Click About getting help while you work. Read the information that displays. Print the information. Click the first two links. Read and print the information for both. Hand in the print-outs to your instructor.
4. Click the Contents tab. Click the plus sign (+) to the left of the Manipulating Objects book. One at a time, click both topics in the Manipulating Objects book. Read and print each one. Close the Microsoft Publisher Help window. Hand in the printouts to your instructor.
5. Click the Save As command on the File menu. When the Save As dialog box displays, click the Question Mark button on the title bar. Click the Save in box. Right-click the ScreenTip and then click Print Topic. Click the Cancel button in the Save As dialog box. Hand in the printout to your instructor.

APPENDIX B
Speech and Handwriting Recognition

Introduction

This appendix discusses how you can create and modify publications using Office XP's new input technologies. Office XP provides a variety of text services, which enable you to speak commands and enter text in an application. The most common text service is the keyboard. Two new **text services** included with Office XP are speech recognition and handwriting recognition.

When Windows was installed on your computer, you specified a default language. For example, most users in the United States select English (United States) as the default language. Through text services, you can add more than 90 additional languages and varying dialects such as Basque, English (Zimbabwe), French (France), French (Canada), German (Germany), German (Austria), and Swahili. With multiple languages available, you can switch from one language to another while working in Publisher. If you change the language or dialect, then text services may change the functions of the keys on the keyboard, adjust speech recognition, and alter handwriting recognition.

The Language Bar

You know that text services are installed properly when the Language Indicator button displays by the clock in the tray status area on the Windows taskbar (Figure B-1a) or the Language bar displays on the screen (Figure B-1b or B-1c). If the Language Indicator button displays in the tray status area, click it, and then click the Show the Language bar command (Figure B-1a). The Language bar displays on the screen in the same location it displayed last time.

You can drag the Language bar to any location in the window by pointing to its move handle, which is the vertical line on its left side (Figure B-1b). When the mouse pointer changes to a four-headed arrow, drag the Language bar to the desired location.

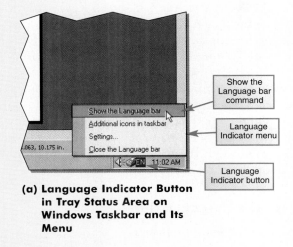

(a) Language Indicator Button in Tray Status Area on Windows Taskbar and Its Menu

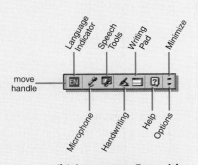

(b) Language Bar with Text Labels Disabled

(c) Language Bar with Text Labels Enabled

FIGURE B-1

If you are sure that one of the services was installed and neither the Language Indicator button nor the Language bar displays, then do the following:

1. Click Start on the Windows taskbar, point to Settings, click Control Panel, and then double-click the Text Services icon in the Control Panel window.
2. When the Text Services dialog box displays, click the Language Bar button, click the Show the Language bar on the desktop check box to select it, and then click the OK button in the Language Bar Settings dialog box.
3. Click the OK button in the Text Services dialog box.
4. Close the Control Panel window.

You can perform tasks related to text services by using the Language bar. The Language bar may display with just the icon on each button (Figure B-1b on the previous page) or it may display with text labels to the right of the icon on each button (shown in Figure B-1c). Changing the appearance of the Language bar will be discussed shortly.

Buttons on the Language Bar

The Language bar shown in Figure B-2a contains eight buttons. The number of buttons on your Language bar may be different. These buttons are used to select the language, customize the Language bar, control the microphone, control handwriting, and obtain help.

When you click the **Language Indicator button** on the far left side of the Language bar, the Language Indicator menu displays a list of the active languages (Figure B-2b) from which you can choose. The **Microphone button**, the second button from the left, enables and disables the microphone. When the microphone is enabled, text services adds two buttons and a balloon to the Language toolbar (Figure B-2c). These additional buttons and the balloon will be discussed shortly.

The third button from the left on the Language bar is the Speech Tools button. The **Speech Tools button** displays the **Speech Tools menu**, a list of commands (Figure B-2d) that allows you to hide or show the balloon on the Language bar; train the Speech Recognition service so that it can better interpret your voice; add and delete words from its dictionary, such as names and other words not understood easily; and change the user profile so more than one person can use the microphone on the same computer.

The fourth button from the left on the Language bar is the Handwriting button. The **Handwriting button** displays the **Handwriting menu** (Figure B-2e), which lets you choose the Writing Pad (Figure B-2f), Write Anywhere (Figure B-2g), Drawing Pad, the On-Screen Keyboard, or the On-Screen Symbol Keyboard (Figure B-2h). You can choose only one form of handwriting at a time.

The fifth button indicates which one of the handwriting forms is active. For example, in Figure B-1a on the previous page the Writing Pad is active. The handwriting recognition capabilities of text services will be discussed shortly.

The sixth button from the left on the Language bar is the Help button. The **Help button** displays the Help menu. If you click the Language Bar Help command on the Help menu, the Language Bar Help window displays (Figure B-2i). On the far right of the Language bar are two buttons stacked above and below each other. The upper button is the Minimize button and the lower button is the Options button. The **Minimize button** minimizes (hides) the Language bar so that the Language Indicator button displays in the tray status area on the Windows taskbar. The next section discusses the Options button.

Customizing the Language Bar

The down arrow icon, immediately below the Minimize button in Figure B-2a, is called the Options button. The **Options button** displays a menu of text services options (Figure B-2j). You can use this menu to hide the Speech Tools, Handwriting, and Help buttons on the Language bar by clicking their names to remove the check mark to the left of each button. The Settings command on the Options menu displays a dialog box that lets you customize the Language bar. This command will be discussed shortly. The Restore Defaults command redisplays hidden buttons on the Language bar.

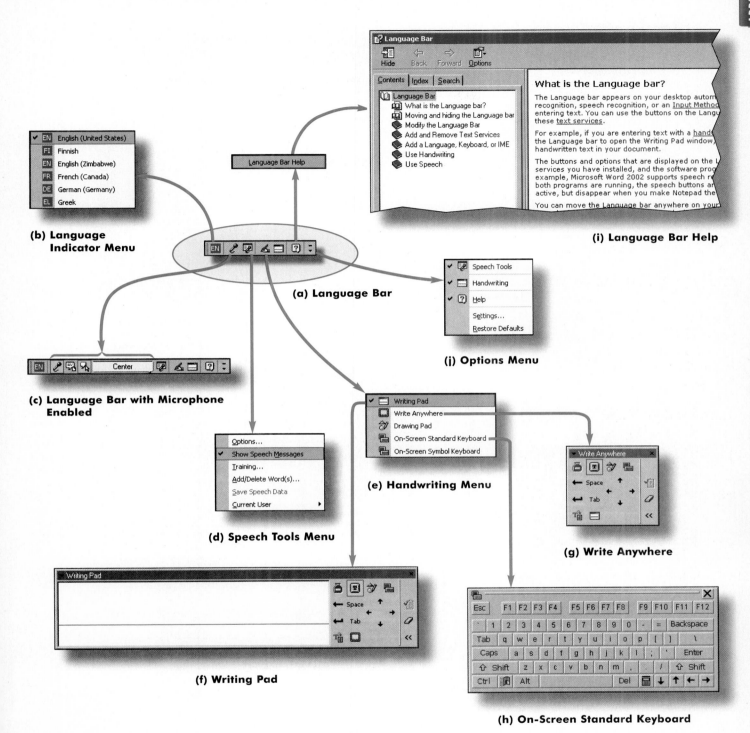

(b) Language Indicator Menu

(i) Language Bar Help

(a) Language Bar

(j) Options Menu

(c) Language Bar with Microphone Enabled

(e) Handwriting Menu

(d) Speech Tools Menu

(g) Write Anywhere

(f) Writing Pad

(h) On-Screen Standard Keyboard

FIGURE B-2

If you right-click the Language bar, a shortcut menu displays (Figure B-3a on the next page). This shortcut menu lets you further customize the Language bar. The **Minimize command** on the shortcut menu minimizes the Language bar in the same manner as the Minimize button on the Language bar. The **Transparency command** toggles the Language bar between being solid and transparent. You can see through a transparent Language bar (Figure B-3b). The **Text Labels command** toggles text labels on the Language bar on (Figure B-3c) and off (Figure B-3a). The **Additional icons in taskbar command** toggles between only showing the Language Indicator button in the tray status area and showing icons that represent the text services that are active (Figure B-3d).

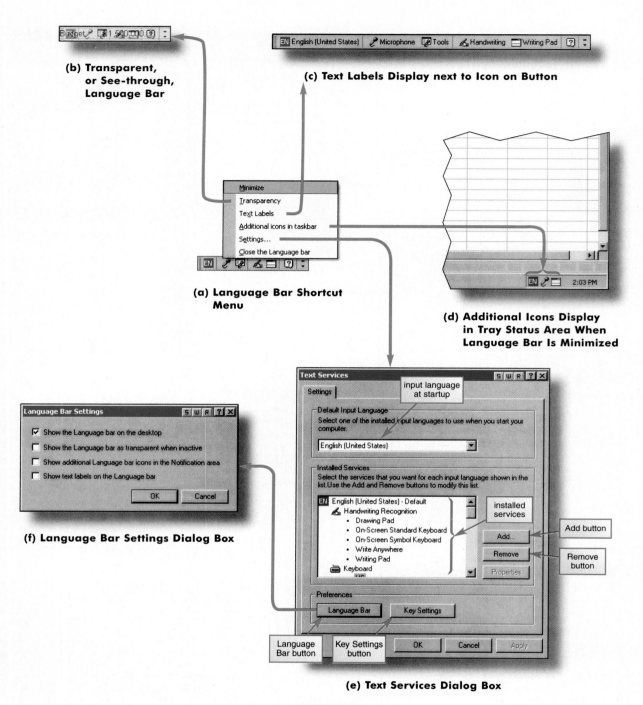

(b) **Transparent, or See-through, Language Bar**

(c) **Text Labels Display next to Icon on Button**

(a) **Language Bar Shortcut Menu**

(d) **Additional Icons Display in Tray Status Area When Language Bar Is Minimized**

(f) **Language Bar Settings Dialog Box**

(e) **Text Services Dialog Box**

FIGURE B-3

The **Settings command** displays the Text Services dialog box (Figure B-3e). The **Text Services dialog box** allows you to select the language at startup; add and remove text services; modify keys on the keyboard; and modify the Language bar. If you want to remove any one of the entries in the Installed Services list, select the entry, and then click the Remove button. If you want to add a service, click the Add button. The **Key Settings button** allows you to modify the keyboard. If you click the **Language Bar button** in the Text Services dialog box, the Language Bar Settings dialog box displays (Figure B-3f). This dialog box contains Language bar options, some of which are the same as the commands on the Language bar shortcut menu described earlier.

The **Close the Language bar command** on the shortcut menu shown in Figure B-3a closes the Language bar and hides the Language Indicator button in the tray status area on the Windows taskbar. If you close the Language bar and want to redisplay it, follow the instructions at the top of page PUB B.02.

Speech Recognition

The **Speech Recognition service** available with Office XP enables your computer to recognize human speech through a microphone. The microphone has two modes: dictation and voice command (Figure B-4). You switch between the two modes by clicking the Dictation button and the Voice Command button on the Language bar. These buttons display only when you turn on Speech Recognition by clicking the Microphone button on the Language bar (Figure B-5). If you are using the **Microphone button** for the very first time in Publisher, it will advise you to check your microphone settings and step through voice training before activating the Speech Recognition service.

The **Dictation button** places the microphone in Dictation mode. In Dictation mode, whatever you speak is entered as text in the text box. The Voice Command button places the microphone in Voice Command mode. In Voice Command mode, whatever you speak is interpreted as a command. If you want to turn off the microphone, click the Microphone button on the Language bar or in Voice Command mode say, "Mic off" (pronounced mike off). It is important to remember that minimizing the Language bar does not turn off the microphone.

(a) Enter Text in Text Boxes in Dictation Mode

(b) Enter Commands in Voice Command Mode

FIGURE B-4

Microsoft **Publisher 2002**

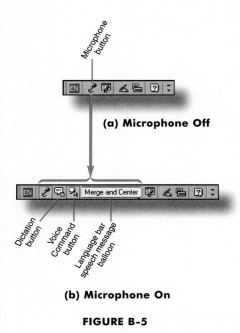

(a) Microphone Off

(b) Microphone On

FIGURE B-5

The **Language bar speech message balloon** shown in Figure B-5b displays messages that may offer help or hints. In Voice Command mode, the name of the last recognized command you said displays. If you use the mouse or keyboard instead of the microphone, a message will appear in the Language bar speech message balloon indicating the word you could say. In Dictation mode, the message, Dictating, usually displays. The Speech Recognition service, however, will display messages to inform you that you are talking too soft, too loud, too fast, or to ask you to repeat what you said by displaying, What was that?

Getting Started with Speech Recognition

For the microphone to function properly, you should follow these steps:

1. Make sure your computer meets the minimum requirements.
2. Install Speech Recognition.
3. Set up and position your microphone, preferably a close-talk headset with gain adjustment support.
4. Train Speech Recognition.

The following sections describe these steps in more detail.

SPEECH RECOGNITION SYSTEM REQUIREMENTS For Speech Recognition to work on your computer, it needs the following:

1. Microsoft Windows 98 or later or Microsoft Windows NT 4.0 or later
2. At least 128 MB RAM
3. 400 MHz or faster processor
4. Microphone and sound card

INSTALL SPEECH RECOGNITION If Speech Recognition is not installed on your computer, Publisher will offer you the choice of installing Speech Recognition when you start Publisher; or, you may start Microsoft Word and then click Speech on the Tools menu to install Speech Recognition.

SETUP AND POSITION YOUR MICROPHONE Set up your microphone as follows:

1. Connect your microphone to the sound card in the back of the computer.
2. Position the microphone approximately one inch out from and to the side of your mouth. Position it so you are not breathing into it.
3. On the Language bar, click the Speech Tools button, and then click Options (Figure B-6a).
4. When the Speech Properties dialog box displays (Figure B-6b), if necessary, click the Speech Recognition tab.
5. Click the Configure Microphone button. Follow the Microphone Wizard directions as shown in Figures B-6c, B-6d, and B-6e. The Next button will remain dimmed in Figure B-6d until the volume meter consistently stays in the green area.
6. If someone else installed Speech Recognition, click the New button in the Speech Properties dialog box and enter your name. Click the Train Profile button and step through the Voice Training Wizard. The Voice Training Wizard will require that you enter your gender and age group. It then will step you through voice training.

You can adjust the microphone further by clicking the **Settings button** (Figure B-6b) in the Speech Properties dialog box. The Settings button displays the **Recognition Profile Settings dialog box** that allows you to adjust the pronunciation sensitivity and accuracy versus recognition response time.

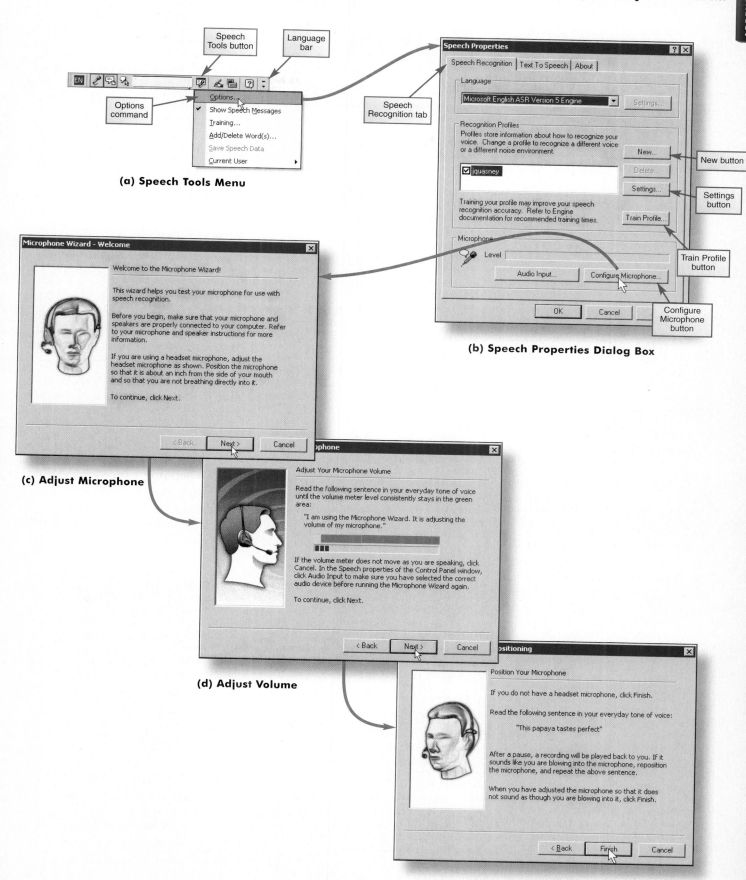

(a) Speech Tools Menu

(b) Speech Properties Dialog Box

(c) Adjust Microphone

(d) Adjust Volume

(e) Test Microphone

FIGURE B-6

TRAIN SPEECH RECOGNITION The Speech Recognition service will understand most commands and some dictation without any training at all. It will recognize much more of what you speak, however, if you take the time to train it. After one training session, it will recognize 85 to 90 percent of your words. As you do more training, accuracy will rise to 95 percent. If you feel that too many mistakes are being made, then continue to train the service. The more training you do, the more accurately it will work for you. Follow these steps to train the Speech Recognition service.

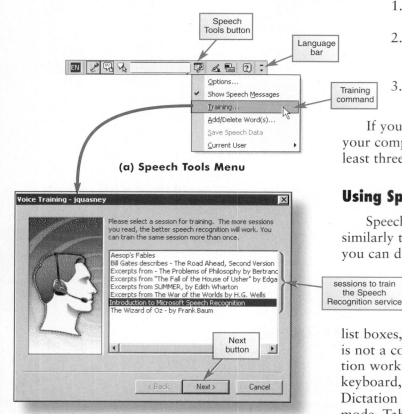

(a) **Speech Tools Menu**

(b) **Voice Training Dialog Box**

FIGURE B-7

1. Click the Speech Tools button on the Language bar and then click Training (Figure B-7a).
2. When the Voice Training dialog box displays (Figure B-7b), click one of the sessions, and then click the Next button.
3. Complete the training session, which should take less than 15 minutes.

If you are serious about using a microphone to speak to your computer, you need to take the time to go through at least three of the eight training sessions listed in Figure B-7b.

Using Speech Recognition

Speech recognition lets you enter text into a publication similarly to speaking into a tape recorder. Instead of typing, you can dictate text that you want to assign to text boxes, and you can issue voice commands. In Voice Command mode, you can speak menu names, commands on menus, toolbar button names, and dialog box option buttons, check boxes, list boxes, and button names. Speech Recognition, however, is not a completely hands-free form of input. Speech recognition works best if you use a combination of your voice, the keyboard, and the mouse. You soon will discover that Dictation mode is far less accurate than Voice Command mode. Table B-1 lists some tips that will improve the Speech Recognition service's accuracy considerably.

Table B-1	Tips to Improve Speech Recognition
NUMBER	**TIP**
1	The microphone hears everything. Though the Speech Recognition service filters out background noise, it is recommended that you work in a quiet environment.
2	Try not to move the microphone around once it is adjusted.
3	Speak in a steady tone and speak clearly.
4	In Dictation mode, do not pause between words. A phrase is easier to interpret than a word. Sounding out syllables in a word will make it more difficult for the Speech Recognition service to interpret what you are saying.
5	If you speak too loudly or too softly, it makes it difficult for the Speech Recognition service to interpret what you said. Check the Language bar speech message balloon for an indication that you may be speaking too loudly or too softly.
6	If you experience problems after training, adjust the recognition options that control accuracy and rejection by clicking the Settings button shown in Figure B-6b on the previous page.
7	When you are finished using the microphone, turn it off by clicking the Microphone button on the Language bar or in Voice Command mode say, "Mic off." Leaving the microphone on is the same as leaning on the keyboard.
8	If the Speech Recognition service is having difficulty with unusual words, then add the words to its dictionary by using the Add/Delete Word(s) command on the Speech Tools menu (Figure B-8a). The last names of individuals and the names of companies are good examples of the types of words you should add to the dictionary.
9	Training will improve accuracy; practice will improve confidence.

The last command on the Speech Tools menu is the Current User command (Figure B-8a). The **Current User command** is useful for multiple users who share a computer. It allows them to configure their own individual profiles, and then switch between users as they use the computer.

For additional information on the Speech Recognition service, click the Help button on the Standard toolbar, click the Answer Wizard tab, and search for the phrase, Speech Recognition.

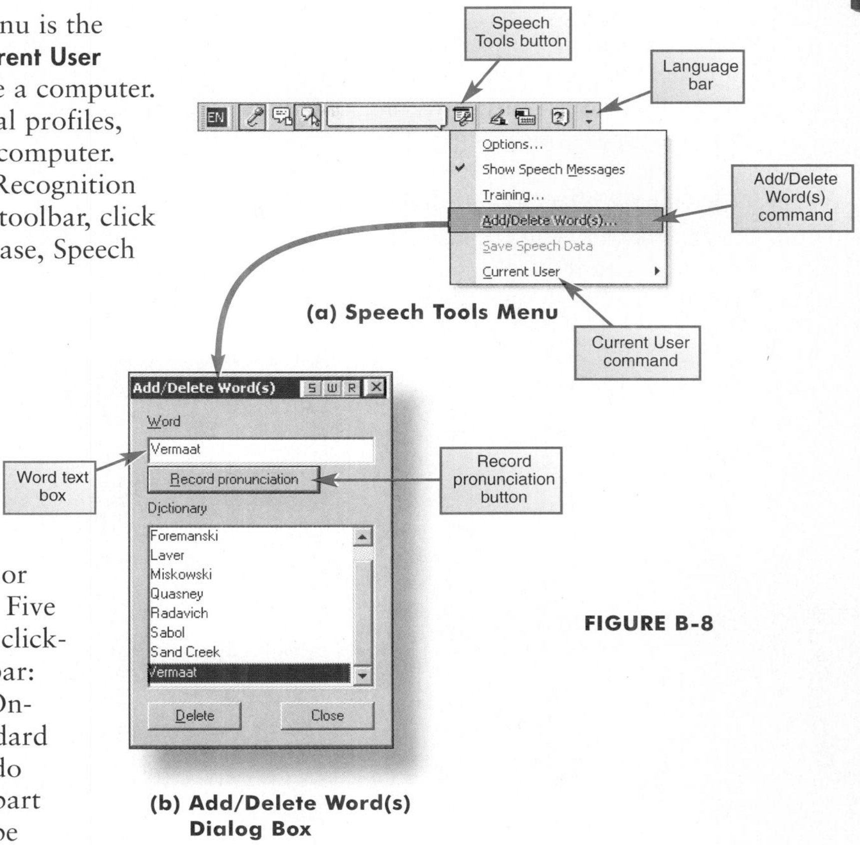

Handwriting Recognition

Using the Office XP Handwriting Recognition service, you can enter text and numbers into Publisher by writing instead of typing. You can write using a special hand-writing device that connects to your computer or you can write on the screen using your mouse. Five basic methods of handwriting are available by clicking the Handwriting button on the Language bar: Writing Pad; Write Anywhere; Drawing Pad; On-Screen Symbol Keyboard; and On-Screen Standard Keyboard. Although the on-screen keyboards do not involve handwriting recognition, they are part of the Handwriting menu and, therefore, will be discussed in this section.

(a) Speech Tools Menu

(b) Add/Delete Word(s) Dialog Box

FIGURE B-8

If your Language bar does not include the Handwriting button (Figures B-1b or B-1c on page PUB B.01), then for installation instructions click the Help button on the Standard toolbar, click the Answer Wizard tab, and search for the phrase Install Handwriting Recognition.

Writing Pad

To display the Writing Pad, click the Handwriting button on the Language bar and then click Writing Pad (Figure B-9). The **Writing Pad** resembles a note pad with one or more lines on which you can use freehand to print or write in cursive. With the **Text button** enabled, you can form letters on the line by moving the mouse while holding down the mouse button. To the right of the note pad is a rectangular toolbar. Use the buttons on this toolbar to adjust the Writing Pad, select objects, and activate other handwriting applications.

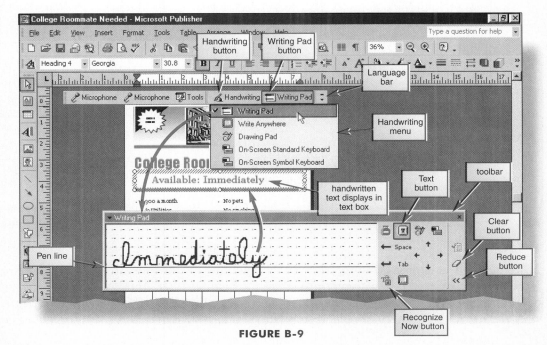

FIGURE B-9

Consider the example in Figure B-9 on the previous page. With a text box selected, the word, Immediately, is written in cursive on the **Pen line** in the Writing Pad. As soon as the word is complete, the Handwriting Recognition service automatically assigns the word to the text box.

You can customize the Writing Pad by clicking the **Options button** on the left side of the title bar and then clicking the Options command (Figure B-10a). Invoking the Options command causes the Handwriting Options dialog box to display. The **Handwriting Options dialog box** (Figures B-10b and B-10c) contains two sheets: Common and Writing Pad. The **Common sheet** lets you change the pen color and pen width, adjust recognition, and customize the toolbar area of the Writing Pad. The **Writing Pad sheet** allows you to change the background color and the number of lines that display in the Writing Pad. Both sheets contain a **Restore Default button** to restore the settings to their preset installation values.

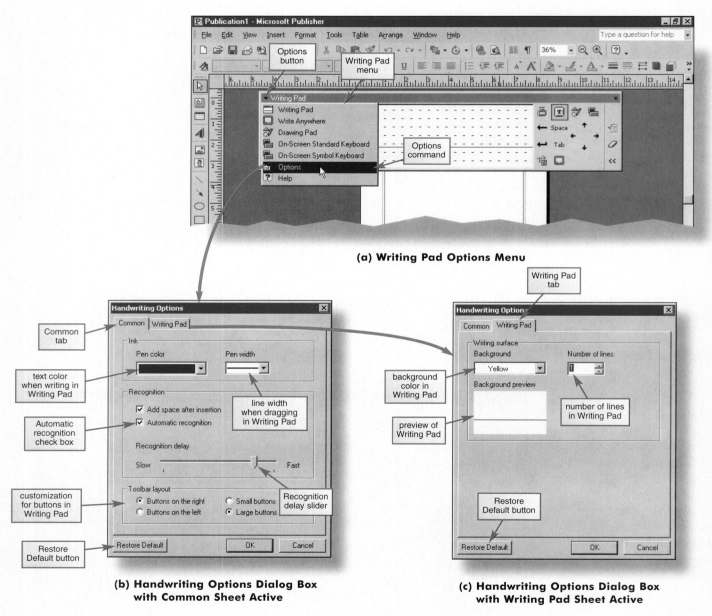

(a) **Writing Pad Options Menu**

(b) **Handwriting Options Dialog Box with Common Sheet Active**

(c) **Handwriting Options Dialog Box with Writing Pad Sheet Active**

FIGURE B-10

When you first start using the Writing Pad, you may want to remove the check mark from the **Automatic recognition check box** in the Common sheet in the Handwriting Options dialog box (Figure B-10b). With the check mark removed, the Handwriting Recognition service will not interpret what you write in the Writing Pad until you click the **Recognize Now button** on the toolbar (Figure B-9). This allows you to pause and adjust your writing.

The best way to learn how to use the Writing Pad is to practice with it. Also, for more information, click the Help button on the Standard toolbar, click the Answer Wizard tab, and search for the phrase, Handwriting Recognition.

Write Anywhere

Rather than use a Writing Pad, you can write anywhere on the screen by invoking the Write Anywhere command on the Handwriting menu (Figure B-11), which displays when you click the Handwriting button on the Language bar. In this case, the entire window is your writing pad.

In Figure B-11, the word, Sale, is written in cursive using the mouse button. Shortly after you finish writing the word, the Handwriting Recognition service interprets it, assigns it to the text box, and then erases what you wrote.

It is recommended that when you first start using the Write Anywhere service that you remove the check mark from the Automatic recognition check box in the Common sheet in the Handwriting Options dialog box (Figure B-10b). With the check mark removed, the Handwriting Recognition service will not interpret what you write on the screen until you click the Recognize Now button on the toolbar (Figure B-11).

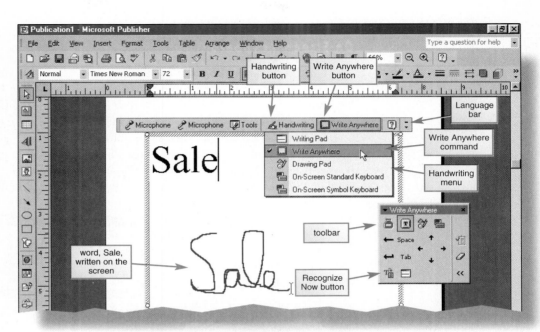

FIGURE B-11

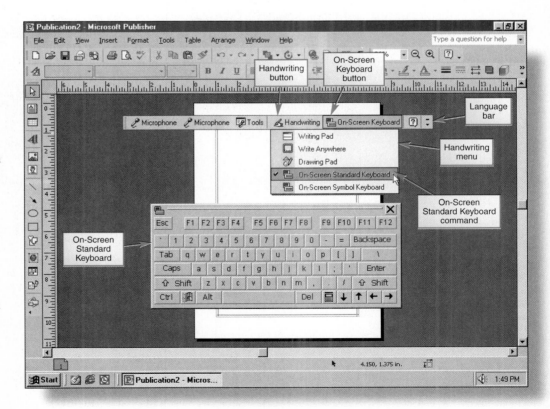

FIGURE B-12

Write Anywhere is more difficult to use than the Writing Pad, because when you click the mouse button, Publisher may interpret the action as selecting another object rather than starting to write. For this reason, it is recommended that you use the Writing Pad.

On-Screen Keyboard

The **On-Screen Standard Keyboard** command on the Handwriting menu (Figure B-12 on the previous page) displays an on-screen keyboard. The **on-screen keyboard** lets you enter data into a text box by using your mouse to click the keys. The on-screen keyboard is similar to the type found on handheld computers.

The **On-Screen Symbol Keyboard** command on the Handwriting menu (Figure B-13) displays a special on-screen keyboard that allows you to enter symbols that are not on your keyboard, as well as Unicode characters. Unicode characters use a coding scheme capable of representing all the world's current languages.

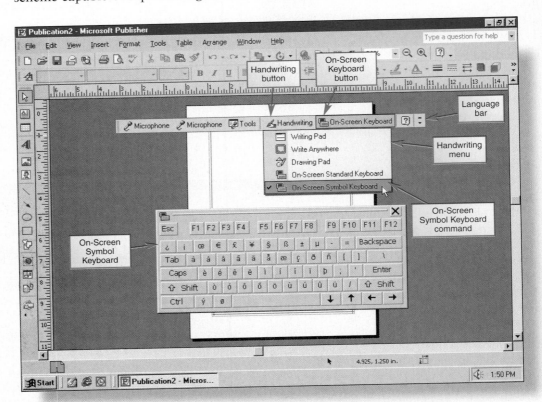

FIGURE B-13

APPENDIX C
Publishing Office Web Pages to a Web Server

With the Office applications, you use the Save as Web Page command on the File menu to save the Web page to a Web server using one of two techniques: Web folders or File Transfer Protocol. A **Web folder** is an Office shortcut to a Web server. **File Transfer Protocol (FTP)** is an Internet standard that allows computers to exchange files with other computers on the Internet.

You should contact your network system administrator or technical support staff at your ISP to determine if their Web server supports Web folders, FTP, or both, and to obtain necessary permissions to access the Web server. If you decide to publish Web pages using a Web folder, you must have the Office Server Extensions (OSE) installed on your computer.

Using Web Folders to Publish Office Web Pages

When publishing to a Web folder, someone first must create the Web folder before you can save to it. If you are granted permission to create a Web folder, you must obtain the URL of the Web server, a user name, and possibly a password that allows you to access the Web server. You also must decide on a name for the Web folder. Table C-1 explains how to create a Web folder.

Office adds the name of the Web folder to the list of current Web folders. You can save to this folder, open files in the folder, rename the folder, or perform any operations you would to a folder on your hard disk. You can use your Office program or Windows Explorer to access this folder. Table C-2 explains how to save to a Web folder.

Table C-1   Creating a Web Folder
1. Click File on the menu bar and then click Save As (or Open).
2. When the Save As dialog box (or Open dialog box) displays, click My Network Places (or Web Folders) on the Places Bar. Double-click Add Network Place (or Add Web Folder).
3. When the Add Network Place Wizard dialog box displays, click the Create a new Network Place option button and then click the Next button. Type the URL of the Web server in the Folder location text box, enter the folder name you want to call the Web folder in the Folder name text box, and then click the Next button. Click Empty Web and then click the Finish button.
4. When the Enter Network Password dialog box displays, type the user name and, if necessary, the password in the respective text boxes and then click the OK button.
5. Close the Save As or the Open dialog box.

Table C-2   Saving to a Web Folder
1. Click File on the menu bar and then click Save As.
2. When the Save As dialog box displays, type the Web page file name in the File name text box. Do not press the ENTER key.
3. Click My Network Places on the Places Bar.
4. Double-click the Web folder name in the Save in list.
5. If the Enter Network Password dialog box displays, type the user name and password in the respective text boxes and then click the OK button.
6. Click the Save button in the Save As dialog box.

Using FTP to Publish Office Web Pages

When publishing a Web page using FTP, you first must add the FTP location to your computer before you can save to it. An **FTP location**, also called an **FTP site**, is a collection of files that reside on an FTP server. In this case, the FTP server is the Web server.

To add an FTP location, you must obtain the name of the FTP site, which usually is the address (URL) of the FTP server, and a user name and a password that allows you to access the FTP server. You save and open the Web pages on the FTP server using the name of the FTP site. Table C-3 explains how to add an FTP site.

Table C-3   Adding an FTP Location
1. Click File on the menu bar and then click Save As (or Open).
2. In the Save As dialog box, click the Save in box arrow and then click Add/Modify FTP Locations in the Save in list; or in the Open dialog box, click the Look in box arrow and then click Add/Modify FTP Locations in the Look in list.
3. When the Add/Modify FTP Locations dialog box displays, type the name of the FTP site in the Name of FTP site text box. If the site allows anonymous logon, click Anonymous in the Log on as area; if you have a user name for the site, click User in the Log on as area and then enter the user name. Enter the password in the Password text box. Click the OK button.
4. Close the Save As or the Open dialog box.

Office adds the name of the FTP site to the FTP locations list in the Save As and Open dialog boxes. You can open and save files using this list. Table C-4 explains how to save to an FTP location.

Table C-4   Saving to an FTP Location
1. Click File on the menu bar and then click Save As.
2. When the Save As dialog box displays, type the Web page file name in the File name text box. Do not press the ENTER key.
3. Click the Save in box arrow and then click FTP Locations.
4. Double-click the name of the FTP site to which you wish to save.
5. When the FTP Log On dialog box displays, enter your user name and password and then click the OK button.
6. Click the Save button in the Save As dialog box.

APPENDIX D

Resetting the Publisher Toolbars and Menus

Publisher customization capabilities allow you to create custom toolbars by adding and deleting buttons and personalize menus based on their usage. Each time you start Publisher, the toolbars and menus display using the same settings as the last time you used it. This appendix shows you how to reset the Standard and Formatting toolbars and menus to their installation settings.

Steps **To Reset the Standard and Formatting Toolbars**

1 **Click the Toolbar Options button on the Standard toolbar and then point to Add or Remove Buttons on the Toolbar Options menu.**

The Toolbar Options menu and the Add or Remove Buttons submenu display (Figure D-1).

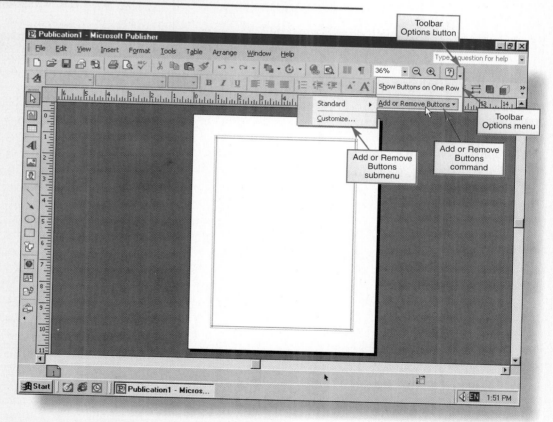

FIGURE D-1

2 **Point to Standard on the Add or Remove Buttons submenu. When the Standard submenu displays, scroll down and then point to Reset Toolbar.**

The Standard submenu displays indicating the buttons and boxes that display on the toolbar (Figure D-2). To remove any buttons, click a button name with a check mark to the left of the name to remove the check mark.

3 **Click Reset Toolbar.**

Publisher resets the Standard toolbar to its installation settings.

4 **Reset the Formatting toolbar by following Steps 1 through 3 and replacing any reference to the Standard toolbar with the Formatting toolbar.**

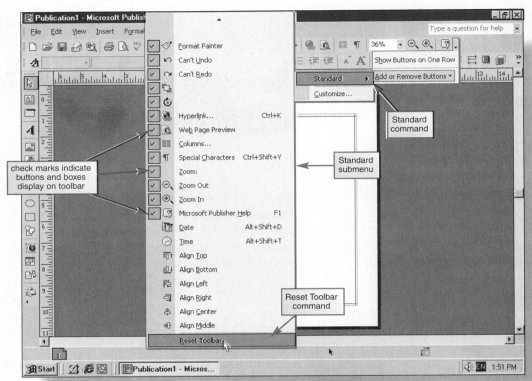

FIGURE D-2

Steps **To Reset Menus**

1 **Click the Toolbar Options button on the Standard toolbar and then point to Add or Remove Buttons on the Toolbar Options menu. Point to Customize on the Add or Remove Buttons submenu.**

The Toolbar Options menu and the Add or Remove Buttons submenu display (Figure D-3).

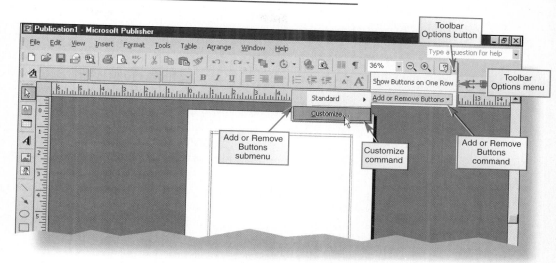

FIGURE D-3

2 **Click Customize. When the Customize dialog box displays, click the Options tab and then point to the Reset my usage data button.**

The Customize dialog box displays (Figure D-4). The **Customize dialog box** *contains three tabbed sheets used for customizing the Publisher toolbars and menus.*

3 **Click the Reset my usage data button. When the Microsoft Publisher dialog box displays, click the Yes button. Click the Close button in the Customize dialog box.**

Publisher resets the menus to the installation settings.

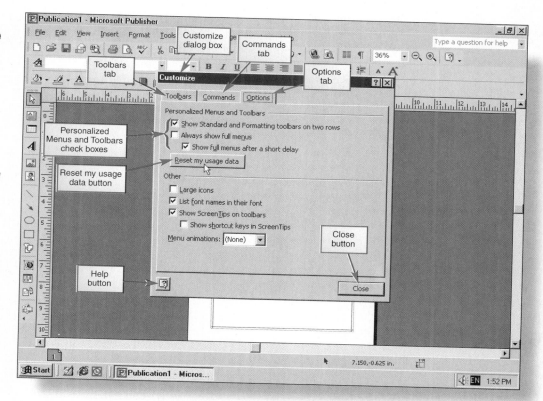

FIGURE D-4

In the **Options sheet** in the Customize dialog box shown in Figure D-4 on the previous page, you can turn off toolbars displaying on two rows and turn off short menus by removing the check marks from the two top check boxes. Click the **Help button** in the lower-left corner of the Customize dialog box to display Help topics that will assist you in customizing toolbars and menus.

Using the **Commands sheet**, you can add buttons to toolbars and commands to menus. Recall that the menu bar at the top of the Publisher window is a special toolbar. To add buttons, click the Commands tab in the Customize dialog box. Click a category name in the Categories list and then drag the command name in the Commands list to a toolbar. To add commands to a menu, click a category name in the Categories list, drag the command name in the Commands list to the menu name on the menu bar, and then, when the menu displays, drag the command to the desired location in the menu list of commands.

In the **Toolbars sheet**, you can add new toolbars and reset existing toolbars. If you add commands to menus as described in the previous paragraph and want to reset the menus to their default settings, perform the following steps.

TO RESET MENUS TO THEIR DEFAULT VALUES AFTER ADDING COMMANDS

1 On the Publisher menu bar, click View and then point to Toolbars.

2 When the Toolbars submenu displays, click Customize.

3 When the Customize dialog box displays, click the Toolbars tab, click Menu Bar, and then click the Reset button.

4 Click the OK button and then click the Close button.

APPENDIX E
Microsoft Office User Specialist Certification Program

What Is MOUS Certification?

The Microsoft Office User Specialist (MOUS) Certification Program provides a framework for measuring your proficiency with the Microsoft Office XP applications, such as Word 2002, Excel 2002, Access 2002, PowerPoint 2002, Outlook 2002, and FrontPage 2002. The levels of certification are described in Table E-1.

Table E-1	Levels of MOUS Certification		
LEVEL	DESCRIPTION	REQUIREMENTS	CREDENTIAL AWARDED
Expert	Indicates that you have a comprehensive understanding of the advanced features in a specific Microsoft Office XP application	Pass any ONE of the Expert exams: Microsoft Word 2002 Expert Microsoft Excel 2002 Expert Microsoft Access 2002 Expert Microsoft Outlook 2002 Expert Microsoft FrontPage 2002 Expert	Candidates will be awarded one certificate for each of the Expert exams they have passed: Microsoft Office User Specialist: Microsoft Word 2002 Expert Microsoft Office User Specialist: Microsoft Excel 2002 Expert Microsoft Office User Specialist: Microsoft Access 2002 Expert Microsoft Office User Specialist: Microsoft Outlook 2002 Expert Microsoft Office User Specialist: Microsoft FrontPage 2002 Expert
Core	Indicates that you have a comprehensive understanding of the core features in a specific Microsoft Office 2002 application	Pass any ONE of the Core exams: Microsoft Word 2002 Core Microsoft Excel 2002 Core Microsoft Access 2002 Core Microsoft Outlook 2002 Core Microsoft FrontPage 2002 Core	Candidates will be awarded one certificate for each of the Core exams they have passed: Microsoft Office User Specialist: Microsoft Word 2002 Microsoft Office User Specialist: Microsoft Excel 2002 Microsoft Office User Specialist: Microsoft Access 2002 Microsoft Office User Specialist: Microsoft Outlook 2002 Microsoft Office User Specialist: Microsoft FrontPage 2002
Comprehensive	Indicates that you have a comprehensive understanding of the features in Microsoft PowerPoint 2002	Pass the Microsoft PowerPoint 2002 Comprehensive Exam	Candidates will be awarded one certificate for the Microsoft PowerPoint 2002 Comprehensive exam passed.

Why Should You Get Certified?

Being a Microsoft Office User Specialist provides a valuable industry credential — proof that you have the Office XP applications skills required by employers. By passing one or more MOUS certification exams, you demonstrate your proficiency in a given Office XP application to employers. With over 100 million copies of Office in use around the world, Microsoft is targeting Office XP certification to a wide variety of companies. These companies include temporary employment agencies that want to prove the expertise of their workers, large corporations looking for a way to measure the skill set of employees, and training companies and educational institutions seeking Microsoft Office XP teachers with appropriate credentials.

The MOUS Exams

You pay $50 to $100 each time you take an exam, whether you pass or fail. The fee varies among testing centers. The Expert exams, which you can take up to 60 minutes to complete, consists of between 40 and 60 tasks that you perform online. The tasks require you to use the application just as you would in doing your job. The Core exams contain fewer tasks, and you will have slightly less time to complete them. The tasks you will perform differ on the two types of exams.

How Can You Prepare for the MOUS Exams?

The Shelly Cashman Series® offers several Microsoft-approved textbooks that cover the required objectives on the MOUS exams. For a listing of the textbooks, visit the Shelly Cashman Series MOUS site at scsite.com/offxp/cert.htm and click the link Shelly Cashman Series Office XP Microsoft-Approved MOUS Textbooks (Figure E-1). After using any of the books listed in an instructor-led course, you will be prepared to take the MOUS exam indicated.

How to Find an Authorized Testing Center

You can locate a testing center by calling 1-800-933-4493 in North America or visiting the Shelly Cashman Series MOUS site at scsite.com/offxp/cert.htm and then clicking the link Locate an Authorized Testing Center Near You (Figure E-1). At this Web site, you can look for testing centers around the world.

Shelly Cashman Series MOUS Web Page

The Shelly Cashman Series MOUS Web page (Figure E-1) has more than fifteen Web sites you can visit to obtain additional information on the MOUS Certification Program. The Web page (scsite.com/offxp/cert.htm) includes links to general information on certification, choosing an application for certification, preparing for the certification exam, and taking and passing the certification exam.

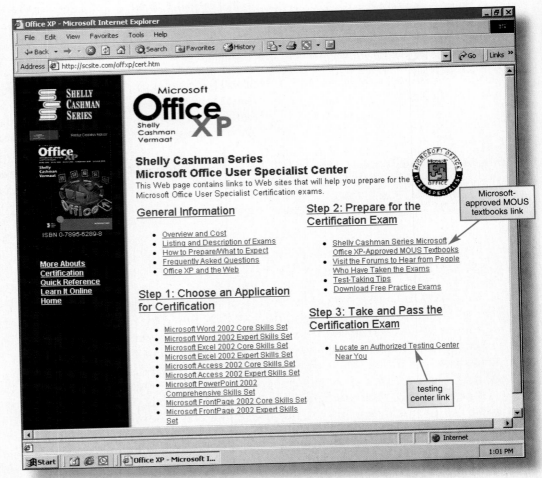

FIGURE E-1

Index

Microsoft **Publisher 2002**

Microsoft
PUBLISHER 2002
Quick Reference Summary

In Microsoft Publisher 2002, you can accomplish a task in a number of ways. The following table provides a quick reference to each task presented in this textbook. The first column identifies the task. The second column indicates the page number on which the task is discussed in the book. The subsequent four columns list the different ways the task in column one can be carried out. Besides using the mouse or keyboard, you can invoke the commands listed in the MOUSE, MENU BAR and SHORTCUT MENU columns using Voice commands.

Microsoft Publisher 2002 Quick Reference Summary

TASK	PAGE NUMBER	MOUSE	MENU BAR	SHORTCUT MENU	KEYBOARD SHORTCUT
Add Border	PUB 5.28		Format	Text Box	Format	Text Box	ALT+O	E
Address List	PUB 4.42		Tools	Mail Merge	Create Address List		ALT+T	G
Align Objects	PUB 3.27		Arrange	Align or Distribute	Align or Distrubte	ALT+O	A
Attention Getters	PUB 1.42	Design Gallery Object button on Objects toolbar	Insert	Design Gallery Object	Attention Getters		ALT+I	D
AutoFit Text	PUB 3.34		Format	AutoFit Text	Change Text	AutoFit Text	ALT+O	X
Automatic Page Numbering	PUB 2.47	Insert Page Number button on Header and Viewer toolbar	Insert	Page Numbers		ALT+I	U
AutoShapes	PUB 3.32	AutoShapes button on Object toolbar	Arrange	Change AutoShapte		ALT+R	C
Bold	PUB 3.21	Bold button on Formatting toolbar	Format	Font	Change Text	Font	CTRL+B
Bullets	PUB 1.26	Bullets button on Formatting toolbar	Format	Indents and Lists	Change Text	Bullets and Lists	ALT+F	I
Cell Diagonals	PUB 5.33		Table	Cell Diagonals	Change Table	Cell Diagonals	ALT+A	C
Center	PUB 3.21	Center button on Formatting toolbar	Arrange	Align or Distribute	Change Text	Font	CTRL+B
Change Calendar Date	PUB 4.34	Change date range button on Calendar Options task pane			
Change Pages	PUB 2.11	Page icon on status bar	Edit	Go to Page		CTL+G or F5
Columns	PUB 2.25	Columns button on Formatting toolbar		Format Text Box	Textbox Sheet	CTRL+SHIFT+ENTER
Copy and Paste	PUB 3.13	Copy button and Paste button on Standard toolbar	Edit	Copy; Edit	Paste	Copy; Paste	CTRL+C; CTRL+V
Convert to Web Site	PUBW 1.04		File	Save as Web Page		
Create a Style	PUB 5.09	Create new style button on Styles and Formatting task pane	Format	Styles and Formatting		CTRL+O	S
Create Table	PUB 5.31	Insert Table button on Objects toolbar	Table	Insert	Table		ALT+ A, I, T
Custom Size	PUB 5.23		File	Page Setup		ALT+F	U

MICROSOFT PUBLISHER 2002 QUICK REFERENCE SUMMARY

Microsoft Publisher 2002 Quick Reference Summary *(continued)*

TASK	PAGE NUMBER	MOUSE	MENU BAR	SHORTCUT MENU	KEYBOARD SHORTCUT
Delete Objects	PUB 1.47	Cut button on Standard Toolbar	Edit	Delete Object	Delete Object	DELETE
Delete Pages	PUB 2.11		Edit	Delete Page		ALT+E	A
Design Checker	PUB 1.49		Tools	Design Checker		ALT+T	N
Drop Cap	PUB 5.14		Format	Drop Cap	Change text	Drop Cap	ALT+O	D
Edit a Story in Microsoft Word	PUB 3.14		Edit	Edit Story in Microsoft Word		ALT+E	W
Edit Graphics	PUB 1.33	Double-click graphic	Format	Picture	Format Picture	ALT+F	P
Edit Layout and Ruler Guides	PUB 4.08		Tools	Layout Guides		ALT+R	D
Edit Linked Worksheet	PUBI 1.08	Double-click worksheet	Edit	Microsoft Excel Worksheet Object	Edit	Microsoft Excel Worksheet Object	Edit	ALT+E	O	E
Edit Orientation	PUB 4.32	Orientation button on Business Card Options task pane	File	Page Setup		ALT+F	U
Edit Personal Information Set	PUB 4.18		Edit	Personal Information		ALT+E	N
Fill Effects	PUB 4.13	Fill Color button on Formatting toolbar	Format	AutoShape	Format	AutoShape	ALT+O	E
Font	PUB 3.21	Font box on Formatting toolbar	Format	Font	Change Text	Font	CTRL+SHIFT+F
Font Color	PUB 3.21	Font Color button on Formatting toolbar	Format	Font	Change Text	Font	ALT+O	F	C
Font Size	PUB 3.21	Font Size box on Formatting toolbar	Format	Font	Change Text	Font	CTRL+SHIFT+P
Form Controls	PUBW 1.11	Form Control button on Objects toolbar	Insert	Form Control		ALT+I	C
Format Painter	PUB 4.23	Format Painter button on Standard toolbar			CTRL+SHIFT+C	CTRL+SHIFT+V
Forms	PUB 3.41	Design Gallery Object button on Objects toolbar	Insert	Design Gallery Object	Reply Forms		ALT+I	D
Group	PUB 3.37	Group Button	Arrange	Group	Group	CTRL+SHIFT+G
Help	PUB 1.52 and Appendix A	Microsoft Publisher Help button on Standard toolbar	Help	Microsoft Publisher Help		F1
Import Style	PUB 5.25	Import new style button on Styles and Formatting task pane	Format	Styles and Formatting		ALT+O	S
Import Text	PUB 2.19	Drag and drop text	Insert	Text File	Change Text	Text File	ALT+I	E
Increase Font Size	PUBW 1.06				
Insert Animated Graphic	PUB 5.42	Insert button on Insert Clip Art task pane			
Insert Date	PUB 5.21		Insert	Date and Time		ALT+I	T
Insert Field Codes	PUB 4.46		Tools	Mail Merge	Insert Field		CTRL+SHIFT+I
Insert Form Control	PUB 5.46	Form Control button on Objects toolbar	Insert	Form Control		ALT+I	F
Insert Hot Spot	PUB 5.44	Hot Spot button on Objects toolbar			
Insert Logo	PUB 4.25		Insert	Personal Information	Logo		ALT+I	R	L
Insert Pages	PUB 2.11		Insert	Page		CTRL+SHIFT+N
Insert Personal Information Component	PUB 4.21		Insert	Personal Information		ALT+I	R

Microsoft Publisher 2002 Quick Reference Summary

TASK	PAGE NUMBER	MOUSE	MENU BAR	SHORTCUT MENU	KEYBOARD SHORTCUT
Insert Tab	PUB 5.19	Double-click Ruler	Format	Tabs	Change text	Tabs	ALT+O	T
Kerning	PUB 4.15	Kerning box on Measurement toolbar	Format	Character Spacing	Change Text	Character Spacing	CTRL+SHIFT+], CTRL+SHIFT+[
Language Bar	PUB 1.21	Language indicator button in tray	Tools	Speech	Speech Recognition		ALT+T	H	H
Link an Excel Worksheet	PUBI 1.05		Edit	Paste Special		ALT+E	S
Master Page	PUB 2.47		View	Master Page		CTRL+M
Mastheads	PUB 2.14	Design Gallery Object button on Objects toolbar	Insert	Design Gallery Object	Mastheads		ALT+I	D
Merge Cells	PUB 5.33		Table	Merge Cells	Change Table	Merge Cells	ALT+A	M
Move	PUB 1.44	Point to border and drag	Edit	Cut; Edit	Paste	Cut; Paste	CTRL+X; CTRL+V
New Publication	PUB 1.10	New button on Standard toolbar	File	New		CTRL+N
Open Publication	PUB 1.40	Open button on Standard toolbar	File	Open		CTRL+O
Pack and Go	PUB 3.40		File	Pack and Go		ALT+ F	K
Photographs	PUB 3.29	Picture Frame button on Objects toolbar	Insert	Picture	From File	Change Picture	From File	ALT+I	P	F
Position Objects	PUB 4.16	Double-click Object Size box on Status bar	Format	AutoShape	Format	AutoShape	ALT+O	E
Preview Publication	PUB 3.45	Print Preview button on Standard toolbar	File	Print Preview		ALT+F	V
Print Publication	PUB 1.38	Print button on Standard toolbar	File	Print		CTRL+P
Pull Quotes	PUB 2.39	Design Gallery Object button on Objects toolbar	Insert	Design Gallery Object	Pull Quotes		ALT+I	D
Quit Publisher	PUB 1.54	Close button on title bar	File	Exit		ALT+F4
Recolor a Graphic	PUB 4.28	Format Picture on Picture toolbar	Format	Picture	Format Picture	ALT+O	E
Resize Graphic	PUB 1.36	Drag sizing handle	Format	Picture	Size	Format Picture	Size	ALT+F	P	S
Rotate Object	PUB 3.25	Click Free Rotate button on Standard toolbar or drag rotation handle	Arrange	Rotate or Flip	Format <object>	Size	ALT+R	P
Save a New Publication	PUB 1.30		File	Save As		ALT+F	A
Save as Web Page	PUB 1-51		File	Save as Web Page		ALT+F	G
Save Publication - Same Name	PUB 1.37	Save button on Standard toolbar	File	Save		CTRL+S
Send a File via E-mail	PUB 5.37	E-mail button on Standard toolbar	File	Send To		ALT+F	D
Select All of a Publication	PUB 2.13		Edit	Select All		CTRL+A
Set Margins	PUB 4.08		Tools	Layout Guides		ALT+R	D
Sidebars	PUB 1.41	Design Gallery Object button on Objects toolbar	Insert	Design Gallery Object	Sidebars		ALT+I	D
Shortcut Menu	PUB 1.33	Right-click object			SHIFT+F10
Smart Tags	PUB 3.21	Click smart tag button	Tools	AutoCorrect Options		ALT+T	A
Spell Check	PUB 2.52	Spelling button on Standard toolbar	Tools	Spelling	Change Text	Proofing Tools	Spelling	F7
Task Pane	PUB 1.10		View	Task Pane		ALT+V	K
Tear-offs	PUB 1.28	Design Gallery Object button on Objects toolbar	Insert	Design Gallery Object	Tear-offs		ALT+I	D
Text Boxes	PUB 3.21	Text Box button on Objects toolbar	Insert	Text Box		ALT+I	X
Toolbar, Dock	PUB 1.20	Drag toolbar to dock			

Microsoft **Publisher 2002**

Microsoft Publisher 2002 Quick Reference Summary *(continued)*

TASK	PAGE NUMBER	MOUSE	MENU BAR	SHORTCUT MENU	KEYBOARD SHORTCUT
Toolbar, Reset	PUB D.01	Toolbar Options, Add or Remove Buttons, Customize, Toolbars tab		Customize | Toolbars tab	ALT+V | T | C | T
Toolbar, Show Entire	PUB 1.20	Double-click move handle			
Toolbar, Show or Hide	PUB 1.20	Right-click toolbar, click toolbar name	View | Toolbars	Toolbars	ALT+V | T
Tracking	PUB 4.15	Tracking box on Measurement toolbar	Format | Character Spacing	Change Text | Character Spacing	
Transparent Objects	PUB 3.34	Set Transparent Color button on Picture toolbar	Format | <object>	Format <object>	CTRL+T
Undo	PUB 1.28	Undo button on Standard toolbar	Edit | Undo	Undo	CTRL+Z
Ungroup	PUB 3.37	Ungroup button	Arrange | Ungroup	Ungroup	CTRL+SHIFT+G
Web Page Preview	PUBW 1.13	Web Page Preview button on Standard toolbar	File | Web Page Preview		ALT+F | B
Web Properties	PUBW 1.09	Background fill and sound in Web Options task pane	Tools | Options | General | Web Options		
WordArt	PUB 2.44	WordArt button on Objects toolbar			
Zoom	PUB 1.24	Zoom box on Standard toolbar	View | Zoom	Zoom	F9